Evangelical
Christianity
in Australia

*For
Harry Goodhew,
Archbishop of Sydney,
in whom is personified so graciously
the evangelical synthesis
of
Spirit, Word and mission*

Evangelical Christianity in Australia

Spirit, word and world

Stuart Piggin

Melbourne

OXFORD UNIVERSITY PRESS

Oxford   Auckland   New York

OXFORD UNIVERSITY PRESS AUSTRALIA

Oxford   New York
Athens   Auckland   Bangkok   Bombay
Calcutta   Cape Town   Dar es Salaam   Delhi
Florence   Hong Kong   Istanbul   Karachi
Kuala Lumpur   Madras   Madrid   Melbourne
Mexico City   Nairobi   Paris   Singapore
Taipei   Tokyo   Toronto

and associated companies in
Berlin   Ibadan

OXFORD is a trade mark of Oxford University Press

National Library of Australia
Cataloguing-in-Publication data:

Piggin, Stuart.

Evangelical Christianity in Australia: spirit, word
and world.

Bibliography.
Includes index.

ISBN 0 19 553538 3.

1. Evangelicalism — Australia. 2. Australia —
Church history. I. Title.

269.2

Edited by Janet Mackenzie
Text design by Cathie Lindsey
Cover design by Cathie Lindsey
Typeset by Desktop Concepts P/L, Melbourne
Printed by McPherson's Printing Group, Australia
Published by Oxford University Press,
253 Normanby Road, South Melbourne, Australia

Contents

Abbreviations   vi

Preface: The Evangelical Synthesis   vii

1 Going into All the World, 1788–1835   1

2 Identifying with the Liberal World, 1836–1870   24

3 The Spirit and Protestant Culture, 1870–1913   49

4 The Word Challenged, 1914–1932   79

5 Holiness above the Word:
   Sinless Perfection in the 1930s   105

6 Word and Spirit, 1933–1959   125

7 The Evangelical Synthesis Attained:
   Billy Graham in Australia, 1959   154

8 Word or Spirit, 1960–1994   172

9 Word Rather than Peace: The Fight over the
   Ordination of Women in Australian Anglicanism, 1992   203

Conclusion   222

Notes   226

Bibliography   257

Index   277

Abbreviations

AAM	Association for the Apostolic Ministry
AFES	Australian Fellowship of Evangelical Students
CIM	China Inland Mission
CMS	Church Missionary Society (Anglican)
CSAC	Centre for the Study of Australian Christianity, Robert Menzies College, Macquarie University
EU	Evangelical Union
IVF	Inter-Varsity Fellowship
LMS	London Missionary Society (Congregationalist)
MBI	Melbourne Bible Institute
MOW	Movement for the Ordination of Women
REPA	Reformed Evangelical Protestant Association
SAOs	Salvation Army Officers
SCM	Student Christian Movement
SSEM	South Sea Evangelical Mission
SUEU	Sydney University Evangelical Union
WMMS	Wesleyan Methodist Missionary Society

Preface: The Evangelical Synthesis

This is a study of Australian Christianity from an evangelical perspective. Evangelicalism has been the commonest expression of Protestantism in Australian history. It is a conservative Protestant movement which grew out of the Protestant Reformation of the sixteenth century, the English Puritanism of the later sixteenth and seventeenth centuries, the Continental Pietism of the seventeenth and eighteenth centuries, and the revivals of the 1730s and 1740s in Britain, Europe and America. Evangelicalism is concerned to foster an intimate, even intense, personal relationship with Jesus Christ. The creation and development of this relationship is understood as the work of the Holy Spirit. It is the Spirit who converts and regenerates believers and gives them the desire for personal holiness. Consistent with the Reformation, evangelicalism holds salvation by faith alone (*sola fide*) as its central doctrine and the Bible, understood as the Word of God, as its sole authority (*sola scriptura*). The evangelical faith is crystallised in the Gospel which the early generations of evangelicals understood not only as the divinely given instrument for the rebirth of the individual soul, but also for the renovation of society and culture. Evangelicalism, then, is experiential, Biblicist, and activist. It is concerned with the Spirit, the Word, and the world. It aims to produce right-heartedness (*orthokardia*), right thinking (*orthodoxy*), and right action (*orthopraxis*). It calls for the consecration of heart, head, and hand. All Christianity is, of course, concerned with Christ, but evangelicalism is passionate about three of Christ's concerns: his Word, his Spirit, and his mission.

How these three concerns worked themselves out in the history of the church and society in Australia is the theme of this book. It is here argued that where these three concerns were held together in synthesis, evangelicalism was strong in itself and made a significant contribution to the shaping of Australian society and culture: 'a cord of three strands is not easily broken' (Ecclesiastes 4.12). But where one was promoted to the neglect of the other two, or even two at the expense of the third, the movement lacked vitality and was even divided against itself. The vicissitudes of the evangelical synthesis are here traced through six periods of Australian history (chapters 1 to 4, 6 and 8). Three case studies explore in greater detail what can happen when the Spirit strand dominates (chapter 5), when the Word strand dominates (chapter 9), and when the synthesis is actually achieved (chapter 7).

Evangelicalism was the official Christianity brought to Australia with the First Fleet (chapter 1). It was the product of that synthesis of Word, Spirit and concern for evangelism and social reform embodied in William Wilberforce[1] and the coterie of well-connected, influential, mainly lay (including a woman!) evangelicals known as 'the Clapham Sect'. Wilberforce's evangelicalism was a step removed from the doctrinaire Calvinism of some of the previous generation of evangelical Anglicans. It was a warm, practical, humanitarian movement which focused on commitment to the world with Word and Spirit to energise that commitment. The evangelical presence with the First Fleet was an early expression of that commitment. The vision of a reclaimed criminal class, a converted Aboriginal race, and the islands of the South Seas evangelised from an Australian base was large, even grand. To reproduce vital religious experience and to cover the southern world with Christian nations were the high aspirations of the first generation of evangelicals in Australia. Word and Spirit were made to subserve an experiment in social reform, the nobility of which has been obscured by the harsh realities of ruling-class culture and convict counter-culture.

From the 1830s, in response to the Catholic revival in Britain which appeared to put the church before the Gospel, and tradition on an equal footing with the Bible, evangelicals were compelled to stress the Word and the Reformation doctrines of *sola scriptura* and *sola fide*. The evangelical synthesis was threatened, and the evangelical programme for the renovation of society more diluted than it might have been. Nevertheless, evangelicals remained committed to the construction of a Christian nation and, for that purpose, made common cause with the political liberals (chapter 2).

The evangelical synthesis was threatened towards the end of the nineteenth century by a preoccupation with the Spirit strand (chapter 3). Evangelicalism came under the sway of an energetic holiness movement, compounded of personal piety and millennial doctrines. Both elements in this compound tended to shift the focus of Australian evangelicals away from action in the world towards devotion in private and fellowship in the church.

But again the world strand was sufficiently strong to hold evangelicals to their vision of social reform, and the last quarter of the nineteenth century saw both a concerted effort to create a culture in Australia consistent with Protestant values and the emergence of a strong commitment to overseas missions. It was also a period of increasingly well-organised evangelistic campaigns.

In the first third of the twentieth century, the unravelling of the three strands continued apace. Evangelical spokespersons were driven by the forces of theological liberalism and secularisation to defend the Bible and doctrinal fundamentals (chapter 4). Devout evangelicals withdrew further into the solace of 'second blessing' spirituality. In disconnecting themselves from the constraints of the Word and rational action in the world, one small group of evangelicals were wrecked on the unforgiving rocks of perfectionism (chapter 5). During the first third of the twentieth century the strand of action in the world was seriously weakened, not only by default, but by a concerted attack on the 'social gospel' and 'liberal evangelicalism'. The evangelical appetite for activism was channelled into missionary work, especially overseas missions and Aboriginal missions which began to work for the first time since white settlement.

The two surviving strands of Word and Spirit became more tightly intertwined in the middle third of the twentieth century (chapter 6). The Bible was studied and the spiritual life cultivated, not only in evangelical churches and fellowship groups, but also in that institutionalisation of Word and Spirit, the 'quiet time', the daily duty of private prayer and Bible reading. The achievement of the evangelical synthesis was rewarded with the effectiveness of the Billy Graham Crusades in 1959 (chapter 7) when Australia came closer to a general religious awakening than at any other time in its history. In the final period of our history (chapter 8), attempts have been made to recover the social activist strand of the evangelical trinity, but this enterprise has been overshadowed by dramatic developments in the other two strands. A resurgence of strongly Reformed theology has so strengthened the Word strand that its adherents have sought to monopolise evangelicalism for themselves, while the even more remarkable flowering of Charismatic Christianity has tempted many Christians to put experience before the Word, and to seek to disentangle themselves altogether from traditional evangelicalism. A particularly instructive manifestation of the dominance of the Word strand was the opposition of powerful Sydney evangelical Anglicans to the ordination of women (chapter 9).

It will be evident to the reader that this book is an extended exploration of an idea. The idea is that evangelicalism is best understood, not as a theology, a party, or an ideology, but as a movement concerned with three major elements—Spirit, Word and world—and that when these three are synthesised the movement is strong, and when they are separated the movement is weak. There are clearly problems with the idea. The historian will want to argue that it is an idea which gives far too much weight to the movement's capacity to control its own destiny. Other, external factors—for example, secularisation or persecution—could determine whether evangelicalism is weak or strong, independently of whether the strands of Spirit, Word or world are bound strongly together or unravelled from each other. David Bebbington, for example, in a recent study,[2] argues that British evangelicalism has been shaped chiefly by prevailing cultural norms. The eighteenth-century enlightenment shaped the surprisingly strong emphasis of Wesley and Jonathan Edwards on reason in religion. The Romantic movement of the nineteenth century was the primary factor in the development of a Pietistic movement in evangelicalism most popularly identified with the Keswick conventions. Finally, since the 1960s, modernism has forged the Charismatic movement, the most conspicuous expression of modern evangelicalism. I think such an interpretation does explain a lot about evangelicalism, but it does not explain its essence—a commitment to the Gospel—which has been surprisingly tenacious since the 1740s revivals. In any case, giving due weight to factors external to the movement is not incompatible with my hypothesis. I would want to argue that the difficulty which the movement too often experiences in achieving the desirable synthesis can reflect the impact of such forces. For example, whenever the authority of the Bible is questioned, the Word strand can become so self-absorbed that, for a time, it can ignore its responsibility to the world. In any event I think my idea deserves a sustained treatment. To my knowledge, understanding evangelicalism as a movement synthesising Spirit, Word and mission has not been used in any other studies of the history of evangelicalism either in Australia or elsewhere. More importantly, it is the only single hypothesis which to me makes sense of the vast and variegated data which the movement has produced. I can only trust that my readers will give the idea a fair hearing.

The foregoing survey of evangelicalism in Australia in six periods over 200 years is similar to a history of the movement in a number of Western nations. The Australian context, however, has presented the evangelical synthesis with unique opportunities and challenges. Hence this study is not concerned primarily with the evangelical movement in its own right, but in the wider context of Australian social and religious history. There is a great need for a study of Australian religious history from an evangelical perspective. A significant minority of Australian Christians are evangelicals, and evangelicalism has made a considerable contribution to the shaping of Australian history, as we shall see.

A second justification for writing a history of Australian Christianity from an evangelical perspective is that hitherto studies of Australian Christianity have been biased towards the Catholic Church,[3] while general studies of Australian society have been biased against all religion. It is a concern that hitherto evangelical Christians have not reflected more on Australian history. Most have believed that they did not need to do that. That we need only the Bible, not history, parallels the Reformation emphasis on the Bible only (*sola scriptura*), not tradition. The very lack of interest in history is evidence of the dominance of the Word strand in Australian evangelicalism. The Spirit and activist strands have not been so happy with this neglect. The European Pietists, who were the immediate forebears of the evangelicals of the eighteenth century, were fascinated by the leadings of God's Spirit in history and in the present world, and collected vast archives of source material which contained evidence of the activity of God in the world.[4] The Pietists, of course, were in the Spirit strand, but they fostered a much greater activism, social and intellectual, educational and cultural, than the orthodox who confined themselves to the Word strand. Not surprisingly, therefore, the first generations of evangelicals—Jonathan Edwards, John Wesley, John Newton, Joseph Milner, and Thomas Haweis[5]—all reflected extensively on the history of the church and rewrote church history from an evangelical perspective.[6] In Australia, it was the Methodists, the most Pietistic of Australia's evangelicals, who were most conscious that, in extending Christ's kingdom in Australia, they were part of God's plan of redemption. Hence, among evangelicals, the Methodists have written most on the history of their movement.[7]

To rewrite Australian religious history, then, from an evangelical perspective is to follow the precedent of the first evangelicals. In 1987 the Evangelical History Association of Australia was launched. I had the honour of delivering the inaugural address and of being appointed its foundation president. The enthusiastic response with which the association has been received by some academics, clergy and church members has demonstrated a dissatisfaction with the way religious history has been written in Australia. On the one hand, the older triumphalist histories of the clergy are considered by professional historians and informed laity to be too narrow in their enthusiasms; whereas the secular insistence on leaving God out of the reckoning, failing to address as important the issues which Christians consider indispensable, and the overwhelmingly negative treatment of Australian Christianity have attracted strident condemnation from non-professionals. There is undoubtedly now a need, perceived since the bicentennial of Australia in 1988, for a new Australian church history.[8]

A revealing attempt to fill the vacuum was made in 1987 by Dr Graham McLennan, a dentist from country New South Wales. McLennan compiled a catalogue of extracts from the first two volumes of Manning Clark's *A History of Australia* to illustrate such themes as the providence of God in the settlement of Australia, the land dedicated to the Holy Spirit, concern for spiritual welfare, the faith of early governors and settlers, and the formation of Bible and missionary societies in Australia.[9] In 1994 he published Elizabeth Kotlowski's *Southland of the Holy Spirit: A Christian History of Australia.*[10] She analyses the religious motivation of missionaries, governors, explorers, and pioneers. Keith Cole is another Australian evangelical who has written extensively on aspects of the history of Australian evangelicalism. His research and writing have been largely devoted to recording the history of Australian evangelical Anglican missions.[11]

To date, however, only one Australian evangelical has written histories which are a sustained celebration of the triumph of grace in the lives of Australian Christians. Marcus Loane, Archbishop of Sydney from 1966 to 1982, has written a large number of biographies of Protestants in the evangelical tradition, both in Australia and beyond, which have fashioned the understanding of church history of Australian evangelicals, especially Anglicans. Loane's writing[12] is in the best tradition of evangelical history writing: it makes the heart glow, nerves the will, and stores the mind with useful truth. It deals with biography, and evangelicals—like most people—love reading about people more than about movements and concepts. It is based on a genuine love of history, for, if its author loves the Gospel most, it is a love which demands a close and penetrating study of the fruits of the Gospel throughout history. It is not just academic, but has heart.

A new religious history is required, however, to supplement Loane's perspectives. Loane is reluctant to explore weaknesses and mistakes. His writing is too clerical, since the clergy are the ones he has known best, and he rightly feels that it is far more difficult to find information on lay people. Furthermore, Loane is more concerned with the incubus of evangelical tradition than with the constraints of Australian culture. The new evangelical history writing will have to deal with structures and movements as well as people, lay people as well as clergy, mistakes as well as successes, and the specific Australian cultural context as well as the international evangelical tradition. Furthermore, since evangelicalism is concerned to do two things with the world, namely to evangelise and reform it, the new evangelical history writing will have to treat not only the evangelist and the reformer, but the groups and people whom they were attempting to evangelise and reform. So, for example, in the first chapter in this book the story is not so much the familiar one of chaplains and missionaries, but is organised around the four groups who were the object of the evangelicals' mission, namely convicts, South Sea islanders, free settlers, and Aboriginal people.

The subject matter of this book is based partly on a survey of most Australian theological colleges conducted in 1993. We asked them what they would like to see in a history of Australian Christianity. Among the topics specified were women and Aboriginal people in the Australian church; missions, both at home and overseas; revival; student work; theological education; regional differences in Australian Christianity; and the relation of evangelicals with Catholics and Anglo-Catholics. We received many requests for an account of pentecostal and Charismatic movements, and I am grateful to Mark Hutchinson, Director of the Centre for the Study of Australian Christianity (CSAC) at Robert Menzies College, who wrote a survey history on these movements which I have drawn upon extensively in this study. Our survey of theological colleges also revealed a demand for an account of Catholic and Anglo-Catholic Christianity. Catholicism has not been treated extensively here because it has been so well done already, and interested students should look at the works of O'Farrell, Campion, and Collins.[13] The history of the Anglican High Church in Australia is covered helpfully in a recent study made by David Hilliard.[14]

Special thanks are due to Mark Hutchinson and my loyal co-workers at Robert Menzies College, Macquarie University. No-one could hope for a better team. Mark, director of the Centre for the Study of Australian Christianity, has worked over most of the chapters in this book. The rest of the team—Richard Quadrio, Geoff Chubb, Graham Banister, Janine Steele, Geoff Treloar, Sue Bartho, Tim Abbey, Dianne Parkes, and Sue Paul—have tried to safeguard my time to allow me to bring this book to completion. Phillip Bell, Richard Hughes and John Russell of the Board of Robert Menzies College have also given themselves unstintingly to keeping the ship on a straight course during those intervals when I was not on the bridge—and, more particularly, when I was! I am very grateful to them all. My thanks, too, to Jill Lane of Oxford University Press for her encouragement to write a book on Australian Christianity which advances some new themes. Jill wanted me to get away from the intricacies of academic debate and bring some freshness to the picture. She also prevailed upon me to write the book around the central thesis which I have enunciated here so that we might produce a book 'which is more than the sum of its parts'.

Another way in which this book is different from most on Australian religious history is that it relies heavily on the over 300 interviews with prominent Australian evangelicals conducted primarily by Margaret Lamb and which are housed at CSAC. My thanks to Margaret for this great labour. Oral history has its own problems, and many will disagree with the opinions expressed in this book—but they are fresh! Thanks are due, too, to the Fairfax Family Trust for the generous grant which has enabled Mark to be employed as CSAC director. The centre seeks to promote scholarly enthusiasm for this neglected subject which promises so much benefit to our church and nation.

This book is the forerunner to a much larger work which I am writing in conjunction with Mark Hutchinson and with Bob Linder of Kansas State University, an authority on evangelicals in politics and in wartime. That book will seek to redress the balance which this one so conspicuously lacks. This study is centred on Sydney and Anglican evangelicalism. The fuller study will give greater recognition to regional differences and to the evangelicalism of other denominations.

1. Going into All the World, 1788–1835

The coming of Christianity to Australia was the work of British evangelical Christians who, fired by the prospect of the expansion of Christ's kingdom over the entire globe, took advantage of an opportunity to plant the Gospel in the southern hemisphere. The Christianity brought to Australia in 1788 with the First Fleet was the product of the Evangelical Revival of the 1740s. It was a Methodist revival and it produced energised, methodical men and women. They tended to dream big dreams and had the will and the endurance to carry them through. The second generation of Anglican evangelical clergy—John Newton, John Venn, Thomas Haweis, Thomas Scott and Charles Simeon—directed their attention to foreign missions, which meant planning and acting on a world scale. While statesmen were provoked by the loss of America in 1776 into rethinking their global strategy and hatching schemes affecting Africa, India, China, and New Holland, evangelicals hitched a ride for the Gospel, and dreamed of schemes to propagate the Gospel in all those areas.

The Evangelical Vision

The world vision of the evangelicals arose partly from the new voyages of discovery which in the eighteenth century opened up the Pacific world. But it was the revival of the late 1730s and early 1740s which gave to evangelicals an unconquerable commitment to the Gospel as the power of God to save. In the revival much was learned of the power of the Gospel as an instrument for renovating whole societies and for converting those drawn from different races and cultures. Little children were converted as well as adults; members of the lower orders were converted as well as those of the upper and middle classes; and in America, 'the poor negro' and the Indians, to whom the revered David Brainerd and other missionaries ministered, experienced revival every bit as dramatic as whites. Demonstrably, the Gospel was divinely designed to rescue all humankind. Accordingly, it had to be conveyed to all humankind. In that process the evangelicals encountered many different types of humans! Never would they accept that any was beyond the reach of the Gospel. A great interest in the world and its peoples developed among evangelicals, which resulted in massive reports and chronicles of the progress of the Gospel among these peoples. This habit of mind was quite different from that of earlier generations of Protestants who, more interested in orthodoxy than in mission, studied propositions in preference to people, philosophy in preference to history, and Oxford in preference to the world. The early evangelicals' synthesis of Spirit, Word and world actually opened them up to the world's peoples and the possibility of reaching them with the Gospel. In Australia this was to translate into a determined mission to the people who inhabited that antipodean world: convicts, free settlers, the peoples of the Pacific islands, and, after many failures, the Aboriginal people of Australia.

A concurrent theological emphasis stirred the evangelical mind. Accompanying the revivals in some Protestant circles was a great interest in the coming of the millennium with its thousand years of spiritual prosperity. In New York, Jonathan Edwards, destined to become the church's greatest theologian of revival, wrote as early as 1724 that, with the approach of the millennium, the Gospel would triumph in those areas where hitherto Satan 'had reigned quietly from the beginning of the world', including Terra Australis Incognita and Hollandia Nova.[1] The large accession of converts into the churches in the revivals fuelled speculation that the millennium was just about to begin and that the earth was about to be filled with 'the knowledge of the Lord, as the waters cover the sea' (Isaiah 11.9).

There was a third development in the British religious scene which was to add momentum to the evangelical movement in Australia. Since the reign of Elizabeth I (1558–1603), the forces of dissent from the Established Church of England were a large and growing problem. Their quest for greater liberties was untiring, and in the eighteenth century their numbers were significantly swelled by the Evangelical Revival. Those adhering to Dissent in response to the revival were known as the New Dissent. They were made up of Congregationalists, Particular Baptists, the New Connexion General Baptists, the Wesleyan Methodists and Calvinistic Methodists. The last two were not strictly dissenters, since they sought initially to work through the national church, but they brought two innovations: the formation of religious societies or classes within the church to nourish spiritual formation and the complementary mission of parish parson and itinerant preacher. They also believed in co-operating with true Christians of other communions.

At the time of Australia's settlement, Calvinistic Methodism was at its peak. Founded on the preaching of George Whitefield, and sustained by the preaching of Thomas Haweis, William Romaine, John Newton and Rowland Hill and the hymns of Augustus Toplady, John Newton, and William Cowper, the movement enjoyed great popular success towards the end of the eighteenth century, and made a significant contribution to early Australian evangelicalism through missionaries who served in the South Seas with the London Missionary Society and who used Sydney as a base for their operations.

The New Dissent and the Methodists were frowned on by the Establishment and by the Old Dissent (Quakers, Presbyterians, Unitarians, General Baptists). They argued that the new enthusiasm was dangerous and against the natural order. It was both heresy and treason, a sin and a crime. Suspicion was brought to a head by the French Revolution. Methodist class meetings and Sunday schools were seen as seedbeds of radicalism and worse. Early governors of New South Wales shared this fear of Methodism and sometimes made trouble for all evangelicals, who were often then all labelled 'Methodists' and 'enthusiasts' or 'Methodistical enthusiasts'. For their part, however, evangelicals, both in England and in Australia, were more interested in co-operating with each other than arguing about whether the purest evangelicals were establishmentarian or dissenting. Thomas Gisborne, an evangelical in the Established Church and friend of William Wilberforce, described the evangelicals who united in the missionary movement as 'parallel columns of a combined army, marching onward, side by side, for the subjugation of a common foe'.[2] The parallel columns were the evangelicals from the church and from Dissent. They were both united and distinct. Despite the unity of heart that undoubtedly existed among evangelicals, they also had the pride of soldiers in their own denominations and, as with military regiments, great rivalry could exist between them.[3] This rivalry was more in the nature of 'holy emulation' than sectarianism.

On 28 October 1786, four days after the appointment of Richard Johnson as chaplain to the First Fleet, the elder Henry Venn, one of the first generation of Anglican evangelicals and now 'stricken in years', enthused in a letter to his daughter:

With what pleasure may we consider this plan of peopling that far-distant region, and other opening connexions with the Heathen, as a foundation for the Gospel of our God and Saviour to be preached unto them; when 'a vast multitude, whom no one can number,' shall, 'call upon his name;'—when ... all the savageness of the Heathen shall be put off, and all graces of the Spirit shall be put on. . . . All heaven will break forth in that song of praise, 'Allelujah! For the Lord God Omnipotent reigneth!'[4]

Venn argued that the Gospel would not only be the salvation of the Heathen. The Gospel and relocation would also be the means of renovating his own society's 'lost creatures', the convicts: 'Those that stole, will steal there no more; for having no receivers of stolen goods, no ale-houses, &c., they will be under no temptation to steal.' Incredible naivety? Not primarily. The evangelicals were then passionately committed to social reform, understood as the reformation of society's outcasts, be it the poor, the criminal, the slave, or the heathen. Because these early generations of evangelicals held together the three strands of Word, Spirit and world, they were determined to take the Gospel to all, whether or not they were perceived to be receptive. The motive of evangelicals for engagement in the Botany Bay enterprise was evangelism and reform, their twin aims for the world.

Three theories are usually advanced by historians to explain the sending of the First Fleet to Botany Bay.[5] The first, the 'convict-dumping' theory, contends that Britain was desperate to find somewhere to export its social problem when, after 1776, convicts could no longer be sent to Georgia or Virginia. A second theory is the Empire and defence argument: that the settlement was founded as compensation for the loss of America, as a base for British penetration of the Pacific, and to serve as an alternative sea-route to China. A third theory is that the colony was set up primarily as a labour camp for young industries, including wine, tobacco and linen for export, thus laying the economic foundation of a new Empire in the Pacific. Captain Watkin Tench, who sailed with the First Fleet, recorded in his journal that 'Extent of Empire demands grandeur of design'.[6]

The evangelicals had their own grand design, and consideration of the evangelical involvement in the settling of New South Wales suggests that a fourth theory ought to be advanced to explain the origins of the settlement, namely that it was an opportunity for a reform experiment. In the evangelical mind, prison reform and missionary activity at home and abroad were easily juxtaposed. Evangelicals sometimes made very effective practical reformers, pioneering, if not perfecting, some of the techniques employed in the analysis of social systems and social problems. Yet evangelicals always aimed to reform individuals, whether they aimed to reform systems or not. To this end, the evangelical prison reformer John Howard (1726–90), favoured the holding of religious services in prisons; he not only endorsed the need for prison chaplains, but he had definite views on the most suitable type of chaplain. Magistrates, he said, should not just take the first clergyman who offers himself:

> They should choose one who is in principle a Christian: who will not content himself with officiating in public; but will converse with the prisoners; admonish the profligate; exhort the thoughtless; comfort the sick; and make known to the condemned, that mercy which is revealed in the Gospel.[7]

Prison chaplains, then, according to Howard, should be evangelicals, and Australia's first chaplain, Richard Johnson, well fitted Howard's prescription. So New South Wales was settled at just the time the burgeoning evangelical movement, with its commercial and shipping cohorts, was ready to embark on foreign ventures, especially those which would facilitate the Gospel's advance into the islands of the sea and which would allow opportunity for ministry to convicts so conspicuously in need of the evangelicals' products: salvation and reform.

Evangelicals have been essentially activistic. Their vision and faith rarely encouraged them 'to let go, and let God'. They became devotees of the 'means' by which God's Gospel could be propagated. Among the chief means were voluntary evangelical societies which were formed in copious numbers at the end of the eighteenth century to implement a vast array of missionary schemes and religious and social reforms. Among those organisations were the Elland and Eclectic Societies, which probably brought about Richard Johnson's appointment as chaplain. The Elland Society[8] was established in 1777 to train poor pious young men for the ministry. William Wilberforce and John and Henry Thornton, members of the remarkably influential evangelical pressure group, the Clapham Sect, were contributors to the fund. Richard Johnson's name is not found in the records of the Elland Society. But those early records are poorly kept, and Johnson was certainly typical of those pious evangelicals of humble social origin whose path into the ordained ministry was laid by clerical education societies such as the Elland Society. In 1783 the Eclectic Society was formed. This was a forum for the discussion of issues of concern to leading Anglican evangelicals, especially reform and missions. Out of the well-connected network represented by the membership of this society grew the Botany Bay chaplaincy.

On 18 August 1786 Treasury was sent 'a Plan' for the settlement of Botany Bay. It included the provision of a chaplain, which appears to have come about through William Wilberforce's friendship with William Pitt the Younger, as is suggested by a letter from Pitt to Wilberforce, dated 23 September 1786:

> The colony for Botany Bay will be much indebted to you for your assistance in providing a chaplain ... Seriously speaking, if you can find such a clergyman as you mention we shall be very glad of it; but it must be soon.[9]

On 15 November 1786, Newton wrote to Wilberforce:

> To you, as the instrument, we owe the pleasing prospect of an opening for the propagation of the Gospel in the Southern Hemisphere. Who can tell what important consequences may depend on Mr Johnson's going to New Holland? It may seem but a small event at present: so a foundation-stone, when laid, is small compared with the building to be erected upon it; but it is the beginning and the earnest of the whole.[10]

The subject appointed for the meeting of the Eclectic Society on 13 November 1786 was 'What is the best method of planting and propagating the Gospel in Botany Bay?' The subject was then debated, but there is no record of what was said, nor was Richard Johnson present, although he was invited.[11] So the Botany Bay chaplaincy was the result of the fellowship of some of the best-known members of a movement which was becoming a mass movement, touching the poor and the multitudes as well as the wealthy and the powerful. They were conscious that in the Gospel they had a potent instrument of social and individual reform, and they had the zeal to use it and the skill to use it effectively.

Just four years after the settlement of Australia, the modern missionary movement was born. In 1792 William Carey and the Northampton Particular Baptists established the Baptist Missionary Society. In his *Enquiry into the Obligations of Christians to Use Means for the Conversion of the Heathens*, Carey, an avid reader of Cook's journals, included a gazetteer of the population of every known country in the world and the known religious allegiance of all the world's peoples. He gives the number of inhabitants of New Holland as

12 million and labels them all pagans, though '1 or 2 ministers are there'.[12] His geographical and demographic enterprise was typical of the evangelical who understood that the Gospel was for the world and all its peoples. Three years later the London Missionary Society (LMS) was formed by a large number of dissenters and 'occasional nonconformists' as Establishment evangelicals who associated with dissenters were known. Evangelicals who felt strongly that the Church of England should have a society supported by members of their own church formed the Church Missionary Society (CMS) in 1799. The LMS founder who most affected Australia was Thomas Haweis, who began and ended his ministry determined to know nothing but Christ and him crucified. He was a Calvinistic Methodist and an 'occasional nonconformist' within the Church of England. Admitted to deacon's orders in 1757, Haweis had been appointed curate of St Mary Magdalene, Oxford. Here he preached fervently the doctrines of the revival, later (1762) published as *Evangelical Principles and Practice*. The diarist James Woodforde dismissed his sermons as 'very stupid, low and bad stuff', but they won a very large hearing among the students. Like Joseph Milner, Haweis was to publish a multi-volume history of the Christian church; it majored on the missionary expansion of the church through the preaching of the Gospel, and he dedicated it to Joseph Hardcastle and the other LMS directors.

In opposition to another LMS director, David Bogue, a learned Congregationalist who wished to see LMS focus its energies on India, Haweis was convinced that God was calling the society to work in the South Seas. The founders of LMS tended to support either Calvinistic Methodism or Presbyterianism, the chief difference being a commitment on the part of the latter to an educated ministry. The important consequence of this was that the best-educated missionaries went to India and those of more humble educational attainments went to the South Seas and often ended up in New South Wales. On 14 May 1798, for example, eleven LMS missionaries arrived in Sydney, dislodged from the Society Islands (which include Tahiti) by the threat of martyrdom.[13] 'If the chaplains began an Evangelical tradition in New South Wales,' observes Ken Cable, 'it was the London Missionary Society men who gave it substance.'[14]

The coming of official Methodist work to New South Wales coincided with a great new fillip to evangelical ambitions unleashed by the defeat of Napoleon. The Wesleyan Methodists, then, came to Australia in significant numbers slightly later than the Calvinistic Methodists.[15] But Wesleyan

Methodism, like evangelical Anglicanism and Calvinistic Methodism, did come to Australia at one of the heights of its power. Wesley died in 1791, but the Wesleyan connexion grew dramatically during the Napoleonic Wars. The Wesleyan Methodist Missionary Society (WMMS) was formed between 1814 and 1818 to capitalise on this surge of missionary interest. At the 1816 Wesleyan Conference it was reported that 116 overseas missionaries had been sent. The last of these to arrive at his post was Samuel Leigh, on 10 August 1815. New South Wales was targeted by the newly created Wesleyan missionary bureaucracy as it was 'supposed there is much missionary work in that Colony'. Leigh was commended to Samuel Marsden by Joseph Butterworth, the influential Methodist MP and friend of Wilberforce, in a letter where, in an outburst of then typical millennial enthusiasm, he waxed lyrical about the peace which had at last come to Europe and the opportunity which that would afford to allow the Scriptures to be spread throughout the world. After detailing initiatives to have Bibles in many languages printed in India, France, Russia, and Germany, Butterworth expressed the prevailing evangelical pneumatology when he wrote, 'We shall only want the Spirit of the Word to be given from on high to accompany the letter and then we may expect great things to come to pass.'[16] This was a perfect statement of the evangelical synthesis of Spirit, Word and world.

How did this confident, expansionist, and reformist movement fare in New South Wales in the years 1788 to 1835? Looked at as a whole, the movement was not strong: successive governors were usually suspicious of non-Anglican evangelicals, namely dissenters and Methodists, thus threatening that evangelical ecumenism critical to the movement's strength. To the evangelicals, the ruling-class culture was seductive at times. But there was always tension between the two. The governors wanted their subjects 'moralised'; the evangelicals wanted them 'Gospelised' as well. Governors tended to come from a higher social class than chaplains, and were suspicious of 'enthusiasm' and 'Methodism', wanting religion to control the will rather than stir the affections. Evangelicals were probably not a significant proportion of the convict population, and women and children, usually more receptive to the Gospel than adult males, were under-represented. Neither the population nor the way it was governed, then, augured well for the evangelicals.

Apart from the convicts, there were other groups among whom the evangelicals expected to minister: soldiers and settlers, Aboriginal people, and South Sea Islanders. The last were to prove receptive soil for the Gospel seed eventually, but early years were a severe trial to evangelical confidence. With few exceptions the soldiers were as committed to debauchery as their more unfortunate charges, and they were not untouched by 'the contagion of infidel philosophy'[17] imported from France and popularised through the writings of Tom Paine. Aborigines were an even more difficult test, usually successfully resisting evangelical overtures for more than a century. Only free settlers were reasonably responsive to evangelical faith, but they had not been motivated to migrate by religious factors, and were few in number in this early period. The aspirations and optimism of the evangelicals, then, were severely tested by their antipodean clientele. New South Wales was 'an awkward, unpromising corner of the Lord's great house'.[18] It is difficult for the historian to assess which is the more remarkable: the extent of their failure or the extent to which, motivated by their desire to reach all with the Gospel, they persisted in engaging with their four distinct mission fields: convicts, South Sea Islanders, settlers, and Aboriginal people. Only among the last did the early evangelicals fail to do a more systematic work of evangelism and reform than has hitherto been realised.

Mission in the Convict Counter-Culture

To address the issue of the relationship between the evangelical and the convict culture, it is necessary to review briefly one of the major historiographical problems in the origins of white Australia. Who were the convicts? Were they rebels, petty thieves, hardened criminals, or working-class victims? The most idealistic view is that they were primitive rebels against an oppressive regime who, in a new land, laid the strong foundations of a democracy. This view focuses attention on Irish convicts, the first of whom were landed in New South Wales in 1791. Irish courts despatched over 20 per cent of all convicts transported to Australia, and many of those sentenced in Scottish and English courts were also of Irish birth. Only a small proportion of all convicts can be regarded as political, but, of them, the majority are Irish. The view that the convicts were petty thieves who made good *petit bourgeois* is held by Manning Clark and Humphrey McQueen,[19] who find therein the principal reason why Australia is not radical, but complacent and conservative. The argument that they were hardened criminals or recidivists is that of L. L. Robson, who shows that most were transported for theft and had previous convictions,[20] while the Schedvins argue that the convicts were hardened members of a criminal class who passed on their loveless and work-shy habits to their offspring.[21] A final view is that they were working-class, wage-earning victims of poverty (not full-time thieves) who fell foul of the law. The casualties of otherwise respectable occupations, they were therefore more likely to possess a sharper class resentment than those who worked in occupations (swindling, prostitution) which had no respectable alternative.

Evidently, there were a number of different types of convict. The convicts had many voices, and it is likely that evangelicalism would have appealed more to some types than others. Since many were working-class victims, the question of the relation of the convicts to organised religion is another chapter in the unhappy history of religion and the working classes. The convicts perceived that the Christian religion was part of the system which victimised them, and were ill-disposed to look on it sympathetically. If they perceived that the exponents of that religion considered them chiefly responsible for their own wretchedness, they were even less inclined to view it favourably. This attitude persisted when transportation was abolished. Convictism, of course, was different from all working-class culture in one important respect. To be transported was, in the majority of cases, not a life sentence. To be working class was. Convictism was a phase which the evangelicals, along with others, did their best to ameliorate and then abolish. The evangelicals understood that their attitude to the convict system was to be like their attitude to slavery. That was easy. What their attitude should be to the working class has always been more problematical.

The impact of the convicts on Australian society helps to explain the conspicuous and often-observed difference between the religious scene in Australia and that in America. America started with convictions; Australia with convicts. America was established by dissenters; Australia by disreputables. American free settlers valued religious liberty; Australian convicts valued personal liberty to practise a more hedonistic religion. The first settlers of America believed America to be the promised land: they did not have to work to make it so. It was already heaven on earth. The first convicts thought of Australia as a God-forsaken hell on earth.

It has been argued that the forces of ungodliness in Australia today are recruited from the ranks of Western secularisation and cannot be attributed to our convict origins.[22] But historical roots sometimes go very deep indeed. Australian secularisation is distinctively Australian, and our convict forebears were so numerous that their legacy is likely to be felt to this day. It was not until 1827 that the free outnumbered the convicts in New South Wales, and nearly half the free were ex-convicts. In 1833 alone, the year after the passing of the Reform Act which signalled the intention of middle-class England to clean up its society, 6779 convicts were sent out, the peak annual figure. In all about 150,000 (including 24,960 women) convicts were transported to Australia, most of them petty thieves. Only about 1800 were transported for political offences: pettiness was therefore more likely to become an Australian characteristic than protest!

It is difficult to establish that there were changes in evangelical attitudes to convicts over time. The first chaplain's own attitude towards the convicts does not appear to have changed. Towards the beginning of his twelve years in New South Wales, Richard Johnson described his charges as the most godless people he had ever seen,[23] and towards the end he characterised them as 'lost to all sense of virtue, and abandoned to every species of wickedness'.[24] He tried to reclaim them primarily by preaching sermons 'upon the awful strain'.[25] This technique appears to have paid some dividends in the Evangelical Revival of the 1740s, but the convicts were not the only contemporaries of Johnson who were unimpressed. William Bull of the Eclectic Society anticipated that Johnson would bore his hearers, and therefore sagely counselled him that his 'copper-hearted companions' must have a Gospel preached to them 'of but few ideas and fireworks'.[26] Governor Phillip, although a stranger to vital religion, may have been referring to the dourness of Johnson's preaching rather than the doctrine, when he advised him to 'begin with *moral* subjects', advice which hurt the sensitive chaplain. John Newton counselled Johnson not to disregard the governor's advice, 'though you and I know that it was like requiring you to cut down a large tree with a wooden hatchet'.[27] Newton later counselled Johnson more firmly about his preaching in 'the awful strain': 'to persons in this state denunciations of wrath too frequently repeated, instead of working savingly upon them, rather tends to increase the enmity of their minds against God'.[28] Newton's advice probably arose from his own experience rather than from any knowledge of the convicts' reaction to Johnson's preaching, which seemed deficient more because it was prosaic than 'awful'.[29]

Very occasionally Johnson's 'awful' preaching found its mark among the convicts. After a service he recorded, 'one at least went away sorrowful and heavy-hearted and some others rejoicing in the Son of God manifested towards them'.[30] Similarly, it is recorded of his preaching to the women who arrived on the Second Fleet that the sermon drew 'tears from many of these unfortunates, who were not yet so hardened as to be insensible to truth'.[31] His efforts on behalf of the sick and dying in the Second Fleet at least were appreciated by one convict who wrote home: 'I believe few of the sick would recover if it was not for the kindness of the Rev. Mr. Johnson, whose assistance out of his own stores makes him the physician both of soul and body.'[32]

It is interesting that the only contemporary criticism of Johnson still extant is that of Francis Grose, administrator from 11 December 1792 to 12 December 1794, who accused him of being a 'Methodist'. If the convicts criticised Johnson, their criticisms have not survived. His was an hospitable home, and his wife, Mary (née Burton), communicated well with the convicts, possibly because she was a Cockney and many of them were London East Enders.[33] Johnson does not appear to have gone out of his way to avoid contact with the convicts. He attempted to visit them when sick and to read to them, and he admitted to finding more pleasure in visiting the convicts from hut to hut than he did in preaching. The convicts appear to have found in their clerical visitor something of a confidant; they complained to him of their treatment, and he sometimes responded to their complaints with as much indignation as he responded to his own hurts.[34] He was something of a bridge between the rulers and the ruled. Perhaps few have proved as unequal to the task set them as Australia's first chaplain, but this is far more of a comment on the enormity of the task than on the feebleness of the instrument. Although sensitive and self-deprecating, he personified the evangelical synthesis of Word, Spirit and world, and he never shirked his responsibilities to his convict flock. He had to endure more persecution than most are called upon to bear. He had little to be ashamed of—he had been tolerant, loyal and dutiful, and, if the converts were not won in any significant numbers to evangelical religion, neither were they turned from it by Johnson. He did not have to turn them; they were already turned.[35]

Samuel Marsden was tougher than Johnson, and he stayed longer. On his arrival in the colony in March 1794, Marsden quickly came to grief at the hands of Grose, who frustrated his efforts to force the convicts to observe the Sabbath. Then, at Parramatta, where he was posted, he came into conflict with the senior officer there, Captain John Macarthur, who dismissed his charge against a drunken emancipist. Historians argue, however, that

Marsden, having thus suffered at the hands of his enemies, suffered far more at the hands of his friend, Governor Hunter, who, in reaction to Grose, reappointed clerical magistrates, including Johnson and himself. Neither the fact that the practice of appointing clerical magistrates was well established in England, nor the fact that it was difficult to find men of integrity to fill the office in New South Wales, could mitigate the dislike felt for clerical magistrates by convicts. Marsden's undoubted severity in that role[36] has been identified as a major factor in the development of anticlericalism in Australia.[37] This is to attribute too much to one villain, however, and Australian anticlericalism is probably better understood as a typical colonial amplification of a social problem at home, namely the rising dislike of clerical magistrates, which was to peak at the 1819 Peterloo massacre when the magistrates ordered a troop of cavalry to charge a crowd at a peaceful reform rally. Australian Christianity was not only shaped by the state of British Christianity at the time of settlement, but continued to be influenced by home developments as much as by local factors.

There is some evidence that Samuel Leigh, the first Methodist minister in New South Wales, was at times accepted by the convicts when the chaplains of the Church of England were not. He comforted a number of condemned convicts who would not allow themselves to confess to Anglican clergy and who, in the case of Catholics, did not have an available priest. Leigh recounted one instance when a group of four condemned Catholics refused the ministrations of an Anglican clergyman, but—one more fully than the others—accepted his help:

> I accompanied them to the place of execution, distant about half a mile. When they came within sight of the gibbet, one of them … turned round and said, with much feeling: 'Sir, I depend on Jesus Christ for salvation. Will you pray for me?' I did pray for him; and never did I see a man more deeply affected, or more earnest in prayer … The other three were exasperated by his conduct, and evidently died under the delusion of a corrupt faith.[38]

This incident, which gives Leigh a success rate of only one in four(!), suggests that to the convicts evangelical Methodism can have been only marginally more acceptable than evangelical Anglicanism. Most convicts were impervious to the subtle distinctions between the sects. Ralph Mansfield, a Wesleyan preacher and publisher, wrote in his *New South Wales Magazine*:

Men in general seem to consider that all religions are the same—that it matters not what sort of opinions they entertain upon subjects of the most vital importance; a degree of apathy which approximates to entertaining no religion at all.[39]

If there is any truth in the stereotype of the Australian as indifferent, even hostile, to doctrinal distinctions and apathetic to all religion, it may be explicable in terms of the emphasis which the convict experience gave to that predisposition inherent in working-class victims of Britain's Industrial Revolution.

Mission to the Islanders of the Pacific

By contrast with the evangelical mission to the convicts, the mission to Pacific Islanders enjoyed remarkable success. Early evangelicals believed that New South Wales would be the base from which the islands of the sea would receive the Gospel. From Sydney would radiate the missionary advance of the church into New Zealand, Tahiti, Tonga and Fiji, Samoa and New Caledonia, New Hebrides and New Guinea, eventually into the countless millions of Asia. 'Let them give glory unto the Lord, and declare His praise in the islands' (Isaiah 42.12). For years Thomas Haweis, the LMS director who pressed most untiringly for the South Seas mission, had laboured to persuade Sir Joseph Banks and others influential with government to establish a settlement in Tahiti. By as early as 1806 the mission, whose missionaries spent much time in New South Wales, had passed through its 'night of toil'. Haweis remained committed to his pet scheme to the end, exclaiming on his deathbed, 'Wonderful things the Lord is doing upon earth!' He was buried in Bath Abbey where his epitaph reads:

> The Southern savage Isles he pitying view'd,
> And urged the peaceful heralds on their way;
> Through fruitless years the patient hope pursued,
> Till glorious conquests crown'd the long delay.
> As good old Simeon, ere his spirit fled,
> Surveyed the promised Branch from Jesse's rod;
> So HAWEIS beheld MESSIAH's kingdom spread,
> And then in peace departed hence to God.[40]

On 17 February 1810 a second group of LMS missionaries arrived in New South Wales, again dislodged from Tahiti. Samuel Marsden found work for most of them, and encouraged them to persevere with the Tahiti mission until within a few years King Pomare had become a Christian and the islands went over to Christianity.[41]

Samuel Marsden was the best-known of the evangelicals who failed with convicts and Aboriginal people, but whose labours among the Polynesian peoples of the South Seas bore gratifying fruit. He had a passion for souls and a vision acquired from his mentor, Charles Simeon of Cambridge, of a Christianised South Seas. In the diary which he kept on his voyage out to Australia, he records his self-doubts and his longings. On the eve of departure he wrote, 'I am about to quit my native country with a view of preaching the everlasting Gospel. O that the end of my going may be answered in the conversion of many poor souls.' This passion made of Marsden a missionary athlete in the tradition of John Wesley, after whose brother he had been named. In 1804 he took charge of LMS missionaries in the South Seas. He pleaded for a civilising mission to the Maoris before the CMS committee in 1807. He consistently maintained that the establishment of commerce with the natives was critical to the success of any mission. In 1814 the mission was launched along lines recommended by him, with the appointment of two artisans, William Hall and John King. He parted with £1400 of his own money to purchase the ship *Active* for the New Zealand mission. Marsden himself first set foot on the mainland of New Zealand at Matauri Bay on 20 December 1814. There was to be no repetition of the shameful first Sabbath at Sydney Cove, and elaborate preparations were made for the solemn ceremony to be held on the following Sunday which was also Christmas Day. Marsden rejoiced to see the English flag flying over Rangihoua, signifying 'the dawn of civilisation, liberty, and religion in that dark and benighted land'. He preached on a text from Luke (2.10): 'Behold I bring you glad tidings of great joy.' In spite of many dangers and a propensity to suffer excruciatingly from sea-sickness, he made seven voyages to his New Zealand mission. He made his last journey when over seventy years of age, lame, and almost blind. The not entirely undeserved epithet of 'flogging parson' has stuck to him like a limpet, disqualifying him from any admiration in the popular history of Australia. But among the evangelicals, his counsel was always sought and his advice usually respected. For three decades his name appears in the minutes of CMS with more frequency than that of any other individual.

Probably the first Australian-born person to become an overseas missionary was James Shepherd, who accompanied Marsden to New Zealand in 1820 with CMS.[42] Another Australian-born missionary, and one destined to greater affection in the Australian evangelical heart thanks to her biographer, was the daughter of an LMS missionary, Rowland Hassall. Mary Hassall married Walter Lawry in 1819 and, during her second pregnancy, accompanied him to Tonga in 1822 to commence a mission there. Walter found the going very hard. It was no easier for him than working among convicts. Indeed, a convict, Morgan, had escaped to Tonga from Sydney and infected the Tongans with a virulent distaste for Christianity. 'To this day,' complained Lawry, 'they remember Morgan's lies and believe them, consequently they detest our acts of religious worship more than anything we do or say.'[43] Walter felt obligated to do missionary things: preach, build schools, and put up with the insensitive, ill-informed, and out-of-date directions from the home secretaries. But he did not know the language, he had no equipment for a school, and the home directors were swayed by the last person who spoke to them. If Walter made heavy weather of it, Mary seemed to 'glide through it' and found herself wondering if it is easier for a woman to be a missionary than a man. She just befriended the mothers and thereby learned their customs and their speech.

In spite of making a better fist of things, Mary was never mentioned in the *Wesleyan Methodist Magazine*: extracts from his diaries were edited to exclude any mention of her, which irritated her a bit. But she never complained or had any feminist paroxysms. She was, her husband said in a burst of alliteration, 'a perfect pattern of passive piety'.[44] In 1824 they left Tonga for England. Mary was pregnant again. They were stunned by the emotion engendered by their departure. Amidst a chorus of much sniffling, one eloquent Tongan said:

> We thank you for coming among us. Before you came, it was dark night in Tonga; now it begins to be light. Your friends in the foreign lands have sent for you. Go, and tell them that Tonga is a foolish land. Let them send us many teachers. Our hearts are sore, we are pained in our bellies, because you are going away from us.[45]

Following the birth of a daughter, Mary Australia, Mary Lawry died in Cornwall, England, on Christmas Day 1825. But Methodism was destined to reap a harvest in Tonga celebrated throughout the evangelical world.

Mission to the Free Settlers

In terms of its future, the most significant mission which the evangelicals had to develop in New South Wales was to the free settlers. The Johnsons and Marsdens may have exercised considerable importance in the colony through their modelling of Christian family life.[46] Among the many reasons why the Johnsons and Marsdens became exceptional farmers was that the wives were eager to provide for their children and delighted in their health as they responded to the excellent and plentiful produce. Marsden's own family was his major solace. He observed that his 'Situation would have been much more intolerable had I been a single Man. My Wife and Family in the Hour of Temptation and Trial have often procured an Asylum of Peace and Tranquility.'[47]

When the LMS missionaries arrived in Sydney from the Society Islands in 1798, they were received warmly by Johnson and Marsden, who felt deprived of devout and responsive evangelical company. Johnson took William Henry and James Fleet Cover and their families to live with him when they first arrived. He especially commended Rowland Hassall, Henry, and Cover, for their diligence in preaching to the settlers.[48] Cover, he wrote to the LMS treasurer, Joseph Hardcastle, 'constantly preaches, and exhorts every Sabbath in different places. His labours are greatly wanted, and I pray God they may be rendered useful.'[49] Governors Hunter and King gave them material aid, and they served the colony as teachers, evangelists, shopkeepers and public servants. They taught and preached in the settlements around Sydney, Parramatta and the Hawkesbury. Although they worked among the convict gangs and with the assigned servants, their main efforts were among the free settlers and emancipists.

Marsden was a little nervous of the LMS missionaries on the issue of authority, but so long as they observed the primacy of Church of England services, he was happy to act as their patron. In 1804 he was appointed LMS agent in the South Seas; he appointed William Pascoe Crook (1775–1846) as his parish clerk, to teach at a school, and to pastor a congregation. A tireless evangelist and a Calvinistic Methodist,[50] Crook had difficulty accepting the Establishment. Marsden observed that he 'shewed great Aversion to the Forms of the established Church',[51] and sometimes went close to tearing the delicate web which knitted together the evangelical workers who monopolised the church scene in the first generation. Another of the LMS missionaries was John Youl, who was also a Calvinistic Methodist lay-preacher.

He returned to England, was ordained and later became the first rector of Launceston in Tasmania. Some LMS missionaries were to return to the islands, but Rowland Hassall was one who remained, becoming Marsden's business manager. He was from the outset a warm supporter of Marden.[52] In New South Wales he founded a dynasty which was greatly to influence the development of the infant colony. His son Thomas trained for the Anglican ministry in Wales, married Ann, Marsden's first-born, and served as a minister and chaplain for many years. He was the founder of Sunday schools in New South Wales, and was known as the 'the galloping parson'. His parish was said to be 'all of Australia beyond Liverpool'.

The Wesleyan Methodists ministered in the same areas as the LMS missionaries, sometimes sharing in the work, and sometimes creating an independent work wherever Calvinism was strongly stressed. They were marginally more separatist than the Calvinistic Methodists and were more impressed by polity issues, so they began to foster a denomination independent of the Church of England. The first Methodist class meetings were held in Windsor and Sydney in 1812. The Windsor meeting was convened by Edward Eagar, an emancipist lawyer, largely because of the strong Calvinism of the Church of England at Windsor. The first Sydney class meeting was held on 6 March 1812 by Thomas Bowden, a teacher, who had arrived in Sydney the previous January. The Sydney and Windsor groups met in Sydney in April for a love feast, and as a result two letters were sent to England requesting preachers. Bowden wrote:

> I am sure Mr Marsden would be glad to see the different settlements provided, and especially if we proceed in the primitive way of Methodism; not in hostility against the Church, but rather in unison with it, not so much to make a party distinct from the Church, as to save souls in the Church. Of course, the Preacher should not be radically a Dissenter; if possible, one attached to the Establishment, as Mr Wesley, Dr Clarke, and most of our primitive Preachers were.[53]

At first Governor Macquarie opposed Samuel Leigh, the first Methodist preacher, but he changed his view when he saw the value of Leigh's ministry. Leigh was a self-sacrificing itinerant evangelist in the tradition of John Wesley. He carried out to the letter the directions of his masters in London: he owned only a horse, and he would accept no land grants except sufficient on which to build a chapel. He was appalled by the heat and the vast distances he had to travel and the sexual temptations he felt. Send no more single missionaries, he advised the home committee of the Wesleyan Methodist Missionary Society, but please send help before he was slain and the sheep scattered. He was lonely. The WMMS had a hard rule not insisted on by the other missionary societies: for a probationary period its missionaries had to remain unmarried. When preaching, Leigh kept losing his concentration if Mary Hassall were in the congregation. Eventually he proposed, but Mary thought him far too earnest. Is it possible, she wondered, to have a husband who is both zealous for God and human at the same time? Warm-hearted Walter Lawry was far more to her liking.

In one area Leigh was content: he was happy to work with Marsden. His two younger colleagues, Walter Lawry and Benjamin Carvosso, were more separatist in their thinking. They were not keen on the Church of England and even less on any Calvinism among the Calvinistic Methodists. Lawry, for example, took Hassall's daughter, but not his theology. In 1819 he complained, 'At Parramatta, Mr H. has everything his own way, our hymns are not sung, and the place of worship is not upon our plan.'[54] By 1821 the Wesleyans had opened their own chapel and Sunday school at Parramatta. In 1821, too, they set up a separate Wesleyan work at Kissing Point (Ryde). Marsden was disturbed, if not greatly distressed, but William Cowper, a Marsden recruit, and Youl, out of their Calvinist commitment, opposed the Wesleyan work bitterly. In 1821, too, the Wesleyans celebrated the Lord's Supper for the first time. Leigh complained to the home committee about these developments, and Lawry and Carvosso were reprimanded. A clear division had developed over the purpose of the Wesleyan mission in New South Wales. Carvosso thought their task was to develop a strong independent Wesleyan work for colonists who had no real link with the Church of England. Leigh and the home committee saw their mission as an adjunct of the Church of England.[55]

Methodist historians have assessed the first Methodist mission to New South Wales as a failure. The mission limped on from one setback to another, until by 1831 when the able Rev. Joseph Orton took over, it had seen very little growth. Leigh and his successor, George Erskine, were both unsuited to their responsibilities as superintendents of the mission. Among the early missionaries, Benjamin Carvosso and Ralph Mansfield were able men, but the latter withdrew from the society in disgust over injustices perpetrated by the home committee of WMMS and took a position with the devout

Wesleyan, Robert Howe, editor of the *Sydney Gazette*. The early Methodists found the convict population among the least responsive they had worked with in any area of the globe, and the scattered New South Wales population was difficult to work and failed to produce adequate lay leadership for the classes and for local preaching. By 1831 only 112 members and 137 Sunday-school scholars were being claimed for the society, and these were considered to be over-estimates. Orton said it was 'little better than a wreck'.[56]

Samuel Marsden realised that the extension of the Kingdom involved more than adding members to the church rolls. Wise policies would have to be developed to lay a broad foundation for the church in the colony. In particular, he foresaw the day when free settlers rather than convicts and their governors would set the political agenda. We have not space to unravel his many disputes with governors, but he was motivated by his desire to maintain the dignity of the clerical office, on which he thought the propagation of the Gospel depended, in a decreasingly penal society. Interestingly, Marsden's clash with Macquarie over the full acceptance into society of emancipated convicts was, at one level, the expression of two strong aspects of evangelicalism. Marsden represented the strong evangelical push towards respectability on the part of the upwardly mobile artisan classes from Britain. Macquarie, on the other hand, through the definite, if high Tory, evangelicalism of his wife, Elizabeth, felt that the doctrine of justification by the atoning blood of Christ, accompanied by the Anglican emphasis on absolution, meant that everyone was redeemable and should be given a second chance. So, it was Macquarie, not Marsden, who, after his death, won the accolade of 'the John Howard or Jonas Hanway[57] of the Colony'. Yet, before concluding that Macquarie's legacy was more 'evangelical' than that of Marsden, we need to remind ourselves that, in supporting the drive for a post-convict, free, prosperous and progressive colony, Marsden came closer to aligning himself with the evangelical legacy. Marsden's evangelicalism must be adjudged to have been a robust expression of the evangelical synthesis of Spirit, Word and world, and so successful was he in his impact on his world, that his critics have condemned him for being more interested in farming than in the pastoral pursuits more appropriate to clergy. But evangelicals from Wesley on have looked on economic prosperity as one of the common, if not guaranteed, fruits of the Gospel. It was just that Wesley was more successful in limiting his acquisition of wealth than Marsden.

Mission to the Aborigines

Official policy towards Aboriginal people began on an optimistic and well-meaning note. In the instructions which he received from the British government, Governor Phillip was directed to 'promote religion and education among the Native Inhabitants'. Phillip responded positively to this challenge. Let us, he decreed, give the Aboriginal people 'a high opinion of their new guests'. Richard Johnson, first chaplain, tried to befriend them, called his daughter Milbah Mary, and tried to adopt a young Aboriginal girl, Abaroo, but after a year and a half she ran away. Settlers and missionaries were encouraged to seek such effective contact with Aboriginal people as would integrate them into the new colony. During this period, proclamations were issued on not maltreating Aborigines. For example, that of 1810 read: 'the natives of this territory are to be treated in every respect as Europeans; and any injury or violence done or offered to the men or women natives will be punished according to the law'.

In practice, Aboriginal people were not protected by the law. Any Aboriginal resistance to the expansion of the white settlement was savagely put down. Despite hundreds of deaths, no white person was punished for killing an Aboriginal person until 1838. Major Paterson boasted of exhibiting Aboriginal heads on gibbets from Parramatta to the Hawkesbury River; Governor Macquarie employed troops against Aboriginal resistance forces, and pitched battles were fought in what are now Sydney's western suburbs. This pattern was repeated throughout the continent. Governor Stirling, for example, dispatched troops against Aboriginal people near Perth in 1834.

Aboriginal people were also largely ignored by the church. This is a critical delay—a generation of Aborigines were brutalised and corrupted by whites before the church did anything.[58] The first official missionary to the Aboriginal people was the Rev. William Walker, who arrived in 1821. He baptised the son of Bennelong. Thomas Coke Bennelong was probably the first Aboriginal adult to be baptised of his own volition. Walker set the pattern of subsequent missions by his theological understanding of Aboriginal people. They were the descendants of Ham, the son of Noah, who was unfortunate enough to catch his father drunk and naked; he reported him to his two brothers, who covered him. For this indiscretion Noah put a curse on the descendants of Ham, said to be the Egyptians, and, by extension, Africans and all black people of the southern hemisphere.[59] The corollary was clear: much could not be expected of Aboriginal people; they were cursed. Then Walker decided that the native people would have to settle down in a permanent mission. One could not wander around and be a Christian.

Following the failure of Macquarie's Native Institutions at Parramatta and Black Town, from 1825 the colonial authorities changed policy from integration to one of separation. Aboriginal people were now to be settled on land reservations where the missionaries would assist in training them in the skills of agriculture and manufacturing. In 1825 Governor Brisbane granted 4000 hectares for a mission of the LMS at Reid's Mistake near Lake Macquarie; in 1826 Darling granted 4000 hectares for a CMS mission at Wellington; in 1827 Earl Bathurst authorised a grant of 4000 hectares for a Wesleyan Methodist mission at Bateman's Bay. These grants were based on an acceptance of the futility of ministering to Aboriginal people in the vicinity of Europeans. The optimism which accompanied this new strategy is evident in the promise of John Harper, an energetic young Wesleyan lay-preacher:

> Let the Mission be established at a place where the Blacks are not in communication with the Whites, and my soul for any man's but his Mission will prosper ... It would also in a short time be able to support itself.[60]

Missionaries had come to see by bitter experience that the greatest handicap to the success of their endeavours was the pernicious influence of the degrading habits of their unconverted fellow whites. The inculcation of proper moral values and manners appropriate to civilisation necessitated that Aboriginal people come in contact only with the best models of Christian civilisation. All too often, other models prevailed. John Harris' considered conclusion is that 'The aggressive and unbridled immorality of white colonial society was the direct cause of the demise of a number of missions, and contributed to the failure of many others.'[61]

The LMS mission at Lake Macquarie was formed in 1826 as a mission to 'the natural Owners of the Country' by Lancelot Threlkeld. He was an experienced LMS missionary, who had worked in the Pacific. He was energetic and a gifted linguist. Yet the LMS withdrew from this mission in 1828, ostensibly for financial reasons. The governor, at the urging of Archdeacon William Grant Broughton (first Bishop of Australia from 1836), picked up the bills until 1841 when the government, too, pulled out. Threlkeld, in a desperate attempt to continue his mission, began operating a coalmine at Lake Macquarie in defiance of the Australian Agricultural Company's monopoly. But in the next year, 1842, he was forced to admit defeat.[62]

In his final report he said that his plan of operation had been to acquire Awabakal, the language of the Lake Macquarie natives, compile a grammar, and translate the Scriptures into it. Whilst these laudable ends were being pursued, the Aboriginal people themselves, however, were fast disappearing. Their disappearance was not his fault. No-one condemned their massacre by whites more fearlessly and vehemently than he, and those whom the whites did not rip open, roast in 'triangularly made log fires', or dash against stones, died of the white man's diseases or were seduced into nearby Newcastle by rum or prostitution. So there was no-one left to read his translations. Threlkeld's final conclusion after seventeen self-denying years:

> It is a melancholy fact, that although much has been done in the way of translation, there are now scarcely any Aborigines left to learn to read, and the few who remain appear determined to go on in the broad road to destruction.[63]

All the other missions continued to fail until the second half of the nineteenth century, when a few achieved a measure of permanence.

Barbara Thiering[64] has indicted the first generation of Australian clergy as a second-rate crew of social misfits who had to be exported to save the evangelical cause in Britain from ruin, just as the convicts had to be transported to save English society from ruin. Hers is partly an anachronistic assessment: our first chaplains may not have been great scholars, but they were good farmers, horsemen, and sheepmen, which may help to explain their success among a population of free settlers, emancipists and children. As Ken Cable remarks of the Church of England at the end of the 1820s, 'it might have done less'.[65] What I have laboured to establish in this chapter is that evangelicals had four difficult mission fields in early Australia: convicts, settlers, South Sea Islanders, and Aborigines. That they stuck to their mission with as much determination as they did and achieved as much as they did is a tribute to the capacity of the evangelical synthesis to empower rather ordinary and unexceptional men and women in their engagement with an unconverted world. Some, such as Johnson and Marsden, were accused by non-evangelicals of emphasising the less palatable doctrines of the Word too frequently in their attempts to reform and save that world, but none was ever accused of withdrawal into a pietistic enclave.

2. Identifying with the Liberal World, 1836–1870

Though the evangelicals were in possession of God's instrument to restore a broken world, it was not so much they as the liberals who were confident in the middle years of the nineteenth century that they would inherit the earth. For liberalism was an idea whose time had come. The liberal ideal was one of harmonious social progress, of religious and political liberty for all, based on a capitalist economy and an educated population, united in a common citizenship with a representative government in a beneficent state. For the most part, evangelicals responded to this strategy to reform society by identifying with it. Evangelicals made good capitalists and liberals. Liberals, capitalists, and evangelicals tended to share the same core values: frugality, moderation, sobriety and hard work. They tended to identify the same enemies: intemperance, sloth and Catholicism in both its Roman and Anglican forms. Liberals did find this one fault with Christians, however: they were factionalised. Sectarianism was the bane of progress, and the liberals opposed its intrusion in the political and social realms, especially the realm of education. But even here liberals were more opposed to Anglo-Catholics and Roman Catholics than to Protestants. In the colonies, liberals who decried sectarianism were not above using it for political advantage.

Evangelicals entered the Victorian age with something of a social engineering programme. They could have developed systems of education, welfare, and hospitals. But they became sidetracked by the need to resist the growing Catholic menace. Only in retrospect have they seen that they may have sustained more damage from their uncritical identification with the capitalist, liberal world. It was a period when, in the evangelical synthesis of Spirit, Word and world, the aim of shaping the world was still prominent, and 'nation-building' would remain an overt evangelical goal until World War I and even beyond. The instrument for shaping the world was not the Gospel only, however, but the Gospel conjoined with 'the Spirit of the Age': liberalism. Consequently, evangelicals in this period had moral power and reinforced the cult of respectability. They had a modicum of political power, although not as great as they would have enjoyed had they resisted sectarian excesses. But they lacked the prophetic power to resist the forces of materialism, always so attractive to the majority of Australians. Their humanitarianism, so conspicuous in the age of Wilberforce, was overshadowed by their triumphalism, and the vital Christianity of the eighteenth-century evangelicals was institutionalised into Victorian respectability. Evangelical dissent developed into prosperous and powerful middle-class denominationalism. The Word strand in the threefold evangelical cord was too weak to divert the energies of liberalism into areas less damaging to the long-term growth of the Kingdom. Evangelical preaching of the Word in this period seems to have accentuated morality rather than the Gospel. This explains why many lay evangelicals appear to have been more interested in mammon than in mission, but as we shall see below it is necessary to view the evangelical emphasis on morality in its appropriate context.

The Spirit strand of the evangelical cord was well represented in this period by the Methodists, who had put their early failures behind them and grew rapidly. Methodism was then committed to the view that faithfulness to the Gospel and seeking to take it to farmers, miners, and labourers as well as the respectable middle classes meant working and praying for revival, and a number of remarkable localised awakenings are a feature of this period of evangelical history. Revivals seem to account for the extraordinary success of Methodism in this period. According to census data, between 1841 and 1871 while the Anglicans increased threefold and the Catholics fourfold, the Methodists increased tenfold. The great increase in population in this period was due to the discovery of gold in New South Wales and Victoria in 1851. At first horrified by the social upheaval occasioned by the gold rushes, the churches, with government help, mounted a significant presence on the goldfields, and the spectre of lawlessness on the scale reported from the earlier Californian gold rush did not eventuate. The Methodists were particularly adept at adjusting to this new challenge: their army of local preachers moved into the goldfields and lived happily under the same conditions as the miners. If the miners can undergo these privations for gold, they argued, we can do the same for Christ. They erected tents and chapels for worship and started Sunday schools. They inherited from their great founder a belief in perfectionism in this life which made them optimistic and energetic in their commitment to social and civic reform. The contribution of evangelical

Christianity to the shaping of this huge new population into a civic-minded community was probably far greater than has been recognised.

In this period, then, the triple mission field targeted by the evangelicals was the state in whose legislatures the future nation was taking shape, the population of a growing capitalist economy (both the exploited and the exploiters), and last, and by all means least, Aboriginal people. With the first they succeeded too well, although they lost through sectarianism much of what they gained through identification with liberalism. In their mission to the free population, they did better with the middle than the working classes, although the success of revivalistic Methodism among working-class people has almost certainly been underestimated by secular historians. Admittedly, there were too few radical evangelical voices such as that of J. D. Lang, who did appeal to the working classes. In their mission to the Aboriginal people, whose time, unlike that of the liberals, had not yet come, the evangelicals failed abjectly in the early part of this period, and then began to taste the fruits of perseverance.

Liberalism

At first sight, it might appear that liberals and evangelicals did not have a lot in common. Atkinson and Aveling have given us a profile of the typical New South Wales liberal of the 1830s. He (for the typical liberal was a male) stood for reform, and joined with those who in 1835 formed the Australian Patriotic Association. He tended to represent the immigrant settler class and campaigned for representative government and trial by jury. He was very likely to be a lawyer and to consort with newspaper journalists. His marriage was probably 'irregular', like that of the leading liberals, William Charles Wentworth, William Bland, Edward Eagar, Sir John Jamison (all of New South Wales), or R. L. Murray of Van Diemen's Land, or William Nairne Clark of Western Australia. He inhabited a masculine world, for reform was a masculine enterprise—it was the work of men who were away from home at public meetings. He was also a Freemason. Atkinson and Aveling make this claim on the connexion between religion, Freemasonry and reform:

> ... freemasonry paid scant attention to religion. Although the ritual of the masons had many Old Testament references—especially to King Solomon and the Temple at Jerusalem—its tone was secular and humanist. In the same way, very few of the reform leaders were religious men.[1]

But this painting shows only some of the colours. The full picture of the New South Wales reform movement has many evangelical hues, to which too many secular historians have been colour-blind.

Edward Eagar, mentioned above, for example, was one liberal reformer who was 'religious'. As we saw in chapter 1, he had established the first Methodist class meeting in Windsor in 1812. An Irish lawyer, he had been condemned to death for forgery. But following a spectacular deathcell conversion in Ireland, he was transported and assigned to an Anglican chaplain, Richard Cartwright. He was pardoned in 1813, but was repeatedly disadvantaged in his business dealing because he had been a convict, so he became an ardent champion of the emancipist cause. His advocacy of emancipists' rights and of constitutional reform for New South Wales both in the colony and in England, to which he returned in 1821, appears to have made a decided contribution to improvements in these areas. He was also a founder of the Bank of New South Wales and the Benevolent Society. But he fell from grace when he refused to return to Australia from Britain. He thus forsook his family and took up with another woman, and Walter Lawry, back in England after his unrewarding mission to Tonga, reported sadly on his pathetic dissipation.[2]

A second fact which modifies the picture of the typical liberal given above is that many Australian evangelicals were Masons. The Masonic movement was identified closely with the Low Church movement in the Church of England, from which a large pool of evangelicals came. As the Protestant denominations were strengthened in this period, evangelicals had to find non-denominational structures for joint enterprise. In the nineteenth century the Masonic Lodge was possibly the most important of all such structures. This is why the lodge assumed such a functional importance, as an inspection of the public buildings in any country town will reveal: it was 'common Christianity', free of episcopal control. The lodge in South Australia is the State's oldest institution, formed in the United Kingdom before the first South Australian settlers sailed! Atkinson and Aveling said of Freemasonry there: 'South Australia, unlike any of the other colonies, was a creation of British liberalism, which partly explains why freemasonry was there so early.'[3] But they fail to see its connexion with evangelicalism. Its membership was made up largely of evangelical Christians. Partly because Freemasonry was condemned by Pope Pius IX in 1863, it became a strongly anti-Catholic movement. But easily the main manifestation of Protestant sectarianism in the colonies was the Orange Lodge, formed in Ulster in 1795. In the 1880s it had 25,000 members in Australia in 180 lodges. The chief voice of Protestant sectarianism was the *Protestant Standard*. Its writers claimed that they were pure evangelicals, fed from Exeter Hall, the oasis of evangelical reform in London.

Third, the architects of reform affecting Australia included those who had been shaped decisively by evangelical Christianity even if they had departed from it. One who made a major contribution to the development of Australia's free political institutions was James Stephen, son of the Clapham Sect Stephen of the same name who was a close friend of William Wilberforce. The younger James Stephen married Jane Catherine, the daughter of John Venn, the rector of Clapham, and apparently lived happily ever after. From 1836 to 1847 he was the permanent undersecretary of the Colonial Office, 'one of the greatest civil servants of the nineteenth century'.[4] He was opposed to short-term expediency, and sought to evolve wise policies to promote the stability of overseas dependencies. He insisted that the Westminster government should protect the weak and stand against the exploitation of natives and poor settlers. He opposed the introduction of cheap coloured labour into the Australian colonies on the grounds that the welfare of the many settlers was to be preferred to the immediate advantage of the few large landholders. He believed that colonial governors should be trusted with wide discretionary powers on the grounds that the man on the spot usually knew much more than a remote administration. He favoured the development of colonial self-government, and played an important role in drafting a report on the constitutions of the Australian colonies. James Stephen departed from the evangelical convictions of his father, but none questioned the sincerity of his Christian faith. He wrote the celebrated *Essays in Ecclesiastical Biography* with its sparkling, sympathetic analysis of the Clapham Sect which had shaped him for his life's work. He was a person of great integrity and righteousness, and on this strong moral foundation erected the edifice of colonial policy which so influenced the future development of New South Wales. His firm policies were intruded into the murky darkness of colonial politics like a light.

Another of the major liberals whom it would be wrong to dismiss as antireligious was Governor Richard Bourke (1831–37) who did most to fashion the relations between church and state in Australia along liberal lines. He was a liberal Anglican, which is not to be taken to mean that he was anti-

Christian! In fact, as a governor in the Cape of Good Hope, he had actively promoted Christian missions to convert the Bantu. In New South Wales his Church Act of 1836 subsidised clergy stipends and church building for all the major Christian denominations. The Act had to reflect the social and ethnic realities of the colonial population. In his 1833 dispatch on church and school establishment, he said an established church would create rancour: 'The inclination of these Colonists, which keeps pace with the Spirit of the Age, is decidedly adverse to such an Institution; and I fear the interests of Religion would be prejudiced by its Establishment.'[5] Bourke's Church Act was not anti-religious in intent. It was designed to strengthen the contribution of religion to society. It was not a secular overthrow of the traditional relationship between church and state. 'It modified that alliance in the interests of religious equality and greater efficiency of administration, both cardinal features of 19th century liberalism.'[6]

For a generation, the Church Acts in the various Australian colonies subsidised the expansion of the churches, and were then abolished. The Church of England was clearly unsettled by the abolition of aid, but adjusted by becoming both more democratic and more self-reliant. In 1866 synodical government was adopted in New South Wales, and Frederic Barker, Bishop of Sydney from 1854 to 1882, knew how to run the church on voluntary lines. In England he had worked in a new Liverpool parish financed exclusively by voluntary offerings. In Australia he formed the Church Society, later the Home Mission Society, to raise funds for the erection of churches and clergy stipends. Unlike the Anglicans, Catholics unreservedly condemned legislation abolishing state aid. Pope Pius IX condemned secular, state-controlled education. Hence Catholics were bound to establish an independent education system, widening the gulf which separated them from Protestants. Presbyterianism, divided by the Scottish disruption of 1843 and by the personal ambitions of the first Presbyterian minister, John Dunmore Lang, was reunited by 1865 in New South Wales, and grew healthily, particularly in the wealthy rural areas of Victoria. Methodism, separated from its English parent in 1855, grew vigorously in most parts of Australia over the next two decades. The New South Wales Baptist Association was formed in July 1858, and the New South Wales Baptist Union was formed in 1870 to assist struggling churches, while the Congregationalists formed the Congregational Union of New South Wales in 1866. In sum, the churches were girding their loins, and the race was on for the soul of Australia.

Nation-building in the New Colonies

The most conspicuous offspring of the marriage of liberalism and evangelicalism were the new settlements.[7] Melbourne, settled in 1834, Adelaide (1836), and Brisbane (1859) were Puritan counters to Sydney, not spin-offs. By the close of 1839, there were five denominations under the leadership of ordained ministers in Melbourne: the Church of England, Catholics, Presbyterians, Wesleyans, and Independents.[8] The Baptists had also begun to meet, but had no ordained minister. Early Melbourne was a bastion of Protestantism. Nonconformity and disestablishment were championed by leading pioneers, John Pascoe Fawkner, a Congregationalist, and William Kerr, a Presbyterian. Romanism was opposed by the considerable proportion of Anglican laity who were of Irish extraction. It was therefore appropriate that Melbourne's first bishop, Charles Perry, should be an evangelical.

Within a decade of settlement, Melbourne was observably holier than Sydney, at least in its churchgoing habits: in Melbourne the churches were 'well attended, the people dressed in their best attire, the shops shut, the streets as quiet as in an English town', and there were 'no visible symptoms of riot or drunkenness'; whereas in hedonistic Sydney, most of the churches were less than half full, Sundays were 'spent by many in "boating", driving, riding, drinking, visiting, &c.',[9] and by the working classes in cooking and eating 'roasted meats, of every description'.[10] Russel Ward reports that this distinction between Sydney and Melbourne was attributed by contemporaries solely to the absence of the convict element in the Melbourne population, but he perceptively speculates that other factors might include the relatively larger number of Presbyterians in Melbourne and also the influence of 'newly arrived immigrants from a Britain already feeling the influence of the evangelical movement'.[11]

In the settlement of South Australia, liberal and evangelical parentage is even more evident. 'Paradise of Dissent' is Pike's accurate description.[12] The founders and first settlers of South Australia were passionate about religious and civil liberties. So South Australia became the first colony in the British Empire to separate church and state. Towering above all those who left the evangelical liberal stamp on South Australia was George Fife Angas. He was an ardent exponent of free trade and civil and religious liberties. He maintained an unrelenting search for godly and industrious men to go to

South Australia as his agents. He was the leading authority on South Australia and also on philanthropic and missionary matters. He was forthright, incorruptible and very able, and he believed that, through religion, people could make the best of both worlds, the true mark of the evangelical liberal. He once wrote:

> I have seen a great deal of men and things and have very closely observed them throughout life and the result of my experience is that true religion alone promotes happiness on earth and secures it for ever after ... He becomes faithful, industrious, and economical in the management of his worldly affairs and hence follow comfort and prosperity.[13]

Queensland, too, bore the evangelical stamp, being the colony which was perhaps the chief beneficiary of the policies of John Dunmore Lang. On 30 March 1838 three Germans commenced missionary work to the Aboriginal people in Moreton Bay.[14] The mission was an unofficial Moravian enterprise established by Johannes Evangelista Gossner and Lang. By 1843 the Gossner mission at Zion's Hill (now Nundah) was abandoned, but as with the earlier LMS missionaries in New South Wales, the German missionaries made an important contribution to the colonial religious culture, contributing to Methodist and Baptist churches and pastoring their compatriots in the 1860s and 1870s.[15] In 1846, James Swan, 'an ardent Baptist' then working for the *Sydney Morning Herald*,[16] migrated from Sydney to Brisbane to assist in the publication of the *Moreton Bay Courier*. He was to play a prominent role as an evangelical liberal in Queensland for almost half a century. He was a 'Lang radical',[17] eager to promote Lang's Christian Commonwealth through the immigration of Presbyterian and Baptist settlers, opposed to transportation and the interests of squatters, and he favoured the separation of Moreton Bay from New South Wales.

Wherever evangelicals were strong, then, their religion not only influenced personal behaviour. They stood for a social reform programme which overlapped the liberal reform programme. Free settlers and evangelical ministers of religion, especially in South Australia and Melbourne, denounced the establishment and prelacy, the convict system, state aid for religion and schools, and corruption in public life. They stood for and eventually secured self-government, universal free education, a social welfare system, and self-defence.[18] These were all at heart as much evangelical as liberal achievements,[19] as indeed was the renovation of the convict colonies, itself something of a social miracle. To accord such powers of social engineering to evangelical forces is to rewrite Australian history. Historians, however, may have failed to see the formative power of evangelicalism because they have not studied evangelicalism or, if they have, they have studied clerical evangelicalism. Lay evangelicalism influenced the development of social institutions decisively.

I have argued that the forces of reason, liberalism, and utilitarianism were strongly represented among the evangelicals of this period, and that it is a mistake to regard these as the preserve of more secular forces who alone must be credited with laying the foundations of the new nation. George Shaw is one of the few Australian professional historians who has grasped the truth of this point:

> Utilitarianism and Protestantism were neither utterly opposites, nor totally incompatible; and where moral codes and the civil order crossed paths, they are remarkably accommodating of each other. Laymen, far more than clerics, were able to put aside theological niceties and to agree on workable compromises which, at the level of ethics and public life, were as satisfactory to Utilitarians as to Protestants.[20]

Shaw contends that from 1788 the forces of evangelicalism were stronger in Australia than the forces of scepticism or utilitarianism. By the 1840s the evangelicals were joined by British and Irish Catholic forces to produce a Judaeo-Christian movement which shaped decisively the colonial civil order of the mid-nineteenth century. This was done with the consent of the great majority of the Australian population and with the financial support of governments in the Church Acts. These Acts may have been hailed as the 'Magna Carta' of the non-Anglican denominations, but their greater significance, argues Shaw, lies in the fact that they were the means of multiplying and strengthening the agencies of Judaeo-Christian culture throughout the colonies. Similarly, the significance of debates between denominational and national school systems is lost if the difference between contending parties is emphasised rather than the fact that the great majority wanted a system which would strengthen the role of the Christian religion in developing civic-mindedness in the rising generation. The argument was not between the forces of Christianity and those of secularism, but between the clergy and the laity. Evangelicals were well represented among the laity who wanted non-denominational Christian education, and the state school systems which emerged in every colony at the end of the nineteenth century were arguably evangelicalism's greatest achievement in the realm of social engineering. Shaw concludes: 'There is clear and abundant evidence that there never was that dichotomy between religion and reason in colonial public life required in a general history of Australia putting secularism in the centre and religion on the margins.'[21]

Understanding of the evangelical emphasis on nation-building and social achievement has been befuddled by the anachronistic perspectives of many historians who have worked on this period from 1836 to 1870. First, it is necessary to realise that we are speaking here about an evangelical achievement. Evangelism and the apologetic defence of fundamentals were not then the distinguishing hallmarks of evangelicalism. The fundamentals were not then under attack, and the task was not therefore to defend or propagate the fundamentals, but to apply them to society. It is this application which has been scorned by a number of historians. Gillman has observed that nineteenth-century Australian Christianity was unrelentingly and mercilessly moralising.[22] But this very moralising was then perceived as a route to social respectability or improvement which had long been accepted as a good fruit of evangelical religion,[23] and a fairly important fruit, one would have thought, in an erstwhile gaol or frontier community. While no form of Christianity appealed to convicts, evangelicalism appealed to emancipated convicts because it was a ladder back to social respectability. Nor was it ever the case that evangelicals, born of a reaction to the arid moralising of the eighteenth century, identified religion completely with morality.

Richard Ely advances the valuable hypothesis that 'civic', as distinct from 'corporate', Protestantism dominated the Australian churches in the nineteenth century. Whereas corporate Protestantism stresses the separation of the faithful remnant from a disobedient nation and supports the welfare role of the church, civic Protestants, whilst sometimes favouring the separation of church and state, always favour the unity of nation and religion, and support the welfare role of the state.[24] Civic Protestants often appear to endorse uncritically current social trends. Most nineteenth-century Australian evangelicals were civic Protestants, and that is why they found political liberalism so congenial. Of humble social origins, many Australian evangelicals were sensitive to charges of uncouthness, they prized education, and had great faith in human progress. They honoured those who had been overseas for their education, regarded everything in print as 'Gospel', and were therefore of a receptive rather than a critical disposition. This evangelicalism was inclusive, not narrow or defensive. It was an evangelicalism sensitive to its context in the world, and the world was not then attacking the Word as the foundation for a strong nation.

Sectarianism

The story of sectarianism is yet another aspect of Australian religious history which has been much better told from the Catholic side than the Protestant.[25] So I shall here endeavour to give a largely Protestant perspective on the issue. Sectarian feeling was the habit of the evangelicals which most threatened to disrupt their happy marriage with liberalism. Sectarianism occurs when different denominations or religions compete with each other for state or civil endorsement of their particular beliefs or values or standards.[26] So sectarianism is more than denominational competition purely to recruit members, although there is evidence that Australians do not look approvingly even on that. Here is a significant distinction between Australia and the USA. Americans labelled denominationalism as sanctified competition or holy emulation, and called it a good thing—so good that lots of new competitors were spawned as well. As a result, Americans have always felt free to switch from one denomination to another with relative ease and impunity. In Australia denominationalism was called sectarianism and labelled a bad thing. This may be one of the reasons why Australians have been so impatient with the details of sectarian rivalry and why, until recently, Australians have been reluctant to switch denominations and incapable of giving birth to any native-born Christian denominations.

A number of factors conspired to make Australian sectarianism both distinctive and intense. Bourke's Church Act ended the Church of England's hopes of achieving establishment status, and, by strengthening all the major denominations as well (Catholics, Presbyterians, Wesleyans), it provided fuel for the fires of sectarianism. In Britain, the major religious groups lived in their own part of Britain: the Presbyterians in Scotland, the Catholics in Ireland, the Church of England and Methodists in England and Wales. They hardly ever saw each other. In Australia they all had to live side by side, as they do in Northern Ireland. Some found it extraordinarily stressful that their co-religionists were not the majority. Sectarianism is a symptom of this insecurity. It is also an aspect of capitalism and of ethnic conflict. The English dominated Ireland as an imperial power, and the consequent economic, social and religious relationships which were dominant there were readily exported with mass emigration to Australia. The Irish Catholics became associated with the lower, working classes, while the English, Scottish and Protestant Irish situated themselves in the middling and ruling classes.

Regional differences also help to explain why sectarianism raged more wildly in some colonies than in others. Melbourne witnessed scenes of bitter sectarianism. Its Protestant establishment was confident of building a much more respectable community than the moral cesspools created in the convict colonies of New South Wales and Van Diemen's Land. For their part, the Catholics went to Melbourne as free settlers and not as convicts, and they were not about to see themselves put down as in the older colonies. In 1843 there was an election to the Legislative Council of New South Wales of a representative for Port Phillip (Melbourne). Lang threw himself into the election when he heard that a prominent Catholic, Edmund Curr, was standing. The campaign in Melbourne was marked by the polarisation of the community along sectarian lines, by threats of violence, and by riots. On 12 July 1846 there was another, far more serious riot in Melbourne, when Orangemen convened at the Pastoral Hotel to celebrate the Battle of the Boyne. Provoked Irish Catholics arrived in great numbers, armed with guns and clubs. The military were called out, shots were fired and arrests made.

The advent of the Oxford movement in 1833 provoked anti-Catholic feeling. As early as 1836 Anglican evangelicals joined other Protestants to establish a Reformation Society in New South Wales. Protestant opposition to Anglo-Catholicism and ritualism was always determined. Sometimes it took on bizarre, even sinister, overtones. During the building of the Church of England in Jamberoo, a small town south of Sydney, a journalist reported in 1866 that 'every attempt at decoration is jealously watched by some who regard external symbol as belonging only to a communion which they seem to regard as the highest proof of piety to hate'.[27] That this was no exaggeration was established subsequently when stone crosses on the gables of the church were pulled down in the middle of the night, and one was dragged away and smashed to pieces. Residents were shocked at the sacrilege, and a reward of £50 was offered for the arrest of the offender. Bishop Barker, though an evangelical with no love of Romish adornment, clearly thought that cross demolition was taking anti-Catholicism too far, and himself donated a new cross. But this met a similar fate in January 1867.[28]

The other side to the coin of anti-Catholic sectarianism is the ecumenism among evangelicals, which found interesting expression in this period. In Australia, the sparsity of the population has encouraged Protestant Christians to experiment in 'common Christianity', and union churches came to dot the landscape. In the pioneering days of colonial churches, common Christianity embraced Wesleyan Methodists, Presbyterians, Baptists and Congregationalists, and consisted of the exchange of preachers and buildings, and co-operation in outreach. In 1849, for example, when 600 immigrants, Lang's 'desirable' settlers, arrived in Queensland in a fleet of three ships, they established a union church. They were for the most part convinced evangelical Presbyterians, Congregationalists and Baptists, and in 1849 they established the United Evangelical Church, with one of the ship's chaplains, the Rev. Charles Stewart, as their first minister.[29] This was consistent with Lang's counsel that they should unite 'on a Scriptural basis, and, at the same time, on so broad a foundation as to comprehend in one body and communion members of the different evangelical denominations at home'.[30] 'Common Christianity' seems to have been strongest in South Australia, until the Methodists realised that they could dominate the colony without making any such concessions.

With the simultaneous growth of denominational consciousness and population, the pragmatic need for such union churches diminished. Many members understood from the start that the United Evangelical Church in Queensland was a temporary measure. Just nine months later, a large group of Presbyterians broke away and established the United Presbyterian Church, 'in which the great doctrines of the Westminster Confession of Faith and other standards will be maintained'.[31] In 1855 the Baptists also left to form their own church, and the United Evangelical Church came to an end. The new Baptist Church (formed on 5 August 1855) was a fellowship of those holding Calvinistic doctrines, but it maintained something of the old spirit of evangelical ecumenism by admitting those who believed in infant baptism to membership, reserving the positions of pastor and office-bearers for Baptists.

Within the nonconformist denominations, the Congregationalists and the Baptists, evangelical ecumenism or 'liberalism' expressed itself in a reluctance to emphasise denominational distinctives. The Baptists, for example, began with the non-sectarian evangelicalism of John Saunders in New South Wales, the more denominational but no less evangelical commitment of James Voller to 'extension and usefulness',[32] and the contemporary flowering of interdenominational evangelicalism fostered in the pages of the *Australian Evangelist* (edited by the outstanding, if ill-fated, James Taylor, minister of the Collins Street Baptist Church) in Melbourne, and Silas Mead's 'triumph of liberal denominationalism over fissiparous sectarianism'[33] in South Australia.

The Laity and Evangelical Anglicanism

In mid-century, the colourful barrister and liberal MP, Robert Lowe, prevailed on the Secretary of State for the Colonies to appoint an evangelical bishop to Sydney.[34] English evangelicals were aware that Bishop Broughton's High Church views had met with consistent opposition from Sydney laity, and, by the time of Broughton's death, were convinced that evangelicalism might be permanently institutionalised in colonial Anglicanism.[35] Frederic Barker's episcopate (1854–82) was very successful in establishing the strong clergy-led evangelicalism which characterises Sydney to this day. A preacher and missionary, Barker pleased the laity by being less a Calvinist than the first generation of evangelicals in Australia and less a politician than Broughton. In consequence, he established Sydney Anglicanism on broadbased popular support. He set up effective parishes, funding procedures, and church organisations. Most significantly, he established Moore Theological College. He had tried to procure evangelical clergy from overseas, but they were a naive lot. He was prevented from using the University of Sydney, established in 1850, because it did not then allow the teaching of Divinity, and the Anglican college at the university, St Paul's, was protected against his control. Moore College was his answer. Its first principal was William Hodgson who, as Mrs Barker observed or threatened, 'would utter no uncertain sound'. Hodgson, however, safe from Mrs Barker for the moment in England, did express a doubt: 'In this country Colleges exclusively theological seem to have a tendency to foster a hard narrow repulsive ecclesiasticism'—he had a way with adjectives. So Moore College was born in 1856 with something of its present reputation among its critics: 'merely a narrow Calvinistic Seminary got up in opposition to the more liberal one of St. Paul's'.[36]

By keeping a low profile and nurturing his evangelical clergy, Barker avoided a show-down with his laity and Low Church clergy, who tended to side with each other against bishops.[37] Admittedly, there were signs of greater strains to come. Barker's clergy increasingly shared the views of the laity: they were religiously conservative and politically liberal. Some of them shared their pulpits with nonconformists. A significant number of them were from parts of Ireland where Protestants were in a minority. They came to form the nucleus of the extreme Low Church party for which Sydney was to become proverbial.[38] Yet, apart from minor disagreements over education and synodical structure, there was peace under Barker between bishop, clergy, and influential laity. The greatest achievement of this unity of purpose was the 1866 Enabling Act, which allowed each diocese in New South Wales to control its own properties. The diocese, not the provincial or general synod, was the sovereign body, allowing Sydney to resist takeovers from either the bush dioceses in the nineteenth century or High Church dioceses in the twentieth. The sovereign diocesan synods also allowed the lower clergy and laity a strong voice in the government of the church, and from the beginning were well attended by both.[39] This was a form of church administration which concentrated on internal rather than community issues. The present character of Sydney evangelicalism—clergy-led and concerned with the church first and the community second—was beginning to take shape. In a strange irony, the energies of the civic-minded laity, who had been eager to co-operate with nonconformists to create a society based on a broad-based evangelicalism, were confiscated for the church. Their participation in the synod meant they had to become more involved in matters of the Word and the Spirit at the expense of the world.

In Melbourne, Charles Perry, Bishop of Melbourne from 1847 to 1874, found the going tougher. The mode of Perry's appointment is fairly clear. With a change of government in the United Kingdom, evangelical influence upset the original High Church plan when one of the original nominees dropped out at the last minute and the government acted directly on the advice of Henry Venn, CMS secretary, to fill the vacancy. Perry was given the least promising of a number of newly created bishoprics. It was the subsequent discovery of gold in Victoria which catapulted Perry into a key position. He, too, had his fair share of Low Church Irish clergy, crediting them with zeal and 'more or less of a wrong-headedness.'[40] He never managed to start an evangelical training college in his diocese, sending his men for training to Moore College in Sydney.[41] For this he was constantly criticised, especially by William Wilson, Professor of Mathematics at the University of Melbourne.[42] Loane writes that Perry's 'great insight was the importance of the laity in church affairs whether on a parochial or a diocesan level'.[43] It was, perhaps, an insight forced upon him by the quality and independence of the Melbourne laity. Perry was a stern academic who lacked Barker's common touch, and he provoked opposition from a strong laity made wealthy through pastoral and mining activities.

Revival[44]

If many evangelicals trusted to progress and liberal democracy to transform their society into closer proximity to the Kingdom of God, others longed for an outpouring of the Holy Spirit in revival. The desire for revival has been a relatively common characteristic of Australian evangelicalism, even in respectable Anglican circles. On 16 July 1855, Jane Barker, wife of Frederic Barker, Bishop of Sydney, recorded in her diary that one of the Sydney clergy had influenced the younger clergy by decreeing that 'it is as much a *duty* in the upper classes to attend balls and such places as for doctors to visit the sick'. She immediately added, 'May our gracious God pour out His spirit upon this colony and cause a revival to take place among the dry bones.'[45] On 30 November 1855 the Barkers gathered with their evangelical clergy and their wives recently arrived from England and held the first of what was to become a monthly prayer meeting. Frederic read the most important passage in the Old Testament on revival, Ezekiel 37, on the valley of dry bones. Then they sang Isaac Watts' hymn, 'Come Holy Spirit, heavenly Dove'. The Barkers did not imagine that planning and strategy were any substitute for the Spirit of God. Jane made the point quite explicit in her diary: 'While doing our best to set an efficient agency to work, we must not forget to implore the blessing of the good Spirit who can alone put life into the machinery, or cause the dry bones to live.'[46] The thought was never far from her mind, occasioning prayerful longing. On the prospect of getting a garden going at Bishopscourt, she enthused:

> But how much more earnestly do we desire to see this great moral and spiritual wilderness fertilised by showers of divine grace and yielding fruit a hundred fold to the glory of God. I have no doubt it will do so,

in His own time, and think a crisis is not far off when the powers of light and darkness will be seen in mortal conflict in this very town of Sydney.[47]

One of the many stereotypes about Australian Christianity is that there has never been a religious revival in Australia. But revivals have actually been relatively frequent in Australian history, and although they have usually been localised, their genuineness may by demonstrated from surviving evidence. From a preliminary survey of printed sources, other than church newspapers, I have identified the revivals in the period covered by this chapter as shown in Table 2.1.

There were two main ingredients in the revival recipe in this period. The first was the experience of revival in the Methodist Church.[48] This was the denomination which most expected revivals and experienced most of them. Revival was one of the major components in the unequalled numerical success of Methodism in nineteenth-century Australia.

Membership had stood at 72 in 1818 and was still only 126 in 1831, and Richard Watson, a secretary of the Wesleyan Methodist Missionary Society, said, 'The New South Wales District is the only one of our missions that has been a disgrace to us.' By the 1840s all that had changed, and the reason was that several revivals had swept through the Sydney district.[49] A 'gracious revival' in 1864 in Hobart, arising from a week of prayer conducted by Spencer Williams,[50] was followed by a 50 per cent increase in Methodist membership in Tasmania in a single year.[51] Revivals within Australian Methodism probably explain the growth of that denomination from 6.7 per cent of the Australian population in 1861 to 10.2 per cent in 1901. In 1901 the church buildings of South Australia, where Methodism was stronger than any other state, could seat 167,000 (45 per cent of the population), of which 80,000 were in Methodist churches.[52] The impact of Methodism is perhaps most vividly evident in Victoria (Table 2.2), the colony where the population increased most in the second half of the nineteenth century, thanks to the gold rushes.

Revival in Australian Methodism in this period was often associated with the name of John Watsford, the son of a convict and the first Australian-born Methodist clergyman. Strong emotion accompanied Watsford's ministry wherever he proclaimed his Wesleyan message of entire sanctification and the duty of evangelism.[53] Indeed, Watsford's experience of revival

Table 2.1: Revivals in Australian colonies, 1834–69

Year	Town/City	Colony
1834	Hobart	Tasmania
1835	Sydney	NSW
1839	Albion Park	NSW
1839	Launceston	Tasmania
1840–41	Parramatta, Windsor,	
	Castlereagh, Bathurst	NSW
1843	Melbourne	Victoria
1844		WA
1851	Kapunda	SA
1853	Bendigo	Victoria
1858	Bathurst	NSW
	Manning River	NSW
	Burra	SA
1859	Brighton	Victoria
	Melbourne	Victoria
	Ballarat	Victoria
1860	Bendigo	Victoria
	Geelong	Victoria
	Ramahyuck	Victoria
	Moravian mission	Victoria
	Goulburn	NSW
	Maitland	NSW
	Burra	SA
	Sydney	NSW
1862	Moonta	SA
	Adelaide	SA
	Callington	SA
1864	Hobart	Tasmania
	Kiama	NSW
1869	St Arnaud	Victoria

Table 2.2: Methodist membership in Victoria, 1841–81

Year	Methodist membership	Total population	Methodists as % of total population
1841	650	11,738	5.5
1851	4988	77,345	6.4
1861	40,799	540,322	7.6
1871	80,491	750,528	10.7
1881	97,115	862,346	11.3

began before he started training for the ministry. The 1840 revival at Parramatta had its roots in a prayer meeting convened by two local preachers who, together with John Watsford, resolved to pray three times a day for the outpouring of the Holy Spirit. Watsford explained what happened:

> At the end of the fourth week, on Sunday evening, the Rev. William Walker preached a powerful sermon. After the service the people flocked to the prayer-meeting, till the schoolroom was filled. My two friends were there, one on each side of me, and I knew they had hold of God. We could hear sighs and suppressed sobs all around us. The old minister of the Circuit, who had conducted the meeting, was concluding with the benediction, 'The grace of our Lord Jesus Christ, and the love of God'—here he stopped, and sobbed aloud. When he could speak he called out, 'Brother Watsford, pray'. I prayed, and then my two friends prayed, and oh! the power of God that came upon the people, who were overwhelmed by it in every part of the room! And what a cry for mercy! It was heard by the passers-by in the street, some of whom came running in to see what was the matter, and were smitten down at the door in great distress. The clock of a neighbouring church struck twelve before we could leave the meeting. How many were saved I cannot tell. Day after day and week after week the work went on, and many were converted.[54]

In Ballarat in the 1860s, in Parramatta, in the inner city suburbs of Surry Hills and Balmain, and in country town such as Windsor and Goulburn, Watsford was used to ignite the fires of revival.

Arnold Hunt, historian of South Australian Methodism, while maintaining the cool conclusion that the history of Methodism in Australia is one of 'many missions, no revivals', nevertheless argues that the Methodists came closest to revival because they were the denomination most confident that the Church of Christ must grow and that God was at work in their movement. They were a successful missionary organisation, they had a message which they believed was pure Gospel, they were a spiritual rather than a bureaucratic or liturgical movement, and they were a warm fellowship in which laity as well as clergy were expected to evangelise. The Methodists were confident that God would bless them, and their nineteenth-century vigour is a reflex of that confidence.[55]

A second ingredient in the revival recipe in this period was the experience of revival in 1859, especially in Wales and Ulster. This revival was really exported to Australia, partly through the pages of a newspaper, *The Revival*, published in London, and through the *Christian Pleader*, published in Australia. The revival rain began to fall at Great Brighton, a Melbourne suburb, on 22 May 1859 when at a love feast 'the Sanctuary became a Bochim, a place of weeping'.[56] In the revivals in the Victorian goldfields, miners from Cornwall and Yorkshire remembered the revivals of earlier years and joined with the preachers in earnestly beseeching the divine outpouring. These revivals, it is said, 'followed the pattern of the Irish Revival, with prayer meetings every night in the churches, with all the phenomena of the Ulster movement, except prostrations'.[57] In Ballarat, under the Rev. James Bickford,[58] 'deep searchings before God' and a 'revival of God's work' occurred in 1859; in 1860 'glorious revivals' were reported at Bendigo under the ministry of the Rev. Richard Hart of Golden Square Methodist Church; and in the same year in the Castlemaine district of Victoria the power of the Lord was reported as present 'to wound and to heal'. It was in 1860, too, in the copper mining town of Burra, South Australia, 500 conversions were reported in 'a most glorious revival of religion ... never such a one in this colony before'.[59]

If revivals were imported, they did not have to come from great awakenings such as the Welsh and Ulster revivals. Nor were they exclusively Methodist. On the Manning River, in northern New South Wales, 'one of the most remarkable awakenings of the Spirit of God that we know in Australia's history'[60] was experienced between 1858 and 1860 under the Rev. Allan McIntyre, a Presbyterian. He had arrived in Australia from Paisley, Scotland, in 1854. The Manning River revival[61] may have been connected with a revival at Lochabar in Scotland or other Scottish awakenings, since McIntyre gathered around him a remarkable band of elders who had witnessed such revival blessing in Scotland. Out of the Manning River revival grew three strong congregations at Tinonee, Wingham and Redbank, and also three private schools at Bight, Tinonee and Purfleet.[62] Revival is an expression of the Christian religion which spills over from church life into community life, and the role of revival in shaping individuals and communities went far deeper than historians have suspected. Revivals often change people decisively and permanently, and send streams of powerful spirituality underground from where they can surface in the most unpredictable places.

Missions to Aboriginal People and Overseas

In 1833 and 1834 the British House of Commons had conducted an inquiry into the condition of native peoples in British settlements. Henceforth indigenous peoples were to be accorded justice, rights, civilisation, and Christianity, accepted voluntarily. This was the Age of Improvement, an age so constructed by those great optimists: evangelicals, liberals, and utilitarians. It was intolerable for a Christian civilisation to admit defeat on the Aboriginal question. Lord Stanley, Secretary of State for the Colonies, wrote to Governor Gipps in 1842:

> I should not, without the most extreme reluctance, admit that nothing can be done—that with respect to them alone the doctrines of Christianity must be inoperative, and the advantages of civilisation incommunicable. I cannot acquiesce in the theory that they are incapable of improvement, and that their extinction ... is a necessity which it is impossible to control.[63]

A decade earlier, in 1832, the government footing the bills, the Church Missionary Society had sent out three ordained missionaries, including William Watson and also a farmer, William Porter, to the Wellington Valley. Porter cultivated more than the land and was dismissed for gratifying himself with a native woman. Watson was a faithful stayer and earned from the Aborigines their highest compliment: 'You were a blackfellow once.' Their behaviour in church was exemplary. The most indecorous thing of which they were guilty was falling asleep occasionally, 'an impropriety not altogether unknown outside coloured congregations'. A number of Aboriginal adults pleaded to be baptised, but Watson would not oblige. They always had some habit or custom of which he disapproved, such as a bad temper or a mixed-race child, or, in the case of Fred, who seemed to work overtime but in vain to please, 'going bush to fetch a wife'. Snort, said the missionaries, you'll choose one of those 'wild, wicked women'. 'Well,' replied Fred, 'I put her in playground with the girls and you make her good.' But the missionaries did not relish the task of taming Fred's woman.

Another exchange conveys something of the hopelessness of the atmosphere which prevailed at the mission. Watson taught the Aborigines the cosmogony of the book of Genesis: creationist, anti-evolutionary. They thought it only right to teach him their cosmogony in return.

GOONGEEN: Have you ever seen something like stars fall? That always come down when black fellow going to die.

MR. WATSON: Pshaw! Not so I think.

GOONGEEN: Hy! Hy! Hy! You won't believe blackfellow! blackfellow won't believe you.[64]

Watson's authority was diminished by his scepticism, for, in matters of religion, scepticism is often ignorance. In 1840 Watson was dismissed and left in a huff, distressed with CMS, not the Aboriginal people, and the CMS mission collapsed two years later.

A Wesleyan Methodist mission, at Buntingdale in Victoria, commenced in 1839; it looked promising at first. It was 130 kilometres west of Melbourne, where 26,000 hectares was set aside on vacant territory. It began with two energetic young missionaries, Benjamin Hurst and Francis Tuckfield. A number of different tribes were attracted to the mission, but they soon began to bicker among themselves. Hurst left in despair, but Tuckfield continued on a new plan. It was a scheme which in 1845 the assistant protector of Aborigines, James Dredge, thought must succeed, namely that the mission would be limited to just one tribe. Nevertheless, it collapsed just three years later. Tuckfield had sold off half the land to settlers to raise the capital to continue. The white settlers were far more pernicious than the different tribes, and the mission closed with little to show for ten years of labour.

Why the chronic failure? The history of Christianity is a record of many fatal delays, and the first generation of white settlement in Australia did not bring the same determination to the Aboriginal problem as it did to the convict challenge. It would have been better if missions to the Aboriginal people had begun with the First Fleet, not thirty years later. Evangelical labour among Aboriginal people was a case of too little, too late. Aboriginal missions have never been accorded top priority by evangelical missionary societies, even those based in Australia. New Holland was seen by the mission boards in Britain not as a great object of missionary endeavour, such as Africa, India, China, and the South Seas, but rather as a platform or base from which to send missionaries. Missions to the Aboriginal people have probably never attracted the investment of money and personnel which they deserve or need. The government looked to the missionaries to solve horrendous problems created by a rapacious white presence. But by the 1820s Aboriginal people realised that the whites were different from what the missionaries wanted them (the Aborigines) to be. A related reason for failure was that the early missions were too close to white settlements. The Aboriginal people were too easily contaminated, too easily infected, and too easily swamped. The more successful missions of the twentieth century were established in areas with a large Aboriginal population and a small white one.

Probably the most important reason for failure was that no white person, and therefore no missionary, came anywhere near understanding Aboriginal culture or religion. And they did not have a critical understanding of their own culture or religion. They insisted on behavioural changes which bespoke British culture rather than the Christian religion. Samuel Marsden, though admirably ahead of his time when it came to the Maoris, was totally pessimistic about doing anything for the Aboriginal people, whom he labelled 'the most degraded of the human race.' He added that 'the time is not yet arrived for them to receive the great blessings of civilisation and the knowledge of Christianity'.[65] Marsden was one who thought it necessary to civilise a race before attempting to Christianise it. He was prepared to comb England to find a twinespinner for the benefit of the Maoris, who he thought were just waiting to get their hands on the instruments of the Industrial Revolution. But the Aboriginal people were very different. The difficulty with them was that they 'had no wants, they lived free and independent, and thought little more of tomorrow than the fowls of the air or the beasts of the field, and put no value upon the comforts of civil life'.[66] Their great crime seems to have been that they lived a life closer to that prescribed by the Sermon on the Mount than any people on earth!

James Dredge, the assistant protector, contended that Marsden and those who thought like him had it back to front. You should Christianise first; then civilisation would result. But again, Dredge sought to measure success in terms of the adoption of British ways: 'For no sooner does the Gospel begin to operate upon the mind of the heathen, than it leads to the first step in civilisation—the necessity of a decent covering—thus clothing is introduced.' Then to attend to the ordinances of religion, that is, to go to church, they will want a settled mode of life and will give up wandering. Then, to read the Bible, they will have to learn to read, and therefore they will desire an education. Next, Christianity teaches a man to love one wife as his own flesh, therefore 'it raises women *from* that state to which heathenism invariably depresses her'.[67] And so on.

John Dunmore Lang, the turbulent Presbyterian minister, held a third position on the relationship between Christianisation and civilisation, namely discontinuity. Lang admired this free and independent race of black men and women who owed no allegiance to Great Britain. He was appalled by the decimation of the race at the hands of the white man. All the waters of New Holland, he said, would be insufficient to wash away the stain of blood from the hands of some gentlemen of good repute. He did not believe that Aboriginal ignorance of the arts of civilisation was an indication of intellectual inferiority. Aboriginal schoolchildren, he observed, learned to read and write with facility. He admired their strong parental and conjugal affections. Then he made an observation which Marsden and Dredge would have considered anathema: the only way to Christianise the Aborigine was

> to find some zealous missionary who was willing to conform to the Aborigines' wandering habits, who would follow them in a bark canoe as they skimmed across the lakes, who would go hunting with them for possums and bandicoots in the depths of the forests, who would join with them in singing their tribal songs by the evening fire and in mimicking the gambols of the kangaroos in the dances of their corroborees. Only such a person might secure their confidence and so be able to win them for Christ.[68]

To modern ears it sounds as if Lang got it about right, but here, as in many other respects, Lang's voice, though often heard, was almost as often rejected.

Far more 'successful' were two Moravian missions in Western Victoria which lasted from 1858 to 1905, when they became self-governing and financially independent communities. The first conversion, that of Nathaniel Pepper at the Ebenezer Mission in the Wimmera in 1859, was celebrated at thanksgiving rallies in Melbourne and London. Frederick Hagenauer, a Moravian minister and founder of Ebenezer, began a Presbyterian Church of Victoria mission to the Aborigines at Ramahyuck near Stratford in East Gippsland in 1862, and activity continued there until 1909. There were also missions whose 'success' must be attributed to the charismatic men who ran them: for example, Carl Strehlow at Hermannsburg in the Northern Territory, Dom Rosendo Salvado at New Norcia in Western Australia, and John Gribble of the Warangesda Mission in New South Wales.

What were the ingredients in their successful recipe? John Harris suggests that there were five ingredients in these more successful missions: some recognition of Aboriginal culture; a willingness to accept that Aboriginal people did have a spiritual basis to life; some acceptance that not all Aboriginal patterns of behaviour were inherently evil; a concentration on Aboriginal languages, expressing the Gospel in the words of the people; the early recognition of the Aboriginal people's faith and the acknowledging of their spiritual gifts, particularly the recognition of Aboriginal Christian leadership.[69] The common element in all five ingredients is acceptance, the essential first step to that cultural congruity, from which bridges can be built for the Gospel.

As for overseas missions, it was not until the last decades of the nineteenth century that the foundation of the Australian base for overseas missions was laid in the various evangelical denominations. But there were conspicuous successes in this earlier period. From 1844 to 1853 John Watsford worked in Fiji as a missionary and witnessed the power of the Gospel in revival every bit as dramatic as he had experienced in Parramatta. Of the first revival in Fiji, that at Viwa in 1846, Watsford wrote:

> The news of the revival spread everywhere, and the natives came from far and near to see what they called 'the fire of love from heaven.' It exerted a blessed influence all through the islands, and it gave hope and faith to many Christians in pleading for the success of Mission work elsewhere.[70]

One of the greatest publicisers of the missionary cause in the nineteenth century, John Gibson Paton, had also already made his mark before 1870. Within months of his arrival in the New Hebrides (Vanuatu) in 1858, this 33-year-old Scot from the Reformed Presbyterian Church of Scotland lost his young wife and son, and could never dislodge from his mind that grave which 'held mother and son locked in each other's embrace till the Resurrection Day'.[71] On leave in the Australian colonies, he spoke of his harrowing missionary experiences at 470 meetings. He was described as 'more addicted to flowery rhetoric than blatant inaccuracies';[72] his deputation made his name a household word. In 1866 the Presbyterian Church of Victoria, which had at last put its house in order through union in 1859, and which reflected Victoria's material prosperity following the gold rushes, appointed Paton and James Cosh as its own missionaries to the New Hebrides, where Paton then saw much reward for his labour.

3. The Spirit and Protestant Culture, 1870–1913

The period 1870–1913 was the high noon of Australian Protestantism. About 40 per cent of the population attended church each Sunday, double the percentage of the earliest and the most recent decades of Australia's history since settlement. The English author, Anthony Trollope, visited Australia in 1871–72 and observed that 'wherever there is a community there arises a church, or more commonly churches ... the people are fond of building churches'.[1] They were especially fond of doing that in Adelaide, which was indeed the city of churches. In 1895 there were 908 churches in Adelaide alone, while there were only 770 hotels in the whole of South Australia. They were also fond of building churches in the South Australian mining town of Moonta. In 1899 seventeen church buildings could be seen from one spot in the centre of town. Apart from two small Church of England and Catholic churches, they were all varieties of Methodist denominations: Wesleyans, Primitives, Bible Christians, and the Salvation Army. Voluntaryism (following the abolition of state aid to religion) and denominationalism do not appear to have weakened the churches, and identification of the welfare of the church with regional progress created a decidedly religious society. Evangelicals sought to forge a Christian nation through a wide range of means: political involvement and social reform; education, temperance and women's movements; evangelism and missions; conventions and revival. Some began lifetime service in missions to Australian Aboriginal people, to the Kanakas of Queensland, or to people overseas (the Pacific, China, Japan, India, Ceylon and Africa). The reflex advantage to the churches of engagement in the foreign missionary movement became increasingly evident in this period: evangelical churches were linked in valuable networks, and church members of all social classes acquired both an appetite for evangelism and mission and an aptitude for stewardship. Some evangelicals devoted the best part of their energies to a need which became more urgent in this period, namely to defend the Bible against Biblical criticism, Darwinism, and ritualism.

So the world, the Spirit, and the Word were all energetically championed in this period. This made it a relatively successful Protestant age, but for all that it was not a great age of evangelicalism. This was because few individuals embodied the evangelical synthesis. The three strands were all present and each was strong, but they were not intertwined. The Word was ably defended, but the theology of the Word was not robust. Unwelcome changes were challenged on moral rather than theological grounds. It was an age in which evangelicals came to think of themselves as either liberal or conservative. Liberal evangelicalism was a confident, inclusive style of evangelicalism arising from the conviction that history was on its side, that society and progress were its debtors, and that the Bible should be understood in ways which made it compatible with the verities of the best, sober scholarship. The conservative evangelicals, on the other hand, thought that history was passing them by, that society was in the grip of the forces of darkness, and that the answer was not involvement with the institutions of modern liberal democracy, but evangelistic missions and holiness conventions, and prayer for revival in this age and for the imminent arrival of the next age. Conservative evangelicals tended to withdraw from the enterprise of shaping civil society and were positively suspicious of progressive Biblical scholarship. They were enthusiasts for the Spirit and champions of the Word, understood devotionally. In retrospect it would seem that most evangelicals were reacting to the forces of secularisation, albeit in different ways, rather than acting out of a strong theology of the Word. The bifurcation of evangelicalism into its liberal and conservative wings took place along regional and denominational lines. The Methodist and Baptist Churches of Victoria and South Australia, for example, were confident in their civic-minded, liberal evangelicalism. New South Wales evangelicals tended to be more conservative and pietistic.

The World: Forging a Christian Country and a National Identity

Having abolished state aid to the churches, New South Wales politician Henry Parkes turned to the more difficult task of phasing out state aid to denominational schools. This culminated in the Public Instruction Act in 1880 in New South Wales and its equivalent in other colonies in other years. Again, the abolition of state aid to churches and church schools did not signify any decline of religious belief: the government was anti-sectarian, not secular, though the legislature seemed determined to make the state the symbol of a common citizenship.[2] The evangelical Protestants, with their high view of the state, were not unhappy, and at this time the church, reinforced by the school and the family, was very effective in the socialising process, an arrangement which lasted for almost a hundred years. 'The church was responsible for denominational and doctrinal instruction; the state was responsible for a general education that was practical, civic, and Christian.'[3] On this foundation a Christian nation would continue to be built.

A significant number of politicians were evangelicals in this period, and, among their legislative concerns, Richard Ely catalogues:

> sabbath observance, education, adultery, divorce, the care of orphans, charity for the poor, aged and sick, the use and misuse of intoxicants, prostitution, sodomy, blasphemy, the swearing of oaths on the Bible in court, gambling, prayers in the legislature, and communal penitence (for instance in the declaration by the governor of a day of prayer for rain). The range was so extensive as to lend some credence to the claim that Australia was 'a Protestant country'.[4]

England's Sunday Observance Act of 1780 remained in force in New South Wales until 1966. David Bollen has argued that the Protestant push for legislation against drink and gambling was only part of a broader social improvement programme: 'Christian humanitarianism was a significant influence on social welfare provision in the nineteenth century, and inspired the little that was benign in the dealings of governments and settlers with Aborigines.'[5]

Whether in the civic sphere of legislation or in the preaching in evangelistic missions, Australian Protestants emphasised individualistic morality rather more than many in the population found palatable. In one of the more interesting responses to the Protestant presence in Australia, the moralisers were saddled with the label of 'wowser'. This term was coined in 1899 by John Norton, Sydney editor of *Truth* magazine (which had a reputation for everything except its title). By 'wowser', he meant a hypocrite, a Wesleyan, a puritanical kill-joy. The term caught on like wild-fire, along with 'wowserism', 'wowserites', 'wowseristic' and the verb, 'to wowse'. The wowsers attracted Henry Lawson's mockery:

We must not kiss in the gardens,
We must not sing in the street,
We must not jump with a joyous shout
When a long-lost friend we meet.
We must not race by the sea-shore,
We must not sit in the sand.
We must not laugh on a New Year Night,
For this is the Wowsers' land.[6]

Catholics were never wowsers. True, they were just as puritanical as the Protestants over sex. The Pope declared that cycling on the newly invented bicycles was destructive of female virtue and modesty. But gambling and drinking were quite popular in Irish Catholic circles. Hugh Mackintosh, who built the stadium at Rushcutters Bay to house prize fights, was startled when, on sharing a two-berth railway compartment, he witnessed John Wren, the wealthy Catholic gambler enshrined for ever in Frank Hardy's *Power without Glory*, kneel to say his prayers. So Catholics did not make very good wowsers, and when in 1910, Labor won office for the first time, Cardinal Moran rejoiced in the defeat of the wowsers, those of a liberal disposition whom he thought of as enemies of the Catholic Church. For their part, the wowsers thought of Catholicism as synonymous with corruption. In 1902 a Methodist minister at Thirroul, New South Wales, said that Methodists should not have to pay taxes to support prisons, since prisons were full of Catholics.[7] This provoked a pitched battle between Protestant and Catholic youths at nearby Figtree. In 1916, in the course of the debates which gave Australia six o'clock closing in pubs, the *Bulletin* magazine suggested that there should be a tax on wowsers. Since there were taxes on drinking, smoking, gambling, and entertainment, all of which helped the war effort but none of which was engaged in by the wowsers, the wowsers could not be deemed to be pulling their weight in the national emergency.

A substitute creed had to be found by those whose interests were not served by wowserism—hence 'mateship'—a genuinely indigenous, working-class creed championed by Henry Lawson and W. G. Spence, the devoutly Christian union organiser.[8] In the comparative absence of women in rural Australia, men came to rely on each other for emotional support as well as physical labour. Mateship was for men. Manliness was a major concern of the churches in this period. In England Charles Kingsley had initiated the cult of 'muscular Christianity', which had great appeal in Australia where, it was said, 'the men are men and the women are, too'. There was much debate in the press as to why more women attend church than men. One argument advanced by the secularists was that religion had clearly been proved false, that men were brave enough to say so, and only women continued to be cowed. Churches, it was commonly said were for women and the elderly:

> Attend your church, the parson cries
> To church each fair one goes.
> The old go there to close their eyes,
> The young to eye their clothes.[9]

How Christian was mateship? Henry Lawson contended that it was the essence of Christianity. A true Christian, says the national bard, was 'one who is sorry for most men and all women and tries to act to it to the best of his ability, and if he ain't a Christian, God knows what is—I don't'.[10] To Lawson, mateship was not only the essence of Christianity, it was also the answer to the problems created in society by the bickering churches:

> They tramp in mateship side by side—
> The Protestant and 'Roman'—
> They call no biped lord or 'sir'
> And touch their hats to no man![11]

But mateship has not always been a force for consensus. T. Inglis Moore tells us that there are two types of mateship: the inclusive and the exclusive. The inclusive is directed 'against the hazards or hardships of an environment, against loneliness, danger and death', and it tends to view all men as equals and is therefore a force for democracy. That is a positive thing, and appears to have served the same social purpose in Australia as revivalistic religion did on the American frontier. But the exclusive type of mateship pits one class, such as the working class, or group, such as convicts, larrikins, bodgies or vandals, against another. Here mateship creates a weapon which is used in community warfare.[12] Mateship is a very limited religion. It is an essentially masculine creed, arising out of the experience of the bush and the war—experiences alien to most Australians. It has one doctrine—loyalty, and even that devolves easily into sentimentalism. Mateship is at its most degenerate in the 'beery brotherhood' of the urban barbecue brigade, superficial, pleasant and harmless, unless you live next door to its devotees.

Unionism was mateship in an organised form, and unionism, too, was thought to have captured the essence of Christianity. 'Unionism', said W. G. Spence, 'came to the bushmen as a religion … It had in it that feeling of mateship which he understood already … Unionism extended the idea.'[13] The socialism of the 1890s may have owed as much to Christ as to Marx. Rod Quinn was addressing Jesus, not Marx, when he wrote of the new Eden being built in Australia:

> We built for Thy glory
> Thy wisdom beseeching
> We founded and fashioned
> Our house on Thy Teaching.[14]

And Henry Lawson wrote:

> Christ is coming once again,
> And his day is drawing near;
> He is leading on the thousands of the army of the rear!
> We shall know the second advent
> By the lower skies aflame
> With the signals of his coming, for he comes not as he came—
> Not humble, meek, and lowly, as he came in days of old,
> But with hatred, retribution for the worshippers of gold![15]

Of course, such language may be the rhetoric of Christianity without the substance, as when Victor Daley depicted Christ as the embodiment of labour:

> I am the Crucified
> I am He for whose garments the world's cut-throats have diced.
> Lo, I die every day, as on Calvary I died,
> And my true name is Labour, though priests call me Christ.[16]

With the spectacular failure of unionism in the Maritime Strike of 1890, the working man turned to politics, and in 1891 the New South Wales Labor Party was formed. The role of the Catholic Church in the history of the Labor Party has been noticed by historians, but typically the contribution of evangelical Protestants to its formation was much greater than has been acknowledged.[17] There are two stereotypes about the formation of the Australian Labor Party. The first stereotype is that it was primarily the product of the impact of Marxist thought on the working class. The second is that it was formed as a Catholic pressure group, and that the Protestants gave up on political processes because they were outmanoeuvred by the Catholics. These two stereotypes do not sit easily together, and it would appear that both are wrong.

As to the first stereotype, that the Labor Party was Marxist, the leading Marxist in the movement was the fiery, outspoken Billy McNamara. He was very anti-Catholic, and he influenced Henry Lawson and Jack Lang, Premier of New South Wales. But for all that he was essentially a side-player. He could not get himself elected. It must be said that the Labor Party was not then, and never has been, revolutionary, and its campaign to civilise capitalism[18] is consistent with Christian idealism. The question then is: which form of Christian idealism, Catholic or Protestant?

The second stereotype, that the Labor Party was formed as an ally of the Catholic Church, was fixed in the Protestant imagination very early in the party's history. Catherine Mackerras, née MacLaurin, born in 1900, before she was ten took it as an axiom that the two were firm allies.[19] She believed that, unlike the English Labour Party which was full of intellectuals, the ALP was made up entirely of Irish Catholics. It is true that the Catholic Church, during the pontificate of Leo XIII (1878–1903), addressed the 'Social Question'. In the celebrated encyclical *Rerum Novarum, or The Condition of the Working Class*, Leo committed the Catholic Church to solidarity with the working class in its quest for justice and a decent standard of living. It is also true that the stridently sectarian *Protestant Standard* whipped up fear of a great Catholic vote which would sweep the Irish Catholic working class into power. But the argument that the Labor Party was strongly Catholic does not agree with the evidence. Cardinal Moran, although an outspoken supporter of the Labor Party, had very little personal influence on its formation. He just thought it would be a very good thing if it could be used for the Catholic Church rather than against it. *Rerum Novarum* was published only four weeks before the 1891 election at which the first Labor Party members were elected, and therefore cannot have had the impact on it which has been claimed. The number of Catholics elected in the 1891 election is disputed. E. J. Brady said there were three. Ford says there were four.[20] Bede Nairn says there were five. In any case, it was few in number. In the 1894 election no Catholics were elected for the Labor Party. There was no great united Catholic vote which was just waiting to spell the end of Protestant political ascendancy.

The truth is that the early Labor Party owed more to the evangelicals than to the Catholics.[21] In the inner suburbs of Sydney, the population did not consist mainly of the Catholic Irish working class, but of Protestants. Anglican and Primitive Methodist churches far outnumbered Catholic churches in Redfern, Darlington, and Glebe. In 1891 the new Labor Party won thirty-five seats in the New South Wales election, heralding the emergence of highly organised and disciplined parties (in the ecclesiastical as well as the political spheres). Among the Labor Party candidates elected in 1891 were a number who fitted into the evangelical camp. J. S. T. Mc-Gowen, who was to become New South Wales' first Labor Premier, was an Anglican lay preacher and Sunday-school superintendent at St Paul's Redfern, an evangelical stronghold under the Rev. Francis Bertie Boyce. John L. Fegan was a Wesleyan Methodist lay-preacher and Sunday-school superintendent at Carrington. He had a political pilgrimage every bit as dynamic as his religious one. He was elected Labor member for Newcastle in 1891, stood successfully as an Independent in 1894 when he refused to take the Labor pledge, joined Labor in 1899 to topple the Reid Government, became a Liberal in 1904, and in 1920 stood successfully for the conservative Nationalist Party. He was a Sunday-school teacher and NSW Grand Chief Templar in the International Order of Good Templars. Alfred Edden was yet another Methodist lay-preacher, elected to parliament in the seat next to Fegan's. He too refused to sign the pledge, but he rejoined the party and became Minister for Mines in McGowen's Government. Another ex-miner, Joseph Cook, was a teetotaller who studied for the Methodist ministry. He became member for Hartley, west of Sydney, and Prime Minister of Australia, 1913–14. Frank Cotton mediated in the Shearers' Strike of 1890, was a founder of the Single Tax League, and editor of the *Democrat*. A Methodist, Cotton may have written the first manifesto of the NSW Labor Party. Other Labor Party men elected in 1891 and known to be evangelicals were Thomas Bavister, G. D. Clark, and John Hindle. Among other evangelicals to represent Labor was the Rev. G. W. Smailes, who was elected in 1894. In South Australia, the paradise of Methodism, three Primitive Methodist local preachers entered parliament, and two of them became State premiers.[22]

The decline of the churches in Australia has been attributed to the growth of organised labour, since its leadership, which at first owed much to Christian inspiration, drifted towards secularism.[23] The ideal of the brotherhood of man was secularised to become a utopian, socialist, co-operative society. But it is probably true that a strong secular emphasis on the brotherhood of man can only be erected on a previously laid foundation of the Christian belief in the fatherhood of God.

The Spirit: The Holiness Movement, Conventions, and Revival

The prosperous years 1860–89 coincided with the new revivalism of Moody and Sankey in the USA. These years saw the emergence of the holiness movement and its English evangelical manifestations: the Mildmay and Keswick conventions, the China Inland Mission, the Children's Special Service Mission and the Scripture Union, the Salvation and Church Armies, evangelical public schools, and evangelical theological colleges at Oxford and Cambridge, the 'Forward Movement' in English Methodism in the 1880s, training colleges for laymen, and numerous large churches and welfare institutions. Perhaps the most influential of these developments, the Keswick Convention, was born in the little town of that name in the Lakes District in England in 1875.

This spiritual floodtide was soon to lap the shores of Australia, which was considered one of the most favourable soils for evangelistic and revivalistic experiments. Many of international evangelicalism's most celebrated evangelists visited Australasia: William 'California' Taylor (1863–65), Henry Varley and Dr A. N. Somerville of Glasgow (1877), Emilia Baeyertz (resident in Australia and evangelist from 1878), Thomas Spurgeon (1878 and 1880), John MacNeil (resident in Australia, evangelist from 1881 to 1896), Margaret Hampson (1883), Dr Harry Guinness (1885 and again in 1901), George Muller (1886), Hudson Taylor (1890), Henry Drummond (1890), Francis E. Clark, the founder of Christian Endeavour (1892 and 1904), Thomas Cook and Gipsy Smith (1894), John R. Mott and the Rev. Charles H. Yatman from New York (1896), T. Champness of the Methodist Cliff College and the Joyful News Mission (1898), R. A. Torrey in 1902, Charles Alexander (1902, 1907, 1909, 1912) and J. Wilbur Chapman in 1909 and 1912. Among the most successful was the Rev. George Grubb, a Keswick missioner, whose 'rip-roaring wild Irishness' prompts the observation that

Australian evangelicalism owes much both in tone and in potency to Irish Protestants. George Grubb spoke at the first Australian Keswick in Geelong in 1891. His message was vintage Keswick: 'If our church members were to receive clean hearts there would be a wonderful revival of true religion. It is defilement in our hearts that keeps us from witnessing.'[24] At the Geelong convention, forty people offered for missionary service. The convention movement took deep root in Australian soil. Generally, these conventions were funded by moneyed laymen and were characterised by contempt for theological precision. The speaker had to have fire, and a personal Gospel without political overtones.

Towering over all the evangelists of the nineteenth century were Charles Haddon Spurgeon and Dwight L. Moody, neither of whom visited Australia, but both of whom influenced it enormously. A missionary with the Bush Missionary Society (formed in 1857) reported in 1871 that Spurgeon's sermons were more popular in the Australian bush than any others: they created most interest and seemed to do most good, perhaps because they were cast in an earthy style which would presumably appeal to bush folk. These sermons, printed in tracts and the newspaper *The Sword and Trowel*, were read at house meetings in bush settlements every Lord's Day morning.[25] Between 1863 and 1892 the majority of Baptist ministers who came to Australia from Britain trained at Spurgeon's college, far ahead of those trained by the Baptist Missionary Society or the Baptist Union. More young ministers went to Australia and New Zealand from Spurgeon's college than to the United States or South Africa, the two other destinations most favoured of British migrants and settlers. The college graduates were committed to evangelism, church expansion, and—unlike their mentor, who smoked and drank—teetotalism. 'Advance Australia' was their aim. Rough diamonds, Spurgeon's preachers laboured with the Bush Missionary Society and championed what they understood as 'General Evangelicalism'.[26]

Ministry in the bush should not be romanticised, however. The outback could be lethal, especially to families. Between 1899 and 1902, for example, Maude Rochardson, married to the Anglican minister Reginald Smee, lived at Brewarrina in western New South Wales, in a galvanised-iron shed where she lost one baby after the other in the dreadful heat. She often contemplated suicide.[27] The church hierarchy had to accept that the outback was too harsh for young families, and from 1897 Anglican High Churchmen formed bush brotherhoods and staffed them with young, unmarried, English ordinands in search of adventure and self-sacrifice in the newly opened northern and western outback of Australia. This was a hard problem for the evangelicals, who were not admirers of celibacy; the Bush Church Aid Society, the evangelical answer to the bush brotherhoods, was not formed until 1919.

Moody's impact on Australian evangelicalism was also vast. Dwight L. Moody (1837–99) is characterised by J. Edwin Orr as 'the greatest of world evangelists'.[28] But there was a problem. The Gospel according to Moody was less exacting than that of Jonathan Edwards and John Wesley, and preaching was made more palatable: more entertaining and simpler. Strongly reasoned, doctrinal sermons and catechising all but disappeared. This was bound, together with rationalistic anti-supernaturalism compounded with Darwinism, to eat into the foundations of the strong Reformed formulations of the faith stemming from the Reformation and the seventeenth century, represented most clearly by the Westminster Confession. The child of the one, fundamentalism, and the child of the other, liberalism, were themselves to produce sickly offspring: theological illiteracy and indifference. Nevertheless in Moody's campaigns in London in 1875 and Cambridge in 1882 the churches were greatly encouraged by an unprecedented response to the preaching of the Gospel. It is estimated that he travelled more than a million miles and preached to more than a million people on his evangelistic campaigns.

Moody never visited Australia, although a petition, inviting him to evangelise Australian cities and signed by 15,381 people, was given to him in 1899, the year of his death. The invitation to Moody, extended by the Australasian Evangelisation Society established in 1891, was made the subject of prayer at the Moody Bible Institute. The president of the institute, Reuben A. Torrey, was present at that prayer meeting and he was deeply moved by the call to Australia. In April 1902 he arrived in Melbourne, heralding probably the greatest evangelistic campaign in Australia's history prior to the 1959 Billy Graham Crusades. The Melbourne mission was preceded by prayer, work, and unity on a staggering level. The evangelical churches drew together in support of the committee of seventy which organised for every house to be visited twice in Melbourne, divided the city suburbs into fifty mission centres with fifty local evangelists preaching in halls and thirty large tents, while in the city, they used the town hall, several theatres, and the 7000-seat Exhibition Building. A Melbourne doctor, William Warren, reported:

> Within a few weeks the Spirit of God laid hold of the Christians, and there was a conscious assurance that the city and its suburbs of nearly five hundred thousand population was going to be moved as never before ... Whole families were brought to Christ, as well as infidels, publicans, and actresses ... A policeman averred that since the mission opened in his district, he and his fellow constables had had practically nothing to do. Theatrical managers declared that if the mission continued they would have to close their establishments ... Do you wonder? God's people were in earnest, the Holy Spirit was given His way and sway, and believers greeted each other with: 'The big revival has begun. Glory to God.'[29]

Attendances totalled a quarter of a million each week, when the population of the whole of Victoria was only one million. Torrey invited Charles Alexander to accompany him as his singer. Alexander returned to Australia in 1907 and again in 1909 with J. Wilbur Chapman when the four months of meetings were characterised as 'a time of Pentecost for the whole Commonwealth'.[30] In 1912 Chapman and Alexander held yet another campaign.[31]

Behind Dr Warren's reference to 'the big revival' above is a story of one of the most concerted prayer efforts known in Australian evangelical history, as Reuben Torrey himself explained:

> When Mr Alexander and I reached Australia we found that there was a group of about ten or twelve men who had been praying for years for a great revival in Australia. They had branded together to pray for 'the big revival,' as they called it in their prayers, to pray for the revival no matter how long it took. The group was led by the Rev. John M[a]cNeil, the author of *The Spirit-Filled Life*, but he had died before we reached Australia. A second member of the group, Rev. Allan Webb, died the first week of our meetings in Melbourne. He had come to Melbourne to assist in the meetings, and died on his knees in prayer. A third member of the group, even before we had been invited to Australia, had been given a vision of great crowds flocking to the Exposition Hall, people hanging on to the loaded street cars wherever

they could; and when that vision was fulfilled he came a long distance to Melbourne just to see with his own eyes what God had revealed to him before.

We also found that a lady in Melbourne had read a book on Prayer and had been very deeply impressed by one short sentence in the book, 'pray through,' and that she had organised prayer-meetings all over the city before we reached the place; indeed, we found when we reached Melbourne that there were 1,700 neighbourhood prayer-meetings being held every week in Melbourne ... In the four weeks, 8,642 persons made a definite profession of having accepted the Lord Jesus Christ as their Saviour ... The report of what God had done in Melbourne spread not only all over Australia, but to India, and England and Scotland and Ireland, and resulted in a wonderful work of God, ... the outcome of the prayer-meetings held in Chicago, and of the prayers of the little group of men in Australia.[32]

Occasionally, the evangelistic missions of this period do appear to have been accompanied by genuine revival. In some cases, these revivals (see Table 3.1) influenced entire communities, shaping the way people viewed their own environment. In 1873 and 1874 two Brethren missionaries from British assemblies, William Brown and Edward Moyse, commenced missionary work in northern Tasmania at Circular Head and Scottsdale. Some 450 people professed faith in Christ at their meetings, and several assemblies were commenced in these areas. Then the evangelists moved to the Kentish district in the central north of Tasmania. During the day the evangelists visited settlers' homes, and at night the people came to hear them preach. When the crowds were too large for the settlers' houses they moved to their barns:[33]

Great interest was aroused in the whole district as night after night the people came to hear the evangelists. From the vantage point of Duggan's barn on the hill could be seen the flickering lights carried by the people walking along bush tracks and across the paddocks, converging on the barn from every direction. These torches were made from the bark of trees soaked in fat. So powerful was the preaching ... that one person, upon seeing a possum on the ridgecap of a barn declared it to be the Devil. When quite a few people began to get converted the excitement became so great that they couldn't go about their normal

Table 3.1: Revivals in Australian colonies/states, 1871–1905

Year	Town/City	State
1871	Goulburn	NSW
	Brisbane	Queensland
1873	Bendigo	Victoria
	Geelong	Victoria
	Warwick	Queensland
1874–75	Moonta	SA
	Wallaroo	SA
1875	Ballarat East	Victoria
1875–76	Kangaroo Flat	Victoria
	Inglewood	Victoria
	Bendigo	Victoria
	Ballarat	Victoria
1877	Toowoomba	Queensland
1878	Bulli	NSW
	Wagga Wagga	NSW
	Kentishbury	Tasmania
1879	Taree	NSW
	Manning River	NSW
1880	Taree	NSW
	Cobar	NSW
	Glebe	NSW
1880s	Marrickville	NSW
1881	Ballarat	Victoria
	Marburg	Queensland
1886	Armidale	NSW
1887	Geelong West	Victoria
1891	Launceston	Tasmania
	Geelong	Victoria
1894	Maitland	NSW
	Waverley	NSW
	Bendigo	Victoria
	Port Pirie	SA
	Broken Hill	NSW
	Moonta	SA
1902	Melbourne	Victoria
	Illawarra	NSW
1905–06	Among the Kanakas	Queensland

work but went instead to urge others to believe. Many were young married couples in their twenties and thirties, and some were teenagers and children.[34]

The whole community was moved. Nearly half of the 400 pioneer settlers responded to the evangelists, and just under 100 were baptised. These converts expressed their new faith in the names they gave to the surrounding districts: Paradise, Beulah, Garden of Eden, the Promised Land. Around Mt Roland, which towers over Sheffield, 'over thirty Bible place names are found in these few square kilometres'.[35]

In 1902–03 a tent meeting crusade in rural New South Wales was paid for by a Methodist philanthropist, the Honourable Ebenezer Vickery, Member of the Legislative Council, who lived in the Sydney suburb of Waverley. He had given the Lyceum Theatre to the Methodist Church, and this became the home base of the Sydney Central Methodist Mission. He had also been the principal donor of the Waverley Methodist Church, which was described as 'the most beautiful belonging to the denomination in the southern world'.[36] But he was as interested in giving money for ministry as for buildings. He was a foundation member of the Evangelical Council of New South Wales, formed in 1899, which organised the Simultaneous Mission in Sydney in 1901. Vickery reasoned that if tents could be so effectively used in reaching the unchurched for Christ in Sydney, how much more successful would they be in the country towns of New South Wales.

It was a correct calculation. The 1902-03 crusade in rural New South Wales resulted in the professed conversion of 25,000. It was nowhere more clearly a revival than in the coal mining villages of the Illawarra, when 2735, or some 15 per cent of the region's population, professed conversion. The fire of the Spirit fell on each coal-mining village in a work described as 'gloriously monotonous': at Mt Kembla 131 professed conversions; Mt Keira 214; Balgownie 183; Bulli 292; Helensburgh 234 and so on. At Mt Kembla 'an intense emotion with an evident assent to the Preacher's burning words were imprinted on every face and feature'. The revival made an impact on the moral tone of the community. At Mt Kembla, the Workers' Club, which was a drinking club, lost many of its members. At Balgownie, the local dancing salon lost its grip on the young. At Mt Keira swearing disappeared and the pit ponies in the mines stopped work as they could no longer understand their instructions, a phenomenon also reported in the Welsh revival three years later. Asked what was the evidence to 'the man in the street' that the revival was genuine, the Rev. D. O'Donnell replied that the question was a very proper one, since there should be 'works meet for repentance'. He catalogued four evidences:

> First, payment of debts. Tradesmen report the settlement of accounts they had long regarded as bad. Second, a pure language ... It is said that in the Mount Keira pit an oath has scarcely been heard since the Mission ... Third, a fair day's work. The proprietor of one of the mines told me that the biggest day's output of coal they ever had, followed the Mission. Fourth, attendance at Church. All the churches report greatly increased congregations and increase in the membership.[37]

Among the successful missions taken during this period were a number conducted by women. In 1907, for example, the Rev. R. L. Wartheim, a woman evangelist of the Methodist Episcopal Church in Denver, was invited to conduct a mission in a small church in Wyee, New South Wales, preaching her message of entire sanctification. Nearby is Bethshan, the home of Elliott John Rien, who arranged a Holiness Convention at his property the following Easter. This led to the formation of the Bethshan Holiness Mission, which continues to this day.[38]

The Origins of Pentecostalism in Australia

The great majority of the evangelists who visited Australia in this period were careful to keep in with the mainstream holiness movement in Britain and thus avoid some of the more bizarre extremes of that movement. But from the holiness movement emerged pentecostal and tongues movements in Australia possibly as early as anywhere in the modern world.[39] As Don Dayton has shown, 'the whole network of popular "higher Christian life" institutions and movements constituted at the turn of the century a sort of pre-pentecostal tinderbox awaiting the spark that would set it off.'[40] The first known reported instances of speaking in tongues (glossolalia) in Australia occurred during a prayer meeting at Portland, Victoria, in 1870. The Azusa street revival in Los Angeles, from which American pentecostalism is traditionally dated, did not begin until 1906. Australian pentecostalism, then, was not founded by Americans, and to this day retains a distinctive character.

Another important, and essentially Australian, underpinning of pente-costalism, was provided by John Alexander Dowie. Born in Edinburgh in 1847, he came to Adelaide in 1860. In 1872 he became Congregational Pastor in Alma, South Australia. By 1875, after pastoring successfully in Manly, he moved to Newtown, Sydney, where he developed divine healing teachings in the face of an epidemic, probably measles or scarlet fever. Dis-appointed by the doctrine of his own church, and not a little ambitious to build a large work in divine healing, Dowie resigned from the Congrega-tional Church in 1877, and started out on his own. By 1883 he was in Mel-bourne, where within a year he had built a large tabernacle, was drawing large crowds to open rallies, and had a healing ministry marked by a num-ber of notable miracles. Dowie moved to the United States in 1888, built a huge following, constructed Zion city and founded the Christian Catholic Church. He descended into financial ruin and error, claiming to be Elijah the prophet. He toured Australia in 1904, drawing large crowds and pro-voking considerable controversy and popular antipathy. Many of those con-verted at his rallies later entered pentecostal congregations. More impor-tantly, Dowie contributed to the formation of the international healing strand of the holiness movement, which was developed by A. B. Simpson, founder of the Christian and Missionary Alliance, into the 'four-fold' Gospel teaching of Christ as saviour, healer, sanctifier and coming king. This in turn fed back into Australia through the visits of Aimee Semple MacPherson, Fred Van Eyk, Kelso Glover and Donald Gee, shaping the theology of the youthful movement.

As with many movements in evangelical Christianity, the best claimant to the title of 'founder' of Australian pentecostalism was a woman. Janet Lan-caster was born in 1858 as Sarah Jane Murrell, and became an active Methodist. When challenged in 1902 over why healing was no longer taught in the Church, she began to search intensely for the power promised to Christians in the Book of Acts. In her search, she 'herself was healed of a broken and disfigured arm'.[41] Receiving in 1906 literature from England telling of 'back to Pentecost' experiences, she began to seek 'the baptism' earnestly, culminating in a Gethsemane experience in 1908, which was fol-lowed after some time by ecstatic tongues. Gathering a number of people around her, Lancaster went on in 1909 to buy 104 Queensberry Street, North Melbourne, an old temperance hall, which she called Good News Hall. Australia's first permanent pentecostal congregation was born. *Good*

News, the journal of Good News Hall, eventually circulated to more than 3000 people all over Australia and was a key factor in the spread of early pentecostalism in this country. From 1909 to 1930, Good News Hall supported missionaries in Japan, India, South Africa, Hong Kong, China, and Central Australia. But there were problems. Good News Hall was loose in its theology and allowed a variety of opinions. Janet Lancaster herself did not believe that the world is a globe. She believed that God and the Holy Spirit are identical, and that Christ is the Divine Son of God, but not equal to God. She did not believe in eternal punishment, preferring the view that the wicked are annihilated. These views shocked other pentecostals, and caused Good News Hall to be divorced from the mainstream of pentecostal life. The birth of Australian pentecostalism was bound to be attended with many complications.

Reaching the World: Missions to Aboriginal People, Chinese, Kanakas, and Overseas

It had long been argued among evangelicals that the highest form of Christian service was foreign missions.[42] Accordingly, the most prestigious institutions of the evangelical movement and the accepted thermometer of its spiritual temperature were overseas missions. The growing strength and maturity of the evangelical movement is nowhere more evident than in its commitment to missions. Whereas the period covered by the previous chapter did produce individual missionary efforts which stirred the evangelical heart, this period saw the laying of solid foundations for missions which managed to tap the evangelical dollar (or pound as it was then). In the foreign missionary movement, evangelicals also found an efficient means of tapping the energies of evangelical women, who often outnumbered men in the missionary societies by more than two to one. For good reason, foreign missions may be thought of as the first feminist movement.

Missions within Australia to Aboriginal people, to the Chinese on the goldfields and in the cities, and to the South Sea Islanders on the cane fields, did not enjoy the same prestige as foreign missions. Denominational missions to the Australian Aboriginal people continued to fail in the white-populated south and east of Australia, where they were closed down or taken over by government or pastoralists. They were replaced by non-denominational missions such as the United Aborigines Mission and the

Aborigines Inland Mission. These were 'faith' missions, and many of their missionaries lived and died in conditions which were virtually identical to those of the Aboriginal people. Among their founders were men and women who deserve to be remembered and honoured. For example, at La Perouse on Botany Bay where the tragic relationship between black and white had commenced over a century earlier, Retta Long witnessed numbers of genuine conversions among Aboriginal people, who, 'born in fire', became 'powerful witnesses' to their faith.[43] The dedication and heroism of these faith missions, however, were not always matched by their wisdom, and their Gospel did little to liberate Aboriginal people from lives of inferiority and self-deprecation. Harris[44] suggests that such missions were run on narrow principles which identified salvation with harsh discipline and petty rules. Neither missionary discipline nor governmental law could stem the tide of Aboriginal declension. By the end of the nineteenth century, Aboriginal deaths outnumbered births five to one. Massacres still continued inland, birthrates were sadly depressed, and survivors succumbed to disease, alcohol and opium. Missions and government co-operated in 'smoothing the dying pillow'.

Early in the present century, however, a more enduring work was started among Aboriginal people in the sparsely populated parts of Australia. In 1908 the Church of England began its Roper River Mission, the Catholics began work on Bathurst Island in 1911, and in 1916 the Methodists established a mission in Goulburn Island. These missions were started in areas where Aboriginal people were in a majority and were able to maintain more of their customs and culture. The success of the northern missions was also due to the fact that Aboriginal people there had a central occupational role in the pastoral industry. It became apparent that the Aboriginal population was increasing again. Missionaries sent to Arnhem Land were asked to impart to the Aborigines 'the benefits of our Christianity and civilisation'.

In the last three decades of the nineteenth century, thousands of Chinese immigrants moved to the cities from the worked-out goldfields. There they became market gardeners, launderers and furniture makers, shopkeepers and merchants, owned cafés and ran boarding houses. They faced increasing hostility from the majority of the white population. Churchgoers shared the prejudices of the majority, and especially condemned the Chinese pastimes of opium smoking and gambling, and gave little support to attempts to reach the Chinese 'heathen' with the Gospel. Nevertheless, impressive evangelistic work was done among Chinese city-dwellers by the Presbyterians and the Church of England, a testimony to the missionary zeal of the few and to the character of the Chinese missionaries themselves. From 1872 until 1880 George Ah Len, who had worked for five years as a catechist for the Presbyterian Church in the Victorian goldfields, worked in Sydney for the Heathen Missions Committee of the United Presbyterian Church. He visited Chinese in their homes and workplaces and held services in a ragged school in the north of the city, with upwards of thirty Chinese braving the insults from ill-disposed labourers who resented the threat they posed to their employment. From 1879 a catechist of the Church of England, Soo Hoo Ten, visited the Chinese at the southern end of Sydney, including the market gardeners of Waterloo and Botany. He established Chinese services in Waterloo, at St Andrew's Cathedral schoolroom, and at Botany where a church was built especially for the Chinese. By 1892 he had baptised nearly 100 converts. He established English classes for the Chinese, a Chinese YMCA, conducted missions in Brisbane and Melbourne, and by 1891 was conducting thirty-eight services a week all over Sydney. In 1898 he was ordained to the priesthood and retired in 1912. Another long ministry to the Chinese was that of John Young Wai, who, beginning in 1882, worked for more than three decades in Sydney for the Presbyterian Church. James Kem Yee, trained in the Victorian gold town of Ballarat, commenced in 1888 a ministry to the Chinese in Newcastle and Maitland, north of Sydney, which lasted until 1920. Significant ministries to the Chinese were also conducted in Tasmania, Victoria, Western Australia, and in the Church of England dioceses of Brisbane, where Kum Jem won many converts, and in Riverina in southern New South Wales where Le Ung Pong ministered to the Chinese of Narrandera and Hay. The Presbyterians encouraged the Chinese to develop their own church and become financially independent. By contrast, the Church of England kept their work among the Chinese in mission mode, and, in Sydney and Melbourne, argued among themselves as to whether the Australian Board of Missions, founded by the Church of England in 1850, but which could never supply the Chinese mission with sufficient funds, should continue to run the mission or hand over to the newly formed Church Missionary Association. In the event, the Presbyterian policy proved the more long-sighted, and Presbyterian work among Chinese peoples survived in an unbroken ministry to the present day.[45]

Meanwhile, another sad chapter in the history of racism in Australia was being written in Queensland, where from 1868 demand for cheap labour for the sugar industry led to the immigration of 62,000 Pacific Islanders, known as 'Kanakas' (from the Hawaiian word for 'man'). In 1901 the new federal Australian government adopted a white Australia policy and decreed that all the Kanakas would have to return to their island homes by 1906. The immigration had resulted in the formation of the Queensland Kanaka Mission, and the deportation led to the formation of the South Sea Evangelical Mission. Both were the work of Florence Selina Harriett Young (1856–1940), a splendid exemplar of the evangelical synthesis of Spirit, Word and world, and one of the most remarkable of all Australian evangelicals. Blessed with a fine mind and great natural gifts, her most distinctive characteristic was her determination which she understood as her consecrated will. She fortified it daily by feasting on the Bible. She loved the Psalms and read all of them through monthly, and read through the entire Bible twice every year. She was born in New Zealand in 1856. At the age of eighteen, she attended a prayer meeting where a hymn was sung about the second coming of Christ. It made her miserable because she knew that she did not want Jesus to return yet. Then the words of Isaiah 43.25 came to her. She said they were well-known and oft-heard, which says something about the revivalistic background to her life: 'I, even I, am He that blotteth out thy transgressions for Mine own sake.' She continued: '"*For Mine own sake.*" Those four words brought peace, abiding peace to my soul. The Holy Spirit had done His blessed work; HE knew I was truly united to Christ.'[46]

In 1882 Florence Young went to Bundaberg, Queensland, to live on the family sugar plantation. She was told that Kanakas were animals and that it was useless to try to teach them anything. She started schools for them, and resolved to make the Bible the basis of the curriculum, and she put salvation ahead of civilisation or education. Thus the Queensland Kanaka Mission was born. At its peak it employed nineteen missionaries in eleven mission centres, and many thousands professed conversion through it. In 1890 Hudson Taylor, founder of the China Inland Mission, came to Australia, and Florence heard him speak. He brought home to her conscience the fearful state of the perishing millions in China. She said to herself, 'It is dreadful. But why do not the Christians go to them?' Immediately a voice replied, 'Why don't you go?' She argued, 'I could not leave the boys.' The voice said, 'If I want you in China, do you think you will be any use in Queensland?'[47]

In 1891 she went to China and in the following year at Shanghai she entered into a deeper experience of the Holy Spirit. This she described as a personal knowledge of the 'Filling of the Holy Spirit'; a moment-by-moment filling that was practised till she died.

After three years' work in China, word came of the great needs of the Kanaka Mission, and Florence discussed with Hudson Taylor whether or not she should return to Queensland. He told her she must be always 'at the Lord's disposal', so she went back to Australia.[48] It was three years before she was able to return to China, where she lived through the Boxer Rebellion. Then she heard of the decision to deport the Kanakas. This, reinforced by appeals from Kanakas who had already returned and were finding it difficult to witness in their homelands—indeed, a number had already been martyred for their faith[49]—gave great urgency to the mission. At the 1904 Katoomba Convention, the Solomon Islands Mission (later the South Sea Evangelical Mission) was founded. Florence herself sailed to the cannibal island of Malaita and was the first white woman to land there. In 1905 a prayer revival came to the Queensland Kanakas and a deepening of interest in the life of faith. Then from Christmas 1905 to Easter 1906, it seemed to Florence that the heavens opened and the Spirit poured out in a wonderful season of revival.[50] It ensured that those who had to return to the islands were not timid Christians, but rather great believers in the power of prayer. It was the memory of that revival which was drawn on in the Solomons when revival came in the 1940s and again in the 1970s, since when it has been endemic until this day.

The South Sea Evangelical Mission (SSEM) was a genuinely indigenous, non-denominational overseas missionary society. It reflected the growing maturity of the evangelical movement in Australia that it was now capable of creating its own overseas missionary societies. Denominations established their own colonial or state missionary boards, and the main British missionary societies established their own autonomous Australian divisions if they had not already done so. The Baptists were typical of evangelicals in maintaining that foreign missions constituted 'the proof of the denomination's excellence'.[51] Addressing the First Australasian Baptist Congress in 1908, the elderly Baptist patriarch Silas Mead enthused:

> Our young people must be drenched with Missionary knowledge.
> Our Christian Endeavour members must be so saturated with Mis-

sionary enthusiasm that they shall cease to ask—'Ought someone to go?' but rather,—'Dare I stay at home and fail to listen to the Saviour's command to go into all the heathen lands and proclaim His salvation to the ends of the earth?'[52]

Mead had a great heart for missions. He had migrated to Adelaide in 1861, following rejection for foreign missionary service by the Baptist Missionary Society. He opened the Flinders Street Baptist Chapel in 1863, and the next year formed the first Baptist missionary society in Australia (South Australian Baptist Missionary Society). It established an Australian Baptist Mission at Furreedpore, India. In Victoria an auxiliary of the society was established in 1865, following the deputations of two missionaries from India, James Smith and John Page. In 1885 it merged with the auxiliary of the Baptist Zenana Mission of Great Britain to form the Victorian Baptist Foreign Mission, and sent the first Victorian Baptists as missionaries to India. A similar development occurred in Queensland. Ellen Arnold, a South Australian missionary in India, visited Queensland in 1885, and as a result the Queensland Baptist Missionary Society was formed and Martha Plested, a member of Jireh Baptist Church, accompanied Arnold to India.[53] Arnold was the greatest of the Baptist missionaries, labouring in Bengal from 1882 to 1931.[54] In 1885 she recruited four other women and two men, labelling them the five barley loaves and two fishes. It was a significant symbol of the numerical superiority of women over men in the mission field. Up to 1914, fifty-five Australian women and sixteen men served with the Australian Baptist Missionary Society.

It was in 1885 also that Hudson Taylor sent George Nicoll to Australia from China to recuperate from an illness. His visit ignited great interest in China, and Mary, the eldest daughter of Henry Reed of Launceston, volunteered to go to China as a missionary. Henry Reed was a great embodiment of the truth often illustrated in evangelical history that those most zealous for the Gospel at home are also those who most support overseas missions. A true Wesleyan, Henry Reed was very committed to relieving poverty and social distress, a concern which found practical expression in his support for the Salvation Army and his funding of the beautiful Mission Church in Launceston, built for the 'working classes'. Reed had helped the Rev. George Brown to establish in 1875 the New Guinea Mission, a Wesleyan Methodist mission in New Britain.[55]

In 1889 Mary Reed returned to Tasmania on sick leave. She persuaded her minister in Launceston, George Soltau, to write to Hudson Taylor, urging him to visit Australia. On 22 May 1890, on receipt of a telegram from Hudson Taylor, an Australasian Council of the China Inland Mission (CIM) was established in Collins Street Baptist Church. The first chairman was the Rev. H. B. Macartney, Church of England minister of St Mary's, Caulfield. The secretary was a Baptist minister, Alfred Bird, and the treasurer, Philip Freeman Kitchen. The Kitchens were Brethren, and the Brethren were in the forefront of evangelical initiatives in this period. The Brethren movement had emerged during a period of great missionary activity within other denominations, which may explain the major emphasis Brethren have placed on mission. Brethren groups were functioning in Melbourne in the 1850s, that is, well within thirty years of the movement's commencement. By the 1870s the thriving Brethren assembly in Melbourne comprised some of 'the leading Christians of the city', including Philip Kitchen, who was owner and editor of the Christian Brethren journal, *Willing Work*.[56] The Kitchen family dynasty became the backbone of the CIM in Melbourne. Philip Kitchen, the mission's first treasurer, was succeeded on his death in 1898 by Dr John James Kitchen, who gave up his medical practice to devote himself fully to the work of CIM and the Upwey (later Belgrave Heights) Convention.[57] Kitchen was one who combined with Anglican evangelical layman, H. P. Smith, to form the Melbourne Bible Institute. James Howard Kitchen was the first 'Upwey missionary' and worked in China with the CIM.

In August 1890 Hudson Taylor himself arrived in Australia. His visit was accompanied by great spiritual blessing, especially in Launceston and Hobart. He returned to China with twelve Australian missionaries, including Florence Young, as we have noted above. In 1891 Keswick sent its own missioner, George Grubb, to Australia where his evangelistic rallies and holiness conventions were a spectacular success. By 1913, 176 Australians and New Zealanders, of whom 101 were women, had served in China with the CIM.

It testifies to the unity of purpose of evangelicals at this time that while in Sydney, Grubb combined with Robert Stewart and Eugene Stock to reconstitute the Church Missionary Association of New South Wales, an independent branch of CMS. New associations were formed in Victoria and New Zealand. Within three years these three associations had sent out 13 missionaries to India, Ceylon, Japan, China, Africa and Persia. Between 1892 and 1931 70 per cent of the 247 missionaries that went out with the

CMS were women, and 66 per cent of those were single.[58] The first two women to serve with the Victorian Church Missionary Association were Nellie and Topsy Saunders from Macartney's Church at Caulfield. They were murdered, with Robert Stewart and eight other missionaries, in Fukien Province on 1 August 1895.[59] 'It is not the wine that is kept that counts, but the wine that is poured out in loving sacrifice.'[60] News of the martyrdom galvanised Australian evangelicals to increase their numbers in China, among them Mrs Saunders, the mother of the murdered sisters. But worse was to come. The Boxer Rebellion of 1900 in China cost the lives of 135 missionaries and 53 children. Of these 188 martyrs, 79 were associated with the CIM. Among these was David Barrett, a missionary for only three years, who, on hearing of the massacre of some of his fellow missionaries on 30 August, wrote that, along with theirs, his blood, which was soon to be shed on a desolate mountain, would be the means by which God's kingdom would increase:

> Extermination is but exaltation. God guide and bless! 'Fear not them which kill', he says . . . We may meet in the glory in a few hours or days . . . Not a sleep, no dinner, a quiet time with God, then sunset and evening bells, then the dark . . . Let us be true till death.[61]

Not all the significant missionary societies formed in Australia in the nineteenth century were evangelical. The Melanesian Mission was started in 1850 with the formation of the Australian Board of Missions, and includes the work of Bishop Selwyn and the heroic life and martyrdom of Bishop John Coleridge Patteson.[62] The first half-century of this mission did not see much fruit. Whiteman explains this partly in terms of churchmanship—that the missionaries were not evangelicals and did not seek a lasting conversion experience for the members of their flocks.[63] But there is another side: in World War II they did not desert the islands as did the missionaries of the South Sea Evangelical Mission, and this gained them a new respect among the indigenous peoples. The active support of foreign missions by Anglo-Catholics is also seen in the formation in 1891 of the New Guinea Mission. In 1884 the eastern part of New Guinea was annexed by Great Britain. H. H. Montgomery, Bishop of Tasmania and father of the Field Marshal, reminded the Christian public of the destruction of Australian Aboriginal people, especially in his own diocese, and called for the creation of a Christian mission to New Guinea to help avert a similar outcome. The

mission was established by Albert Maclaren, an Anglo-Catholic, and Cop-
land King, an evangelical, at Dogura in Bartle Bay in 1891. It was an impov-
erished mission and appealed to the celibate Anglo-Catholics rather than
the evangelicals.[64] The Mission to Torres Strait Islanders, begun in 1871, is
justly celebrated for the work of Gilbert White, Bishop of Carpentaria from
1900, and also for the amazing ministry of the 'little deaconess', Florence
Buchanan.[65]

Defending the Word against Ritualism, Darwinism and Liberalism

If Australian evangelicalism grew stronger and more mature during this period, it also became a more defensive movement. It had not only to contend
with secularism and materialism, but also with ritualism, which Anglo-
Catholics sought to insinuate into Church of England liturgy, and with Darwinism and Biblical criticism, to which theological liberalism demanded
the church accommodate itself.

In the Presbyterian and Baptist denominations, evangelicals fought two
highly significant battles against the growing forces of theological liberalism.
In 1875 Charles Strong was inducted at Scots Presbyterian Church in Melbourne. Infected with liberalism from Germany (neology), he challenged the
evangelical Calvinist orthodoxy of the Presbyterian Church of Victoria,
which, formed in 1859 from a union of three strands of Presbyterianism in
the colony, was 'the strongest, wealthiest, loudest and most influential of the
churches in Victoria'.[66] Strong taught that substitutionary and other theories
of the atonement were 'figures of speech', not to be mistaken for 'exact defi-
nitions'.[67] Among the leaders of the fight against Strong[68] was J. Laurence
Rentoul, professor at the Theological Hall of the Presbyterian Church of Victoria. This theological college had been formed in 1866 and was characterised by 'a warm evangelical ardour for the salvation of men',[69] as befits a
church which had been more influenced by the evangelicalism of the Free
Church of Scotland than the Presbyterian churches in most other Australian
colonies. The campaign against Strong was led by the warm-hearted evangelical minister of St Andrew's Presbyterian Church, Carlton, D. S.
McEachran (1828–1915). He was to be made Moderator of the Presbyterian Church in Victoria in 1885, a sure indication of the support he had in the
General Assembly for his stand against Strong. The Presbytery of Melbourne
considered Strong's arguments amidst a great demonstration of public inter-

est in the press. The Presbytery affirmed what they claimed Strong denied: the miraculous and the supernatural; the infallibility and authority of the Scriptures; and the substitutionary atonement.[70] Strong also publicly supported the Sunday Society, which sought to break the iron grasp of the Sabbatarians, and on 1 August 1883 he chaired the meeting at which Justice Higinbotham delivered a notorious lecture attacking credal and supernatural religion. McEachran charged Strong with heresy. Strong resigned and left for Scotland, pursued by a declaration that he was no longer a minister of the Presbyterian Church of Victoria and that Scots Church was now vacant. Strong's supporters, having failed to withdraw Scots from the denomination, established on 11 November 1885 the Australian Church, which declared itself to be 'comprehensive, non-dogmatic, liberal'.[71] The evangelical Calvinists appear to have won this first round with the liberals, but the fight brought to light a number of worrying trends for the Presbyterians. Orthodox Calvinism seemed now to be very unpopular with a significant number of Melbourne's articulate laity, and the Strong case was the incubus for starting the slide into liberalism which the Presbyterian Church was to suffer in Australia.

Among the Baptists, C. H. Spurgeon himself sounded the trumpet against the advancing forces of liberalism. In the August 1887 issue of the *Sword and Trowel*, Spurgeon endorsed two earlier articles by the Rev. Robert Shindler, sounding the alarm at Modernist attacks on the atonement, the personhood of the Holy Spirit, Hell, the Resurrection, Higher Criticism and Darwinism and the infiltration of these teachings into the Baptist pulpit. Spurgeon labelled this slide into liberalism the 'downgrade', and he led an exodus from the Baptist Union with the words 'fellowship with known and vital error is participation in sin'.[72] The downgrade controversy was followed with great interest in all Australian colonies[73] and was not limited to the Baptist denomination. The Brisbane response is typical. There, on 13 November 1887, the Rev. William Osborne Lilley, minister of the Ann Street United Methodist Free Church, preached a broadside against Spurgeon, charging him with a refusal to accept 'the new light from Heaven which had come upon the world during the last thirty years'.[74] William Whale, pastor of the Wharf Street Baptist Church in Brisbane, attacked Lilley the following Sunday in a sermon entitled 'Mr Spurgeon and his Critics'. This so-called 'new light from Heaven', he suggested, 'may in fact not be light at all'.[75] Prominent Brisbane Congregationalist and Presbyterian ministers weighed in on the side of the liberals, and the fight was joined.

The evangelical fight against ritualism had a more formative impact on the shape of the Church of England in Australia than the fight against liberalism. In the period covered by this chapter, churchmanship became a primary concern of Anglicans, and the politicisation of the church paralleled the politicisation of a society embarking simultaneously on the road to Federation and party politics. Within dioceses, High, Broad, and Low Church parties struggled for supremacy. The Diocese of Sydney continued to build doggedly on the evangelical foundation laid by the first chaplains and by Bishop Barker (1854–82). Sydney never became a monochrome evangelical diocese: its clergy always numbered among its ranks some non-evangelicals who were often extremely able men—they had to be. But every success they enjoyed, and every expression of competing traditions, whether it be the moderate Broad Church measures of Bishop Barry (1884–89) or the High Church ritualism of Thomas Ernest Hill, principal of Moore Theological College (1885–88), only galvanised evangelicals in their determination to maintain and consolidate Sydney in its evangelical heritage.

If Sydney was not a monochrome diocese, the evangelicals within it were not monochrome either. George Grubb, the Keswick missioner, taught that a person is made holy or sanctified by a second experience of the Holy Spirit after conversion. This 'second blessing' understanding of holiness was typical of the revivalists of the period. It was a theology of sanctification which seemed to have the future on its side, and gave the Anglicans some prospect of duplicating the successes of the Methodists. Nathaniel Jones, principal of Moore Theological College (1897–1911) and Mervyn Archdall, rector of St Mary's, Balmain (1882–1908), provided a second evangelical option. They were also champions of holiness, but not via the second blessing route down which Grubb wished to lead the evangelical movement. Jones and Archdall were strongly futurist in their theology, preoccupied with millennial considerations, especially unfulfilled prophecies.[76] They were staunchly Calvinistic, which Jones, in particular, combined with Brethren thinking, to emphasise that the church's role was to be the small flock of the elect gathered from a sinful and doomed world. A third option was represented by F. B. Boyce and R. B. S. Hammond: this-worldly, socially engaged, and convinced that holiness consisted mainly of the elimination of social evils, especially those associated with alcohol.

Each of these three evangelical options was Biblicist, but only the second was based on a systematic theology of the Word. The Grubbites, to coin a phrase, approached the Word devotionally, while the Boyceites approached it pragmatically. Nathaniel Jones pounded into his students that the Bible, not experience or reason, was the Christian's only and absolute authority. Jones held the doctrine that Scripture was the inspired, full, plenary and authoritative revelation of God. He did not attack publicly the Grubbites as their passions (holiness and evangelism) were too close to his own heart, but he did attack unrelentingly the rationalist critics of the Scriptures. In this enterprise, he was assisted by Archdall, who became the diocese's most published critic of Darwinism and Biblical criticism. But Jones' and Archdall's hermeneutic (their principles of Biblical interpretation) seems to have militated against that active commitment to the transformation of the world which had characterised Wilberforce's generation when the evangelical synthesis had worked so effectively. It was not only that their hermeneutic was too literalistic; it was also too futuristic to meet the needs of the present. Before coming to Australia, Archdall had worked for the London Society for Promoting Christianity among the Jews. He came to believe in the future spiritual restoration of the Jewish people, and he emphasised that one of the most important aspects of the Scriptures was the prophecies which remained to be fulfilled. Jones and Archdall were powerful exponents of the Spirit and the Word, but they were chiefly interested in the future world where the elect would reign, rather than the redemption of this one where all are suffering. In the perspective of history, we can see that it is not sufficient to believe in the sufficiency of the Word if one's interpretation of the Word is itself deficient.

In 1870 four dioceses had evangelical bishops: Sydney, Melbourne, and two other New South Wales dioceses, Bathurst and Goulburn. By the beginning of World War I there were still four evangelical dioceses, but Bathurst and Goulburn had seceded from the evangelical camp to be replaced by two Victorian dioceses, Bendigo and Gippsland. James Moorhouse, the Broad Churchman who succeeded Perry as Bishop of Melbourne (1876–86), eroded the conservatism of the Perry tradition. Moorhouse's successor, Field Flowers Goe (1886–1902), was an evangelical and a strong CMS supporter, but on his appointment as bishop is reported in the oral tradition to have said, 'I've been known previously as an evangelical—henceforth I will not be known as anything.'[77] He became known as an 'advanced evangelical',[78] because of his fairmindedness and tolerance. Robust evangelicalism did surface in Goe's episcopate. One prominent evangelical cleric was Digby

Berry, who carried the fight to the adversary by writing a series of tracts to set out the Gospel and refute Anglo-Catholic error, and who built up a devoted and well-instructed congregation at Holy Trinity, East Melbourne.[79] This evangelical rearguard action of the first decade of the twentieth century,[80] however, was too late for the evangelicals to recover lost territory. The diocesan culture—liberal, evangelical and pluralistic—had been fixed. St Mary's, North Melbourne, where H. S. Begbie was vicar from 1905 to 1908, was the evangelical flagship of a dwindling fleet.

Whereas the evangelical clergy in Sydney assumed control of the Church of England, evangelical laity in Melbourne, discouraged by a growing army of non-evangelical parish clergy, assumed control of the evangelical movement. Melbourne lay evangelicals often took the initiative in inviting leading evangelists to Australia from Britain and America. The Grubb mission of 1891, for instance, had a much greater impact on Melbourne than on Sydney.[81] Melbourne evangelicalism's acceptance of lay mercantile leadership, with a corresponding non-theological pietism, found Grubb's revivalism a congenial product. Then, during Torrey's 1902 mission in Melbourne, the manager of the Federal Coffee Palace, Hervey Perceval Smith, was converted, and thereafter his considerable administrative gifts were channelled into a variety of evangelistic activities. One such was the Melbourne Gospel Crusade, which operated out of the Federal Coffee Palace.[82] Something of the atmosphere of these times is conveyed in the minutes of the crusade which speak of meetings opening and ending with 'good seasons of prayer', occasionally disrupted by disorderly opposition from '(chiefly) irresponsible youths' for which a constable needed to be on hand for a few weeks to break the pattern. To provide the crusade's converts with good Bible teaching, H. P. Smith and his Melbourne Gospel Crusade Council established the Upwey Convention (1918) which later moved to Belgrave Heights. The convention movement, together with the Melbourne Bible Institute, founded in 1920, were the evangelicals' chief response to the worrying scepticism about Biblical inerrancy based on Darwinism and Higher Criticism.

4. The Word Challenged, 1914–1932

The Great War and the Great Depression which convulsed the Western world were crises threatening the fundamentals both of civilisation and of faith. Almost 60,000 young Australians were killed in the war. The idealism of most Australians died with them, and its orphan child, public-spiritedness, died for want of nurture in the ensuing materialistic age, making money in the 1920s and surviving in the 1930s. It was a difficult time for the churches. But there were signs of strength: Bible colleges, conventions, university student work and overseas missions all thrived. The more the evangelical churches measured their health in terms of their engagement in foreign missions, the more dependent on women the movement became, because women greatly outnumbered men in the missionary task force, and this was not only because so many young men had died in the war.

The Word in Opposition to the World

Spiritually, the decade between the war and the depression was an ebb-tide. In the 1920s liberalism's star was in the ascendant, and evangelicals were tempted to respond either by adopting fundamentalism or by forsaking their evangelicalism. Fundamentalism, a twentieth-century development within conservative evangelicalism, was a movement to defend Protestantism against Biblical criticism, theological liberalism, the theory of evolution, and the social gospel. It is best understood not as an anti-intellectual movement, but as an anti-Modernist movement. In America B. B. Warfield and A. A. Hodge ably defended Biblical inerrancy, and between 1910 and 1915 twelve volumes known as *The Fundamentals* were published and widely distributed to Protestant clergy throughout the world. These volumes clearly identified the enemies of evangelicalism: Darwinism, Higher Criticism, liberal theology, modern philosophy, socialism, materialism, atheism, spiritualism, Romanism, Mormonism, and Christian Science. Fundamentalists affirmed as well as condemned. The 'essentials' they affirmed were the virgin birth, atoning death, bodily resurrection, miracles, and second coming of Christ, together with Scriptural inerrancy. As distinct from the inspiration of Scripture, inerrancy was actually a recent development, a fundamentalist reaction to Modernism.

Fundamentalism came quickly to Australia: there was a conference on 'Fundamentalism' in Sydney as early as 1921 and another in Melbourne in 1922. But it did not put down the deep roots of its American parent. The chief institutionalisations of fundamentalism in Australia were the Bible college and convention movements, although it is important to remember that both predated fundamentalism and existed primarily for positive reasons rather than defensive ones. Under the influence of fundamentalism, evangelicalism became narrower and defensive. The Bible was defended before it was obeyed, and society was to be evangelised—it was beyond reformation. Fundamentalism dulled the cutting edge of evangelical commitment to social reform, for the social gospel became identified with liberalism and therefore it had to be wrong, an attitude which held sway in evangelical circles until the 1970s.

Evangelicalism was now saddled with the negative overtones of fundamentalism: obscurantism, anti-intellectualism, intolerance, pietism, and separatism. To escape association with fundamentalism, some Protestants ditched their evangelicalism. Congregationalists, among the most enterprising of nineteenth-century evangelicals, went liberal, as did many Presbyterians and Methodists. Other evangelicals became self-absorbed, concentrating on the inner life of their own branch of the movement. Such evangelicals also displayed a tendency to be preoccupied with certain doctrines in which the wider populace had no interest, including Biblical inspiration, dispensationalism, and premillennialism. The last—the belief that Christ will reign on earth for a thousand years before the final judgment—thrives on deprivation, and it is therefore not surprising that it became an evangelical preoccupation during the war and the depression. Any decline of eschatological beliefs among conservative evangelicals usually reflects their improved socio-economic standing. In all this the evangelicals were reflecting the world rather than reshaping it.

In a concerted attempt to resist the world in the area of the family and human relationships, committed evangelicals encouraged their children not to marry unbelievers, opposed many of the new freedoms which women were flaunting since the war, stiffened their opposition to divorce, and fostered the ministry of women. It was by now becoming evident that

Australian evangelicalism was perpetuating itself through generations in family dynasties.[1] There were disasters as well as dynasties—some children of evangelicals fell from grace and forsook their parents' faith—but there is no doubt that there was a high correlation between evangelical parentage and getting on in the world. The nurturing of prominent Australian citizens, with or without faith, by Protestant clergy has been a conspicuous fact in Australian history. Phillip Derriman maintains[2] that 1 per cent of all the people listed in *Who's Who in Australia* are sons or daughters of Protestant clergymen, compared with 0.1 per cent of the population as a whole.[3]

Evangelicals raised rather than lowered their standards on divorce. From its beginning in 1876, the Mothers' Union of the Church of England had allowed divorced women to belong if they were the 'innocent party', but in 1920 the rules were changed to exclude all divorced women. This was to harden 'the cement which held our social structure together'.[4] Divorced women were not readmitted until 1974. The 1930 membership of the Mothers' Union stood at 10,000. Its influence extended beyond its members, however, through its magazine *Mothers in Australia*. Much to the delight of the Mothers' Union, the Royal Commission on the Basic Wage recommended in 1920 that married women should be encouraged to stay at home and rear their families as thriftily as possible.[5] At the 1923 annual meeting of the Mothers' Union in St Andrew's Cathedral, Sydney, the Bishop of Goulburn spoke of the 'new womanhood'. Girls now earning their own wages were tempted to 'precocious and perilous pleasures'. The spiritual purpose and character of the Mothers' Union, he concluded, were more needed than ever. Its object was to protect the foundation of home life and the sanctity of marriage. It should not be used merely as an instrument of parochial finance. In fact, women were now making a larger than ever contribution to parish life through the growing work of deaconesses, encouraged first by Archbishops J. C. Wright and then Howard Mowll of Sydney and by Geoffrey Cranswick, Bishop of Gippsland.[6] It was not even unheard of for women to preach! In 1926 the Congregational Church of Colonel Light Gardens in Adelaide received Winifred Kiek, a former Quaker, as their minister, the first woman to be ordained to a parish in Australia.[7] In 1928 Maude Roydon, the English feminist preacher, was invited to enter the pulpit of St Mark's Darling Point, the first woman so to do in the Church of England in Australia.

One of the highlights of evangelical church life in this period—the strength of the overseas missionary movement—must be attributed to the growing acceptance of women as missionaries combined with their continuing exclusion from leadership in the home church. Between 1914 and 1932 the CMS sent out 153 missionaries, of whom 104 were women. Between 1915 and 1938 the Methodists sent out 223 missionaries, of whom 141 were women, while in the period 1914 to 1938 the Baptists sent an extra 58 missionaries, of whom 43 were women, to their celebrated mission in Bengal. The predominance of women in the Baptist mission may be attributed partly to the inspiring leadership of Ellen Arnold, who brought medicine, education, and the Gospel (she did a lot of preaching) to India for fifty years. One of the most significant mission fields to develop in this period was Central Tanganyika, of which Anglican diocese George Chambers from Sydney became bishop in 1927. He was reputedly a dynamic leader of men and especially women, including Katie Miller (the real founder of the Church at Berega), Narelle Bullard (who established Kongwa Hospital and who was also pastor, evangelist and preacher, believing that she had received a definite call to preaching as well as nursing), and Ruth Minton Taylor (a teacher at Mvumi School). By 1938 Chambers had a team of 24 Australian missionaries, of whom 17 were women.

Some of the implications of the strength of the female presence on the mission field was beginning to be brought home at least to mission boards. In 1918 a celebrated LMS missionary, Florence Garnham, reported (as she had been commissioned) to the all-male Australian Methodist Overseas Mission Board on the work of 'missionary sisters' as they were then known, much to the displeasure of the women themselves:

> I am not a suffragette ... but it strikes me that your Women Missionaries are not given the status that should be given them ... In the LMS every woman is given the same status as the men ... The result of it has been that the women realise they are truly missionaries, as much as the men—preachers of the Gospel—and that their responsibility is equal to that of the men ... I think you should give your Women missionaries the same status as the men. It may not be possible—the principles of Methodism may be against it; but after all, Christ's Kingdom comes first; Methodism second.[8]

Missions to Australian Aboriginal people did not have the same prestige as overseas missions, but some important mission stations were established in this period: Mornington Island (Presbyterian, 1914); Croker Island, NT

(Methodist, 1915); Goulburn Island (Methodist, 1916); Groote Eylandt (CMS, 1921); Mt Margaret, WA (United Aborigines Mission, 1921); Milingimbi (Methodist, 1921); Elcho Island (Methodist, 1922); Lockhardt River, Queensland (Australian Board of Missions, 1924); Oenpelli (CMS, 1925).[9] As of old, the missions established schools, churches, and gave some medical help. The churches continued to find the going hard with Aboriginal missions, but they did a lot better with whites in the outback. It was in 1912 that John Flynn was appointed foundation superintendent of the Australian Inland Mission of the Presbyterian Church of Australia. Through its medical work, later supplemented by patrol padres, nursing hostels, aircraft and the pedal radio, it sought to maintain a 'mantle of safety' over the people of the outback. Flynn was not an evangelical, and the mission, consistent with the inclination of its founder for ecumenicity, was careful to insist that creed was not its primary concern. In 1919 a group of Anglican evangelicals, who were concerned with creed, formed the Bush Church Aid Society in conjunction with the Commonwealth and Continental Church Society, which had a long and distinguished history of evangelical work in Western Australia and country districts of the Australian colonies.[10] The Bush Church Aid Society appointed Sydney James Kirkby, a convinced and flag-carrying evangelical, as its first secretary.[11] The Mail Bag Sunday School was started in 1922 by Fred Harvey, who served with the society in Wilcannia. It developed into a series of 600 lessons over eleven grades, and, at its peak in 1939, 4500 children were being serviced by 60 volunteers.

The World at War

Historians have tended to castigate the churches for their unexamined and enthusiastic endorsement of the war, pointing to the role of the churches in recruiting and conscription, to the foolish notion that war would refine the nation and revive the church, and to the shallow theology which saw the war as the result of human sinfulness and a visitation of God's judgment. The churches, we are told, thus lost a great opportunity to bring a deeper vision and a more challenging morality to bear on the development of the Australian spirit. Much of this condemnation is anachronistic. It is inconceivable that significant numbers of churchmen could then have thought any other way about Empire or war. Sweeping generalisations about the churches are often seen as unreliable when detailed studies of particular clergy and regions are concerned. True, one Methodist clergyman declared that Jesus would have voted 'yes' to conscription.[12] But the clergy of Illawarra, for example, were deafening in their lack of support for conscription. Neither did they share the unrealistic optimism of many Australians at the beginning of the war that it would all be over soon.[13]

John Moses is one historian who has sought to illuminate the convictions and values of those who supported Australia's war effort in general and conscription in particular. He has shown that Australian churchmen, particularly Anglicans, were imbued with a theology of war and Empire, and which enjoined on the British nation the responsibility of protecting the weak, by force if necessary. This was the British version of the 'just war' which has enjoyed long support in Christian theology. By contrast, many German intellectuals and theologians endorsed Prussian militarism, seeing Germany as the hammer of God and war as the holy means by which Germany would defend the superiority of the German *Kultur*. The liberal theologians Albrecht Ritschl, Adolf von Harnack and Martin Rade 'championed the ideology of cultural Protestantism'.[14] So the Civic Protestantism of Britain with its just war was ranged over against the State Protestantism of Germany with its holy war.[15] British and Australian Anglican churchmen came to the conclusion that the Germans were serving Odin, the God of War, not the Christian God. They therefore felt ample justification in supporting the war as a crusade against a pagan and Satanic ideology.

Many clergy undoubtedly reduced the international problem to an individualistic and moral dimension. War was looked on as a judgment of God on sinful man who connived at the ugly spirit of militarism and who provoked the wrath of God through Sabbath-breaking, taking his name in vain, horse-racing, gambling and drinking. The war made militant wowsers of the clergy. A Presbyterian minister, Robert Cordiner, reported the desire of a friend of his 'to fly over the great crowds of Randwick racecourse and drop bombs on them to wake them up'.[16] In 1918, when the Hughes Government approved the use of lotteries to meet the shortfall in subscriptions to the war loans, Dr Alexander Leeper, warden of Trinity College in the University of Melbourne, responded, 'We would rather lose the war than break a moral law.'[17] The South Australian women's temperance lobby opposed compulsory armed service before the war, and conscription during it, on the grounds that their sons would be corrupted in the army by boozing and debauchery. The Methodists, in particular, were worried by 'wet canteens' for the soldiers, and established huts where recreational alternatives were available. King George V said he was going off drink for the duration of the war. At a 'Follow the King' meeting in Wollongong, a speaker said that anyone who 'treated a soldier to a drink, we are entitled to regard as a German spy'.[18] In June 1916 New South Wales electors, in opposition to the wishes of their Labor premier, William Holman, voted overwhelmingly for 6 p.m. closing in a referendum, and the six o'clock closing of pubs then introduced lasted for fifty years. The most notable of all temperance campaigners was a Sydney Anglican rector, R. B. S. Hammond. An interjector once shouted during one of his speeches, 'You're talking through your hat, Hammond. You've never been drunk and you don't know what you're talking about.' Hammond replied, 'True, I've never been drunk. Also I've never laid an egg, but I know a bad one when I smell it.'[19] Hammond argued that the Americans and Canadians were serious in their prosecution of the war, as was demonstrated by their determination to introduce Prohibition. In 1918 the *Australian Baptist* asked if Australia was ready for peace since it had not introduced Prohibition.[20] If the war had lasted much longer, it is likely the Prohibition movement would have taken deeper root in Australia.

At first the churches sought to maintain a business-as-usual mentality. J. C. Wright, Anglican Archbishop of Sydney, decreed that the first consideration of his clergy in wartime 'should be the maintenance of religious life'.[21] So church building and activities appear to have continued unabated throughout the war years. The very continuity was important to the war effort: normality was considered basic to civilian morale. Historian Michael McKernan is one who criticises the churches for the inadequacy of their contribution: 'Even in their charitable work, the churches were clearly outstripped by bodies like the Red Cross'.[22] But this is an unfair criticism. The Red Cross would have been much weaker without the support of the churches, especially church women. Rectors' wives were very frequently office-holders in the Red Cross, and offertories and the takings from church concerts were frequently given to the Red Cross. More than 550 clergy enlisted for war service, as Table 4.1 shows.

Applications for chaplaincy positions far outnumbered appointments. The frustration which some clergy had at not being appointed chaplains is reflected in the number of clergy who enlisted in the ranks. Only Catholic chaplaincies remained unfilled for any length of time. Catholic bishops put the maintenance of parish life ahead of the needs of the forces. Chaplains

Table 4.1: Clerical enlistment in World War I (Australia)

Denomination	Chaplains	Ranks
Church of England	175	51
Catholic	86	1
Presbyterian	70	6
Methodist	54	80
Other Protestant denominations	27	n.a.

tended to be older than the ranks and were not as able to take the roughest of army life, and were more frequently replaced after relatively short periods of service. They had the privileges of officers without the same level of danger, since they were not expected to engage in combat. For both these reasons they tended to be looked down on by the men, who dubbed the chaplains as 'Cook's tourists'. There were heroes among the chaplains, however. John Fahey (Catholic), 'Fighting Mac' McKenzie (Salvation Army), and Andrew Gillison (Presbyterian) were three celebrated chaplains who identified fully with their men, living under the same conditions and facing the same dangers. The first and second became national heroes, while the last was killed trying to rescue an injured soldier.

The clergy were for the most part zealous supporters of voluntary recruitment. After all, volunteers would be fighting 'for God and humanity in the cause of righteousness and truth'.[23] There was little opposition to conscription by clergy, although they were not all such ardent advocates of it as McKernan suggests. Many preferred not to speak of it, others allowed for conscientious objection, and a minority took a pacifist line. They much preferred to think of enlistment as a matter of conscience and a test of character and faith, desirable qualities of a voluntary system which would be lost with conscription. The conscription referendums of 1916 and 1917, both of which were lost, divided the churches along sectarian lines, a division fostered unscrupulously by Prime Minister Billy Hughes. The adverse impact of the referendum debates on Christianity in Australia is asserted explicitly by Lionel Fletcher, who was to become the most prominent evangelist Australia has produced. Fletcher was converted in 1896 at Peak Hill (NSW) Methodist Church, and the next year at a conference in Petersham in Sydney he learned from Archdeacon Tress the importance of yielding his whole life to God in order to be filled with the Holy Spirit. 'My life was never the same again,' he later testified, 'and every blessing I have received since, every soul won, and every Church revived in my ministry, is the result of that night.'[24] Fletcher was the pastor of Port Adelaide Congregational Church from 1909 to 1915. This period covered the Chapman–Alexander missions of 1909 and 1912, mentioned in chapter 3. Not many from his own church had attended those meetings because they were so far away, but Fletcher prayed desperately that he would be used by God to bring many souls into his Kingdom just as Chapman was doing. Soon 250 were attending the weekly prayer meeting, all praying earnestly for revival. So great was the blessing which followed that when he left to evangelise first the State of South Australia, then Britain, America, and New Zealand, it was the largest Congregational Church in Australia in terms of membership. Fletcher later wrote: 'I firmly believe that Australia would have been swept by revival in those days, but the Great War brought the conscription issue to the people, and in the controversy and bitterness which followed, the spiritual blessing was stayed.'[25]

In Brisbane, Canon David Garland (1864–1939), a very able High Church Anglican, sought to capitalise on the war by devising a form of memorial service which would unite all Australians in the recognition of the spiritual dimension to the commemoration of the dead. Anzac Day came to be looked on by many Australians as a sacred day. It took on a form devised, not by the Returned Servicemen's League, but by Garland, whose Anglo-Catholicism gave him a sensitivity to the emotional significance of requiems and which enabled him to stand between Catholics and Protestants, hoping to bridge the gap between them in the interests of a civic Christian ceremony acceptable to all Australians. He deliberately sought to set Anzac Day up as Australia's All Souls Day, a day for national meditation. It had to be a holy day, not just a public holiday with horse races and open pubs. Not until the 1930s did the RSL wrest control of Anzac Day from the control of the churches, and it was not until 1964 that hotels were allowed to be opened on Anzac Day.[26]

The eternal state of soldiers killed in action was an issue every clergyman had to deal with in order to advise anxious relatives and friends. Protestants had always taught that the only way to salvation is through faith in Christ, but there were those who argued that the love expressed by an unconverted man in giving his life for his country would be counted to him for righteousness. Another argument was that those who would have been converted in the course of their lives, had not battle shortened their lives, might be saved.[27] There was an increased demand for prayers for the dead and reservation of the Sacrament in fields and hospitals. By the end of the war there was a relentless push for a new Church of England prayer book to accommodate these 'developments'.

It is difficult to analyse the reciprocal influence of evangelicalism and war. Some evangelicals appear to have glorified war. Perhaps the most amazing was the Irishman of Huguenot origin, Dr Everard Digges La Touche. A champion of the doctrine of grace, he had written in 1912 *The Person of Christ in Modern Thought*, and in 1914 *The Need for an Evangelical Revival*. 'Generous, handsome and scholarly, La Touche flashed across the Sydney scene like a meteor.'[28] So great was his love for the Empire that he enlisted as a private soldier and died at Gallipoli. It is easier to get inside his heart than his head. The view that World War I was a denial of Australian nationalism, rather than the expression of it, seems to prevail in modern thinking. But La Touche would challenge this thinking with the argument that nationalism does not mean isolationism when moral issues are at stake. Militarism was probably stronger amongst the High Church folk than evangelicals, and, in the competitive struggle for chaplaincy appointments, evangelical Anglicans may have been by-passed. Digges La Touche enlisted in the ranks, while David Knox of Adelaide went as a welfare worker, putting his evangelical leadership in South Australia at risk. Later, his courageous membership of the Gladesville RSL earned him profound respect. Judd fairly points out that evangelicals were slow off the mark in World War I.[29] This accounts for Archbishop H. W. K Mowll's care not to be caught out again in World War II.

The World in Depression

It is easy to criticise the churches for their band-aid work in the Great Depression and their failure to address the underlying structural causes. There were liberal evangelicals in this period, such as the Dean of the Cathedral in Sydney, A. E. Talbot, and the principal of Moore Theological College, D. J. Davies, who did debate the underlying causes of economic malaise and made pronouncements on social issues, supporting radical and political changes. But they may not have done a lot except talk.[30] It was the conservative evangelical, Archdeacon R. B. S Hammond, rector from 1918 of St Barnabas, Broadway, who, more than any other Anglican clergyman, was able to achieve relief for the poor and unemployed through political and commercial means by enlisting the support of both Sir Philip Game, the State governor, and the business houses. Hammond always attached his social welfare work to evangelism, thus winning the support of conservative evangelicals for his relief programme. He found housing for significant numbers of homeless men and families. By 1934 there were eight hotels with accommodation for 1000 and five Hammond Family Hostels offering shelter to 114 families. He also arranged loans to get people started in new employment. The hungry were fed—more than a quarter of a million meals were served in one year alone—and many of the inebriated contacted at the courts signed the total abstinence pledge and became members of the St Barnabas brotherhood. It is said that over 4400 men came to Christ through Hammond. Most imaginatively, he created a rural settlement near Liverpool, just out of Sydney, where families could buy a house for £100. By 1939, 110 cottages had been built, and the area came to be known as the suburb of Hammondville. This inspired similar experiments in other States.

The Methodists did most to succour the poor through the central missions which they had established in a number of Australian cities. When the depression struck, the Sydney central mission transferred expenditure from its established ministries such as the girls' residential, the Seamen's Mission, and its immigration ministry to more emergency relief-oriented ministries such as the refuge, hostel, and the aged homes. The pursuit of mild reform coupled with energetic rescue work was the aim of the central mission, rather than radical change and political involvement.[31] A. B. Lalchere, minister of the Five Dock Church in Sydney, established in November 1929 the Methodist Unemployment and Relief Fund. It sought to offer men a period of casual work and pay them for it, and continued to operate beyond World War II. In Melbourne, Os Barnett, a Methodist lay-preacher, campaigned for a babies' home to care for those whose parents were indigent. He knew how to win the support of people of all religions and none, and represented the position, earlier adopted by Wilberforce, that it does not matter who is with you at the barricades so long as the cause is right. He made an impact on the Victorian premier, Albert Dunstan, and became a member of the Victorian Housing Commission.[32]

In the Catholic Church, the depression, especially in Melbourne, stimulated the programme called Catholic Action launched by Pope Pius XI in 1925. The depression had resulted in a new interest in Catholic social theory and resulted in the publication of the *Catholic Worker* in 1936. Catholic Action had radical elements. Based on the slogan 'All should own and all should work', it wanted co-operative ownership of all resources. In New South Wales the Catholic Church fostered movements which favoured the development of piety under the control of the hierarchy as the best route to reclaiming the favour of God for the poor and needy. The St Vincent de Paul Society, started in Australia in 1881, was a major arm of the Catholic Church for relief work in the depression, especially in conservative New South Wales.

The Salvation Army established soup kitchens in many parts of Australia and labour bureaus to seek work for the unemployed. Accommodation was found for the homeless. SAOs knocked on the doors in the slums ostensibly to distribute *The War Cry*, but really to seek out the destitute too proud to ask for help. The Salvation Army was trusted then as now, and schoolteachers regularly reported evidence of needy families to it.[33] But its efforts did not go uncriticised. The unemployed put a black ban on the Bennett's Lane soup kitchen in Sydney, on the grounds that the soup was always the same and the men had to wait outside in the cold because the premises was too small to accommodate them. SAOs shared one thing with those they were trying to help, namely poverty. As did many ministers in other denominations, they took repeated cuts in their own salaries, and were often unable to draw a regular salary at all. In 1929, the first year of the depression, Eva Burrows, destined to become the General of the Salvation Army from 1986 to 1993, was born at Tighes Hill, an industrial suburb of Newcastle, New South Wales, where coalminers and steelworkers made up most of the workforce. She was the eighth of nine children. Her father held her aloft and declared, 'I dedicate this child to the glory of God and the salvation of the world', which was 'a rather tall order for a little baby' as the general later observed.[34] Her father drew a low and irregular salary, and the family depended on 'angels' for food, charity for shoes, and her mother's ingenuity.

Most leaders in the church were very cautious about departing too dramatically from individualistic morality towards broader social analysis and remedies. The social gospel, however, did appeal to those working in areas which suffered most during the depression, especially mining and industrial centres. E. H. Burgmann, the Anglican Bishop of Goulburn, was radicalised partly through his links with the Newcastle miners, and became an ardent advocate of the social gospel.[35] The socialist seed took deepest root in the fertile soil of Australian Methodism, which from its founder owned a commitment to the poor. Radical Methodist ministers, such as Ralph Sutton, Bill

Hobbin, Alan Walker, Alan Brand and Dudley Hyde, publicly denounced capitalism as a system of exploitation, and endorsed socialism as more consistent with the teaching of Jesus. One of the most interesting of church responses to communism was that of the 1929 Cessnock revival.[36] In 1929 the coalfields had been the subject of first a miners' strike and then a lockout by the management. Conditions were desperate: miners and their families were living on rabbits; the communist leaders of the Miners' Union were stirring up the miners to use direct action to promote the rule of the proletariat. The commanding officer of the 35th Infantry Battalion was contemplating calling out the militia. In the midst of this anxiety, the Protestant churches of Cessnock (Baptist, Methodist, Presbyterian, Salvation Army) promoted an evangelistic campaign with F. B. Van Eyk and Albert Banton as evangelists. The meetings had phenomenal success, with hundreds converted. In pentecostal folklore many of the 'red' activists were converted and revealed their caches of explosives stored in readiness for the insurrection. The loss of so many men defused the situation, and deprived the unions of so many communists that they never recovered their dominance.

The Word Defended and Propagated

The evangelical movement in this period, threatened by the division between conservative and liberal evangelicals, was greatly helped by the foundation of Bible colleges. These took the heat out of theological disputation, by leaving the older theological colleges to liberals who were then in the ascendancy. The Bible colleges dealt so effectively with this problem precisely because they were not established directly for such a negative purpose. They are better understood as a response to the missionary and revivalistic enthusiasm at the turn of the century. William Lockhart Morton, a Presbyterian minister influenced by Hudson Taylor, founded the first missionary training college in Australia, Angas College, in Adelaide in 1893, and in 1914, also in Adelaide, the Chapman–Alexander Bible Institute was established. The Sydney Missionary and Bible College was formed in 1916 by a Congregationalist minister, Charles Benson Barnett, who had returned from missionary work in China. Its purpose was to provide 'the opportunity for any young man of consecrated life and character, to fit himself by definite study, and training in the knowledge of the things of God, for any service he may wish to undertake'.[37] He served there until 1937. Similarly, the

Melbourne Bible Institute,[38] formed in 1920 under the brilliant if controversial C. H. Nash, had special links with the China Inland Mission. Its aim was to train men and women through the study of the Bible, for which purpose no text book was to be used except the Bible itself. It set out its 'Position' with unmistakable clarity:

> The Melbourne Bible Institute stands four-square for the wholehearted acceptance of the entire sacred volume of the Old and New Testaments as from God. This is God's book for the plain man, and to such He will interpret its full meaning progressively by His Holy Spirit.[39]

The only other Bible college formed in this period was the Perth Bible Institute, founded by the Baptist, Carment Urquhart, in 1928, the only Protestant college offering Bible instruction in Western Australia before 1957.

The Australian Bible colleges have been remarkable for the continuity they have achieved in evangelical doctrine, Keswick piety, and interdenominational comity. They also enjoyed until recently a distinctive constituency: faith missions, conventions for the deepening of the spiritual life, evangelistic organisations, independent churches, and laymen and women who felt the need of systematic Bible knowledge.[40] The stature and long tenure of the early Bible college principals—Morton, Nash, Barnett, Urquhart, and Rolls—gave the colleges a critical influence in shaping Australian evangelicalism in the first half of the twentieth century and protecting it from Modernist inroads. Of the 8000 students enrolled in Australian Bible colleges to 1980, it has been estimated that 40 per cent became full-time Christian workers.[41]

In the 1920s the rising tide of Modernism was represented by the giant figures of H. E. Fosdick of New York and H. D. A. Major of Oxford. Within the New South Wales Presbyterian Church it was represented by R. G. Macintyre's 'potential immortality', John Edwards' 'theological reconstruction', and Samuel Angus' 'Christianity bigger than the Bible'. From 1914 to 1943, Angus[42] was Presbyterian Professor of New Testament at St Andrew's College, University of Sydney, and he taught in the United Faculty, where Presbyterian, Methodist, and Congregationalist clergy were trained. He had been recommended by Professors Andrew Harper of Sydney and James Orr of Glasgow, two liberal evangelicals. The latter even said Angus' theological standpoint was that of evangelical Christianity,[43] a clear abuse of the term which no conservative evangelical would ever make! Angus affirmed a religion 'of Jesus' as distinct from the orthodox religion 'about Jesus', a distinction beloved of Angus' mentor, Adolf von Harnack (1851–1930), the architect of liberalism and the social gospel. On his own admission, the areas in which Angus claimed he was in controversy with orthodoxy and which he indicated were the 'total' of such areas, were more than enough to give evangelicals apoplexy:

> the Virgin birth; the physical resurrection of Jesus and the empty tomb; the death of Christ as a 'propitiation' and 'all-sufficient sacrifice' for the sins of the world; the deity of Christ; the Trinity, not of the New Testament, but of the fourth century speculation; the authority of Scripture; and whatever the Westminster Divines excogitated and systemised during the years of codification of their statements of Christianity.[44]

The move against Angus was made reluctantly and after much delay by Robert McGowan, the evangelical Presbyterian minister at Ashfield. That liberalism enfeebles and eventually kills churches was a conviction which moved McGowan to tears in his opposition to Angus. He was not the only one who wept over Angus. Alan Whitham, a Sydney Anglican minister, in a recollection which might tell us more about the folk-memory of conservative evangelicalism than about what actually happened, recounts that in 1965 he was travelling home in the train with Ivan Stebbins, an impressive old gentleman who was chairman of the Congregational Union in 1943–44. Alan was bemoaning the decline in interest in doctrine:

> Old Ivan was looking out the window and when he turned to look at me, there were tears on his cheeks. He said, 'I killed the Congregational Church.' He explained that in the 1930s a committee of which he was chairman sent seven of their best students for the ministry to Germany for theological training and when they returned they were all liberals. They destroyed the Church.

The impact of Angus has been traced on a number of NSW Methodist ministers: Bill Hobbin, Dudley Hyde, Alan Brand, Cecil Collard and Eben Newman.[45] Angus appears to have had a greater impact on the emotions of Methodists than on the intellects of Presbyterians, and it is probably easy to exaggerate the impact of the Angus case on NSW Presbyterianism. But it did raise insuperable questions about the legal procedures by which the Presbyterian Church sought to safeguard orthodoxy. The battle over Angus was long, inconclusive, and divisive. It was not until 1942 that the General Assembly of the Presbyterian Church resolved to delete from its agenda all matters relating to Angus, who died in the next year after eight years of painful illness.

The weakening of the Methodist, Presbyterian and Congregationalist Churches by Angus was an object lesson to all the other churches, and conservatism and orthodoxy came to be defended by most New South Wales denominations with greater determination than in many other areas of Christendom. The forces of Sydney evangelical Anglicanism, deftly marshalled by the conservative evangelical triumvirate of D. J. Knox, R. B. Robinson, and H. S. Begbie, responded to Angus by deposing the liberal evangelicals in their own church. The Baptist response to Angus was led by G. H Morling, for forty years principal of the Baptist Theological College. By nature eirenic and moderate, Morling was probably forced to commit himself and the college more peremptorily to a conservative view of Biblical inspiration than he might otherwise have done. 'The College', he declared in his first 'policy speech' as acting principal in 1922,

> stands for the Bible as the authoritative Word of God. Because it is a denominational College it cannot stand officially for any particular theory of interpretation but just because it is a denominational College it must stand officially for the divinity of the Bible.[46]

With reference to the Angus controversy, he affirmed that the college's policy was 'one of sound evangelical teaching as opposed to modern theological conceptions',[47] but he left it up to C. J. Tinsley, Baptist minister, to boast that the college 'had one of the strongest evangelical platforms of any college in the world, being based wholly and solely upon the Word of God'.[48]

Reaching the Student World with the Word

One area of the world where the Word was most successfully defended and propagated between the wars was the university. Many very able students entered the University of Sydney from the public and Catholic high schools with the exhibitions which the government awarded under the University Amendment Act of 1919. Student Christian work before World War I in Australia did enjoy some success, but the fundamentalist controversy of the 1920s resulted in the establishment of specifically evangelical student societies. John Mott, an American secretary of the YMCA, had visited Australia in 1896 to help form the Australian Student Christian Movement (SCM) at a conference at Ormond College in the University of Melbourne. Having a near monopoly in the field, the SCM set the pattern for student work which would later be followed by other groups: annual conferences, systematic Bible study circles, missionary conferences, small group meetings, work in Christian Unions in private schools, and, later, camps and the use of the 'quiet time'. As the Modernism/fundamentalism debate hotted up through the 1920s, the SCM's choice of leadership imported an increasingly liberal theology, which necessarily divided its broad membership. The reaction of Paul White (later to become famous as 'the Jungle Doctor') to his under-graduate experience of SCM at the University of Sydney was indicative:

> When I got up there the one Christian organisation that I heard about was the Student Christian Movement. I went along to a study circle, and the leader (a prominent Methodist minister) started to tear leaves out of the Bible, and tell me that I really needed to rethink the whole of my faith; that I had swallowed too much without thinking. I didn't like it, and I told him so. I was at the advanced age of nineteen, and perhaps I was a little bit *gauche*, because after three or four of those particular Bible studies, it was suggested that perhaps they would go more smoothly if I didn't attend.[49]

Not all of the tension among Christian students was doctrinal, however. There were questions of style and social class. As one member of the 1930s noted in her choice of the SCM at university over the Evangelical Union (EU):

> I had become very upset about the evangelical movement coming into my local church, because they used to all be 'saved', and they used to sing these most dreadful choruses, which I thought were infantile and not worthy of the Christian religion. So when I got to the university … I became very interested [in the work of SCM]. I joined the study groups and used to go to all the meetings. I finally went to a confer-ence at Corio, which was wonderful.[50]

The Inter-Varsity Fellowship of Evangelical Unions (IVF) was born in England in 1928, the culmination of ten years of opposition by evangelical students to the liberal tendencies of the British SCM. From its inception, its leaders, inspired by Norman Grubb of the Worldwide Evangelisation

Crusade, were eager to establish Evangelical Christian Unions, not only in every British university, but in every university in the British Empire. As its first missionary it selected Hugh Gough, then IVF chairman and later Archbishop of Sydney, and charged him with the task of introducing the IVF to Canada. Gough was unable to accept, but the vice-Chair, a young medical student called Howard Guinness, accepted. It was an ideal appointment: Guinness was a pioneering, individualistic maverick. In the middle of his hugely successful tour of Canada, Guinness received from notable Sydney evangelical philanthropist, J. B. Nicholson, a telegram which read something like 'Come under and help us.' Guinness arrived in January 1930, and by April, the Sydney University Evangelical Union (SUEU) emerged out of the pre-existing Sydney University Bible Union. Then, in Melbourne on 14 May 1930, as we read in the minutes, 'the Evangelical Union was launched in utter dependence upon God'. In Guinness' second visit to Australia in 1933, IVF branches were established in every Australian university.

The basic diet which the IVF deemed essential to the growth of robust Christian students was Bible study, prayer, evangelism, and interest in missionary work. During the 1930s the IVF emphasised defending the 'fundamentals' against Modernism in general, and against the Sydney SCM backed by Samuel Angus in particular. That it was not always easy to be a member of the SUEU in its early years is suggested by the debate held in June 1935 among members on the motion to change its name to the Sydney University Christian Fellowship. In supporting the motion it was argued that the name created confusion for students who thought SCM was what they were looking for, whereas the EU was what they really wanted. Furthermore, it was acknowledged that there was a 'natural dislike' to the name, 'especially in the colleges'. Those opposed to the motion argued that the name formed a reproach which was 'so necessary in keeping members up to the mark'. Thirty-five attended the meeting which debated the motion. The motion was lost very narrowly, by seventeen to fifteen with three abstentions.[51]

Reaching the World with the Word

The Modernist threat actually inflicted major casualties on the evangelical armada. The chief casualty was the old evangelical commitment to the transformation of society. Most evangelicals now focused exclusively on the transformation of the individual. The Presbyterian and Methodist ships were severely damaged and fell behind. The Congregationalist ship was scuttled: 'unable to regroup in the post-liberal age',[52] it declined absolutely.[53] The Baptists, especially in New South Wales, took over from the Methodists as the flagship in the evangelical fleet. Indeed in the period from 1914 right up to the Billy Graham Crusades of 1959, it was chiefly the NSW Baptists and the Brethren who kept evangelicals to the mark.[54] Since evangelicalism is strongly influenced by role models as well as by a steady diet of the Bible in evangelical churches, NSW Baptists were now an inspiration to the rest of the movement largely because they had a glorious trinity in G. H. Morling, the archetypal college principal, C. J. Tinsley, the archetypal pastor, and John Ridley, the archetypal evangelist. Their ministries coincided with the dominance of Keswick spirituality in Australian evangelicalism. Morling and Ridley were both Keswick men, and frequently spoke at conventions which were modelled on Keswick,[55] and their reputation and therefore their influence spread far beyond their own denomination. It was on 14 November 1932 that John Ridley cried out at Burton St Baptist Tabernacle: 'I wish I could shout "Eternity" through the streets of Sydney.' Present was Arthur Stace, who two years earlier had been a metho-drinking derelict when he was converted at an Anglican Mission Hall. For thirty years, Stace wrote the word 'Eternity' in large elegant copperplate, before dying in 1967, a Sydney icon.[56]

Baptists in this period are normally said to have been rather conservative, less educated than evangelicals from other denominations, and more suspicious of an educated ministry.[57] Morling used to speak of the Thalaba Baptist who informed him that every graduate in Arts he had ever known had gone to hell, on which Morling's biographer, E. R. Rogers, comments that it is remarkable 'that he should have been so certainly acquainted with their ultimate destination'.[58] Anti-intellectualism, ironically, helps to explain the Baptists' importance to wider evangelicalism, for when other denominations—seduced by the education harlot—were succumbing to liberalism and secularism, the NSW Baptists were not. Less sensitive to the charge of fundamentalism, they helped to preserve evangelicalism during the liberal decades.

Morling was not primarily an apologist for the Bible. He was primarily an exegete and homilist who thought that the best defence of the Bible was to teach it exegetically and experimentally in conventions, in his Thursday-night Bible school in which up to 200 people of all denominations enrolled, and in the pages of the *Australian Baptist* where he conducted the Australian Baptist Bible School for a decade. But the most important thing he did for the defence of the Bible was to train his students to share his passion for it. Morling's college, galvanised for its evangelical purpose by the proximity of Samuel Angus, sent an increasing stream of Bible-believing and Bible-preaching ministers into the Australian church and beyond. But does Morling's rather devotional approach explain why few of his students became what John Thomson, who grew up an Anglican, called 'really solid'?[59] They preached the Word, but neither their doctrine nor their theology was ever robust, and they rarely made hearty controversialists. Morling's was a soft evangelicalism which allowed sinless perfection into some of the ranks in the late 1930s[60] and the Charismatic movement into many more of the ranks a generation later.[61]

Meanwhile, there developed in Melbourne in this period the strongest, the best-organised, and the most determined network of lay evangelicals in Australian history. Some of its members traced their spiritual ancestry to Reuben Torrey's visit to Melbourne in 1902, and others beyond that to the Geelong Convention of 1891 and even to the Evangelisation Society of Victoria, established in 1883. It grew out of the deep fellowship of visionary and able evangelicals; it expressed itself in voluntary interdenominational institutions which evangelicals are so adept at running and which multiplied in Melbourne for the next half century; and it focused on the simplest evangelical aim, to evangelise and teach the Bible. Yet members of the network were often so able that they rose to the top of their professions or businesses and made considerable contributions to civic affairs and government instrumentalities.

Something of the network's genius may be traced back to a wild, wintry night in June 1900 when Edwin Lee Neil, an accountant in his father's drapery firm in the city of Melbourne, was interviewed by the Rev. C. H. Nash for the position of organist at St Columb's Church of England in Hawthorn. Reflecting on this interview, after Lee Neil's untimely death in 1934, Nash wrote:

> Ideals were set before the young applicant to which in his natural modesty he felt himself entirely unequal, but the impression stamped on my mind was unmistakable and from that hour a friendship began which has continued and grown without one single ripple of misunderstanding for more than thirty-four years. His last conscious com-

munication to me from his sickbed was 'Carry on with your proposals, for I am sure to be in agreement with them.' Such friendship is too sacred for discussion. For me it has been the most formative, inspiring and protective influence in the latter half of my lifetime.[62]

Nash went on to become arguably the most influential clergyman of his generation, devoting all his attention to the nurture of lay people through the Melbourne Bible Institute, the Upwey Convention, the Bible Union of Australia of which he was founder in 1923, and the City Men's Bible Class. Lee Neil became the managing director of the Myer Emporium, Melbourne's leading department store, and was instrumental in the conversion to Christianity of its proprietor, Sidney Myer, who had been raised in Russia as an orthodox Jew.[63] Neil was made a Commander of the British Empire in 1926 for his service to Australian trade, and became involved in the conservative political movements which led to the victory of the United Australia Party in the 1931 federal election. He was founding president of the MBI from 1920 until his death.

Another who warmly supported the MBI was Hervey Perceval Smith, whom we met in the previous chapter as the founder of the Melbourne Gospel Crusade dedicated to the proclamation of the three Rs: Ruin by the fall, Redemption by the Blood of Christ, and Regeneration by the Holy Ghost. In 1924 he opened the Keswick Book Depot. Among other worthies of their generation were William Buck (a Melbourne firm of chartered accountants still bears his name), Alex Eggleston (a Melbourne firm of architects still bears his name), T. Graham, James and John Griffiths (importers of tea), Horace John Hannah (a remarkable bibliophile), A. Kenny, Dr John James Kitchen, Dr D. Stewart MacColl, David Ernest Renshaw, Charles Alfred Sandland, and Frank Varley (son of Henry Varley, the evangelist). Two evangelists, Walter Betts[64] (and his song-leader, Harry 'Hallelujah' Dyer) and George Hall, were associated with the group, but did not have the same responsibility for decision-making. It was Kitchen's vision to establish the Melbourne Bible Institute to train missionaries, and it was Hall's vision to establish the City Men's Bible Class in 1927 to bring to the commercial young men of Melbourne the challenge of life-long service to Christ. The class met in the Griffiths Brothers Tea Rooms in Elizabeth Street Melbourne, and was attended by between 140 and 200 men. These young men were soon put to work, notably at first in open-air preaching. The logical development from that was the formation of Campaigners for Christ through which the next generation were trained for leadership and evangelism. Out of the MBI also grew the Borneo Evangelical Mission (1928) and the Australian Council of the Unevangelised Fields Mission (1931).[65]

Out of the convergence of the activist evangelicalism of Nash, H. P. Smith, the Melbourne Bible Institute, the Upwey Convention, the Bible Union, and other lay-led evangelical societies, grew the CMS League of Youth, which began in Melbourne in 1928. Max Warren, the celebrated English missionary statesman, said: 'From the League of Youth in Australia and New Zealand has come a stream of recruits for missionary service which has no parallel in the church life of those countries'.[66] The intensification of spirituality encouraged in this evangelical world resulted in that apogee of Keswick spirituality, something of a mini-revival in the 1930s.[67] Howard Mowll, evangelical Archbishop of Sydney from 1933, was overheard to remark that the weakness of the Diocese of Sydney in its commitment to Keswick spirituality compared with Melbourne was a great concern and disappointment.[68] In Melbourne, too, the Methodist Local Preachers' Branch was very vigorous and had an impact on evangelical life in Australia. Teams of these local preachers went all over Australia and New Zealand. For many years the group held a Holiness Convention each King's Birthday weekend in Melbourne. It was conducted entirely by laymen. George Hall, who had been trained in America under Dr R. A. Torrey and Dr Campbell Morgan, and who knew evangelical life in USA intimately, said that the Holiness Convention of the Methodist Local Preachers' Melbourne Branch was the greatest spiritual force he had ever experienced.[69]

Reaching the World with the Spirit

Baptists were evangelical archetypes in this period, the flagship of the evangelical fleet, not only because they preserved the fundamentals doctrinally and were committed to evangelism, but also because they were encouraged by word and example to allow the Holy Spirit to develop a vital spiritual life in the individual soul. The synthesis of Spirit and Word was a Baptist imperative. Principal Morling of the Baptist Theological College was the greatest model for the Baptist denomination of the synthesis of Spirit and Word. Allan Tinsley said of Morling:

> He was a man who not only taught the doctrine of the Holy Spirit, but he lived the doctrine of the Holy Spirit. That was his major teaching.

Not the present razzmataz, but the old time genuine understanding of the indwelling Spirit of Christ in a man's life and it was reflected through him.[70]

To read Morling's *The Quest for Serenity* is to realise that this Christocentric lover of the Word of God was something of a mystic.[71] He did his master's thesis on Francis of Assisi, and was a devotee of the Quakers.[72] Young Morling delighted in the sealing of the Spirit which he called 'the sunrising from on high', the gift of assurance.[73] In 1942 he confided in his diary that he longed to be filled with the Holy Spirit:

> I must be filled with the Holy Spirit;
> I cannot lead my life without His fulness.
> I may be filled;
> The promise is for me.
> I would be filled;
> that is the point reached.
> I shall be filled

If I entrust myself to Jesus He cannot disappoint me. It is His very nature; it is His work in heaven. It is His delight to give souls the Holy Spirit.[74]

Morling longed for 'definite power above mere influence';[75] for him truth had to be on fire, doctrine had to be experimental, and spirituality had to be efficient,[76] by which he meant effective in the real world. He created an evangelicalism so vital that the need for pentecostal razzmatazz was not felt by the average Baptist.

Pentecostal razzmatazz, however, did continue to develop in Australia in this period. Two 'big names' toured Australia in 1920–21. Smith Wigglesworth, a rough-and-ready plumber who had been an evangelist for the Methodists and the Salvation Army before his baptism in the Spirit in an Anglican church in Sunderland, England, in 1907, had an extraordinary healing ministry. It was his style which became so normative for much of Australian classical pentecostalism.[77] Aimee Semple McPherson, on the other hand, was a winsome, attractive preacher, who had developed a large following in the USA. In Melbourne, the crowds she attracted filled the giant Wirth's Olympia. While McPherson won many of the mainstream clergy over along with thousands of converts to evangelical Protestantism, Wigglesworth polarised opinion. Excommunications of pentecostals became more frequent through the 1920s and 1930s, as the pentecostal message began to take hold in Australia, resulting in to the formation of denominational structures, including journals, Bible schools, and annual conferences.

An overseas visitor who had less impact on the Australian public at large, but who was probably more important for the internal life of the movement, was A. C. Valdez, Senior. He had felt called to go to Australia for some years, and finally made it to Melbourne in 1925. There he had a vision indicating that he should go to Sunshine, a Melbourne suburb. Within a few weeks, Valdez had the Sunshine Hall packed with people of all denominations, hundreds receiving 'the baptism', hundreds more receiving healing or simple conversion. 'Trains running from Melbourne to Sunshine were crowded with people attending the meetings. As they journeyed, they sang favourite hymns such as "Joy Unspeakable" … Some were converted on the train before they arrived at the meeting.'[78] The news of the Sunshine Revival spread around the country, and people came from Sydney, from Western Australia, Queensland and South Australia. They in turn went back and founded new works.

In the twelve months of his ministry in Melbourne, Valdez brought about a sea-change in the nature of pentecostalism in Australia: the movement had clearly moved from being a mission to being a church. This was due to the need to institutionalise and defend the gains of the revival. Valdez chose and ordained people into elderships, and the Pentecostal Church of Australia was organised as a focus for the people from around the country who had been through the fires of revival together. Meanwhile an opposition movement was developing.[79] C. H. Nash's Melbourne Bible Institute placed a ban on talking about or evincing pentecostal practices in the college, leading a number of students to resign. This was part of a general mainstream movement: Keswick closed its doors to pentecostalism, as did the World's Christian Fundamentals Association, in 1928.[80]

Generally, through the 1920s and 1930s, pentecostals either went quiet within their own denominations, or separated to form their own church organisations. In 1926 Frederick Van Eyk organised a number of congregations into a loose grouping called the Apostolic Faith Mission, some of which was a reaction to the formation in the same year, under the inspiration of Valdez and Greenwood, of the Pentecostal Church of Australia. This latter was a name which was clearly interchangeable with that of the Assemblies of God. To unite these works under a common name and constitution, in 1937 an All Australia Conference was held in the Sydney suburb of Red-fern, and the largely east-coast movement took the name of the Assemblies of God in Australia. Shortly before this, two other groupings began to take hold in the still loosely defined pentecostal world. In 1929 Frederick Van Eyk was forced out of the Apostolic Faith Mission and, on his way back to South Africa, linked up with Albert Banton and a number of small indepen-dent pentecostal groups in Adelaide. Banton and Van Eyk began evangelis-ing in New South Wales, a campaign which resulted in the formation in Cessnock of the first Four-Square Church. In 1930 the Wales-based Apos-tolic Church was founded in Australia by William Cathcart. Out of the As-semblies and Apostolic movements came Cecil and Leo Harris, who (after being converted to British Israelitism in 1941) came to blows with the older movements over their theology. Harris brought the National Revival Cru-sade from New Zealand to Australia in 1945, after which it was renamed the Commonwealth Revival Crusade, and then the Christian Revival Cru-sade, taking local church autonomy as its form, the Bible as its only consti-tution, and British Israelitism as one of its distinctives. Although still small in number, then, organised pentecostals were maintaining an emphasis on the Spirit strand which would develop from the 1960s into a major chal-lenge to the evangelical synthesis of Spirit, Word and world.

One entry-point for pentecostals into mainstream Christianity was the healing movement, which had become respectable in Australian Christian-ity long before the 1960s. In 1923 J. M. Hickson, an Anglican layman, toured Australia, preaching that 'salvation was a divine work in the whole of man—including the body'.[81] In Sydney, Hickson's teaching was pursued among the Anglo-Catholics and among those open to influences from out-side their own church, especially missionary groups. Father John Hope, Anglo-Catholic rector of Christ Church, St Laurence, from 1926 and dri-ving force behind the interdenominational Order of Saint Luke, carried on the Hickson tradition by holding 'healing services' with 'laying on of hands and Holy Unction'.[82]

The period covering the Great War, the 1920s, and the depression was a testing time for the nation and a nervous time for the churches. Neither in the nation nor in the church was leadership strong. The churches might have done worse. The evangelical wing of the church energetically support-ed Bible colleges, conventions, missions both at home and overseas, stu-dent work, open-air evangelism and Bible distribution, and battened down the hatches against the storms of liberalism and Biblical criticism. But significant changes had come over the movement. It was now narrower in its social commitments, more defensive in its theology, and less confident about its significance in the shaping of the Australian nation. Even the overseas missionary movement, which served to open the horizons of many conservative evangelicals, may be understood partly as an opportunity to express orthodox faith in an environment uncontaminated by liberalism. Evangelicalism had become more self-absorbed, more concerned to meet the needs of its own supporters, and more anxious to keep their approval. Its openness to the world was reduced; its commitment to obey the Word was less evident than its determination to defend it; and its understanding of the role of the Holy Spirit in the Christian life was fragmented. The evangelical synthesis, then, had not been in great shape in this period. The next age, however, culminating in the 1959 Billy Graham Crusades across Australia and New Zealand, was to witness a resurgence of the evangelical synthesis.

5. Holiness above the Word:
Sinless Perfection in the 1930s

In the late 1930s some of the leaders of Sydney's non-denominational evangelical organisations—the Inter-Varsity Fellowship (IVF), the Sydney University Evangelical Union (SUEU), the Children's Special Service Mission, the Crusader Union, and the Inter-Schools Christian Fellowship—started to propagate 'sinless perfectionism'. This was the doctrine that, by an instantaneous experience of the Holy Spirit, sin is eradicated in believers so that they are able not to sin any more. This experience was not called 'the baptism of the Holy Spirit', the term beloved of modern Charismatics to describe the post-conversion experience of the Holy Spirit which they claim is necessary to empower the believer for ministry. The sinless perfectionist doctrine was sometimes called by its adherents 'entire sanctification', 'uttermost salvation', 'perfect love', or, most frequently, 'walking in the light',[1] or 'walking in the Spirit'.[2] The teaching split the evangelical organisations, who eventually expelled its adherents. Eventually a commune of perfectionists was established in Sydney. Marriages were there arranged and broken, and members lost their assets, their children, and their sanity.

This apparently strange phenomenon has a history almost as old as Christianity itself.[3] It is one expression of a heresy known as 'antinomianism'. Antinomians claim that, since they have been set free from sin through the blood of Christ, they are no longer bound by the moral law. They can therefore do as they like. The moral law and the penalties for breaking it will not apply to them. There are two types of antinomianism—one has to do with the doctrine of justification (the means by which we are saved), the other with sanctification (the means by which we are made holy after we are saved). The antinomianism which is a distortion of justification argues that since, through Christ's blood, we are set free from the penalty of sin, we are thereby at liberty to sin. The antinomianism which is a distortion of sanctification argues that the blood of Christ can eradicate sin entirely from believers, who are therefore able not to sin. This latter is 'sinless perfectionism'. It is an aberration of the holiness movement of the nine-teenth century, a caricature of evangelicalism, and a bastard growth of re-vivalism. It is an exotic growth which can luxuriate in the hothouse of doc-trines of the Spirit when uncorrected by the clear evidence of the Word and untested by the need to evangelise effectively in the real world. It is one of the weeds which can grow in the evangelical garden when the three strands of Spirit, Word and world which make up the evangelical cord are separated out from each other.

Theologically, the root of modern perfectionism lies in John Wesley's teaching that Christians can attain 'entire sanctification' resulting in 'Chris-tian perfection'. Wesley described this as replacing the will to sin with a de-sire to love God with all our heart, mind and strength, and our neighbours as ourselves. The great movement towards holiness which swept America, Britain and Australia in the last third of the nineteenth century, usually la-belled the Keswick movement, actually rejected Wesleyan perfectionism. The suggestion that sin could ever be eradicated in this life was condemned as illusory. But both Wesleyan and Keswick holiness teaching were designed to satisfy the desire for greater holiness, and both rejected the teaching of the church on sanctification which may be traced back through Calvin and Luther to Augustine and to Paul. Keswick teaching stressed sanctification by faith, maintaining that justification and sanctification were two separate ex-periences. Though both were to be appropriated through faith, the second (sanctification) is to be appropriated passively rather than actively. Believers were to rest in God, to 'let go and let God'. Insofar as they abide in Christ, they will be sanctified. If they choose to reassert their own wilfulness, they will forfeit the presence of the Lord and power over sin. Evan H. Hopkins, 'the theologian of the Keswick movement', used the famous illustration of a poker to convey the essence of Keswick spirituality. Put a poker in the fire and keep it there and it will become hot, red, and malleable; withdraw it from the fire and it will be cold, black, and hard. If Christians sinned it was because they were not living in the Spirit's fire; they were not walking in the light. The effect of the Keswick doctrine of sanctification by faith was to en-courage Christians to withdraw from society in the quest for a self-induced holiness. It tended to divide Christians by encouraging spiritual elitism. Its champions said they had discovered the truth of sanctification for the first time. Following the interpretation advanced by H. C. G. Moule's volume on the Epistle to the Romans in the *Expositor's Bible* (1894), they had argued that in Romans 7, Paul was describing the preconsecration experience of converted but carnal Christians, and that by consecration to Christ one can travel out of the defeat of Romans 7 to the victory of Romans 8. 'The Keswick message asserted that the Reformed teaching produced miserable Christians, people who were living in Romans 7. But they had found a message which could enable you "to pass over Romans 7 to Romans 8!"'[4]

This doctrine had the capacity to create a strong desire for consecrated living. Evangelical activists, such as Howard Mowll, Archbishop of Sydney, were greatly attracted to it as the means of fostering greater commitment to the service of Christ. As we have seen in the previous chapter, Mowll regretted that Sydney evangelical Anglicans seemed to be lagging behind Melbourne evangelicals in their acceptance of Keswick spirituality. As we shall see in the next chapter, he was an ardent exponent of consecrated Christian living. Mowll, however, was able to avoid the damage wrought by an excessive emphasis on this one doctrine because he was a practitioner of the evangelical synthesis. He was a student of the whole Word and not just part of it, and he was driven by the pragmatic desire to be effective in his communication of the Gospel to the world. He therefore had little time for elitist doctrines which were the preserve of those sufficiently honoured to be in the cult. By contrast, the adherents of the sinless perfection movement in Sydney in the late 1930s were so committed to their one doctrine on sanctification that they were prepared to break fellowship with other Christians and to deny other truths. 'Instead of trying to relate the truths so that they modify each other,' explained theologian, Broughton Knox, 'to get a united whole, you pursue your own show.'[5] Sinless perfectionists were certainly students of the Word, but only of part of it, and they rejected any corrections from contemporary evangelical theologians such as T. C. Hammond, C. H. Nash, or G. H. Morling, all of whom attempted to put them straight and prevent more keen, young evangelicals from joining the cult.

The Families Involved

Six families, all related through descent and intermarriage, were at the core of the evangelical circles from which the perfectionist movement developed: the Agnews of Waverley, Oatlands, Tasmania; the Grants of Sydney; the Decks of New Zealand; the Griffiths of Griffiths Teas fame in Melbourne; the Neils from Melbourne; and the Youngs, whose wealth was made through the Colonial Sugar Refinery. We have already met the Griffiths, Neils and Youngs in previous chapters. Though the catalyst came from the Agnew family, each of the family dynasties brought an important element to the sinless perfectionist mix.

Henry Young (the great-grandfather of Sydney Anglican theologian, Broughton Knox) adopted Plymouth Brethrenism, and was influenced by the dispensationalist premillennialism of Brethren theologian, J. N. Darby. This most systematic of evangelical views of the end time, with its graphic vision of the forthcoming rapture of the church, was to become the most popular of all Protestant eschatologies through the publication in 1909 of the Scofield Bible. The Youngs' premillennialism and strong sense of the Lord's imminent return made them ardent evangelists, reaching out to the islands around Australia through their agency, the South Sea Evangelical Mission (SSEM), the foundation of which we covered in chapter 3. As a family, the Youngs were larger than life. When she landed on one of the Solomon Islands, Florence Young[6] was approached by Islanders flourishing spears. She sufficiently disconcerted them by opening and closing her umbrella. Florence was influenced strongly by Keswick. In speaking of the Katoomba Christian Convention, which had been established in 1904 in her brother's house in Katoomba, she rejoiced that 'the distinctive Keswick principles, the meeting of spiritual needs according to the doctrine of sanctification by faith, were clearly stressed in the Australian movement'.[7] The Youngs, therefore, added Keswick intensity to premillennial fervour and brewed the potent mixture across the years in the crucible of the convention movement.

The premillennialism of the Youngs was reinforced by that of the Deck family. They also were Plymouth Brethren who had migrated to New Zealand, and had taken an active part in the South Sea Evangelical Mission. The SSEM was a family mission. It began in Henry Young's son's home in Fairymead, Queensland, and cousins Cathy, Connie, Norman and Northcote Deck went there to assist. In the next generation, two Deck brothers worked with the mission and played an active part in the sinless perfection movement led by their cousin, Lindsay Grant. One of these brothers would later extricate himself from the movement, at the cost of his marriage, while the other ran the cult's property, Lochnaw, in Scotland.[8] Of the eleven children of John Field Deck and Emily Baring Young, seven went out as missionaries, five to the Solomons with the SSEM.

Also active in the SSEM were Alan Neil, scion of the Melbourne commercial family of Edwin Lee Neil, managing director of Myer, and Ken Griffiths, of the Griffiths Teas family. The Neils had grown up with the Griffiths in St Columb's, Hawthorn, C. H. Nash's Melbourne church. Alan married Frances Grant and had six children.[9] Alan's sister Phyllis married Leslie Griffiths, later first president of the Melbourne University Evangelical Union, and brother of SSEM member Ken Griffiths. Ken drew the tie even closer by marrying Alan's sister-in-law, Margaret Grant. The Grant girls were daughters of 'a dear Christian man',[10] and this connection brought their three brothers, Lindsay, Ronald and David, into contact with the Anglican hierarchy, Brethren theology, and SSEM missionary commitment.

Into this mix came the Agnew family, of Tasmania. Vera Agnew's father was a member of the Charley family, who were involved with the Broken Hill Proprietary company through the Cherbolds, a connection which might help to explain their wealth. The Charley family lived at Mt Tomah, and at least some of them were singularly unimpressed by the activities of the perfectionists.[11] Vera's husband added the spice of British Israelitism, which strengthened the millennial and racist tendencies later found in the Sydney group. Vera's two daughters, Nancy and Del, married the Grant brothers, Ronald and Lindsay. Del soon severed all links with the Melbourne group, led by Ronald and Nancy. The Melbourne group, including a number of Presbyterian ministers, remained orthodox evangelicals. The Sydney group, with Del as high priestess, became a cult.

Chronology

The debate over liberalism which racked Presbyterianism in the 1920s and 1930s divided the church into conservative and liberal wings. The Grant family attended the Ashfield Presbyterian Church in Sydney where the minister was Robert McGowan, a conservative leader, whom we met in the previous chapter. The Grants were therefore in the front line of attack against the arch-liberal, Samuel Angus. Staying with the Grants were Allan and Bruce Bryson, whose parents were missionaries in Africa, serving with the non-denominational Africa Inland Mission. The Bryson boys[12] were then attending Trinity Grammar School, which in 1930 was visited by Howard Guinness on his first visit to Australia to establish the work of IVF. Trinity was the first school to establish a Crusader Fellowship, which was led by

Bruce Bryson and Ian Holt.[13] Interdenominational student work, Sydney evangelicalism, and Brethren theology were thus well mixed in the experiences of quite a number of the rising stars.

The 1930s saw an expansion of important interdenominational evangelical ministries, especially EU, IVF, the Crusader Union and the Inter-Schools Christian Fellowship. In the Crusaders in 1932 were David Grant, Jack Deck, Neville Babbage, Charles Bellingham, the son of W. R. Angus, the Open Air Campaigners' founder, Campbell Begbie, Bruce Bryson, and Paul White, all to become household names in Sydney evangelicalism. In the warm, heady atmosphere of the student evangelicalism of the 1930s it is not surprising that plants of the intensity of sinless perfection should have taken root. In 1935, Graham Scroggie in Melbourne and the fierce Irish evangelist, W. P. Nicholson in Sydney held dynamic missions among university students. A genuine revival broke out among young people in Melbourne,[14] while in Sydney there was a great response both to Nicholson's appeal to become a Christian and to his subsequent appeal to Christians to come forward to receive the fulness of the Holy Spirit. The SUEU committee minutes record that revival was longed for and expected, but did not eventuate.[15] It was a great year for student Christian work: in March the campus of the University of Sydney was visited by the Japanese Christian celebrity, Dr Toyohiko Kagawa.

The Inter-Varsity Fellowship of Evangelical Unions was inaugurated at a conference at Culverden, the Deck family home in Katoomba, in January 1936. A committee of fifteen appointed Lindsay Grant as general secretary.[16] The conference coincided with the Katoomba Convention, which (shaped around the intensely pietistic writings of Keswick greats such as Andrew Murray) aimed at inculcating true holiness and so was fertile soil for inward-looking doctrines to take hold. Meanwhile, in Tasmania, a convention for the cultivation of holiness and sanctification was established by Vera Agnew. At this convention it was prophesied that one of Vera's daughters would be given a divine mission and would walk in the light. When Lindsay Grant married Vera's daughter, Del, there was something of an expectation that he was marrying a sinless prophetess.[17]

Katoomba was not only a holiness convention; it was also a missionary convention. So it is not surprising that the sinless perfectionist movement in Sydney received additional nourishment from the mission field, especially through the labours of the Neils and Grants who worked with SSEM. In the Solomons, Alan Neil and Ronald Grant came to the realisation that the objective teaching of the Christian faith had not penetrated deeply into island cultures, and that a more subjective experience of the Spirit-filled life was required for effective ministry. They themselves sought a deeper experience of God. They were encouraged in this through the teaching of a world-wide movement centring on Paget Wilkes, known as the Honour Oak movement. Wilkes (the founder of the Japan Evangelistic Band in 1903) taught that sanctification was a twofold process: first the eradication of sin, and then the baptism of the Holy Spirit.[18] In the Solomons, Alan Neil and Ronald Grant experienced a special post-conversion cleansing of heart and life, after which they saw the power of the local religious leaders broken and witnessed deliverances from demon possession. This theology of the spiritual life was brought back to Australia, where it reinforced developments already taking place in the SUEU. There was a rapid acceleration towards perfectionism.

On 10 June 1938, a new evangelical paper, *The Edifier*, published an article entitled 'The Reality of Entire Sanctification', by Alan Neil. In a return to the full-blown Wesleyan view of sanctification, Neil wrote of 'uttermost salvation' and the need for to be 'fully sanctified':

> the searching of the Spirit goes on till there comes a time when the searching ceases, and the Holy Spirit gives the witness that the whole of the self life is experimentally crucified, put to death, with Christ, and it is no longer I but Christ living within ... [and] you know you are cleansed from all sin.[19]

The article caused a furore which stunned *The Edifier's* editor, Eric Daley. Neil's former principal at the Melbourne Bible Institute, C. H. Nash, responded with a series of articles on the Holy Spirit insisting that no-one reaches perfection in this life, but that did not lessen the onus on the Christian to lead a holy life. Nash could see the spiritual potential in Neil, and consoled him in a constructive and healing manner.[20] The SSEM, however, at the instigation of the vigilant Dr Northcote Deck, examined the pair at a special meeting of the Sydney Council in March 1938. It found their views to be incompatible with those held by the SSEM. Alan and Ronald resigned immediately.[21] The committee of the Katoomba Christian Convention, persuaded by the interpretation of Romans 7 advanced by Norman Deck, a fine theologian, also took drastic steps, rejecting all further association with them.[22] Florence Young herself had enjoyed a deeper experience of the Holy Spirit while serving as a missionary in China,[23] but it was a personal knowledge of the filling of the Holy Spirit rather than something which made her instantaneously perfect, and she dissented from the extreme claims of the youthful enthusiasts. It was not the practical missionaries, who were away much of the time, but mostly the younger generation of Decks, Neils and Grants who were caught up in the movement. The alarm of absent parents explains the expulsion of Ronald Grant and Alan Neil from SSEM. The children had gone to unacceptable extremes.

Nash's role in the containment of perfectionism was probably critical. Alan Neil's father, Edwin Lee Neil, as we saw in chapter 4, was a close friend of Nash and a leading Melbourne layman in the forefront of the convention movement. Nash had almost certainly been aware of a 'charismatic' clash at the beginning of the century at the Eltham Holiness Convention, he had sought to contain his young protégés during the Sunshine pentecostal revival of 1925,[24] and now he had to temper their enthusiasm for perfectionism. He had himself experienced controversy in the early 1900s and had suffered times in the wilderness.[25] Influenced deeply himself by the Keswick teaching of Bishop Handley Moule, Nash came to reject firmly all optimistic views about our power over sin. 'As long as I remain in a mortal body,' he wrote, 'I expect to have to endure the conflict between flesh and spirit and how human love for human beloved can be delivered from that conflict except by a moment by moment hiding in God's grace I have not yet discovered (to my shame).'[26] Nash's commitment to the older Augustinian view that sanctification involves lifelong conflict explains in part why Melbourne perfectionists remained in their churches (a strong Nash teaching) and why sinless perfectionist teaching was contained within a small group, known as 'the Royal Family'.

Sinless perfectionism was thus excluded from *The Edifier*, the SSEM, and the Katoomba Christian Convention. That left the IVF, EU, Children's Special Service Mission, Scripture Union, Crusaders, and CMS League of Youth. Lindsay Grant held the position of IVF general secretary from 1936 until 1943, when he was replaced by another medico, Paul White. Grant's significant position in the EU in the 1930s and his involvement in Crusader circles paved the way for confrontation. In 1935 he was howled down by the students at a university mission. This was in striking contrast with the performance on the same occasion of the rising star in the evangelical firmament, Marcus Loane, who with strong delivery and forceful argument commanded a respectful silence. Not that he faced the same opposition. Three students had been suspended by the Senate for their rowdiness, and Loane spoke to an altogether more subdued gathering. Grant seems to have earned his position by virtue of his activism, by an appearance of Bible knowledge, by his association with the big names in evangelical student work such as Howard Guinness, and by the fact that he was a university blue. Guinness' archetypal Englishness impressed Grant, who became very interested in all things British, including the British Israelite movement. A further complication is that Grant's leadership appears to have been endorsed by female prophets; by Alice Smith while at university,[27] and by his wife, Del Agnew, in the movement's subsequent communal activities. He was reported to have had 'sex appeal' and was reputedly very attractive to women. When in 1952 Del was to divorce him, at least three women hoped to marry him. He was rather egotistical. He enjoyed the limelight and was given to bluffing and bullying. When he spoke or expounded the Scriptures, he did so with the great confidence that his position was correct. It has been observed, however, that as well as he knew his Bible, neither he nor Alice Smith were well grounded in Christian doctrine.[28] The holiness movement had devalued doctrinal precision in favour of experiential religion, and it had also fostered a non-critical attitude to the Bible. Grant's doctrinal position and religion were far more matters of practice than of theology.[29] The practice had echoes of the Oxford Group with which the Evangelical Union had earlier wrestled, including group confession of weaknesses and failings; the 'four absolutes' with their perfectionist overtones—absolute honesty, purity, unselfishness and love; deliberate targeting of the social elite; and a preference for their own intimate groups over regular church services, attendance at which became very rare.[30] Lindsay and Del practically banned churchgoing, mainly because the cult's members had too much work to do.

Lindsay was always longing for a second blessing, always hankering after a deeper Christian life. One of his cousins is reported to have said to him, 'First it was the Oxford Group, now it is this [sinless perfectionism]. What will you go in for next? Mormonism?' He was the sort of person who, with great sincerity, is always wanting to go one step further, but with a theological foundation inadequate to support the flamboyant superstructure.[31] By 1939 the SUEU was divided down the middle over Grant's perfectionist teachings. Some members later reported that in those tense days, they were conscious of being bound by evil when they prayed in the daily prayer meeting. Allan Bryson's missionary father, Stuart, who had seen Paget Wilkes' teachings in action in Africa, predicted, 'Families will be broken up and all sorts of scandals will result from this.' Allan thought his father exaggerated, but all his predictions and worse happened.

When, however, sinless perfectionism burst on the Sydney scene in the late 1930s, some keen young Christians wondered what all the fuss was about. Alwyn Prescott was one who thought that the sinless perfectionist position was very plausible: it was based on ample Scriptural foundation (especially Romans 6.11 and 1 John 3.9, 5.18). The view that 'by faith you could be perfect' was very attractive to a young Christian who wanted to be the best for God. Neither perhaps was it a large step to move from justification by faith alone—the most honoured of Protestant doctrines—to perfection by faith alone. Indeed, the keenest Christians were fair game for the new teaching, whose champions sought to recruit the pick of the crop by flattering their keenness. Ian Holt, who felt that his friends were being 'got at',[32] told Grant at a 1939 houseparty that 'I can't find anything in what you are trying to teach me that I'm not experiencing already.' The next year, he expressed the same view to Vera Agnew at a houseparty in the Tasmanian midlands: 'There's nothing new in your teaching.'[33] Though Holt could not see the difference in terms of living the victorious Christian life, his views were vintage Keswick, while Mrs Agnew's views were extreme Wesleyan.[34]

In September 1939 the SUEU resolved its problem with a spill and an election for all committee positions. Harvey Carey, later Professor of Obstetrics and Gynaecology at the University of New South Wales, was president of the SUEU in the critical year 1939–40, and he led the coup. He was then in his fifth year of medicine—the EU was led by five medical presidents in succession: Ian Holt, Allan Bryson, Arthur Reddell, Harvey Carey and then John Hercus. The medicos believed that once EU got out of the control of medical students 'it would go to the pack'.[35] In a student movement dominated by medicos, it took a medico (Carey) to withstand a medico (Lindsay Grant). Alwyn Prescott, then in engineering, was secretary.[36] As it was the custom for the outgoing committee to nominate the incoming, five of the seven nominated by the committee of 1938–39 were committed to the sinless perfectionist position, including Humphrey Deck as president, Philip Deck as secretary, and Lloyd Sommerlad.[37] But Carey had other ideas. He decided to stand for the presidency and lobbied support from those op-posed to sinless perfectionism, including the pragmatic Prescott, who had looked at those who professed to be sinless, and concluded that it was quite obvious that they were not. Furthermore, the perfectionists themselves were changing. They were moving from the ardent pursuit of personal holi-ness to the strident assertion of personal perfectionism. They were no longer open to debate. An exclusive, cultic, Gnostic mentality, foreign to evangelicals and Australians, was beginning to infect the movement: only those who were ready were to be further instructed in the higher wisdom. Their opponents, such as Carey and Prescott, were dismissed on the grounds that they were insufficiently spiritual to grasp perfectionist truth. Carey believed that there was a danger that the preoccupation with perfec-tion would displace the more traditional commitment of the EU, namely evangelism, and that the EU would become a perfectionist coterie powerless to witness for the Gospel. He was convinced that such teachings would de-stroy the EU and that it would be preferable to deny the perfectionists any more opportunity to propagate their views. Carey was astute, skilled in apologetics, and a clear thinker. He only asked Prescott to be present at the 1939 annual meeting to elect the new committee, but Prescott felt he had to do more than that. He stood as secretary, and his future brother-in-law, Noel Stephenson, stood as prayer secretary. Each of these three was elected by just one vote. The elected committee had three opposed to sinless perfec-tionism, two perfectionists, and two neutral. It was a difficult year. When they could not avoid meetings, Prescott and Carey became 'devious', moving motions against which no committed Christian could vote.

Meanwhile, the evangelical big-guns were trained on the sinless perfec-tionist position. The advent of T. C. Hammond as principal of Moore Col-lege in 1935[38] brought a sledge-hammer down on the perfectionists. Ham-mond expounded the Epistle to the Romans, rejecting all notions of perfectionism and reasserting the orthodox Augustinian understanding of sanctification. In particular he taught that Romans 6, so beloved of the per-fectionists, was followed by Romans 7, which described the mature Christ-ian life as a great struggle against sin. In a typical display of withering logic, he destroyed the perfectionists' exegesis of Romans. All Lindsay Grant could do was to look on helplessly and protest of Hammond: 'He's a fine man, but …'. As they searched the Scriptures, the anti-perfectionists developed a new insight on Scriptural interpretation, namely that 'no scripture is of its own interpretation'.[39] They began to see that the weakness in the perfectionists' case was the very thing which they thought at first was its strength, namely its dependence on a few prominent verses of Scripture. In the heat of disputation, the young members of the EU were strengthening the Word strand in their evangelical synthesis.

At the 1940 annual general meeting of the SUEU, 86 members were present. The attendance was ominous, as the perfectionists were not popular and could not win elections. They attempted to limit the number of voters by refusing to allow postal voting and disenfranchising evening students.[40] They might have been perfect, but that did not put them above politics! It was a vain move. Though the perfectionists put up a full team, their ticket was defeated resoundingly. John Hercus was elected president over Alan Lane by 66 votes to 20, and Donald Robinson secretary over Philip Deck, by 65 votes to 21.[41] Hercus informed the Grant-dominated IVF executive that it had lost the confidence of the SUEU.

As the perfectionists became elitist, the orthodox despaired of bringing their erring brothers and sisters back to middle ground. It became increasingly 'we and they', and the perfectionists were isolated. Indeed, most of the affected evangelical organisations did not wait for the perfectionists to withdraw of their own accord. While the EU attempted to keep membership open to all who would subscribe to the doctrinal basis, including perfectionists, in other organisations the axe fell more swiftly. In the CMS League of Youth, perfectionism was directly attacked by Campbell Begbie. The Scripture Union and the Children's Special Service Mission had the structures and constitution necessary to contain the problem: the latter's staffworker, Heather Drummond, was asked to resign by a more experienced and mature council than was available to the EUers.[42]

In the IVF and the Crusaders, the infection was more difficult to eradicate. The infant IVF had as yet no graduates of long standing, and so became 'the very hotbed of the movement'.[43] In the Crusader Union, some teachers threatened to have the union excluded from schools if the problem were not dealt with. Jack Dahl, a member of the Crusader Union's council, sought to organise gatherings at which T. C. Hammond would refute the tendency. When Roger Deck and his brother, Brian, had to take a stand against their brother Philip, perfectionism's capacity to split families became evident. The Grants, too, were divided over the issue. David Grant, a 'top quality' Christian leader and a close friend of Ian Holt, was incensed when asked to leave the Crusader movement. That finished yet another friendship: 'It was a terribly, terribly sad business', recalled Holt. Friends and relatives parted, rarely to see one another again, and the divisions kept happening for decades as the movement managed to get its hooks into new members. There is no doubt that some of the orthodox felt as betrayed as the perfectionists felt rejected. In Sydney the Crusader Union leaders imposed a rigorous discipline on those who espoused perfectionism, not permitting them to teach it in the meetings of the union. Any who did not agree to accept this discipline had to move out, so losing their most fruitful source of new recruits.[44] Marcus Loane, chairman of the Crusader Union from 1944 to 1949, gave clear teaching against perfectionism, as did Basil Williams, a New Zealander, who in 1944 became IVF travelling secretary. While the evangelicals attempted to exclude the teaching, rather than the individuals, Grant and the perfectionists withdrew from their old friends. It was a peremptory, hurtful separation. The group dropped right out of active Christian involvements.

After she married Lindsay Grant in 1947, Del Agnew began exercising an autocratic rule over the members of the movement which, in the time-honoured manner of cults, had become a commune. The basis of her power was that she had a prophetic capacity to discern evil in the lives of others and the spiritual power to eradicate it. Del's control was exercised over every detail of the family lives of commune members, including marital relationships and the care of children. Family break-ups were engineered. Couples were ordered to break up, with no appeal. In 1952 Del's marriage with Lindsay ended in an arranged divorce which scandalised his former friends. Lindsay married another from the inner circle, Margaret Debenham, and they all continued to live in the commune. The scandal split the group. Lindsay's two older brothers, David and Ronald, and their wives detached themselves from the hard-core centre of the movement. David's wife, Mary, never saw Del again after 1949 when Del spent a day with her talking over her intention to divorce Lindsay. Heather Drummond was another who never accepted the divorce. She detached herself from the group and returned to the church.

Ronald Grant had married Nancy Agnew, who was never as committed to perfectionism as Del. This sub-group went to Melbourne, where C. H. Nash had been teaching Biblical and Augustinian views on sanctification for decades, and had retained the near adulation of young zealots. So the

Melbourne group stayed within the fellowship of the churches: it was not so closed to friends and relatives as the Sydney group, and did not commit the same excesses. Known as 'The Group' or 'The Royal Family', the Melbourne movement started meetings attended by about 50–60 people (today about 160), where they taught 'perfect love' as Wesley taught it. Occasional visitors have been impressed by the Christian calibre of those who attended and could not fault the Scriptural teaching.

Today they meet in about seven home groups, are all members of their local churches, and come together quarterly for a meeting of the entire group. Wesleyan in theology, they are also somewhat Wesleyan in organisation. They constitute a church within a church, *ecclesiola in ecclesia*. Some are members of St Hilary's Anglican Church, Kew, which was founded by Edwin Lee Neil. The funeral of his son, Alan, was a glorious, remarkable one. Though they combine their remnant mentality with a revival one, they are essentially Quietist, waiting on the Spirit, fearful lest they over-organise. Others are at St Stephen's Presbyterian Church in Surrey Hills and at Trinity Church, Camberwell. In each of these congregations they are a power group, but they have never penetrated Melbourne University. There 'the leaders debated the theological issues and rejected the emphasis coming from the IVF executive'.[45] In Queensland there appears to have been no similar manifestation. The charismatic Fred Schwarz had tremendous influence in the EU, but clearly no desire to go down the sinless perfectionist track.

Religious and Psychological Factors

Religious aberrations are normally difficult to explain. They are often an unholy mixture of holy things. Sydney's sinless perfectionism was compounded of the search for holiness, the loyalty of family dynasties, the individualism of the people involved, a role for women and laity which went beyond current conventions, and the strong leadership qualities of Del Agnew and Lindsay Grant.

Family loyalty easily degenerates into family pride, and individualism into elitism. The Young, Grant, and Deck families have made a large and substantially positive contribution to the life of the evangelical community in Sydney. The Grants were 'saintly and generous people', and, if they had a fault, it was perhaps that in some way they developed in Lindsay a perception of the great family, even Christian aristocracy, of which they were a part.

The wealth of the Youngs and Griffiths, the sacrificial missionary service of the 'much used family of Decks', contributed to this sense of spiritual elitism. Lindsay Grant grew up unconsciously seeing himself as an aristocratic spiritual leader, as the inheritor of the mantle of Howard Guinness. Lindsay believed he had 'an impeccable spiritual bloodline'.

Both Del and Lindsay grew up in a community where people toed a strict social line, but enjoyed a legacy of personal spiritual liberty free of denominational discipline. It may be significant that not one of those who became perfectionists appears to have come from an Anglican church. Lindsay was a member of St John's, Balmain, for a short time, but that has not been a strongly evangelical parish. It may be that the Anglican esteem for traditional orthodoxy was a safeguard. The interdenominationalism of the group was reinforced by their individualism: Lindsay had the habit of changing churches when the preaching did not suit him. The freedom of the interdenominational student world (IVF, Crusaders, etc.) provided a situation in which such spiritual dilettantism, linked to Christian responsibility beyond the theological competence of the individuals involved, was clearly dangerous. Such evangelical parachurch organisations generally contain an element of protest against denominational bureaucracy. They are usually therefore not very democratic, tending to selection by and for the elite. Ironically the 'freedom' they generated was the very environment that bred spiritual dictators.

Women were strongly evident on both sides of the debate. On the one side were the three Agnew women; Alice Smith; Dr Alice Hare (née Adam); and (more as followers than leaders) Heather Drummond and Hilda Hungerford. Alice Smith, though a small woman, was as big a name as Lindsay in the SUEU of the late 1930s. She was co-opted to its committee on 17 December 1935, along with Ronald Grant. Her influence on the women was reputedly unchallenged. She continued to defend the movement fiercely, disputing bitterly with Paul White in IVF committee meetings, and only in the last year of her life did she recant her perfectionism. On the other side were women who founded movements and provided the backbone of mainline organisations: Florence Young; Margaret Young (Ernest's wife); Anna Hogg who graduated with first-class honours and the university medal in philosophy; Jean Porter, a future headmistress of Macarthur Girls High School; Doris Roy, who had been dux of Fort Street Girls' High School and was brilliant in languages; and Win Dunkley, a valued Bible teacher, and later the backbone of the Teachers' Christian Fellowship. On both sides, the Brethren influence was strong, leading to strong lay control, and almost no clerical influence. Brethren influence can also be seen in the fact that the perfectionists were content to be small and elitist and to cut off fellowship with other Christians.

The positive and genuine element in the movement should not be denied. As Alwyn Prescott insists: 'You must not imagine that these people were doing their own thing, wanting to please themselves. They were people who were committed to pursuing holiness.' And although they 'never gave much evidence of having attained it', the perfectionist movement had some very fine Christian people in it. They were well educated, and very often from among the professional elite, doctors, dentists, teachers. Heather Drummond was a splendid Christian—'an extremely able and good woman'.[46] When Ian Holt met Lindsay Grant at a function at Trinity Grammar School, he was struck by the 'lovely look on his face' and concluded that Grant 'still loved the Lord'.[47] Alan Neil and Ronald Grant were fine missionaries. They were not the only people to have their ministries destroyed through the impact of this insidious teaching.

Lindsay Grant's leadership style contributed to the disaster. He did not seek guidance on major issues, or if it were offered, he rejected it if it did not agree with the superior level of guidance which he enjoyed. Knowing he would get no support from theologian T. C. Hammond, Grant's tactic was to veer away from his influence, and to indicate that advisers such as Hammond, Harvey Carey, Paul White or Prescott were insufficiently spiritual to grasp perfectionist truth.[48] More robustly, Del Agnew always dismissed Lindsay's opponents as 'creeps'. Allan Bryson's refusal to submit to Lindsay's authority in the late 1930s led to a blazing row on the roof of Sydney Hospital and the breaking of their friendship.

It was a social movement as well as a religious movement with an inner sanctum of esoteric knowledge. It was not the doctrine of sinless perfectionism which split the marriages, but the fact that the movement acquired a group mentality. Only the elite were invited to join the leadership. As we have seen, Del, the high priestess of the cult, exercised an autocratic and all-pervasive rule over the commune which extended into every detail of daily life. Allan Bryson observes: 'It was here that family breakups were engineered, and we knew of cases where couples were told they had to separate, and that was that. No argument!'[49] Lindsay and Del practised with some of their followers what they labelled 'love in the Spirit' in order to demonstrate what true love was. It was their exclusive ministry, not to be emulated by their followers. Broughton Knox spoke of Del as having very great charisma: 'she's not feminine, but she certainly has a real power to influence people, holding them, making them obedient'. Disobedience or knowledge unbecoming of one's station has been reported to lead to beatings and even, in one case, mental derangement resulting in death.

Sequel [50]

In the end, it was World War II which helped the IVF to remove its sinless perfectionist executive. War-time restrictions on travel (and therefore conferences) restricted the spread of the movement. In 1943, as soon as he had finished his residency at North Shore Hospital, Lindsay Grant enlisted in the army, while the orthodox Paul White was invalided home. The combination of a coup led by Harvey Carey in SUEU and White as IVF general secretary meant that the sinless perfectionist virus in IVF was dead. [51] Partially to survive, in Sydney the movement developed its business interests outside Christian circles, starting restaurants and catering centres including the Commonweal in Sydney and Lochnaw Castle in Scotland. [52] In the late 1940s the group formed itself into a company called Tinker Tailor. In Hunters Hill, they acquired Passey, a nursing home where Margaret Debenham (Lindsay's second wife) was matron. The real centre, however, was Wellings, a substantial residence in Woodside Avenue, Burwood, where the group expected to await Christ's second coming. Del said the Lord would return while they were there. They invited prestigious religious people to their various religious communes to add lustre to their movement. David du Plessey and Ian Paisley were two people who received invitations—du Plessey walked out in disgust. From about the early 1960s most of those who had been involved in the movement and got out had re-established fellowship with other Christians and were involved in some kind of meaningful Christian service. This was particularly true of David Grant.

It was difficult for some to leave, and some have still not managed to extricate themselves from the movement. This was not only because of psychological pressure, but also because some had invested their life's assets in the commune and were even at risk of losing their children. One who managed to extricate herself after experiencing terrible trauma and coming

121

close to a nervous breakdown, said, 'I don't want them to know where I am living.' All members lost their savings and their assets to the group. Evidence emerged of psychological repression, physical abuse, violations of the Christian sexual ethic, and doubtful business dealings. Such repercussions resulted, not surprisingly, in a police inquiry into the business activities of the group in the early 1960s and the public exposure of the cult by the media in the early 1990s.[53]

It has been a sad demise for a movement genuinely devoted to the pursuit of deeper consecration. Their theology may not have gone beyond that of Wesley's perfect love, but their claim that they had attained it certainly went beyond Wesley's claim. So discredited have the Wesleyan and Keswick views of holiness become that the churches seem to be little interested in holiness at all. Even pentecostals seem to be interested in every aspect of the Holy Spirit except his holiness. At the Keswick Convention 'Keswick theology' is no longer taught, having given way to the older evangelical view of sanctification as an unrelenting struggle. For modern Christians, higher life and victorious living are not an issue. But this has created a vacuum where the church does not have 'a more excellent way'. Such 'Easy-believism' is consistent neither with Scripture nor with the great reforming or Puritan founders of evangelicalism, who insisted that it is never wrong to long to be as holy as a forgiven sinner can be.[54] A faith which does not issue in holiness is not true saving faith, they insisted, for while we are saved through faith alone, the faith which brings salvation is never alone.

While perfectionism alone cannot be blamed for the decline of holiness teaching, orthodox evangelicals certainly took fright at it. Hurstville Baptist Church was split down the middle by the debate over perfectionism, and a breakaway Hurstville Christian Fellowship Centre was established. R. C. M. Long, rector at St. Michael's, Wollongong, preached strongly against it in the 1940s, while the repercussions of the perfectionist movement in Sydney, in particular, have meant that experiential movements, like Charismatic and pentecostal renewal, are particularly suspect, and the battle against them acrimonious. T. C. Hammond in particular became fierce about perfectionism, rightly insisting that sanctification was not the same thing as sinlessness.[55]

Geoff Bingham,[56] missionary, evangelist and writer, found himself put at arm's length for emphasising the experiential character of Christianity. Yet Bingham's intense pursuit of holiness in the 1950s proved very attractive to many, including those still influential in the ministry today. His personal following was so great that some—with the Australian aversion to tall poppies and the Anglican aversion to loners—feared that there was danger of a personality cult emerging. His critics feared that he might lead his considerable following down perfectionist paths.

As the 1950s and 1960s progressed, however, the experiential nature of the Christian life was increasingly sought, by the young in particular. Helen North, a CMS missionary in India, brought back to Australia the emphasis of the powerful revivalist, Bakht Singh. His holiness teaching linked up with the Honour Oak movement and Watchman Nee. It flowered brightly at Kuring-gai Gospel Chapel, a Brethren meeting place. Here a number of promising pupils of Shore Grammar School were attracted to perfectionism; they linked up with the Hurstville fellowship, attracted a number of the able sons of well-to-do families, and carried the doctrine back to Sydney University via St Paul's College. One such was Tony Golsby Smith, who became the leader of one of the numerous satellite groups which the movement spawned. He taught at Barker College, where he exercised a major influence on some pupils who still attended his meetings long after he left the school. Some King's old boys have been caught up in the same movement, and have undergone rebaptism in the Hawkesbury near Smith's home at Wilberforce. Sinless perfectionism will continue to break out in such local efflorescences, Canon Len Abbott suggests, as long as 'the orthodox declare the truth without mercy'. In the evangelical cord of three strands, sinless perfectionism has strengthened the Word strand as theologians, ministers and interested laity have studied the Biblical foundation of the belief. It would be good to report that the Spirit strand has been strengthened, too, by the development of a more fully rounded, Biblical understanding of the role of the Spirit in the Christian life. No doubt, some, who have borne the task of defending people and institutions against this cult, believe that they have taught God's truth on the matter. But many, by their hunger for charismatic experiences, suggest that the sinless perfectionist movement has weakened the Spirit strand and unravelled it from the evangelical synthesis to its lasting impoverishment, increasing the nervousness which evangelicals have of aspirations after holiness and of movements which focus much on the Holy Spirit in the life of the believer. It should be concluded, however, that the circumstances which gave rise to the cult influenced evangelicalism more than the cult itself. For it is not as if the cult were large, and the few evangelical leaders who knew about it preferred not to talk about it. It almost seems that the greatest impact of the cult has been felt in more recent years, rather than in the 1930s and 1940s. The generation in which the cult arose embodied the evangelical synthesis of Spirit, Word and world as successfully as any in the history of Australian evangelicalism, as we shall see in the next chapter.

6. Word and Spirit, 1933–1959

Australia was a more confident and united nation in this next period as it pulled out of the Great Depression, mounted another highly disciplined war effort, and then faced the threat of communism and the Korean War in the 1950s. National and church leadership was conspicuously better than in the previous period, the economy strengthened, and there was broad consensus on social and cultural values. At war without, Australia was at peace within. In the 1950s an age of equipoise was reached, a balance of individual freedoms and community responsibility. The churches themselves contributed to the development of this happy state. The balance of freedom and responsibility is consistent with Catholic social theory which was closely studied and energetically applied to Australian society in the 1940s and 1950s by the National Secretariat of Catholic Action. It is also consistent with conservative Protestantism which espoused a social system based on three New Testament norms: order, freedom, and justice. Not surprisingly, in this environment, the churches, both Catholic and Protestant, thrived.

The 1950s was arguably the most successful decade for the evangelical synthesis of Spirit, Word, and world in Australian history. True, the Spirit strand wrestled with millennarian and perfectionist excesses and remained largely unenergised by fledgling pentecostalism. But it still had sufficient fire to ignite scores of local revivals in the 1950s, which was a decade of unusually effective evangelistic campaigns; they culminated in the 1959 Billy Graham Crusades when Australia came closer than at any time before or since to a general spiritual awakening. The Word strand was conspicuously strengthened by the contributions of able, conservative Bible scholars and by an increased provision for Biblical theological education in the Reformed tradition. The world strand was also stronger as the evangelical churches retreated from the fundamentalism which had so tempted them in the previous period. The determination to make Australia a Christian nation or to keep it Christian was stubbornly sustained throughout this period, and the evangelical investment in overseas and Aboriginal missions was increased markedly.

Leading the Christians onward in this period was a new generation of generals who had greater ability than their predecessors. The Melbourne evangelicals continued to be led by C. H. Nash and his keen lay devotees, while the Sydney Baptists still enjoyed the deeply spiritual leadership of Principal Morling and the evangelistic successes of John Ridley. But the new evangelical leaders were remarkable. In Sydney, Howard Mowll became archbishop in 1933, one of the greatest evangelical statesmen of the twentieth century. At Moore Theological College, T. C. Hammond, with a mind like a rapier and a tongue like a whip, reigned supreme. In 1947 the exuberant orator Stuart Barton Babbage became Dean of Sydney. The Methodists in Sydney were ably led by Frank Rayward, superintendent of the Wesley Central Methodist Mission, and by Alan Walker who won a national reputation through his leadership of the Methodist Mission to the Nation in the 1950s. Student work in universities, critical to the future of evangelicalism, was headed by Paul White, 'the jungle doctor', and North American Charles Troutman.

From Sterility to Stability

If Australia had been like a small country town prior to 1939, the war made all Australians aware of the rest of the world, opening people to consumerism and internationalism to an extent previously inconceivable. The agents for this were twofold. First, the great religio-political edifice of the Empire crumbled as the Japanese advanced on Singapore, and as that great bastion of Australia's defence collapsed in a matter of days. Everything that had seemed sure and stable was undermined—Australians had to rely on their own strong arms, and had to wrench themselves out of British control in order to bring their troops back from Africa. On the other hand, after the fall of Corregidor and the American forward bases in the Philippines, Australia became the main supply base for the Pacific War. When MacArthur stepped down from his plane like some military messiah, Australians took him to their hearts. They also took in a million American soldiers, and the ground was laid for post-war Americanisation.

The post-war churches made their plans for growth and expansion in a period of social stability and economic prosperity. Australia in the period

1949 to 1966 was dominated by a Menzies Government made up of ministers who were of long standing and a modicum of competence. Robert Menzies himself, an arch-royalist and an imposing orator, was the perfect figure-head for a government which wanted to project an image of patriarchal security. This was underpinned by auspicious circumstances in politics and the economy. In the 1950s and 1960s capitalism, having overcome the challenges posed by depression, war and the Labor Party, regained dominance both economically and politically in Australian society, with the middle classes as the chief beneficiaries. It had the advantage of having a common enemy which united the nation—in Korea, Australian troops joined the United Nations forces in opposing the communist trio of North Korea, China and the USSR. With the threat of nuclear annihilation expanding as the decade progressed, the unifying theme of 'us against them' was often played, usually to the electoral disadvantage of the Labor Party in such scandals as the Petrov Affair. Furthermore, there was a wool boom, which encouraged the growth of mixed farming, and at the same time a dramatic growth in secondary industry spurred on by immigration, infrastructure accumulated during the war, and protective tariffs. Unemployment hovered at an unbelievable 1 per cent or less for much of the period, with fluctuations in the early years of both decades.

At the 1954 census, 89.4 per cent of the population professed adherence to one of the Christian denominations. Of these 41.9 per cent were Church of England, 25.4 per cent were Catholic, Methodists constituted some 12 per cent, while Presbyterians were the smallest of the 'big four' with 10.7 per cent. Gallup polls on actual church attendance showed that 35 per cent of those canvassed in 1947 and 33 per cent of those canvassed in 1955 claimed to be 'regular churchgoers', though what this category meant in the minds of the respondents was not tested. These figures are unremarkable, perhaps, except for the fact that this was about twice the English percentage: 94 per cent of all Australians in 1948 claimed to believe in God, as against 84 per cent of the English. These figures must challenge the view that Australia is somehow a *peculiarly* godless country.

A variety of influences underlay the resurgence of evangelical Christianity which occurred in Australia in the 1950s. This was a period of tremendous religious vitality in European and American Christianity. The year 1948 saw the formation of the World Council of Churches, which brought Protestant groups closer together across denominations, and there were similar movements world-wide within denominations (such as the Baptist Bible Fellowship, which had one million members in 1975). This was the period in which the Southern Baptists in America began their incredible growth. In the mid-1950s there were celebrated debates in both the London *Times* and the Chicago *Daily News* on fundamentalism, as evangelist Billy Graham took his leave from the fundamentalism of his youth and established 'the new evangelicalism', which was tolerant, accommodating, and amazingly successful. The liberal–fundamentalist debate in the United States, which produced what looked like a hopeless muddle in the 1930s and 1940s, settled down in the 1950s with all sides coming to defined positions. Three basic positions evolved in American Protestantism: liberal, fundamentalist, and neo-evangelical.[1] Many who had been in the fundamentalist movement from the start, but were disillusioned with the intolerance it spawned, followed the strong leadership of such worthies as Billy Graham, Carl Henry and Edward Carnell. At the same time, clarification of the evangelical position was coming from such English evangelicals as Martyn Lloyd-Jones, James Packer, and F. F. Bruce, and this flowed into Australia largely through the IVF network.

The Evangelical Synthesis in Action: The Mowlls

Howard Mowll, Archbishop of Sydney from 1933 to 1958, and his wife Dorothy, were archetypal evangelical activists. In the tapestry of their lives, the world strand was the most conspicuous thread, but the Spirit and Word strands harmonised with it, producing consecrated lives. So perfectly did they embody the evangelical synthesis, and so effective were their ministries, that they are still revered as the greatest gift to evangelical Anglicanism in Australia's history. A product of the revived, intellectual evangelicalism which issued from the Cambridge Inter-Collegiate Christian Union (of which he was president), Howard Mowll was ordained in England, became a lecturer at Wycliffe College, Toronto, and Bishop of West China from 1922 to 1933. He married Dorothy Martin in 1924. Her father was the principal of the Diocesan Theological College in Foochow, China. Set on a missionary career, she had sailed for China in 1915 and served there for a total of eighteen years. She became known as 'Miss Henry Martyn'[2] after the legendary missionary chaplain, and was a woman of great vision and determination, mixed attractively with merriment and vitality. She was in many ways the power behind the power, and the strategist behind the visionary, always devising new schemes and carrying a notebook and pen with her everywhere so that she could keep track of the flow of ideas.

As befits those whose ministries encircled the globe, they were both missionaries at heart, and together they girded the loins of their church for evangelism and mission at home and abroad. The strong reliance on the Word and the Spirit which Howard Mowll had in his mission to the world is evident from a perusal of his personal Bible. Here is a theology and a spirituality efficiently harnessed to the evangelistic task. In the front of the Bible he wrote, 'Life is a Mission. Its end is service. Its law is self-sacrifice. Its strength is fellowship with God.' Of all the books in the Bible, the Letter to the Romans was easily the most heavily annotated by Mowll, suggesting that Mowll had studied closely the primary document of evangelical Protestantism. The pages of his Bible are interleaved with the poetry of piety on which, together with the Word, he nourished his soul, and the Bible's margins contain many a pithy sermon summary. At the beginning of the Book of Acts, for example, Mowll wrote on the subject of being filled with the Holy Spirit, one of the keys of consecrated Christian living:

> Five reasons why men were not filled with the Holy Ghost:
> 1. Lack of Conviction. The Twelve.
> 2. Desire of Power. Simon.
> 3. Need of Instruction. Cornelius.
> 4. Lack of Seeking. Ephesus.
> 5. Love of Sin. Epistle? Whitsunday.

In his Bible, too, we find the record of his struggle with his own besetting sins as he monitored his own soul and his effectiveness as a soul-winner. He prayed to be delivered from lethargy, both spiritual and mental, from his quick temper, lack of patience and irritability, and from his 'self-consciousness and great difficulty in speaking personally to people'.[3] There is perhaps no finer proof than Mowll that the evangelical synthesis of Spirit, Word and mission produces consecrated service.

He was elected Archbishop of Sydney in 1933 at the height of the Modernist controversy, due to the clear understanding of a distinction between liberal and conservative evangelicalism. He was nominated by H. S. Begbie, and supported by D. J. Knox, R. B. Robinson, and S. E. Langford Smith, all conservatives. Although himself a conservative, he was no fundamentalist sectarian. He refused, for example, to allow the Bible Churchmen's Missionary Society, a conservative breakaway from the English CMS, to be established in Australia. Instead, he revitalised the moribund CMS, gave it a new constitution, and as its president himself gave it strong leadership. He placed conservatives in key diocesan positions, especially R. B. Robinson as General Secretary of the Home Mission Society and S. M. Johnstone as Diocesan Registrar. D. J. Knox did not need a special diocesan appointment: he was one of the brains behind the Anglican Church League which had orchestrated Mowll's election. Langford Smith was the chief brain! H. S. Begbie was the rector of three strong parishes during Mowll's episcopate: Willoughby, Parramatta, and Church Hill.

Mowll's first priority, however, was training evangelical clergy at Moore Theological College and placing them in strategic parishes. As Moore's principal, he appointed the celebrated conservative Irish evangelical, T. C. Hammond. In 1926 Hammond had been on a lecture tour to Australia, under the auspices of the Anglican Church League, to help stem the move to prayer book revision then strong in England. He made such an impact that, when in 1936 a new principal was required, two of the three college trustees, H. S. Begbie and H. L. Tress, prevailed on the third, Archbishop Mowll, to appoint him. Hammond had been born in Cork, Ireland, in 1877. Emilia Baeyertz, an Australian evangelist of Jewish parentage, was present in Cork for his second birth in 1892. He was always appreciative of the contribution which women evangelists could make to the mission of the church, and prevailed on Monica Farrell, an amazingly gifted speaker, to migrate from Ireland to Australia to engage in the work of evangelism. Hammond grew up in an environment where the tiny Protestant minority was often fiercely persecuted by the Catholic majority, and many converts to Protestantism emigrated to escape persecution. Australia was one of the chief beneficiaries of this exodus, and staunch anti-Catholic feeling was thus infused into Australian evangelicalism. Hammond was a well-trained champion in the Protestant cause, and from 1919 to 1936 was superintendent of the Irish Church Missions. He possessed a sharp intellect, a photographic memory, a robust sense of humour, plenty of courage, and a heart for evangelism. In defence of persecuted Protestants, he had become adroit at invoking the law, which was to stand him in good stead in the legalistic atmosphere of Australian Anglicanism. His powers of disputation were formidable. In Ireland he introduced the agnostic Everard Digges La Touche to faith in Christ, and in Australia he engaged

Sydney University Philosophy Professor, John Anderson, in memorable combat, greatly heartening the evangelical student troops.

Mowll was at first nervous of appointing such a practised controversialist. This same controversial style has raised questions about his piety. His strongly objective theology did not express itself in the style of spirituality then in vogue, but he set a new fashion which has come to be thought of as the acceptable face of Sydney evangelicalism. Hammond has been characterised as 'a genuinely Anglican theologian in the evangelical tradition, with a deep respect for both Calvin and Butler and arguing for what he on more than one occasion termed a "moderate Calvinism"'.[4] Once having taken the plunge to offer Hammond the job of Moore College principal, Mowll did everything to make it work, including having the students up at 4.30 in the morning to make sure they were ready to welcome their new head when his ship docked in Sydney Harbour. Mowll came to depend very heavily on Hammond, since he had little time for thinking deeply on theology. The partnership became of great value to the diocese, but it was not without its negative side. Hammond advised Mowll on how to handle a group of fifty 'central' churchmen who in 1938 petitioned the archbishop for greater sympathy for their position. It was not wise advice, and Mowll had to work hard for years to recover lost ground.[5] The remainder of the Anglican Church outside Sydney responded to the conservative evangelical takeover by further isolating the diocese. In 1935 Mowll was snubbed for the primacy; Archbishop Henry Le Fanu of Perth was elected instead, a slight which Mowll and Sydney evangelicals felt deeply.[6] Sydney, too, was out of step in its resistance to any constitution which centralised the Australian church. Neither the clergy nor their lay supporters thought that a strongly centralised denomination under tight episcopal control was healthy.

Meanwhile, in 1936 Dorothy Mowll threw herself into plans for the centenary of Broughton's consecration as Bishop of Australia. The extraordinary pageant in the Sydney Town Hall involved 760 people in twenty-two scenes depicting the history of the Anglican Church 'from its earliest days until the coming of Bishop Broughton to Australia'. It was said to be the biggest gathering of Anglicans ever held outside England. But the key thing for her was not that it was big, but that it was Biblical. Her great desire was to demonstrate that the Church of England has been a Bible-loving church, a church which has held fast to the Gospel of Jesus Christ throughout its history. The next year she put on another church history pageant, 'General,

Anglican, Australian', around the theme of the warrior pilgrim Church of God 'marching down the centuries to win the world for Jesus Christ'. It ended with the singing of Blake's 'Jerusalem' and with the sentiment that 'God's own Jerusalem' might be built in 'this our beloved Australia'.[7] It all sounded rather English, but the hope was to take this English Australian Gospel to the world. The Mowlls were essentially internationalist in perspective, and not afraid to think big. Like all archbishops before him, Mowll saw his role as that of Christianising Australia, and reaching out to Australia's region in Asia and the Pacific.

It was during the war years that Mowll's greatness as a leader became evident. Conscious of the criticism that the Church of England in Sydney had not been as supportive of the war effort in World War I as it might have been, Mowll went to extraordinary lengths to meet the needs of soldiers, both spiritual and recreational. At the same time, he foresaw the future rapid expansion of Sydney and he sought to strengthen the church's presence in every population centre through the provision of church buildings and ministry. It required great energy to achieve both goals together. The reality was that the number of available clergy declined as many joined the armed forces as chaplains or soldiers. Finances were short as every penny was dedicated to war work and charities. Materials for building and maintaining churches were extremely scarce. Worse, areas of church activity were decimated by the demands of total war. Mowll established the Church of England National Emergency Fund. Its auxiliary, the Sydney Diocesan Churchwomen's Association, mobilised 2000 women under Mrs Mowll's leadership. The grounds of the cathedral were covered with makeshift huts for servicemen. There they found food, a bed, and friendship. It was a service described by the Governor-General's wife as 'pure Christianity'. At her funeral in 1957 a man, standing outside the cathedral on the site of the huts, stopped a passer-by and said, 'There are not many in the world like her. Many a time she put her hand on my shoulder and gave encouragement during the war.'[8]

In 1947 Mowll was appointed Primate of the Church of England in Australia. He relished the responsibility, and in spite of his convinced evangelical churchmanship, carried if off with great acceptance to all parties. Just as he had visited every parish in Sydney early in his episcopate to get them moving, so now he visited every diocese in Australia. He led the Australian delegation to the Lambeth Conference; he was accompanied by future archbishop, Donald Robinson, at the inaugural meeting of the International Fellowship of Evangelical Students (IFES) meeting at Harvard, Boston in 1947; and he attended the inauguration of the World Council of Churches in Amsterdam in 1948. It was his well-known interest in the formation of this body which cost him the privilege of being the foundation president of the international fellowship, since evangelicals have always been ambivalent about the ecumenical movement. Neither did Martyn Lloyd-Jones, who was also at Boston, accept his advice to resign from his pastorate in London to become a promoter of international evangelicalism. He must have been one of a tiny minority who ever said 'no' to the archbishop. In 1953 Mowll realised a long-held ambition by launching an appeal through both the Church Missionary Society and the Australian Board of Missions to send missionaries to South-East Asia. In 1956 he visited China.

On the eve of Christmas Eve, 1957, Dorothy Mowll died of Hodgkinson's disease. A diocesan bishop wrote: 'In her we saw exhibited the finest traits of the evangelical tradition, with its call to personal dedication to our Lord and to the work of extending His kingdom.' Three weeks before she died, though ill, she attended a function on board HMAS *Melbourne*. One young officer later described her as 'a ball of fire. She is so vital and so interested and so friendly.' In her diary in the year of her death she wrote: 'In Christian work, if we go back, we die; . . . it is only by going forward when the challenge comes that the lamp of faith burns more brightly, and courage and vision are kept strong and virile'.[9] A year later the archbishop lay close to death's door. Students at Moore College were invited to his bedroom to take their leave of the great man. He asked them if they were reading their Bibles and saying their prayers. He rallied, went back to work, and then suddenly died. In 1959, the year after Mowll's death, Billy Graham came to Sydney. On the last day of the Sydney crusade, buoyed by the sight of the largest crowd that he had ever addressed, Billy looked up into the heavens and addressed Mowll: 'I believe . . . Sir, your Grace, you can see this day . . . your heart is rejoicing. A part of what we are seeing here is a result of your many years of faithful ministry in this city.'[10] Evangelicalism is not above hero-worship, and Mowll's after-glow reaches into the present. This 'initiating Father-in-God' still represents the evangelical ideal of the consecrated life, made up of activism, orthodoxy, and spirituality.

The Renaissance of Scholarship in the Word

The Modernist dispute continued to wreak havoc throughout this period. One who suffered from the tension engendered in conservative denominations by liberalism was W. H. Holdsworth, principal from 1911 to 1938 of the Baptist College in Melbourne. He became president of the Melbourne College of Divinity in 1924, but felt it unwise to allow any of his students to enrol in its courses until 1933 because of Baptist suspicion of Modernism. Then, when he came to retire in 1938, his succession created a furore. The evangelical Christian weekly, *The Edifier*, intervened robustly at a delicate stage in the appointment process on behalf of one of the two candidates for the position, making out that he was loyal to evangelical faith whereas his rival, if appointed, would mar the future of the church. The intervention rendered both men unappointable, and after a cooling-off period, the college appointed a complete outsider, unknown to members of the rival factions.[11] The bitterness engendered by this dispute was to linger in the denomination for years.

But in the mortal combat between liberals and fundamentalists, both sides were critically wounded, and not always by each other. The English version of Karl Barth's commentary on the Epistle to the Romans appeared in 1933. It was a refutation of both liberal Protestantism and fundamentalism. Many Australian Protestants, who had been led into dangerous waters by the liberalism of Samuel Angus, scrambled on board Barth's lifeboat and paddled their way tentatively back towards the safety of the evangelical shore. Evangelicals liked much of what they heard from Barth. Not only did he affirm the rebelliousness of humankind beginning with Adam, 'the man who sinned at once', and the righteousness and omnipotence of the transcendent God, who revealed himself through Christ alone and saved by grace alone, but he insisted that the Bible was the sole source of knowledge about God. His position was distinguished from that of the fundamentalists in that he insisted that the Bible only became the Word of God when it was interpreted by the Holy Spirit in the life of the believer. Evangelicals believed in the necessity of Word and Spirit, but the fundamentalists among them were not the only ones who felt uneasy at Barth's apparent downplaying of the authority of the Bible in its own right. Barth appealed to them because he had the uncompromising style of the preacher rather than the balanced moderation of the theologian. But when they unpacked what he affirmed and denied, they were not so certain that they wanted to deny as much or affirm so little. T. C. Hammond, more disposed than most evangelicals to detecting the heresy in the fairest-sounding words, perceived immediately that Barth was no ally of evangelical truth, and warned that 'it would be dangerous to allow so stout an opponent to remain unassailed in our rear'.[12]

Barth wanted to rescue the Christian faith from any dependence on human culture, on history, reason, experience, the visible church, or political power. He argued that the resurrection of Christ should be thought of as a 'non-historical event' because it was too central to the revelation of God to be subjected to the lawlessness of historical relativism. He denied that human society had any affinity with the Kingdom of God, and encouraged the church to ignore the world. He exalted God by obliterating man. Evangelicals were happy to use his ammunition in their bombardment of the liberals, but they doubted if the Word should be so divorced from the world. In developing a considered Biblical response to Barthianism, they brought about a resurgence in Calvinism. It became important for them to be known as 'Reformed' as well as 'evangelical'. Such Reformed evangelicals in Australia relished Hammond's strong, objective Calvinistic theology; the edge went off their appetite for the subjective pietism which had previously characterised the Spirit strand, along with revivalism and second-blessing holiness teaching, and they fellowshipped with those of Calvinist traditions, including members of the Presbyterian Church of Australia, the Free Church (the Presbyterian Church of Eastern Australia), the Reformed Presbyterian Church, and the Reformed Churches of Australia.

Symptomatic of the revived Calvinism was the advent of the *Reformed Theological Review* in 1942. It was conceived by Robert Swanton, a Melbourne Presbyterian, who was to serve as its editor for over forty years. It fostered evangelical scholarship and Reformed convictions. Swanton had studied history at Melbourne University, writing a thesis on John Dunmore Lang, and in the late 1930s had studied theology at Basel, Switzerland, with Karl Barth himself. He was parish minister of Hawthorn in Melbourne from 1940 until 1968. In the universities, while the SCM took wholeheartedly to Barthian theology, the IVF in the 1940s witnessed the birth of a more confident evangelicalism as more able scholars came to its aid. Evangelical students grew more literate Biblically as they worked through *Search the Scriptures*, a three-year Bible-study programme written by leading

English evangelical clergy such as A. M. Stibbs, H. E. Guillebaud, F. D. Coggan, R. J. Cobb, and Basil Atkinson. IVFers were also better equipped theologically owing to T. C. Hammond's 'systematic theology for non-theologians', *In Understanding be Men* (first published in 1936), on which generations of Australian evangelicals cut their theological teeth. The IVF ethos continued to be set by Paul White who applied a threefold formula to student work: Entertain, Educate, Evangelise (or, less alliteratively: 'humour, cricket, souls'). White also saw the need for a continuous leadership training scheme for short student generations, and practised a programme of nurturing BWW: 'Blokes Worth Watching'.

In 1951 Howard Guinness, founder of the IVF in Australia, was the speaker at a mission at Sydney University. Dudley Foord, a young evangelical layman with an instinctive capacity to support men of initiative, believed that 'this man can do something' and spent a year preparing for the mission, which has gone down in evangelical lore as one of the great university missions. It was a harbinger of probably the most successful decade in Australia's evangelical history. The 1950s saw a decline in liberalism, the rebirth of Biblical theology, and the coming to life of evangelical scholarship. Out of this academic revival, modern Australian evangelicalism has been constructed. Indeed, the Australian experience was part of the world-wide renaissance of evangelicalism, allowing evangelicals to regain in more recent decades something of the initiative in theology and Biblical studies and to begin to make inroads into the university system as more young evangelicals received university appointments.

For much of the 1950s, culminating in the Billy Graham Crusades which won many students to Christ, the IVF was imaginatively led by Pennsylvania-born Charles Troutman. He arrived in Australia in 1953, intending to work for only a brief period of time as an IVF staffworker. His wife and two of his three children, however, contracted polio in the epidemic of that year. Troutman therefore had to protract his stay until 1961. In 1954 he was appointed IVF general secretary. Perhaps because he was a foreigner, Troutman was always conscious of the distinctiveness of the Australian environment and character. His family's predicament made him ponder the divine purpose in allowing him to come to Australia. He looked, he listened, and he thought. He prayed for a fresh vision of the nature of the Christian presence in Australia; he wanted to work out what needed to be done locally. He was not only a thinker; he was also strategist. He committed himself to bringing Christian groups together in the cause of evangelical Christianity, and developed White's concept of the unbreakable Scripture Union–IVF circle. Formed in Britain in 1867, the Scripture Union in Australia established annual beach missions which reached many young people for Christ. Troutman received the wholehearted support of the Scripture Union secretary, Colin Becroft, and school pupils from the Inter-School Christian Fellowships graduated into the EUs which staffed the beach missions and camps. Following graduation, many EUers became teachers, who in turn supported the fellowships. A great encourager, Troutman also brought Ian Burnard into the movement. Burnard succeeded Troutman as general secretary and led it for the next fifteen years.

Theological colleges of all doctrinal complexions also contributed to equipping the saints with new weaponry in the battle for the mind. By 1963 there were fifty-six theological colleges in Australia. Each of the main denominations had at least one, while the larger denominations tended to have at least one in each of the larger States.[13] Standards at the Melbourne College of Divinity and the Australian College of Theology were raised, and in the late 1940s Semitic Studies were introduced into the University of Melbourne. St Patrick's Catholic college in Manly was erected into a Pontifical Faculty of Theology, offering postgraduate study for its best students. Theology, it was claimed, could here 'be pursued for its own sake in a strictly scientific fashion'.[14] Staff included Thomas Muldoon, Professor of Dogmatic Theology, and W. Leonard, Professor of Sacred Scripture, the architect of vital Australian Catholic Biblical scholarship. Scholarship easily broke down denominational barriers, and in 1953 the Fellowship for Biblical Studies, made up of Catholics and Protestants, launched the *Australian Biblical Review*. Dr J. A. Thomson became director of the Australian Institute of Archaeology, which specialised in Biblical archaeology, and later Reader in the Department of Middle Eastern Studies at Melbourne University. In 1947 the Society of the Sacred Mission, an Anglican religious community dedicated to training men for ordination, established St Michael's House at Mount Lofty, near Adelaide. Under its Australian Provincial, Father Basil Oddie, the community modelled the religious life and took in ordinands until the house was destroyed by the 1983 Ash Wednesday bushfires, after which the society moved its headquarters to Melbourne. Its greatest scholar in its Adelaide days was Gabriel Hebert, author of *Fundamentalism and the Church of God* (1957). Hebert was quite candid about his aim:

> It is with conservative evangelicals in the Church of England and other churches, and with the Inter-Varsity Fellowship of Evangelical Unions, that this book is to be especially concerned. It will be therefore only common courtesy on my part to refrain from calling them by a name which they dislike and repudiate.[15]

Hebert's attack provoked many refutations, including an article in the *Reformed Theological Review* from Alan Cole, who had been baptised in Ireland by T. C. Hammond and who was himself a fine scholar and brilliant linguist. Cole quoted the evangelical apologist John Stott on the three characteristics of fundamentalism from which conservative evangelicals insist on distancing themselves: 'a bigoted rejection of all Biblical criticism, a mechanical view of inspiration, and an exceptionally literalist interpretation of Scripture'.[16] The most extensive refutation came from the pen of J. I. Packer. His *Fundamentalism and the Word of God* (IVF, London, 1958) became an evangelical classic. The dispute revealed the concern which evangelicals now clearly had to be considered intellectually respectable. More important, it demonstrated that Biblical interpretation had become the key concern of evangelicals. It has remained so ever since.

In 1954 the synod of the Reformed Churches of Australia resolved to establish a theological college and Christian university modelled on the Free University in Holland, founded seventy years earlier by Abraham Kuyper.[17] The Rev. J. A. Schep was appointed as foundation Professor of New Testament. He retired in 1964 when he adopted a pentecostal position. The college's most venerable scholar was Klaas Runia, Professor of Systematic Theology from 1957 until 1971. He had been a minister of the Reformed Churches of the Netherlands, and had written his doctoral thesis at the Free University under the supervision of G. C. Berkouwer on aspects of Karl Barth's theology. Runia was to write a major study of Barth's doctrine of Scripture and was a valued contributor to the *Reformed Theological Review*.[18] Reformed dogmatics, he declared in his inaugural address as theology professor, must be Scriptural, church-confessional, and theocentric. With reference to the last he rejected Barth's theology as ultimately false because it was Christocentric rather than theocentric. For the Reformed scholar, the science of theology was clearly the treasure of the church, and Runia enthused in his peroration to his 'dear Students': 'Theology is a queen, beautiful as the dawn, adorned with many mysteries. I tell you honestly: theology has the love of my heart. I can only see it as a privilege to infuse into others this same love.'[19]

It is clear that the Calvinist revival which began in the 1940s and gained momentum in the 1950s would result in the strengthening of the Word strand and with it the growing appreciation of doctrine and theology in the churches with Reformed confessions. In 1963 the formation of the John Knox Theological College in Melbourne reflected this revival of Reformed theology. Also in Melbourne, the ever innovative Stuart Barton Babbage, principal of Ridley College from 1953 to 1963, gathered around him lecturers who were to achieve international recognition. Among them Leon Morris and Frank Andersen were as committed in their evangelicalism as they were brilliant in scholarship. A New Testament theologian and exegete, Morris, himself principal of Ridley College for almost three decades from 1964, focused on Christ and his cross in his more than forty scholarly books and commentaries. Andersen stunned the academic world with his erudition in the ancient languages bearing on the Old Testament, and was destined to be appointed Professor of Studies in Religion in the University of Queensland.

Meanwhile, also in Queensland, Thomas Warriner, trained under the distinguished Old Testament scholar, Wheeler Robinson, presided over the Baptist college until 1966. He incurred the wrath of the fundamentalists, but he was much loved, and the college really grew for the first time. In Sydney the Baptists enjoyed the eirenic rule of Principal Morling until 1960 and the respected scholarship of John Thomson, whose decade at the Baptist college, beginning in 1957, made a considerable impact on both the denomination and the university scene. He was one of the foundation assistant editors of *The Journal of Christian Education* launched in 1958, and contributed an article to the first number of the journal entitled 'Education in the Qumran Community'. Its first editor was Dr Anna Hogg, senior lecturer in Education at Sydney Teachers' College, and she explained that professional teachers could not be content merely to practise their craft and achieve results. Professionals, she wrote, have to understand the principles on which their practice is based.[20] Evangelicalism has always been involved in the development of professionalisation,[21] one of the cultures in which it most thrives is in the professions, and evangelical professional groups sprang up like mushrooms. Sometimes evangelicals were associated with more robust enterprises which reached well beyond the evangelical world. For example, also in 1958 Edwin Judge, a young New Zealand evangelical lecturer in ancient history at the University of Sydney and an authority on early Christianity, discussed with Bruce Mansfield, a Reformation historian, and Ken Cable, historian of Australian Christianity, the possibility of an academic journal on the history, not of the church nor of theology, but of religion. The prestigious *Journal of Religious History* was born two years later. So by the end of the 1950s the burgeoning scholarship in the Word was buttressed by scholarship in ancillary disciplines and in the professions.

Strategies for the Conversion of the World

This period began with one of the most amazing episodes in the history of Aboriginal missions, referred to in the media Australia-wide and beyond as 'the Peace Expedition'. In 1932 five Japanese fisherman were killed at Caledon Bay on the eastern coast of Arnhem Land. A police party was sent from Darwin to investigate, and one of their number, Constable A. S. McColl, was speared to death. A credulous white population was told that the Balmattum tribe of Caledon Bay was wild and highly dangerous, that, unless taught a lesson, the whites of the north could be massacred, and that police planned a punitive expedition. Missionaries in Arnhem Land were appalled at the prospect, realising that it would be a major set-back to their labours. The Commonwealth Government was pressured by the police to allow the punitive expedition and by the missionary forces to disallow it, and eventually consented to a party of CMS missionaries embarking on the expedition unarmed and unprotected. The Prime Minister, Joe Lyons, gave them six months to complete the exercise. In the party were Hubert Warren, who had been one of the early missionaries at the Roper River Mission, and Alf Dyer, who was then at the Oenpelli Mission. Dyer, given to visions and rash of judgment, had already resolved to go on the expedition alone, having taken the matter to the Lord in prayer. He was given a verse from Scripture to affirm this leading: 'For if thou altogether holdest thy peace at this time, then shall ... deliverance arise ... from another place; ... who knoweth whether thou art come ... for such a time as this?' (Esther 4.14). Dyer was also driven by the strong principles which motivated his decades of work among the Arnhem Land Aboriginal people, to 'preserve for these lovable people all that is good in their natural way of life, while at the same time effectually fighting superstition, disease, malnutrition, dirt, ignorance, and the degrading influence of low-grade whites'.[22] He also hoped that the foundation could be laid for a mission to this unreached tribe at Caledon Bay. When Dyer joined the other members of the mission party in Darwin, one of them wrote:

> Having heard that CMS had had to restrain him from going overland, on horseback, entirely unaccompanied, to quieten the Caledon Bay blacks, and that he ranked with Warren in experience of the wild tribes, I had pictured Dyer a man of gigantic physique. Instead, he proved to be a thin little, malaria-ridden scrap of humanity who, especially in the shorts, shirt, and skull-cap which he wore aboard the lugger, looked like a wizened-up pirate.[23]

When they eventually arrived at Caledon Bay, they were greeted with cheers rather than spears. They found that the Japanese had been killed for interfering with the women, but that Constable McColl had been killed by one Dagiar from a different tribe, from Blue Mud Bay, south of Caledon Bay. When found, Dagiar too claimed that he speared the policeman when he witnessed him molesting his youngest wife. The missionaries persuaded those who confessed to killing the Japanese together with Dagiar to go to Darwin to face the trial which they were confident would acquit them. Warren returned south to a hero's welcome, while Dyer accompanied the accused to Darwin on an eleven-day voyage, during which the Aborigines frequently abandoned ship and had to be retrieved. When they landed in Darwin, the Aborigines were immediately seized by the police and clapped in irons. They were demented with terror, expecting instant execution. Dyer received hostile letters from all over Australia, denouncing him for having deceived and betrayed the Aborigines. 'These letters I took and laid on the Litany desk in Christ Church like King Hezekiah "to cast them upon the Lord".'[24] After disgraceful trials in which the accused were not even permitted to speak in their own defence, the killers of the Japanese were each sentenced to twenty years and Dagiar was sentenced to death. An appeal to the High Court, initiated by Warren, led to the quashing of all the sentences. Dagiar was released into Dyer's care, but disappeared and was never heard of again.[25]

So vociferous were the complaints about the treatment of the Aborigines following the peace expedition, that a beginning was made in changing the procedures in court cases involving Aboriginal people. At about the same time, a more significant change in governmental policies towards Aboriginal people was being mooted. It is a debated point whether this change resulted from all the publicity received from the peace expedition.[26] At the Conference of Aboriginal Authorities meeting in Canberra in 1937, it was resolved:

> That this conference believes that the destiny of the natives of Aboriginal origin, but not of the full-blood, lies in their ultimate absorption by the people of the Commonwealth, and it therefore recommends that all efforts be directed to that end.[27]

When this policy of assimilation displaced segregation, it was considered a major humanitarian breakthrough. Admittedly, to the historian 'ultimate absorption' looks like a return to the earliest policy of 'integration', and to the socially aware of today it looks like a patronising and racist policy. But it signified a major shift in understanding about the destiny of the Aboriginal people. They were no longer seen to be a dying race, but a race of survivors who were therefore to be regarded as fellow Australians, and to be treated like any other Australians. The shift in attitude was the result of the labours of such scholars as the Anglican clergyman and Professor of Anthropology at the University of Sydney, A. P. Elkin, and of some influential Aboriginal people themselves.

The missions, champions of Aboriginal 'uplift', anticipated the policy of assimilation long before it was adopted by government and they were also among the first to express dissatisfaction with it. Keith Cole, Anglican minister and foundation principal of Nungalinya, the theological training college for Aboriginal people in Darwin, labelled assimilation 'beneficent genocide'.[28] In 1959 the major Christian missions, meeting in the National Missionary Council of Australia, adopted an agreed policy on Aboriginal people, urging that all existing reserves be retained for Aboriginal use and ownership.

At the other end of the continent from Caledon Bay, the evangelical businessmen of Melbourne were strengthening the home base for a rash of evangelistic and missionary enterprises. The powerful evangelical network which had gathered in Melbourne after World War I around C. H. Nash inspired the next generation by holding before them the ideal of the lay evangelical saint. Nash was the teacher they loved to obey, they took to heart his every word, and they heard him say, 'Go and do and be likewise.' It is not difficult to imagine how they warmed to his characterisation of the true Christian, such as the following of his intimate friend, Edwin Lee Neil:

> He had the wide vision of the statesman, the judicial balance of the judge, the quick insight of the physician, the unerring dexterity of the surgeon, the practical sagacity of the man of affairs, the knowledge of human capacity of the wise teacher, the love of his fellowmen of the true spiritual pastor. And to these qualities were added an innate purity of soul and moral sensitiveness, which gave to ordinary men a sense of his 'aloofness' from all baser things, and an exquisite love of beauty and fine taste in form, colour and harmony, which made the tawdry, the shoddy and the 'make-believe' a positive torture to his being. He had no real propensity for, rather an indifference to, commerce and the daily details of the merchant's career; but as a business manager, taking long views of the trend of affairs and directing operations on scrupulously fair and sound principles, he was acknowledged and respected as a foremost authority in the business world.[29]

But if they were greatly influenced by C. H. Nash, he influenced them to be wary of the influence of others! He was a scholar and he did not throw his weight behind everything called evangelical. He was critical, for example, of anything which could be called 'Hollywood evangelism'. He taught them to be discriminating. He also taught these competent young men to be humble. At one meeting of the City Men's Bible Class, he sat with a group of young businessmen at a meal before the study began, talking about their girlfriends. To one who was very quiet, Nash asked, 'And what about you?' The response, 'I am waiting for one who is worthy of me', made Nash's lips and nose twitch before he said, 'Young man, you'll not have far to look.'[30] They were aware of his weaknesses, that he was a poor administrator, that he was unhappily married, and that he had the sort of warm-blooded temperament which may have made him prone to the temptations to which he was accused of yielding on a couple of occasions. Some of his closest friends resolved to investigate those charges fully and concluded that he had done nothing serious.[31] On the other hand that same temperament made him beloved of many because he was intensely human and was fiercely compassionate to the needy and those who suffered any injustice. He was not sinless, and he taught vigorously and effectively against sinless perfection, a current temptation among committed Protestants, as we saw in the previous chapter. He fostered obedience in mind and body to the Scriptures, but he always insisted that his disciples were not to form 'a little holy club'.

Nash's disciples formed instead a small army, drilled in the Bible, in the spiritual discipline of prayer, and in a vision for the Gospel, and at the end of World War II they readily assumed the reins of the evangelical institutions started by their forebears. Edwin Lee Neil fell off a ladder and was killed in 1934, but it was not until the 1947–48 Upwey Convention, when Dr J. J. Kitchen resigned as Chair and H. P. Smith died within hours of Kitchen's announcement, that the evangelical army knew that it was changing generals.[32] The new order included Bruce Bryson, Len Buck, Bill Clack, Alfred Coombe, Eric Daley, Ralph Davis, Alan Kerr, Ridley Kitchen, J. Harold Mc-Cracken, John Nimmo, George Pearson, Arthur Pocklington, David and Will Renshaw, John Robinson, J. Oswald Sanders, Charles Sandland, Howell Swanton, Stan Waddingham, and Keith Walker. The last, for example, one of the Brethren and chartered accountant, audited many of the interdenominational organisations in Melbourne for forty years, including the Melbourne Bible Institute, Upwey/Belgrave Heights Convention, Asia Pacific Christian Mission, Campaigners for Christ, Missionary Aviation Fellowship and a number of missionary societies, including the United Aborigines Mission. Among the clergy who came from the same generation were J. Beatty, Archdeacon Moroney, R. V. Merritt, John Renshaw, and Alf Stanway. Many of them had fathers in the first generation, for it was a movement calculated to produce evangelical dynasties. Something of the atmosphere in which they grew up is conveyed in a testimony which John Renshaw, son of David Ernest Renshaw, gave at the Melbourne Evangelical Union in 1947:

> I clearly remember how, at the age of four, my brother [David] came home from a Gospel Crusade meeting determined to convert his brothers, and so, in a room at home, he moved up the chairs and preached a very sound Gospel message. He was 10 years old and I was four. I still have the little scrap of paper on which I registered my decision to follow the Lord Jesus Christ.[33]

Nash's disciples constituted something of a male club, reflecting perhaps not only the times, but also Nash's own all-male education, and his difficulties with his wife. There was a Christian Women's Bible Class, but it never reached the heights of the men's class. Occasionally one glimpses the influence of the strong and Godly women in their lives if not in their schemes: the mother, for example, of the Renshaw brothers, or Sabina, the wife of Alfred Coombe. Something of the role of women in the lives of their husbands and sons as they struggled for faith is seen in the case of Ralph Davis, the Chair of Mayne Nickless, who was converted long before his father, Norman. Ralph[34] was converted in 1925 at the Were Street Methodist Church, Brighton, through the agency of Daniel James Draper, great-grandson of the great man of the same name. In the 1930s and 1940s Ralph's father, Norman Charles Davis, struggled to keep Mayne Nickless afloat. He spent a lot of time at clubs, and his neglected wife sought the solace of the congregation at Were Street Methodist Church. At the 1947 June Young People's Convention, John Robinson, an evangelist with Campaigners for Christ, preached on the text 2 Kings 4.26, 'Is it well with thee, is it well with thy husband, is it well with the child?' She accepted the invitation to come to the front to renew the faith she received years before at her church in Hurstville. She had suffered badly from neuralgia, but from that moment suffered no more for thirty-five years. She wrote to her husband that night about her conversion. He was in Brisbane on business. Ralph later wrote:

> I was not aware of her letter nor was she of the one I wrote to him telling him of what Mum had done. Both letters reached him two days apart. The impact of the letters plus the prayers of years for Dad was tremendous. He was nonplussed and told Mum she should not do that kind of thing without reference to him. He was made to think about himself and could not dismiss the Spirit of God moving in his heart. He was besieged by his own conscience at the memory of his failures, by the clear message of Mum's testimony, her pleas to him to follow her and the knowledge that he was in a crisis. He became unapproachable to me, whereas we were on easy terms up to that time. He did not acknowledge my letter, but talked, argued and opened his heart to Mum. But he was not easy to get on with—conviction of sin—the appeal of Christ—the sense that he was caught in a net with only one escape— his desire to keep on good terms with his friends etc. After some weeks I asked him if I could help him. He said, 'No. I am going to work this out for myself. I have tried twice before to be a Christian and I failed. I don't want to fail this time.' We (Joe, Sheila and Joan) all prayed. Mum bore the brunt of Dad's unhappiness. He did not read a newspaper for weeks on end. He came straight home and read the New Testament

constantly asking Mum what it all meant. The Lord was helping him answer his own questions—would he fail again—how can I deal with my friends—do I have to give up drink completely—Is there anything wrong with little drinks—Can I make it?

But he was already a changed man. No way could he refuse to proceed. Mother helped him more than any one could have known. They talked it all over time and time again. Finally he accepted all that it meant to follow the Lord as best he knew how and peace gradually came to him. With that peace came contact again with the family.[35]

C. H. Nash moulded all such material into a formidable force for the Gospel, made up mainly of laymen. He 'taught us a lot about leadership', said Len Buck, 'and the place of laymen in it'.[36] To his numerous disciples, he was 'The Chief'. Frequently, it was young laymen with fire in their bellies who set the agenda ahead of the clergy, who 'approved' programmes after the event. They were prepared to make public stands on matters of conscience. H. P. Smith, manager of the Federal Hotel in Melbourne, resigned when the owners obtained a liquor licence. Howell Swanton, a loss assessor in the insurance industry, did not count it too great a loss when he was fired for refusing to refrain from open-air preaching. Charles Sandland took on the Methodist Master of Queen's College in the University of Melbourne, Raynor Johnson, and won. Johnson had denied the virgin birth in a book entitled *A Religious Outlook for Modern Man* (1963). At the Methodist Conference, Sandland was comprehensively defeated, but shortly afterwards 'the back room boys got at the Master of Queen's, and he resigned'.[37]

This second generation spawned many new evangelical organisations, including Campaigners for Christ, the Christian Leaders Training College in Papua New Guinea,[38] Everyman's Welfare Service, the Missionary Aviation Fellowship,[39] Steer,[40] Prison Fellowship Australia, and the influential evangelical newspaper, *The Edifier* (now *New Life*). They also supported Melbourne branches of a host of other evangelical agencies, including those of their own denominations.[41] In 1945 the Interdenominational Missionary Fellowship was established to support missionary societies 'not substantially attached' to any denomination. When it was acknowledged that denominational missionary societies experienced many of the same problems as those in the interdenominational stream, a wider organisation was required and the Evangelical Alliance of Victoria was developed as a result. It was a plank in the platform of both societies that the evangelisation of the world was the responsibility of all believers. To belong to this Melbourne group was to take that responsibility seriously. Alan Kerr vividly recalls the interview he had with Ralph Davis in the early 1950s when Ralph told the younger businessman that he should have 'a foreign missionary interest'. Kerr protested that he was too busy, but Davis responded that he was the model for the many young people in the Scripture Union, and it was not good for them to see that he did not have a foreign missionary interest.[42] Hence they all strategised for the evangelisation of the world. Len Buck, for example, in his capacity as secretary of the Hawthorn Circuit of the Methodist Church, made an enormous contribution to Methodist missions in the Pacific.

Members of the network tended to take over from each other, thus avoiding dislocation. They took at least one society as their special responsibility, and then they served on the boards of others. They were a very tight-knit group, and the administrative structure of these evangelical agencies was identical to the interlocking directorships of the business world in which most of them were conspicuously successful. They were very determined and disciplined: it was said that you did not get far if you opposed them, and that they were very black and white. They remained true to their churches so that they were not a thorn in the flesh for their denominations. Their faithfulness to their own churches was often in the wider interests of the evangelical cause, such as the support given by the Anglicans to Ridley College. All were very big donors. 'You give away a lot of money,' C. H. Nash once observed to John Griffiths. 'As fast as I shovel it out, the Lord shovels it in,' Griffiths replied.[43] Their impact on the 1959 Billy Graham Crusade in Melbourne was enormous. They were treasurers and chairmen of the various sub-committees. Alfred Coombe was chairman of the planning committee, Ralph Davis was the crusade treasurer, while Len Buck gave great leadership in the prayer committee. They were not just lay administrators, competent as they usually were in this area. They engaged in up-front ministry, in evangelism, pastoral care and teaching. Most were open-air preachers, and some, such as Len Buck, a Methodist lay-preacher for over fifty years, were outstanding speakers. Charles Sandland was a lay-preacher for over seventy years! The achievement was great, the fruit plentiful, and the Lord seemed to smile on their endeavours. They witnessed times of revival in the mid-1930s, in 1943 at the Upwey Convention, in 1959 with the Billy Graham Crusades when the amazing Melbourne scene set the pattern for the rest of Australia, in New Guinea in 1970 and 1971 and in Borneo in 1973.

How do we explain the success of this evangelical network? They were Bible-centred, evangelistic, focused, spiritually disciplined, and able. They embodied the evangelical synthesis of Spirit, Word and world. A significant number of them were Methodists who resisted the liberalism of their denomination, whilst retaining the practical concern for a needy world and the longing both to be filled with the Holy Spirit and to experience revival. They were all consistently encouraged at the Upwey Convention to allow the Holy Spirit to control and direct their lives. They studied the Bible alone in jealously guarded 'quiet times' each day, and together they studied the Bible under the direction of a great Bible teacher. They resonated when Nash commented on Jesus' instruction to his disciples who had caught nothing in a night's fishing to 'Cast your nets out into the deep', 'If you stay in the shallows you will catch shrimps'.[44] His every aside was received with respect and stored in the memory, there to forge character. When Neville Chamberlain sold out Czechoslovakia before World War II, and Nash mentioned Great Britain, he added, 'No longer great'.[45] The evangelical army Nash produced in Melbourne testifies to the importance of a steady diet of great Bible teaching. They prayed as hard as they planned. There was not a cynical bone in any of their bodies, and they delighted to 'give a strong lead and follow a difficult one'.[46] Their positive, healthy attitudes made them confident, energetic and happy. They avoided aimlessness and wastefulness. They had a tremendous sense of strategy and of the ultimate reasons for engagement in any enterprise. They did not engage in business for its own sake, but because it gave them the means, the power, to effect great ends. It all sounds too good to be true, but theirs was the intense conspiratorial pleasure which all enjoy who band together to plot for eternity.

Acts of the Spirit

The evangelistic campaigns of the 1930s and 1940s in Australia were not the work of revivalist technicians, but of remarkable characters who aspired to be filled with the Spirit. William Booth-Clibbon, grandson of William Booth, Gavin Hamilton, Hyman Appelman, Lionel Fletcher, Oswald Smith, Garry Love, W. P. Nicholson, William 'Cairo' Bradley, J. Edwin Orr, John Robinson, Alex Gilchrist, and the Rev. Bill Watts (known as 'Hallelujah Bill') were all strongly individualistic evangelists in their style and methods. Perhaps because there was then no dominant evangelist on the world scene as there had been with Spurgeon and Moody and there was to be with Billy Graham in the 1950s, evangelists did not look to emulate human techniques as much as they looked to the Holy Spirit for success. Revivals were reported at Woombye and Toowoomba in Queensland, at Kingscliff in northern New South Wales, at Nhill in Victoria, and again in the mining communities of South Australia. Among those converted in these revivals were future Aboriginal pastors, Rodney Minniecon and Peter Morgan. Minniecon claims to have been involved in a dozen revivals since. Morgan's experience is further evidence that the evangelical movement in Australia has long witnessed phenomena consistent with full-blown pentecostalism. In a sermon in 1993 he testified:

> I come from the Atherton tablelands. Where I come from, revival broke out in 1934 so it's a long time. 1934. Now the Holy Ghost fell upon our people and they were drunk for weeks. They couldn't go to the shops to the supermarket otherwise they speak in tongues. They were drunk, they were drunk, you would think they were under the influence, but they were drunk in the Spirit, and they couldn't speak a word for weeks in English. They spoke in tongues.
>
> So I came from that background. I came into that experience in 1949 and I was never the same again. I was so hungry after the Spirit. You ever get hungry? You eat and eat and eat until you're full. Now, it's the same way with the Spirit. Now when I have received ... I wanted more. So, I said, 'Lord, I want more. You said there is more, there is rivers to swim in.' See. Ezekiel[47] saw the flow of the Spirit. He saw there's rivers to swim in. So if you only paddling round on the shores, walking round on the beach, there's rivers to swim in ... My cousin who came through this revival in 1934, I said to him, 'Your face is shining.' He says, 'Yeah.' He says, 'I know that.'[48]

Meanwhile, the influence of a revival which began in 1933 in Gahini, in the Rwanda CMS mission, was to be felt throughout the evangelical world. The East Africa Revival resulted in the outflanking of Islam in Africa and in much constructive nation-building in the post-colonial era in the 1950s and 1960s. Australian Christianity was significantly influenced by this revival, chiefly through three instruments: CMS missionaries in East Africa and Australian church leaders, such as Marcus Loane, took news of the revival back to Australia with them; African pastors, such as Festo Kivengere, visited Australia and spoke at conventions; and the revival produced a great classic of evangelical spirituality, namely Roy Hession's *Calvary Road*, which was widely read and faithfully followed. The principle of this revival was the importance of 'walking in the light', of being open with one another, of mutual confession. Its theme text was 1 John 1.7: 'If we walk in the light, as he is in the light, we have fellowship one with another, and the blood of Jesus Christ cleanseth us from all sin.'

Among those influenced by the East African revival in Australia was the Rev. Geoff Bingham, who had been a prisoner of war in World War II. In Bingham the evangelical synthesis of Spirit, Word and world was powerfully exemplified. He discussed the East Africa Revival with Marcus Loane and others, and thought long on the power of Christ's blood. He reflected on the foundation premise of Keswick theology, that the believer is 'crucified with Christ' (Galatians 2.20). He saw that the centrality of the cross was not to be understood in any cultic sense, but in a personal sense. At the same time he read the works of Andrew Murray (1828–1917) who infused the Reformed faith with the pietism of the Evangelical Revival. He also studied Walter Marshall's *The Gospel Mystery of Sanctification* (1692) and discussed it with T. C. Hammond who declared that it was 'spot on', and *Born Crucified* (1945) written by L. E. Maxwell, an American fundamentalist. From these he concluded that the Gospel promised more than the forgiveness of sins. It offered transformation through being crucified with Christ. Through the cross, guilt is destroyed, and through the destruction of guilt, the power of sin is destroyed. Living in the freedom which results from the destruction of the penalty and power of sin is the holy life. This resulted in 'a very personal living experience of the holiness of God' which expressed itself in extraordinary prayerfulness:

> What happened then, regularly, week in week out, was that I couldn't go to bed before midnight or even one or two o'clock in the morning, then I'd sleep for a couple of hours and then I'd be up and into the Word and prayer; the whole thing was quite incredible, really.[49]

Each Sunday, Bingham packed out Holy Trinity, Miller's Point, where he was minister. With a number of his fellow ministers he held all-night prayer meetings, which just 'went like a flash'. He then went to Pakistan as a missionary, because he saw that his new experience of the holiness of God had global significance. Indeed, it had cosmic significance, and in Pakistan he developed his understanding of Christ as the Lord of history. Remarkable scenes of revival accompanied his ministry in Pakistan.

Nourished by the experience of its missionaries in the East African and Pakistan revivals, a number of Sydney clergy followed Bingham's lead and forged a unity of Keswick-inspired spirituality with Reformed theology. From this highly combustible compound, the fires of revival began to smoulder in a number of Sydney parishes. Parish missions were more than usually fruitful. Two laymen, subsequently clergy, Ray Wheeler and Dudley Foord, held a mission at St John's, East Willoughby. 'It was the closest I ever came to witnessing a revival,' Wheeler recalled. 'Many were under conviction long after the mission was over.'[50] The 1955 Katoomba Christian Convention was addressed by Harold Whitney, the Presbyterian evangelist who attempted to swing his denomination behind Billy Graham. So unprecedented were the manifestations of prayerfulness and conviction of sin at that convention that a number of Sydney Anglican clergy attribute to it their calling to the ministry.[51] Attendances at churches grew, sometimes remarkably; the membership of the mainstream churches generally rose throughout Australia in the 1950s and peaked in the next decade.[52] There were probably more large congregations in Australia in the 1950s than at any other time in our history. Sunday schools in the 1950s were huge: it was before TV or Sunday sport. Some very fine church buildings were erected in Australia in the 1950s, including chapels at Barker, Trinity and Knox grammar schools in Sydney. These fine non-utilitarian buildings signify that at least some Australians aspired to the transcendental and to the beauty of holiness.

In Melbourne Anglicanism in the 1950s, only the CMS League of Youth seemed to exhibit the spiritual vitality evident more generally in Sydney. In the late 1950s and 1960s there was a strong anticlerical feeling in the League of Youth,[53] and as the main clerical brotherhood in Melbourne Anglicanism was then Anglo-Catholic, evangelical clergy seemed to keep to themselves, nervous of being labelled 'party men'. Frank Woods, Archbishop of Melbourne from 1957 to 1977, endeavoured to break down the isolation of parties by the doubtful means of placing evangelical curates with Anglo-Catholic incumbents. As a result, in the forty years following 1950, over sixty of Melbourne's parishes changed their churchmanship from evangelical to liberal Catholic.[54] The sending of a number of Sydney clerics to Melbourne—H. M. Arrowsmith to Toorak in 1945, followed by Thomas Gee, Leon Morris, and S. B. Babbage—did not stem the tide.

Beginning in 1953, the Methodists, headed by Alan Walker, conducted their Mission to the Nation.[55] Alan Walker's Gospel was socially aware and intellectually respectable, but it was not the great departure in Christian history for which many Methodists hoped. A subtle twist was coming into the desire of the churches—now the aim was 'to *keep* Australia Christian'. Nevertheless, the Mission to the Nation was a mark of the vigour of post-World War II Methodism, which, as was evident from the 1947 census, had become the third-largest denomination in Australia, behind the Anglicans and the Catholics and ahead of the Presbyterians. In 1958 Alan Walker became superintendent of the Sydney Central Methodist Mission. He fearlessly denounced social evils and unhesitatingly embroiled himself in politics if needed. It was not the 'social gospel' so much as the 'whole Gospel'. This has been described as the

> combination of the traditional spiritual life of the church (expressed through worship, prayer and evangelism) with Christian humanitarianism in such a way that the philanthropic activity is seen to be the logical outpouring of the church's inner life.[56]

The marks of spiritual vitality were not observable only in Protestant churches in the 1950s. The study of Catholic popular piety reveals a similar increase in religious devotion. A remarkable flowering of devotion to the Virgin Mary was prompted by the centenary of the promulgation of the dogma of the immaculate conception in 1854. There were Marian conferences and huge rallies: Marian processions attracted tens of thousands of Catholics in the capital cities. In 1953 the World Rosary Crusade arrived in Australia, headed by Father Patrick Peyton with his famous slogan, 'the family that prays together stays together'. During this period, Corpus Christi processions of 100,000 were not unknown.

Such spiritual energy threatened to have political implications, and Catholics have not been as reluctant as Protestants to seek to take the world by political processes. In Queensland, where the Catholics, under Archbishop Duhig, were both more conspicuous and better organised than the Protestants, the majority voted in the September 1951 referendum to ban the Communist Party, one of only three states to do so.

In Melbourne in 1941 the National Secretariat of Catholic Action established the Catholic Social Studies Movement, popularly known as 'the Movement'. Headed by B. A. Santamaria with the blessing of Archbishop Mannix, the Movement concentrated on gathering cells of interested Catholics to discuss important social issues in the light of Catholic social theory. This rejected both the atheism of socialism, and the greed of capitalism, and called for a third way of relating labour and capital through a corporate ethic of social and interpersonal responsibility. By organising through the Industrial Groups, the Movement came to control the Victorian State Labor Party, and to a position of near control in other states. At the initiative of H. V. Evatt, the Federal Labor Executive announced its intention to dissolve the Victorian Executive and to inquire into the activities of external organisations which sought control of the party for their own ends. The Industrial Groupers withdrew and in 1957 formed their own party, the Democratic Labor Party (DLP), which garnered enough support to split the Labor vote and to deny the Labor Party office for some two decades. The long post-war boom and the attendant upward social mobility during this period had broken the traditional nexus between Catholicism and labour and this provided the DLP with a base of voters. The DLP thus also acted as a bridge between yesterday's Catholics who 'always voted Labor' and today's Catholics, who often vote Liberal.

In retrospect the 1950s, the decade of equipoise, was really a bridge to the globalisation of culture which was to be the inevitable result of a war which had all but destroyed the old world. The 'drift towards America' and increasing ease of travel made it possible for American religious influences to have an increased impact on Australia. The state in Australia began to step away from its tacit support of mainstream denominations, in particular loosening Anglicanism's hold on public culture. The truth was that the post-war Australian way of life was becoming inevitably less British, and even less fundamentally Christian. With the undermining of establishment Christianity, the way was opened for forms of Christian faith more suited to a fragmenting, pluralistic, post-modernist society, especially the Charismatic movement. The Spirit and the Word, whom God had put together, were to be put asunder violently by the next generation.

7. The Evangelical Synthesis Attained: Billy Graham in Australia, 1959

The founders of modern evangelicalism were George Whitefield, Jonathan Edwards, and John Wesley. Their ministries were accompanied by scenes of revival which, particularly in the 1740s, greatly surprised even them. Multitudes came to a personal experience of the risen Christ in the power of the Spirit. Evangelicalism cannot rise higher than its source, and when the dimension of revival drops out of the thought and experience of Christians they have allowed themselves to devolve into something less than evangelicals. The best-known evangelical in the twentieth century, Billy Graham, understands that clearly. He longs in his evangelistic campaigns not only to bring many to faith in Christ, but to see whole communities concerned with the things of God, and national practices and institutions transformed by Gospel values. Never before and never since the 1959 Billy Graham Crusades[1] in Australia's capital cities have Australians been so concerned with the Christian religion. The crusades were the most effective engagement with the Australian community ever achieved by evangelicals in Australia. Evangelicals were then almost totally united behind the crusades, and there was very little opposition even by non-evangelicals. Here was the most conspicuous expression of the evangelical synthesis of Spirit, Word and world in Australia's history. Did Australia experience genuine revival in 1959 as Billy himself prayed that it would be?

Billy Graham himself was far more reluctant to claim that revival had accompanied the crusades than he had been to encourage people to pray for it before the crusades. He said you cannot judge the real results of a crusade until thirty years later.[2] Now is the time to attempt such an assessment. Many who participated did not consider that revival came. Gordon Powell, then the most prominent Presbyterian minister in Australia, said six months after the Sydney crusade, 'I haven't any doubt in my own mind that revival is coming.'[3] He was never prepared to say that it had come. Anglican Archbishop Marcus Loane, at the twenty-fifth anniversary of the Australian crusades, said 'For a short while during those four weeks in 1959, Sydney seemed to stand on the edge of an authentic revival.'[4] He has nowhere said that it went over the edge.

The crusades did not look like the authentic revivals of the past. There does not appear to have been any generalised conviction of sin as evidenced by the mass weeping which characterised some earlier revivals. Graham does not appear to have had the emotional impact of Edwards, Whitefield, or Wesley. Harold Whitney, the Presbyterian evangelist, whom we met in chapter 6, toured Britain and America in 1956 'to assess Revival potential',[5] and doubted that Graham had the potential: 'Frankly my reaction was unfavourable. ... I could not see why the people responded ... Night after night people came forward without undue pressure.'[6] For some then, Graham's crusades were too unemotional to be revivals. Others, such as the prominent English preacher, Martyn Lloyd-Jones, declared that organised campaigns are just not compatible with revival: 'As long as you go on organising, people will not fall on their knees and implore God to come and heal them.'[7]

Let us look at these two objections. Observers at his meetings monotonously remark on the surprising atmosphere—not overt emotion, but a deep hush and remarkable concentration on the preacher's message from people of all ages. What were they thinking as they concentrated? So frequently are we told of the entire absence of fear-inducing techniques by Graham that it is surprising to learn that fear was felt in those quiet, engrossed hearers. As one convert said, Graham 'frightened me because I had heard nothing like it ever before,'[8] Another reported:

> I shall never forget it. Mr. Graham had preached on Noah, and I shook as he said, 'And God shut the door!' ... When the appeal was given for people to come forward I just stood there resolved that I could never do that ... But as the crowds moved to the front, Billy kept repeating Ephesians 2.8, 9 'For by grace ...'. Almost imperceptibly ... it dawned on me ... Salvation was something God gave me. It was as though I was let out of a box. I was free. I wanted to run, and I did.[9]

Graham's own understanding was that such convictions came from God's Spirit and not from crowd suggestion. Counsellors were advised,

> Without any attempt to stir people emotionally, and without using human pressure to bring people to a decision, [the evangelist] will

invite all of those in whose heart the Holy Spirit has been working to come to the front for further counsel and prayer.[10]

Graham endorsed the teaching of Jonathan Edwards, the church's chief theologian of revival, that the work of the Spirit 'is not to be judged of by any effects on the bodies of men; such as tears, trembling, groans, loud outcries, agonies of body, or the failing of bodily strength'.[11]

Opposition to Graham was often grounded in the fear that organisation quenched the Spirit, and even by American standards it must be admitted that the Billy Graham Evangelistic Association was organised. The association developed 'an intricate technology of soul-saving'[12] on the philosophy that 'You can't get anywhere with any kind of business these days without organisation.'[13] A Billy Graham Crusade was a mammoth feat of organisation run according to military-like standard operational procedures (SOPs). The process was very masculine. Of all the twelve committees, only the prayer committee was required to have a lady vice-Chair. The team, comprising primarily business associates, knew how to enjoy themselves with men. For example on 30 May 1959 Grady Wilson, associate to Billy Graham, wrote to an executive of the Chrysler Corporation, thanking him for taking the team hunting: 'The kangaroo hunt was tops ... Every member of the team got a kangaroo.'[14]

But is all this organisation incompatible with prayer and revival? Pollock, Graham's biographer, claims that the basic facts of organisation were taught the team by Willis Haymaker, a veteran who had organised crusades for many evangelists between the wars. He attached primacy to prayer, emphasising that the secret of revival was to get thousands to pray. Graham urged his workers on with the vision that the Australian crusade could be 'one of the largest Protestant meetings in the history of the Christian church. What a tremendous witness for Christ it would be throughout the world.'[15] Surveying the enormous crowd, the largest in Melbourne Cricket Ground history[16] and the largest he had ever addressed, Graham said 'This is the Lord's doing, and it's marvellous in our eyes ... This crowd is due to the work of the churches of Victoria ... to hunger and to the sovereign move of God.'[17] Graham was inspired by John Eliot, missionary to the American Indians, who spoke of prayer *and pains*. Efficient bureaucracy is not incompatible with revival. The emphasis is not on the pains at the expense of the prayer. It was all the prayer that gave Graham all the confidence. His appeal at the first meeting in Melbourne included the words: 'You cannot come to Christ any-time you want to. You can only come when the Spirit draws you. Millions have been praying. You'd better come now.'[18] We cannot, therefore, rule out the possibility of revival on the *a priori* grounds that it was too organised.

Revival Defined

Before determining whether or not the Billy Graham Crusades in Australia were accompanied by revival, it is necessary to define revival.[19] This is not an easy task. Neither Christians in general, nor theologians or historians in particular, agree on a definition. Revival is such a historical phenomenon that historians seem to be incapable of defining it without also commenting on its cause. What causes revivals? They are sovereign outpourings of the Holy Spirit sent from heaven; they are 'merely the routine activities of evan-gelists enthusiastically in pursuit of souls';[20] they are caused by the business cycle and social and natural disasters;[21] they are interludes of hysteria attrib-utable to psychic insecurities;[22] they are attempts to resolve anxiety, includ-ing the sexual tension of the young.[23] My own definition is also based on my understanding of its cause:

> Revival in the Christian tradition is a sovereign work of God which consists of a powerful intensification of the ordinary work of the Holy Spirit in convicting, converting and regenerating sinners, poured out upon large numbers of people at the same time, and is therefore a community experience. It is occasionally preceded by an expectation that God is about to do something exceptional; it is usually preceded by an extraordinary unity and prayerfulness among Christians; and it is always accompanied by the revitalisation of the Church, the conver-sion of large numbers of unbelievers, and the diminution of sinful practices in the community.

This definition calls for a theological understanding of revival, but allows for historical analysis of revivals in terms of the six antecedent and accompany-ing characteristics. The theological understanding is conveyed in the first sentence of the definition. As a Christian I can believe that revival is a work of God. As an evangelical Calvinist I can believe that it is a sovereign work of the Spirit of God which consists of the conviction, conversion, and rebirth of sinners. But as a historian I have to find evidence of those things in the lives of human beings. The phenomenon of revivals throughout history appears to have been generally associated with six forms of human behaviour which the historian can identify from evidence: they are longed for; they draw Christians together in unprecedented unity; they are born of ardent prayerfulness; they renew the Church; they convert many sinners; they restrain sinful social behaviour.

There will be some who object that this definition is too spiritual for a historian to use, and there are many mundane factors to account for Graham's unprecedented success: the superb organisation; the higher proportion of Protestants or churchgoers in Sydney and Melbourne compared to New York or London; the concentration of the population in a few, easily reached cities; the relative lack of deep-seated divisions between Australian Protestants; and the openness of post-war Australia to things American.[24] But why must the historian's attention be confined to these mundane factors? If there were such a historical phenomenon as revival and if it had occurred in Australia, these mundane causes would not be sufficient to establish it, because they are specific to Australia and cannot account for the revivals in other countries in other ages. This chapter explores, with reference to the 1959 Billy Graham Crusades, each of the six factors in my definition, with a view to establishing whether or not the phenomenon identified as revival in other places at other times occurred in Australia in 1959.

1. The Expectation of Revival

A deep longing for, and expectation of, revival developed strongly in Australia in the 1950s. True, there was still room for doubt about city-wide campaigns in the tradition of American revivalism. In 1956 'Oral Roberts had come to Melbourne with the largest tent in the world only to have it pulled down ignominiously around his ears.'[25] In spite of this setback, as has been shown in the previous chapter, the 1950s was a decade of unusually successful university, parish, and denominational evangelistic missions, while at the annual conventions, too, the spiritual temperature rose. A desire for, if not expectation of, revival of sorts was nurtured, too, by those, numerous at Moore Theological College in Sydney in the 1950s, who were strongly interested in eschatology[26] and who sought holiness within the second blessing, entire sanctification, sinless perfection tradition.[27] Graham did not do a lot to foster this understanding of revival, his being an altogether more robust, wholesome, happy, outgoing expression of the Christian faith.[28] His expectation of revival was centred neither in eschatology nor in sinless perfection, but in human need and its remedy, the cross.

While he often preached on the second coming, and still writes on Armageddon, anyone who organises like Graham and cultivates friendships as he does, expects to be around for a while. A Billy Graham Crusade is not a convention for the deepening of the spiritual life. I dare say it is not revivalism. With its addressing of current issues, it is closer to the optimistic postmillennialism of Jonathan Edwards in the eighteenth century and Howard Mowll in the twentieth. It is addressed to the world, not some spiritual elite. Still, Moore College students of the 1950s, before the theological revolution promoted by Knox and Robinson,[29] talked revival, even if it was not exactly what Graham had in mind.[30]

The rather modest campaign that the Graham team had in mind[31] did not anticipate that the Australian crusades would follow the trajectory of his previous crusades, especially New York (1957), where Cliff Barrows exclaimed as he surveyed the 125,000-strong crowd: 'We cannot see the end of the crowd ... spiritual hunger draws people together like this ... let us tell the world that we Americans believe in God'.[32] The team's preliminary research suggested that the Australian campaign would be small because the population was scattered and Australians had a reputation for being sports-loving, prosperous, and hitherto resistant to evangelists.[33] The preliminary report made for the Sydney crusade was 'based on the assumption, somewhat arbitrary, of an upper limit of 7,500 decisions over a 9-day crusade'. In the event, all the projections were surpassed. The number of inquirers was eight times that early projection. The cost of the follow-up operation was put at £2750. The actual expenditure was £21,818. The finance committee who had to allow ten shillings for every inquirer was advised that a two-week crusade would be expected to result in not less than 3000 commitments to Christ.[34] The response rate was double that. Team director Jerry Beavan expected that 2500–3000 counsellors would be needed. By the end of January, Canon H. M. Arrowsmith reported that 8000 had enrolled in Sydney. The Federal Executive produced material for 20,000 decisions, but that was to prove one-third of Sydney's requirements alone. If expectations were high before the crusades began, they were not high enough.

That something special was afoot, however, was perceived by Jerry Bea-van, Australian crusades team director, whom Graham later concluded had done his best work in Australia.[35] 'Bill,' he wrote in August 1958,

> I really believe that we are on the verge of a national spiritual awaken-ing here in Australia ... There are so many evidences that God is doing an unusual thing that we are constantly overwhelmed by his blessing ... There is more prayer right now in Sydney than there was in New York City at the height of that crusade.[36]

Motivating Christians to pray and work for revival was built in to every Billy Graham Crusade. On 27 October 1958 a luncheon was held in the Melbourne Town Hall to announce the Billy Graham Crusade. The pro-gramme sported a special picture of Graham with a one-page biography, ending with the words, 'The Goal ... The Prayer: Revival in our Time!' Gra-ham encouraged his readers:

> There is a great deal you can do. First, if you have not done so, make an open confession of Christ, and a definite decision for Christ. Join a church, and put your time, your talents and your money at God's dis-posal. Begin to live a positive, whole-hearted Christian life, witnessing to others of your faith in Christ. Pray earnestly for a revival in your church, your community and your nation.
>
> Read and believe the promise of God in Isaiah 57.15.[37] Remember that God is the author of renewal.

A dodger entitled 'Hear Billy Graham in Melbourne' has a message from Billy Graham on the back:

> 'We need ... we must have REVIVAL'
> says Billy Graham
> Thinking men in every walk of life are agreed that our civilisation ... our way of life ... has little hope for survival on a local, national or international level unless we see, and soon, a return to God ... to the faith of our fathers.

Graham's concern for the regeneration of the nation did not go unno-ticed or unappreciated by the national press. The Melbourne *Age* reported:

> The most significant and arresting feature of the evangelistic crusade ... is the obvious fact that ... it has demonstrated a passionate desire

on the part of widely differing sections of the community for a revival
of true religion comparable with the great revivals of history.[38]

In 1956 Canon Loane, then principal of Moore College, predicted revival
was coming to Australia,[39] but the success of the 1959 crusades still took
everybody by surprise.

2. Unprecedented Unity

The sociologists of religion tell us that it is normally sects, not churches,
which are conversionist. Conversion work and revival are most frequently
found among the sects, and while there have probably been hundreds of 'little revivings' in Australian history they go unreported because of disinterest
and because they are sectarian, not mainstream. By 1959 Graham had already turned his back on the sectarianism of fundamentalism. He was not
concerned to dwell on what divides Christians, convinced that in church
history 'the great divisions have always resulted from somewhat minor differences'.[40] He was building the 'new evangelicalism' which favoured inclusive evangelism. In the interests of evangelistic success, Graham's ecumenical pragmatism drove him towards the harnessing of the support of all the
clergy, rather than offend any of them. He did not just clean up the reputation of revivalism, by insisting on calling his campaigns crusades instead of
revivals, and by taking steps to ensure that he would not succumb to the
three great temptations assaulting revivalists—sex, money, inflated statistics—but he adapted evangelism to the churches instead of making it the
scourge of the church as it had been in the hands of the old-time revivalists.
Revivalism had divided the churches. Billy's crusades united them.

The Australian crusades marked the beginning of the near unanimous
support for his crusades by the major Protestant organisations, though some
smaller groups were not included.[41] The Sydney churches elected to exclude
the Assemblies of God for 'local considerations', while the Melbourne executive decided to accept them in the choir, counselling, and ushering.[42] The
South Australian and Queensland committees followed the New South
Wales example in disallowing involvement to groups not represented in the
invitation to Graham.[43] One evangelical group who elected not to support
Billy Graham in 1959 was the Australian Fellowship of Independent Evangelical Churches Association. While the Wesleyan Methodists co-operated
with the crusades, the other churches in the group stood by the American

fundamentalism of Carl McIntire and voted against co-operation with Graham.[44] It was a tiny antipodean flick from a large American tail.

The process by which the formal invitations to invite Graham to Australia were developed has been well documented by Loane.[45] What must be added to this picture is all the humbler invitations which Graham received from visitors to America, such as evangelist Harold Whitney,[46] and layman Alan Kerr (who invited Graham to Australia on behalf of Campaigners for Christ, only to be told that he would have to do better than that).[47] Graham's evangelistic ecumenism went beyond evangelical ecumenism, frequently reclaiming for evangelicalism clergy who, like the best-known Methodist minister of the day, Alan Walker, had hitherto avoided an unequivocal identification. Walker had once described a Billy Graham Crusade as 'nineteenth-century evangelism in a twentieth-century world'.[48] On 24 October 1958, the self-confident Walker attempted to stop the holding of crusade meetings on Sunday afternoons as it would conflict with church activities. The advisory committee unanimously recommended the holding of meetings on Sunday afternoons, and Walker withdrew his motion under protest.[49]

The Presbyterian Gordon Powell was the archetypal minister whom Graham delights to get on side with the promise of mutual benefit. Powell is Australia's answer to positive thinker, Norman Vincent Peale and 'a Man called Peter', having preached eighteen times in Peale's church, Marble Collegiate, and once in Peter Marshall's church in the presence of George Bush. A soft evangelical, Powell agreed with a colleague at St Stephen's, Sydney, that 'you don't have to take the Bible literally, but you do have to take it seriously'. Yet Powell's preaching was always based on the Bible. Like Peale, he wrote popular books to make one feel good and positive. In 1959 Powell was vice-Chair of the Sydney Billy Graham Crusade executive committee. St Stephen's received 646 referrals from the Sydney crusade, at that time a world record. A total of 404 new members were added to the church roll.[50] Graham liked people such as Powell and would not have been distressed to learn that Powell was a rank modalist in his understanding of the Trinity.

A critical aspect of Graham's sensitivity to ecclesiastical traditions was his remarkable appreciation of the importance of the Anglican Church. He did not win all Anglicans. One bishop (E. H. Burgmann of Canberra and Goulburn) said that Graham's view of the Bible was 'idolatrous',[51] while another (T. B. McCall of Rockhampton) wrote in his diocesan magazine that aspects of the Graham crusades were 'objectionable, dishonest, distressing, and disgusting'.[52] But Graham's growing friendship with a number of senior Anglican clergy—R. C. Kerle, Marcus Loane, Archie Morton, Leon Morris, S. B. Babbage, Archdeacon Arrowsmith—goes a long way towards explaining the success of the Australian crusades. In an address at the Myer Music Bowl on the text from John 3, 'Have you been born again', Graham said Nicodemus was the sort of person who might be a bishop today—then he added 'Perhaps not here in Australia, but in America'.[53] It was an interesting aside, showing how highly he rated Sydney Anglican bishops. At the last meeting of the Sydney crusade, Graham waxed lyrical on the Sydney clergy. Seldom had he seen 'a city before where one man was so loved by so many from all walks of life as the late Archbishop Mowll', nor a city where the calibre of the clergy has been so high, so devout, so spiritual, so evangelical as in the City of Sydney.[54] The success of the Melbourne crusade was critical to the even greater success of Sydney. Led more by the laity than Sydney's clerical evangelicalism, Melbourne had wider lay experience in evangelistic enterprise and was thus well-placed to initiate the grand campaign. Sydney had more strength to carry the battle higher and further. So the crusades were preceded and accompanied by extraordinary interchurch unity and, as Bishop Kerle observed, left behind 'a memory of what God can do when His people are fully involved in a city and nation-wide campaign of evangelism'.[55]

But even this was not the limit of Graham's ecumenism. He sought and succeeded in obtaining the assistance of the secular arm.[56] Graham brought with him to Australia a letter from Richard Nixon, requesting William Sebald, the American ambassador, to give any assistance that the members of his staff might be able to provide: 'Certainly,' he concluded, 'it would be most difficult to find people who were more friendly in their attitude toward the United States than the Australians.'[57] At the last meeting in Melbourne, Graham read a letter from President Eisenhower, and just a month later he was in London, taking tea with the Queen. What was so special about Billy Graham, demanded the *Daily Herald* that he should be accorded such 'an unusual public honour'? The *Herald* concluded that 'the evangelist's barnstorming, fast-talking, massed-choir approach certainly had royal interest—and possibly royal approval'.[58] The press, too, were united in their praise of the handsome young evangelist, giving 'unprecedented recognition with not one unfriendly voice'.[59] Historian Ken Inglis observed that the newspapers were among the first converts.[60] Graham thought it 'a thrilling ... and a wonderful thing when the newspapers make religion front page copy almost every day'.[61] Unprecedented unity, not only between Christians, but also between secular authorities and the churches, preceded and accompanied the Australian crusades.

3. Extraordinary Prayerfulness

Frequently great revivals have been preceded by a spirit of extraordinary prayer. In the *Crusade Bulletin* for October 1958, Graham wrote, 'If spiritual awakening comes to Australia, it will not be as a result of organisation, publicity, preaching or singing. It will come as a result of prayer on the part of Christians all over the world.' He believed 'that more prayer has been made for the Melbourne and Sydney crusades than for any single event in the whole history of the Christian Church.'[62] The Billy Graham Crusades of 1959 were great prayer offensives. There is more than lip-service in the directive that 'The most vital of all is the Prayer Committee ... [The] personnel for this committee ... should be your most spiritual people.' Hence, Leonard Buck, a prominent Melbourne businessman, whom we met in the previous chapter, who had given decades of service to a wide range of evangelical missions and evangelistic organisations, and who, in 1989, was to be granted the Order of Australia, was chosen to chair the Melbourne crusade prayer committee. He took as the key verse for the united prayer programme the great revival text 2 Chronicles 7.14: 'If my people, which are called by my name, shall humble themselves, and pray, and seek my face, and turn from their wicked ways; then will I hear from heaven, and forgive their sin, and will heal their land.' The purpose of the prayer programme was 'To have the people of the Melbourne Area become "revival conscious"', to become 'aware of their spiritual need' so that the Holy Spirit might come 'in mighty convicting and converting power'. People were to pray 'for a heaven-sent revival'.[63] The participants in the Prayer Partnership scheme were exhorted to pray for 'the greatest moving of the Spirit of God it has ever known ... [to] pray for Revival in Our Time!' On 1 July 1958 there were 48 prayer partners; by April 1959, there were some 40,000. This 'vital National Prayer Offensive' was launched at an all-night of prayer in five centres in Melbourne on 21 September 1958. At least sixteen churches in Sydney and twenty in the country joined in. Each hour focused on a particular need: for 'heart searching and revival among the people of God, beginning with we who pray'; for the 'country areas of Victoria'; for 'a mighty awakening among college and school children, High School and University students'. One leader commented, 'never have I seen such spontaneity in prayer … There was a very evident leading of the Spirit of God throughout.' If the prayers offered for the Melbourne crusade were prodigious both in volume and in zeal, they were exceeded by those offered for the Sydney crusade. The opening of the Sydney crusade was something 'in the nature of a spiritual explosion'.[64] By 10 April the evening of prayer had to be held in fifty-one centres.

An interesting indication of the Billy Graham team's ability to think of everything and everybody is found in this area of prayer. Pasted into the Melbourne Crusade Procedure Book in the section devoted to prayer are two pamphlets. One is a united prayer programme, which opens with 'A sure way to have a revival' by Dr R. A. Torrey, which shows that Graham endorsed this aspect of his revivalist tradition. The second pamphlet is entitled *The Victory of the Veterans*. It was written by Dr F. W. Boreham, OBE. It begins with the words: 'In the course of a very long life I have often heard God speak to the multitude through the lips of an outstanding evangelist.' Boreham was born in 1871 in England, had heard and been taught by Spurgeon, had served as an usher in D. L. Moody's great London crusade, and had achieved an international reputation as author of a series of 125 sermons on 'texts that made history'. Published in five volumes between 1920 and 1928, it has been described as 'one of the most famous series of sermons in the history of preaching and certainly one of the most original'.[65] Having mentioned Spurgeon and Torrey, Boreham continues in his pamphlet:

> And now Dr. Billy Graham is coming; but I shall not be there. The poignancy of my regret is shared by an immense number of old and frail folk and sick folk who must needs be content with watching the dynamic movement from a distance.

The pamphlet encouraged prayer by all those who could not get to the crusade meetings through incapacity, for that was where the battle would be fought and won. Just eight days after the glorious climax to the Sydney crusade, Boreham was called to his reward. Graham was at pains to recruit the help of all such warriors.

4. The Church is Revitalised

In genuine revivals, churches are revitalised and strengthened. Four measurable indicators of the church's revitalisation may be offered: increased numbers of churchgoers, theological students, missionaries, and members of the Scripture Union.

Evidence abounds of increased membership of individual churches after the crusades. Lance Shilton, for example, Rector of Holy Trinity Adelaide,[66] wrote to Graham in 1962, indicating that 'where there is sympathetic and sincere follow-up by the Church to whom they are referred, the majority (75 per cent) go on to spiritual maturity'.[67] Of Gordon Powell's world record 646 inquirers, 404 became church members. Two years later a survey revealed that 52 per cent had not missed a communion, 24 per cent had missed a few, and 24 per cent appear to have dropped out.[68] The percentage of survivors (76 per cent) is remarkably similar to Shilton's experience. The task of the historian, however, is to be more quantitative. Did church membership rise in Australia after the crusades? Readily available statistics give us figures only for 1956 and 1961. They do show a higher than expected increase between those years. Both Anglican and Presbyterian figures reveal a healthy increase between 1961 and 1966, suggesting perhaps that the crusades had fostered a capacity for evangelism in those denominations. The Methodists, however, peaked in 1961.[69]

We might suspect that if any denomination would benefit from Billy Graham's visit it would be the Baptists. Graham himself is a Baptist, and Baptists traditionally are enthusiastic about evangelistic campaigns to increase membership. Further, while the proportion of decisions at the crusade approximated to the denominational strength in the wider population of the other denominations, the Baptist percentage of decisions was five times higher than the population average.[70] With about 2 per cent of the population, the Baptists scored 11.6 per cent of the decisions, exactly the same percentage as the Presbyterians who had 10.7 per cent of the population.[71] The Baptists also supplied nearly 30 per cent of counsellors for the Sydney crusade.[72] The unpublished research of Dr Edward Gibson, onetime president-general of the Baptist Union, shows that up to 1953 a decrease in membership was as likely for Baptist churches as an increase, and that the percentage increase picked up in 1956, peaked in 1959 and 1962, then went into decline until the mid-1970s. The clear conclusion we must draw from this is that the Billy Graham Crusades did not initiate the improvement in the denomination's membership; it appears, however, to have enabled it to grow even more rapidly in 1959 and to reach its highest rate of growth in 1962. The 1959 crusades, then, were a very effective form of harvesting and an effective, but short-term, means of church growth.

Numbers of theological students and missionaries increased even more dramatically in response to the crusades. In 1969 the Adelaide Bible Institute had a student body of 118, 25 per cent of whom were there because of the 1959 crusades.[73] More than half of Melbourne Bible Institute's 160 students in 1969 were products of 1959. The first-year intake of 44 at Moore College in Sydney in 1960 was the largest in its history, and the 1961 total enrolment of 104 students was the peak enrolment before recent years.[74] Deaconess House in Sydney also enjoyed record enrolments just after the crusade, peaking at 62 theological students. In 1961 Deaconess Mary Andrews surveyed the students about the impact of the crusade. Every student said she had either been involved in it or converted at it, even an Indian student from Kerala who had participated in Graham's 1956 campaign in India![75] Missionary training received a similar boost. A great number of people who came forward for CMS service were converted at the 1959 Billy Graham Crusades.[76] Jack Dain, federal secretary of CMS, 1959–65, notes that 'Over my years in CMS there was never a single course of candidates among whom there were not Graham converts.'[77]

The crusades' impact on Bible reading was probably enormous. Scripture Union membership in Australia leaped from 58,000 in March 1958 to 104,400 in November 1959,[78] due not only to the crusades, but to two Scripture Union weeks which were designed to reinforce them. In the weeks which followed the Sydney crusade, it is reported that 183 Bible-study groups were established in the central business district of the city. One of them—led by the Rev. Arthur Deane—lasted for a decade.[79]

5. Large Numbers Are Converted

In genuine revivals of religion, large numbers of the hitherto unconverted are brought to faith in Christ. The 1959 Southern Cross Crusade took in Australia and New Zealand. During its fifteen weeks, nearly 3.25 million people, or one-quarter of the entire population of Australia and New Zealand, attended meetings. Admittedly, many people attended the crusade meetings more than once, so the total number of individuals who attended would have been less than a quarter of the population. But of those who did attend, 150,000 responded to Graham's invitation to accept Christ. This included 130,000 Australians, or 1.24 per cent of the entire population. These were said to be the largest crowds which had ever heard the preaching of the Gospel. To that point it was the largest, most successful evangelistic campaign in human history—and it happened in the land of amiable pagans. 'Never again will I doubt that the Gospel is the power of God,' wrote Bishop Kerle, overawed, 'nor that men's lives can be changed through the foolishness of preaching.'[80]

Melbourne attendances totalled 719,000 with 26,440 inquirers, that is, a response rate of 3.7 per cent. Attendances at the Sydney Crusade totalled 980,000 with 56,780 inquirers, that is, a 5.8 per cent response rate. The crusades in other cities were taken by associate evangelists with Graham speaking at the final meetings, with results as follows: Perth, 5396 inquirers and 106,800 in attendance (or 5.1 per cent); in Adelaide, 11,965 and 253,000 (or 4.7 per cent); and in Brisbane 10,661 and 291,000 (or 3.7 per cent).[81] Among the churched population, the effects were immediately apparent. By the end of the second week of the Sydney crusade, a marked increase in churchgoing was already evident. Graham had never known such a response. 'Spiritual hunger is the greatest I have ever known in my ministry,' he said, 'This is the work of the Holy Spirit.'[82] Ministers were reporting daily miracles of God's grace in changed lives. Homes were being restored, and whole families were dedicating themselves to Christ.

6. Sinful Practices in the Wider Community Are Reduced

The great revivals of the past have raised community standards, sometimes eliminating temporarily whole areas of criminal practice and immorality. At first sight it looks unlikely that the 1959 crusades would have done that. Only 25 per cent of decisions made at the Sydney crusade, for example, were made by the unchurched. Only 5.5 per cent were from so-called depressed residential areas and only 7.5 per cent of those who were employed were in labouring or manual jobs.[83] To look for evidence of the impact of the crusades on the incidence of crime, however, is essential to my definition of revival. One has to work hard to extract the required information from available statistics, which are obscured by the normal break-up of five-year intervals. The changes in the crime statistics do appear in annual and monthly figures, but these are difficult to procure.

At first glance the statistics show that all the crime indices except drunkenness[84] rose dramatically in the 1950s, suggesting that the frequently voiced expressions of fear about juvenile delinquency and moral declension had some basis in fact. This fear was one of the reasons why Australians were encouraged to pray for revival when Graham came. Then, in the 1960s, the indices rose even more steeply, suggesting that the crusades had no quantitative impact on the community's standards and that this was not a revival.

The *Sunday Mirror* which appeared the Sunday after the final great meeting of the Sydney crusade, however, includes an article headed, 'THUG GIVES UP REVOLVER: Burglar hands over tool-kit', in which magistrate A. E. Debenham claimed that 'The Billy Graham Crusade has cut crime in Sydney by an estimated 50 per cent.'[85] This claim was accompanied by stories of a safebreaker handing the instruments of his trade to one flabbergasted counsellor, a gunman surrendering his revolver to another, and the information that businesses were reporting an epidemic of repayments of bad debts, while church attendance in Kings Cross, Sydney's red-light district, had risen to record heights. A keen Anglican all his life, Debenham went to every crusade meeting. The nature of his work involved protracted interviews with people brought before the courts. He did not hesitate to probe their spiritual condition, and on the basis of such intimate discussions, he concluded that Billy Graham was having a deep impact on the human psyche in Sydney.[86] Many a dormant conscience was awakened. A young woman confessed to her university that she had obtained her degree through cheating. A bank employee informed a bank official that he had embezzled a small sum of money. Expecting to be dismissed, he was the means instead of the official's going to the crusade where he, too, was converted.[87]

Such reports were an encouragement to look harder at the crime statistics. The number of convictions for all crimes committed in Australia doubled between 1920 and 1950, and then doubled again between 1950 and 1959 when the population increased by only one-quarter.[88] Then, in 1960, 1961, and 1962, the number of convictions remained fairly constant, resuming its dramatic upward trend in the middle and late 1960s.[89] Something which occurred at the same time as the Billy Graham Crusades slowed, even stopped, the further decline into criminality of community behaviour. The illegitimate birthrate and the *per capita* consumption of alcohol give other rough indexes to non-criminal community standards. Again one is at first struck by the gigantic change for the worse which overtook Australian society in the late 1950s and 1960s. Ex-nuptial births as a proportion of total births fell in the 1940s and early 1950s to a historic low of about 3.9 per hundred. They then began to climb fiercely in the middle and late 1950s, heralding the permissive 1960s. In the period 1955 to 1965 this index rose every year to almost double the 1954 figure, but the year it rose most slowly (0.06 per cent) was in 1960.[90] The illegitimate children not conceived in 1959 were not born in 1960! Again, one can argue that something happened in Australia at the same time as the Billy Graham Crusades which almost stopped the rot, not from existing, but from becoming more rotten. Turning to alcohol consumption: Bureau of Statistics figures show that, contrary to trends, the alcohol consumption for 1960–61 was 10 per cent lower than the 1958–59 figure. Something happened in Australia at about the same time as the Billy Graham Crusades to cause a 10 per cent reduction in the consumption of beer.

How do we explain the success of the 1959 crusades? Successes in history are rarely monocausal. A combination of factors explains the great impact of the crusades. Anxieties about a world threatened by the Cold War, and a society beginning to totter into moral decline after a decade of equipoise, made even softly secular forces approve of revival, thus opening many hearts to the challenge and hope in Graham's message. The gifts, stance, and superb organisation of Billy Graham and his team contributed to the success. The psychologically all-important initial success in Melbourne, fostered by superb laypeople who had been used to decades of parachurch activity, played a key part, as did the re-energising of Methodism in the 1950s ably led by Alan Walker. One could make out a strong case that the critical mass in all of this was evangelical Anglicanism. Billy Graham was the icing on Howard Mowll's cake. It was a rich cake, full of the right ingredients. The leadership of S. B. Babbage and Leon Morris in Melbourne and Kerle, Loane and others in Sydney was consistent and constructive. The evangelical Anglican clergy were frequently passionate in their zeal for souls; they were experienced in evangelism, and they had tasted some success in the many effective parish missions of the 1950s. The laity, both men and women, were capable and loyal. The Anglican Church, like the Catholic Church, has rarely enjoyed revival. But when significant numbers of Anglicans started hungering for it, as they did in England in 1954 and in Australia in 1959, things happened. Graham came to see all that while he was in Australia. That is why he hoped the next great awakening would commence in Australia. Did revival come to Australia in 1959? By all the indicators accessible to the historian, it did. It was a revival, all right, and a great one. That it grew out of an evangelistic outreach to the unchurched and reflected the style and positive personality of the preacher and therefore looked different from past revivals should not obscure the fact. What has become disappointingly clear in retrospect, however, was that the 1959 Billy Graham Crusades were a peak achievement of the evangelical synthesis in Australia, rather than the harbinger of a brilliant new period of achievement for it. In the decades which followed, the three strands of Spirit, Word and world, which had been bound together so tightly in the crusades, were unravelled. Each strand could now be strengthened in isolation, but the strength of the evangelical cord as a whole was to be seriously weakened.

8. Word or Spirit, 1960–1994

Spiritually, the 1960s was a decade when the tide ebbed. It was an age of uncertainty and rampant secularity. It favoured a type of Protestantism which was combative and knew how to take the battle to the enemy, namely objective, scholastic, Reformed Calvinism which toughened the Word strand. Sociologist Hans Mol contends that in the 1960s the hitherto static Australian religious scene became dynamic, first with rapid and then steady decline: Australia, he said in 1971, was either 'a Christian nation in search of a religion, or a heathen nation in flight from one'.[1] Denominational memberships had been rising steadily from 1931 (though still below the population growth), peaking in the early 1960s. From the mid-1960s, mainstream denominational memberships began to slide. In 1961 New South Wales 'Christian' denominational affiliations totalled 3,479,371, while the total in 1981 was 4,082,542, a growth of some 17 per cent. During the same period the Australian population had grown 38 per cent,[2] and those (in New South Wales) who declared themselves as having 'no religion' grew by more than 3000 per cent, indicating, if not increased unbelief, at least an increased willingness to state unbelief. The term usually used for such major shifts in cultural norms is 'secularisation', indicating either a decline of religious activity, or removal of the churches to the periphery of Australian life. In America, modernisation has not meant deChristianisation, but Australia seems to have taken the route of secularised Europe. Polls taken in the respective countries show an interesting contrast: in America, the proportion of the population who believed in God rose from 94 per cent in 1949 to 98 per cent in 1969;[3] in Australia, for the same years, it declined from 95 per cent to 87 per cent.[4]

Christianity was not simply shrinking as a proportion of the total religious profile of modern Australia, however. It was changing and taking on new forms. Numerous denominations, old and new, appeared in strength in Australia for the first time. Orthodox churches expanded and variegated: Greek, Russian, Serbian, Syrian (now Antiochian), Romanian, Bulgarian,

Coptic and others.[5] Catholicism took on a more pluralistic form with the input of hundreds of thousands of migrants, leading to specialist ethnic parishes. Within Protestantism, the growth of the pentecostal movement saw the growth of ethnically specific congregations all over the country, a trend mirrored in the Uniting Church, formed in 1977, with its traditionally strong missionary ties to the South Pacific and Korea. In the 1960s pentecostals grew dramatically and infiltrated the mainstream churches in the form of the Charismatic Renewal. While overall church attendance fell among the general Australian population, from 41 per cent attending at least monthly in 1960 to around 24 per cent in 1985, only the pentecostals managed to avoid and even reverse the trend. The pentecostals and Charismatics were the most successful of the churches in attracting youth.

Some leaders in the mainstream denominations looked to church union as the answer to declension. For decades, the Anglican and Catholic communions had been exploring the possibilities of reuniting their branches of the Christian Church, divided since the Reformation. Donald Robinson, Anglican Archbishop of Sydney (1982–93), reported to his synod that he had voted against the idea at the Lambeth Conference, as 'I think the quest for a universal primacy is on the wrong track. I can only add that I do not think it will get very far if it continues to explore the basis of such a universal primacy in Scripture.'[6] A more successful attempt at union, and one which had a deep effect on the character of church life in Australia, was the merging of elements of the Methodist, Presbyterian and Congregationalist traditions into the Uniting Church of Australia. A draft Basis of Union was voted on in 1972, with the Methodists and Congregationalists both polling over 80 per cent in favour of joining. It was not until May 1974 that the Presbyterian General Assembly decided to proceed to union, though with only seven votes more than the three-fifths majority required. A considerable number of congregations stayed out of the new Uniting Church of Australia. Some of these were Congregationalist, but most were Presbyterian. Hence union in effect further fragmented the denominational scene.

Turning to the world Christian scene: the Catholics staged the Second Vatican Council (1962–65) with ambiguous results. Sectarianism between Catholics and Protestantism, a marked feature of Australian society for over a century, evaporated overnight. That other great movement of concern to conservative Protestants—liberalism—at least in the churches seemed a spent force. Its bold assaults on the citadels of orthodoxy were of decreasing concern either to churchgoers or non-churchgoers. Admittedly, J. A. T. Robinson's *Honest to God* (1963) was a sensation since its 'new morality' rationalised the old immorality as demanded by the permissive 1960s, and Harvey Cox's *The Secular City* (1964), in arguing that secularisation was a fruit of Christianity's liberalising power, stimulated a response which surprised even its author. But from then on, it was downhill for the liberals. The assault of New Zealander, Lloyd Geering, on the resurrection in 1966 created a brief antipodean skirmish, and led to the separation of the Rev. Grahame Kerr of Sutherland in Sydney from the Presbyterian Church of Australia and the creation in 1967 of the Presbyterian Reformed Church of Australia. In the 1970s John Hick took the reins of theological liberalism in England with his *God and the Universe of Faiths* (1973) and *The Myth of God Incarnate* (1979) which he edited. Don Cupitt published *Taking Leave of God* in 1980. In Australia, Barbara Thiering, from the evangelical heartland of Sydney, shocked the conservatives with her increasingly radical reading of the New Testament documents in the light of her interpretation of the Dead Sea Scrolls.[7] Her critics used the same weapons which they had sharpened against her to attack Bishop Spong, who at the beginning of the 1990s denied the incarnation and resurrection and affirmed homosexuality.[8] In the 1980s the issues raised by feminism seemed to create greater interest than those raised by the liberals, which led many evangelicals at first to identify feminism as just another expression of liberalism. As a device to produce a version of Christianity acceptable to the educated, scientifically literate technocrats, liberalism was a failure. Ecclesiastical liberalism found a home in the ecumenical movement and in a creative enclave in the Uniting Church, but overall it was apparently in decline, unable to prevent significant numbers of its adherents from succumbing to the forces of secularism and giving up on the churches altogether. Evangelicals believed that liberalism emptied churches, while conservative, Biblical Christianity grew churches and produced Christian workers.

An Evangelicalism Stronger in Parts than in the Whole

The strength and resilience of evangelicalism in the period 1960–90 has surprised the prophets of Christianity's demise. In the USA, 1976, the middle year of the period, was labelled 'the year of the evangelical'. In Australia, as in America and Britain, evangelicalism has become the strongest movement within the Protestant churches. National and international gatherings of evangelicals of many different theological complexions sought to focus the movement's energies on evangelism, its mission to the world. Significant numbers of evangelicals recovered the movement's social conscience which had been such a conspicuous part of the faith of early generations of evangelicals. The renaissance of Reformed theology produced a growing battalion of evangelical theologians and an army of evangelical preachers, with Sydney increasingly recognised as one of the most fortified of the international movement's command posts. The long gestation period of Australian pentecostalism came to an end with the birth of a thriving infant which grew more rapidly than any other Christian offspring. In 1979 revival, of great power and longevity, came at last to the most needy of the church's flock: the Aboriginal people. More than ever Australian Christians spoke of 'the Great South Land of the Holy Spirit' and prayed and longed for revival.

But with all the evidence of strength and vitality, there were worrying signs of weakness in evangelical ranks. The decline of liberalism within the churches took away one of the chief rallying cries of the evangelicals. Strongly Reformed evangelicals tended to label everything with which they disagreed as 'liberal', but the evangelicals' inability to agree on a definition of liberalism was an indication that the movement was fragmenting. Without a common enemy and with growing numerical support, the movement soon discovered that it was not as coherent and unified as it had hoped. Traditional mainstream pietistic evangelicalism was separated into at least four different channels: Reformed evangelicalism in the Puritan tradition; left-wing evangelicalism, which established such socially aware groups as World Vision, Zadok, and Eremos; right-wing fundamentalism, which championed Creation Science and Biblical inerrancy; and the Charismatic movement and pentecostalism.

The fragmentation of the evangelical movement was accompanied by the separation of the strands of the evangelical synthesis. The Spirit, Word, and world strands each became stronger in this period, but each found it easier to live without the restraint and correction of the other. Evangelicals had always believed that they belonged to the true, invisible church, but they had not spent a lot of time defining what they meant by 'church'. Now, faced by the challenge of the ecumenical movement, which offered to reduce evangelicalism to one part of a world-wide church ultimately under the supervision of the Bishop of Rome, evangelicals turned their minds to the study of the Church. And faced with the rapid growth of Charismatic churches, they turned their hearts to the subject of worship, which they had also largely ignored hitherto. But the more they focused on the church and worship, the less they cared for the world, because it is actually very difficult to care for both the church and the world. Evangelical laity began to complain of being 'clericalised' as their Reformed Bible teachers taught them more about what was required in the church than in the world. Even the socially aware evangelicals seemed to lack a robust theological motivation for their engagement with society, as all theological formulations, evangelical, liberal, and Catholic, seemed incapable of addressing the immediate future.[9] The evangelicals especially stressed the second coming of Christ. Some used this to foster urgency in proclamation and deed, but most felt that their theology was strangely unrelated to the growing pressures on a secularising and increasingly multicultural society.

Evangelicals had always acknowledged that it was necessary to put doctrine ahead of fellowship, the Word before emotion, and to rely for the righteousness which saves on the objective work of Christ on the cross. But when Word and doctrine were emphasised to the apparent total exclusion of fellowship, warm piety, and the energetic pursuit of holiness, whatever was left was not evangelicalism. Christianity was more than experience, but, if not felt, it was nothing. Finding the systematic theology of the Reformed rationalists indigestible and ultimately unnourishing fare, many evangelicals sought an emotionally richer diet in the Charismatic movement. Pentecostals tended to jettison the Word as the authoritative basis of their belief, and instead sought that authority in increasingly emotional and esoteric experiences. The three strands were pulling apart and concentrating more narrowly on their own preferences, thus fostering short-term growth, but long-term disintegration of the evangelical movement. One of the sharpest critics of the direction of evangelicalism before his death in 1981 was that old champion of the evangelical synthesis, Martyn Lloyd-Jones, the Welsh Bible expositor. He regretted the wholesale attacks of conservative, Reformed evangelicals on the Charismatic movement:

> It would be a disaster for evangelicals, and for men of Reformed convictions, if they became preoccupied with answering the new Pente-

costal claims instead of recognising that 'the greatest need of the church is to realize again the activity of the Holy Spirit'.[10]

That disaster is certainly one that has befallen Australian evangelicalism.

At the Second National Assembly of Evangelicals, held by the Evangelical Alliance in London on 18 October 1966, Martyn Lloyd-Jones dramatically called the evangelicals out of their denominations to join a United Evangelical Church.[11] In Australia, evangelicals have never been very interested in that option, not so much because they find it congenial to co-exist with liberals and/or ritualists in the one denomination, but because they prefer to contemplate taking over the whole denomination—or at least parts of it, such as a diocese—for the evangelical cause. In 1966 Hugh Gough, Archbishop of Sydney and the senior evangelical bishop in the Anglican world, on resigning his office complained of those in the reputedly evangelical Diocese of Sydney who put their evangelicalism ahead of their Anglicanism. The majority in the diocese neither agreed with their archbishop nor desired to break away from their denomination. Henceforth the main struggle in the diocese was between those who put their evangelicalism first and sought to reform the diocese further along evangelical lines, and those who had always believed that 'Prayer Book Anglicanism' was one of the finest and firmest expressions of evangelicalism and sought to preserve the rich and tolerant culture it had created and the warm spirituality it had fostered.

Bringing Theology out of the Cold

Theological education cannot outstrip general education. In the 1960s Prime Minister Menzies gave a great boost to tertiary education, and theological education was one of the beneficiaries. Providers of theological education proliferated. Well before the end of this period, theology could be studied in dynamic new foundations established by individual churches with visionary pastors (the pentecostal way), in denominational colleges energised by commitment to a clearer theological mandate (the Reformed way), in consortia of traditional colleges combined to maximise staffing and library resources (the ecumenical way), or in universities (the academic way). Specialised theological training was now provided, for example, for lay people, distance students by extension, and Aboriginal people.

A recent trend in theological education in Australia has been the establishment, particularly among pentecostal churches, of church-based colleges. They are based on the apprenticeship system, a successful minister training a group of tyros in the practical aspects of ministry: worship, leadership, education, youth, counselling, or music ministries. Among important pentecostal colleges is Tabor Bible College, started in Adelaide by Dr Barry Chant, and growing by the early 1990s to embrace four campuses in Perth, Melbourne, Adelaide and Sydney. A genuinely indigenous pentecostal denomination, the Christian Outreach Centre, was established in 1974 in Brisbane by Clark Taylor, and has since added a Bible college and the Christian Heritage College which offers Arts courses accredited by the Queensland Minister for Education. Its determination to provide theological education for the twelve nations of the Pacific and Asia to which the denomination has spread has already led to the creation of Bible colleges in some of those countries and is symptomatic of recent developments in Australian theological education, namely to become a provider for overseas consumption.

Among successful denominational colleges founded in this period is Luther Seminary, Adelaide, which opened on 3 March 1968. In the twenty-five years since then, it admitted 520 students of whom 275 completed the ordination course. In 1977 it introduced the Bachelor of Theology programme, and 230 students received that degree to 1993. The Graduate Diploma in Ministry was introduced in 1990, and 29 students have received the award. More than 60 per cent of the clergy of the Lutheran Church of Australia have been trained at Luther Seminary.

A concerted effort was mounted to establish the study of theology as a fully ecumenical and a fully academic discipline. Vatican II (1962–65) made the ecumenical development possible. In 1966 the Australian Society for Theological Studies was established to bring all theological inquiry to the bar of scholarship (from 1967 New Zealand was included). The society produces *Colloquium* to publish articles which attain this standard. In 1967, too, ANZATS (the Australian and New Zealand Association of Theological Schools) was established. In Melbourne the ecumenical United Theological College, made up of the theological halls of Ormond College (Presbyterian), Queen's College (Methodist), and the Melbourne Congregational College, was expanded in 1972 to embrace the Jesuit Theological College. From the late 1970s consortia of colleges in Sydney, Brisbane, Adelaide and

Perth were established and achieved accreditation of their courses and the right to issue theological degrees from their respective education authorities. In a move to redress the perceived injustice done to the churches in keeping them out of universities in the last century, theological colleges are now having their courses recognised by the NSW Higher Education Board and equivalent bodies in other States. On 15 December 1983 the Sydney College of Divinity was incorporated on the invitation of the NSW Higher Education Board. The six founding colleges were the Baptist Theological College, the Catholic Institute of Sydney, the Churches of Christ Theological College, St Paul's National Seminary, Union Theological Institute, and the United Theological College. These were joined in 1986 by the St Andrew's Greek Orthodox Theological College and in 1989 by the St Mark's College of Ministry in Canberra. Brisbane College of Theology is a consortium of St Francis' College (Anglican), Pius XII Provincial Seminary (Catholic), and Trinity College (Uniting Church). In the case of Perth, Adelaide, and Brisbane consortia, the credentialising authorities are now universities (Murdoch, Flinders, and Griffith respectively).

The view that the denominational training college was the only natural home for the study of theology was now challenged by a revitalised tertiary sector hungry for students in all disciplines. In 1964 the Martin Report was published. With reference to theological education, its most significant recommendation was:

> 15 (iv) Universities, and the proposed Institutes of Colleges and boards of Teacher Education, should consider the provision of courses of a non-dogmatic character which are relevant to theological studies.[12]

'By discussing theological education alongside other forms of tertiary education in Australia, the report has implicitly conferred the kind of status on theological work that only a formal, national and high-level advisory body can confer'.[13] Universities established religious studies departments and courses which increasingly shared with theological colleges the pursuit of theological science and the training of people for Christian ministry. La Trobe University in Melbourne, for example, has had extensive programmes in the history of Christianity, theology and Biblical studies since 1977. The newly established School of Studies in Religion at the University of Sydney developed in 1992 a cross-creditation programme with the Sydney College of Divinity, allowing students access to a wider range of subjects, and in 1993 the Australian College of Theology entered into agreements with Macquarie University and the University of Western Sydney to offer joint degrees in Arts and Theology. The significance of such developments should be underscored. Theology and theological education are now accorded the same status as other disciplines in the universities and will do much to remove the prejudice against theological study endemic to Australia.

In the 1980s, in a development which looks as if it has the future on its side, the theological education of the laity received new attention. The need had long been felt, of course, and in the 1940s Moore College began evening courses to train lay readers. This developed into the correspondence courses for the Certificate in Theology and the Preliminary Theological Certificate, with about 2000 students enrolled annually. In 1986 the Master of Robert Menzies College at Macquarie University, Paul Barnett, later Bishop of North Sydney, commenced the School of Christian Studies, to give evening courses for part-time students in the Licentiate in Theology programme of the Australian College of Theology. The courses have been attracting over 100 students annually. Significant development in theological education by extension also took place in this period. Distance education has actually been provided in Australia for many decades as churches have tried to train rural people and give post-ordination training to rural clergy. Within the Anglican Church, the General Board of Religious Education has been a major provider of courses offered in conjunction with the Australian College of Theology. Another group requiring specialised theological education are Aboriginal people. Since 1974 they have been able to receive training through the ecumenical Nungalinya College in Darwin, or its extension in Queensland, Wontulp-Bi-Buya College. The foundation principal, Keith Cole, moved onto the college campus in Darwin just nine days before all the college facilities were destroyed by Cyclone Tracy, and the building process had to start all over again.[14] Torres Strait Islanders were trained at St Paul's Theological College on Moa Island until 1969 when the college closed. In 1989 it reopened on Thursday Island.

The Ascendancy of Reformed Theology

One of the most conspicuous features of evangelicalism in this period has been the pronounced resurgence in Reformed Christianity which stands for an uncompromising allegiance to historic Calvinism. Reformed churches are gaining in membership, and the Anglican Church, in both Britain and Australia, is being galvanised by a determined Reformed presence.[15] Annual conferences of Reformed ministers in Australia, as well as in Britain and America are now well attended. In 1957 the Banner of Truth Trust was formed in Britain to reprint Puritan classics, to publish Reformed theology, and to publish the journal *Banner of Truth*. Mountains of this historical and theological literature were acquired by English-speaking evangelicals, hungry for the purest and richest reflections on the Word and the work of the Spirit in the Christian life.

The impact of Reformed literature on the tinder-dry hearts, tender consciences, and eager minds of Australian Baptist, Presbyterian, and Anglican evangelicals was swift and powerful. The first tremors were felt in Tasmania and soon spread to Victoria. In February 1960 the Tasmanian Reformation Fellowship was established by a group of Calvinistic Baptists, one of whom, Eric Turnbull, resigned a few weeks later when asked by the Baptist Union to desist from preaching Reformed doctrines. In the same year, J. Laurie Lincolne, principal of the World Evangelisation Crusade Training College near Launceston, and thirty of his fifty students broke away and set up their own college, appropriately called Geneva, since it was committed to the 'five points of Calvinism'.[16] In the following year, the Reformed Evangelical Church was formed in Launceston, and in the same year the Banner of Truth Trust appointed its first official agent in Australia. In 1962 the Reformed Church of Australia opened the first parent-controlled Christian school in the tradition of Abraham Kuyper, the Dutch Calvinist scholar. In 1963 the Reformed Evangelical Church linked up with the Presbyterian Church of Eastern Australia, another small Calvinist denomination, to establish the John Knox Theological College in Melbourne. Both the college and the denominations which supported it continued to be rocked by disputation over such issues as whether or not the Gospel is to be offered to all since Christ died only for the elect.[17] Similar tiny High Calvinist denominations proliferated, amalgamated and separated throughout Australia: the Westminster Presbyterian Church began in Western Australia in 1970; the Reformed Presbyterian Church of Australia was founded in 1974 and the Southern Presbyterian Church of Australia in 1986.

The schism between Reformed Calvinists and Arminian Finneyism[18] in Baptist circles had barely emerged by 1959, hence the near unanimous support which the Australian Baptists then gave to the most celebrated of their fellow Baptists, Billy Graham. The story was different in 1968 at his second visit. By then opposition to Billy was fomented by members of the Banner of Truth Trust, which condemned 'revivalism' and 'decisionism', and by American fundamentalist Carl McIntire who visited Australia and condemned Billy as a compromiser with liberals. From the deacons of Kerang Baptist Church in Victoria, Billy received the following admonition:

> From time to time we have been distressed by the presence on your platform of men who deny the fundamentals ... are you not in danger of violating New Testament principles for the sake of maximum support and outreach? ... We ... wonder if the time has come for you to choose between the slippery road of gracious diplomacy and the painful path of Scriptural separation.[19]

One W. Bradbury of Petersham in Sydney shot off the following missile to the Billy Graham Evangelistic Association:

> I am only an Electrician but I'd love one or two hours with Billy Graham over the Word of God. NO spiritual man would drift like Sir Billy has ... I judge him to be a man of MIXED PRINCIPLES AND NOT FIXED ONES ... I WILL NOT WASTE TIME TO SEE OR HEAR HIM UNTIL HE BECOMES A FUNDAMENTALIST AND NOT A NEUTRALIST.[20]

Admittedly, the Baptists in 1968 remained as they had been in 1959 (after the Brethren) easily the most unequivocal denomination in their support of Billy Graham. In 1968, three months before the Melbourne crusade, 158 Baptist churches had registered at the crusade office; this was only just behind the registered number of the far more numerous Methodist and Anglican churches and way ahead of the Presbyterians.[21] And not all Baptists wrote rude letters to Billy. Consider this gem from Mrs E. Kinnear, a member of Ashfield Baptist Church:

> I felt after hearing your address on Saturday night I must write to you and tell you about my little budgie. You said in your sermon, 'Jesus loves me this I know for the Bible tells me so.' My little budgie now seven years old has been saying that since he has been able to talk. I think most of the day he keeps saying 'Jesus loves me.' Then at times he says the rest. Sometimes he will try and sing 'Jesus loves me.'[22]

Mrs Kinnear aside, it is clear that the increasing difficulty which the Baptists, under pressure from Reformed forces, were having in supporting Billy Graham and which was echoed in other denominations, shows that the evangelical consensus was breaking down. The resurgence of conservative evangelicalism nerved some Protestant denominational organisations to maintain Reformed distinctives, even when not all their members felt strongly committed to them. The Melbourne Baptists, for example, felt unable to support the United Faculty of Theology with its Catholic presence. In 1975 they formed the Evangelical Theological Association, in which Whitley College applied jointly with the Churches of Christ Theological College to teach the Bachelor of Theology for the Melbourne College of Divinity.

From the formation of the Uniting Church in 1977, steps were taken in the continuing Presbyterian Church of Australia to ensure that its ministers were given a solid grounding in conservative, Reformed theology. On the retirement of Professor Crawford Miller, the Sydney Theological Hall was moved out of St Andrew's College in the University of Sydney and relocated first at Ashfield and then at Burwood under the Rev. J. A. Davies as dean, while a number of Presbyterian candidates trained at Moore College. Dr Nigel Lee, a prolific writer, exuberantly led the resurgence of Reformed theology among Queensland Presbyterians, while in Melbourne, the venerable Calvinist, Robert Swanton, filled the Chair of Theology until the late 1980s.

In 1985 the Rev. James Hogg, pastor of Stanmore Baptist Church in Sydney, a Reformed stronghold, protested against the participation of the Baptist Theological College in the Sydney College of Divinity in a manifesto entitled *Triumph or Tragedy*. He questioned participation in a consortium which had Catholics as the largest collaborators. The Baptist Union therefore asked both the Baptist college and Hogg to state their cases. The college and the executive council of the Baptist Union obliged with a pamphlet entitled *Co-operation without Compromise*. To this Hogg responded with *Ecumenism: A Serious Cause for Dissent*. At its meeting on 22 February 1986, the union passed (343–329) the motion that they should stay in the Sydney College of Divinity with certain safeguards (such as 'no exchange of lecturers'). The Reformed magazine *Banner of Truth* observed on this outcome: 'The controversy is clearly by no means over and while some deplore it, others remember the words of Spurgeon, "A dead calm may be our enemy, a storm may prove our helper." '[23]

The pressure of the Reformed forces was too great, and in 1988 the Baptist college withdrew from the Sydney College of Divinity and joined the Australian College of Theology. Furthermore, in the1980s intense controversy among NSW Baptists over Biblical inerrancy drove a number of enterprising ministers to Victoria so that they could get on with the job of growing churches, the new word for evangelism.[24]

D. B. Knox and the Authority of the Word

It was through the Anglican Moore Theological College, however, that Reformed theology was to have its greatest impact, during the long principalship of Broughton Knox (1959–85).[25] His influence was enormous. From the 1960s to the early 1980s, archbishops refused to ordain anyone for work in the diocese who had not trained at Moore College. Born in Adelaide in 1912, Knox was educated at the University of Sydney; there he studied Greek with Gough Whitlam, and demonstrated his independent spirit by not joining the Evangelical Union. He was trained for the ministry and ordained in England, where he joined with Stuart Barton Babbage in the Biblical Research Committee of the IVF and with Douglas Johnson in the production of scholarly evangelical literature. Knox acquired a reputation as an uncompromising champion of Reformation doctrine; when he perceived something was contrary to Scripture, he had the memorable habit of uttering a sevenfold 'no'. He galvanised a generation of evangelicals to say 'no' to the advances of liberalism and the incursions of ritualism.

Within months of his appointment as tutor to Moore College in 1947, he made an unforgettable appearance as an 'expert witness' in a famous trial known as 'the Red Book Case' in which the Bishop of Bathurst was accused of advocating liturgical innovations incompatible with the law of the Church of England. Knox received his doctorate from Oxford in 1953 for a dissertation later published under the title *The Doctrine of Faith in the Reign of Henry VIII*. In an insight which is the key to both his faith and his personality, he observed that human sufficiency (as opposed to faith in God) 'taught the haughty to presume while the humble despaired and it gave little place for Christian joy'.[26] He may have looked and sounded like an academic, but his instincts and his heart were those of a warrior for the truth rather than of a speculator on truth. The truth in the Word of God was to be obeyed—personally—and truth was to be defended and error refuted fearlessly. He was more interested in engaging with God than with other professional theologians, and hence his was a life of faith and prayer. But he loved theology and he loved arguing, and he taught his students to love both. In 1960, the year after he began his term as principal of Moore College on the crest of the Billy Graham Crusades, he established a new theological institute, the Sydney Reformed College, in the hall of the Congregational Church at Leichhardt. He staffed the college with himself and Bill Lawton, a young prizewinning Moore College graduate, teaching there each evening the history and theology of the Calvinist Reformation. Bill Lawton, like many in those days, was passionate about double election, limited atonement and other hallmarks of High Calvinism. But Broughton Knox's commitments were to more central doctrines on the authority of the Bible and the nature of the church.

His belief that the Bible was the sole authority in all matters of faith and doctrine led him to insist that only doctrines found in the Bible should be taught as essential to salvation,[27] that the Bible is self-authenticating, and that the only revelation of God is 'propositional'. In 1960 he developed the last claim in an article entitled 'Propositional Revelation the only Revelation'.[28] He disputed the view that 'the Word of God' is not a series of propositions, but a series of events, that God's revelation is not in words, but in acts. Knox argued that this view is contrary to the revelation of the Bible itself, which affirms that the words, or propositions formed by those words, are the means by which revelation takes place. An event is not revelatory, only the Bible's account of that event reveals God's mind: 'For an event to be revelational, it must be interpreted by God himself.'[29] To affirm propositional revelation was to affirm inerrant revelation.[30] God can and has not only made one inerrant proposition, but a whole series of them in the Bible, and excluded from it any erroneous proposition. Not to believe that is 'the height of impiety'.

It followed that the chief work of the ministry was to teach the Bible where alone God reveals himself; the chief work of the theologian was to defend the inerrancy of Scripture; and the chief glory of the believer was to hear and learn the Scriptures. This emphasis has fashioned Sydney Anglicanism more than any other single influence. The height of piety became the proclamation and defence of the Word. Christ is related to and worshipped through the Bible, which contains the words of Christ, which are life and which come from the Father. In private conversation and in public preaching, Knox loved to emphasise that key to Christian truth and devotion, as supported by such Biblical verses as John 3.34, 6.63, and 17.8. This has become the great strength of Sydney evangelical Anglicanism, and most of its weaknesses stem from the institutionalisation and politicisation of this great truth of *sola scriptura*, the Bible alone. It produced warriors for the Word who could more easily than fairly be accused of living the Bible in their minds through theological disputation than in their hearts by personal obedience.

Almost as influential as Knox's position on the Bible, and far more controversial, was his view of the church.[31] For him the church is primarily a heavenly reality—a gathering in heaven (Ephesians 2; Hebrews 12.8ff). The truest earthly manifestation of this heavenly reality is the local church; not the denomination beloved of the ecclesiastics, nor the world church beloved of the Ecumenical movement which was then in full cry.[32] The local congregation is complete in itself because each congregation is the gathering of Christ's people around himself. It followed that to absent oneself from the local gathering was to cut oneself off from Christ who builds the believer up through the gifts he gives to other believers in the congregation, all of whom, because they are given gifts by Christ, are ministers. The denomination is the servant of the local church and not vice-versa. Denominational structures are no substitute for fellowship in the local body, and the unity of Christians is not to be expressed primarily in loyalty to one denomination.

In this view of the church, Knox was ably supported by Donald Robinson, who joined the faculty of Moore College in 1952, and was vice-principal from 1959 until he became Bishop of Parramatta in 1973.[33] From 1982 to 1993, he was Archbishop of Sydney. Robinson maintained that the unity of the 'one holy Church' of the Apostles' Creed was a heavenly reality. The earthly reality was that the true church, being the local assembly, is many. Church union, then, is neither proper nor possible. His most controversial emphasis was that the church was not an instrument of evangelism, but is rather the result of evangelism. This refusal to put the church at the disposal of the evangelistic cause distressed many evangelicals for whom evangelism is primary. The world strand was weakened and directors of missionary societies complained that Moore College graduates were not as interested in overseas missions as they once were.

When Robinson became archbishop in 1982, two corollaries of his position on the church characterised his episcopate: the insistence that the local church was at the centre of the church's work with the denominational structures but its servants, and the emphasis on 'making Sunday work', the opportunity for Christians to withdraw from the world and be refreshed together for their mission in the world. If these were positives for the archbishop, there was a big negative. The Knox–Robinson ecclesiology reinforced the Low Church evangelical impatience with diocesan bishops and other traditions which were not based obviously on Scripture. Knox produced rectors who preferred a polity of congregational independence, who had trouble with infant baptism, robes, liturgical services and prayer books. It was felt that such traditions were not only unBiblical, but actually impeded the church's outreach to the unchurched. Constant pressure was exerted in synod for relief from these encumbrances.[34] The Rev. Peter Watson, appointed in 1970 to direct the New Areas committee, though considered a safe and conservative evangelical, expressed the view that changes were required in the services of public worship.[35] In the late 1980s and early 1990s a fiercer pragmatism entered the courts of the church with the popularisation of the church growth movement. But even then pragmatism was secondary to theology. It was theology that mattered. The instinctive feelings about what makes for congruity with the unchurched and utility for them were overborne by a concern for the pure church. The instinctively sociological was swallowed up by the theological. Throughout this entire period, a heightened emphasis on the purity of the church, stemming from the Biblicist ecclesiology of Knox–Robinson, coincided with a decline in church attendance.

Perhaps the greatest perceived weakness in Knox's theology was in the area of the Spirit. The Spirit's role in the inspiration of Scripture is acknowledged, but the interpretation and understanding of Scripture is the work primarily of our reason and the self-authenticating nature of the Scripture itself. Similarly, the agency of God the Holy Spirit in human history is not emphasised. This affected the view of God held by Sydney Anglicans. God does not have to intervene in human affairs because he has left his Word (*à la* the clockmaker) as a guide for daily living.[36] At the critical time when the Charismatic movement was flowering and making claims about the Spirit as unfamiliar to evangelical Christians as the doctrine of justification had been to medieval Christians, Knox failed to develop a strongly

Reformed doctrine of the Holy Spirit. Impoverishment in thinking about the Spirit and in holiness of living afflicted evangelical Anglicanism in this period and, instead of knitting the Word and Spirit strands strongly together, put them at enmity with each other. Too often Sydney Anglicans had to make the choice between being evangelical or Charismatic, and, if they chose the latter, they were unlikely to experience much empathy from their clergy trained under Dr Knox.

The consolidation of Reformed theology at Moore Theological College eliminated the revivalist and holiness emphases of previous decades. There was a significant 'narrowing' and withdrawal from the broad stream of evangelical thought, and a massive reduction of influence on the broad Australian church. Moore College came to serve only a school within evangelicalism, and weakened the Spirit and world strands in the evangelical synthesis. But even such serious criticisms seem carping when put alongside Knox's achievements. For a generation of clergy trained by him, theology now mattered, the Bible mattered, and God mattered. It seemed a small price that Anglicanism and bishops mattered less. Thirty-six hours before he suffered a fatal stroke, Knox entertained guests with his wife, Ailsa. The question arose as to where they should go for a walk after lunch. Ailsa suggested that they should wait for a certain bishop to arrive 'as he likes to determine issues like that'. Broughton commented, 'One should always obey a bishop.' Ailsa snorted, 'Oh, Broughton, coming from you that is a bit rich.' Broughton replied, 'I did not say that I should obey the Bishop, I said that you should.' But Ailsa had not been married to Broughton for decades for nothing. She finished the exchange with, 'You said, "One should always obey a Bishop".'[37]

The Fragmentation of Evangelicalism in the Student World

The dynamics of fragmentation in historic evangelicalism is nowhere better illustrated than in the area of student Christian work. During the 1960s, while the Australian tertiary education sector exploded in growth, theological liberalism declined rapidly. In the late 1970s, the SCM had only 100 members Australia-wide.[38] Meanwhile, the evangelical student body, the IVF, prospered. In 1962 Ian Burnard was appointed IVF general secretary in succession to Charles Troutman, and led it for the next decade and a half. The IVF expanded with the multiplication of campuses and the opening of colleges of advanced education, but in the 1970s lost the tight coherence of its earlier decades. Evangelical Unions became enormous, headed by student leaders characterised by maturity and an impressive Biblical understanding. The SUEU in the mid-1960s comprised some 900 members, or about 1 in 17 of the entire student body. The EUs were so large that the zeal at the core, which had been the driving force of earlier days, was diluted by the less keen members. Faced with this challenge, Ian Burnard was clear about the IVF's priorities. First, current issues were to be approached Biblically. Second, the EU's aggressive evangelism was to be maintained, and, in many a union refectory and on many a university lawn, Burnard modelled a fearless evangelism. Third, witness was to be established and maintained in every faculty of the university.

This strategy worked well throughout the 1960s. But by the 1970s evangelicals had become so numerous, and so incapable of identifying a common enemy, that they started to argue among themselves. Hence the one stream of pietistic evangelicalism which the original IVF represented was displaced by a new diversified and polarised evangelicalism. This was partly importing an American problem which had been threatening for decades. In the USA the IVF was often thought of as a foreign import, far too cerebral and lacking in evangelistic aggression. Evangelical sectarianism, which had been avoided in Australia because of the strength of pietism and the relative weakness of evangelicalism, now emerged, and student leaders had no experience in confronting this reality. Student evangelicalism fractured, and six distinct strands emerged, with the IVF, led by Tony McCarthy from 1977 to 1984, represented mainly in the first two. First, the Reformed or Puritan evangelicals, emphasising confessional theology and traditional piety, produced Reformed Objectivists, typified by the *Banner of Truth*. Second, orthodox evangelicalism or neo-evangelicalism reacted against fundamentalist separatism, and was influenced profoundly by the Billy Graham Evangelistic Association. A third group were happy to be designated 'liberal evangelicals' who stress the Gospel's social mandate. Chief among them was Archbishop Penman of Melbourne (1984–89) who had been prominent in student Christian work. Another important liberal evangelical is Christine Ledger, a graduate of the Australian National University who became the director of the world-wide SCM movement, resident in Lausanne. Fourth, the fundamentalists were institutionalised in Australian universities in the early 1970s by the Navigators and Campus Crusade for Christ. Both groups emphasised a rather mechanistic approach, with Navigators centring on a topical Bible memory system, and Campus Crusade around Bill Bright's four laws of life. Fifth, the Charismatics came to be represented on Australian campuses mainly through a group known as Students for Christ. Maranatha is another such group, although much smaller. Finally, some sects mounted aggressive work on some campuses. Chief among them was the Church of Christ, not to be confused with the Churches of Christ denomination.

By the mid-1980s it was argued that the IVF, now the Australian Fellowship of Evangelical Students, was in crisis. Andrew Reid, general secretary from 1984, called for a radical rethink of policy. Based on the premise that modern students must be influenced by the materialistic and apathetic society in which they live, and are therefore less mature, independent, capable and persevering than previous generations of students, Reid proposed a reversion to a more directive stance from better-trained staffworkers and academics in order to procure for modern students the nurture, leadership, and instruction which they cannot supply for themselves. The task of the fellowship was clearly identified as giving students systematic Bible exposition, as increasingly they were coming from churches where the Bible was not systematically taught and where many basic Biblical truths were ignored. Its old guard reacted against this model, arguing that it stultified student initiative. In 1975 a virile new indigenous player entered the game. Phillip Jensen was appointed chaplain of the University of New South Wales. When the IVF workers did not welcome his overtures, he simply started his own meetings. Within a decade his Campus Bible Study was attracting a weekly attendance of 300, while the fellowship had collapsed. Jensen combined great personal skills in evangelism and Bible teaching with a grasp of the strategic importance of programmatic training in evangelism, modelled on the American Christian organisation Student Life, but adapted for the Australian setting. Critics grumbled about the new movement's Biblicism and even Bibliolatry, by which they meant fundamentalism. Emulating the more successful American approaches, therefore, has been divisive of the traditional IVF base, and has further divided the evangelical movement, by strengthening the Word strand and weakening the Spirit strand.

Sounding an Uncertain Note in the Campaign for the World

The Australian churches proved totally unequal to the task of stemming the tide of secularism, materialism and permissiveness which overcame the

Australian community in the period covered by this chapter. Particularly in public and political spheres, the churches seemed half-hearted in their defence of the old ways, which now felt more traditional and paternalistic than Christian. In New South Wales and South Australia highly effective Labor leaders, Neville Wran and Don Dunstan, repealed legislation designed to protect the weak. Sunday observance was the first legally sanctioned practice to go. The opportunities for gambling proliferated; hotels were opened on Sundays and hotel trading hours were extended; censorship collapsed, and pornography became a legal industry; abortion on demand became a legal reality; and homosexuality was decriminalised. Ironically, Wran approached this task with a crusading zeal which could be illiberal and undemocratic. For example, when in 1979 he legalised the opening of hotels on Sundays, it was contrary to the overwhelming wish of the New South Wales public expressed in repeated referendums. In a political arena where special interest groups such as the liquor trade were able to focus pressure through lobbying, democracy was sacrificed.

In South Australia, where Methodism had once withstood the liquor industry, the Festival of Light was formed in 1973 to 'make a stand against moral decline'.[39] It was supported not only by the 'wowsers', but also by Catholics who had never in the past had a reputation for wowserism. In 1974 Fred Nile was appointed full-time NSW director of the Australian Festival of Light. He had graduated from the Melbourne Bible Institute in 1957. The following year Elaine and Fred Nile were married at Revesby Evangelical Congregational Church of the Puritan Heritage, where Fred was converted. From 1958 to 1963 he completed further theological and university courses and rejected 'the foolishness and barrenness of modernism'. He was ordained in the Congregationalist Church in 1964 and in that same year succeeded the Rev. Norman Pell as full-time national director of the Australian Christian Endeavour Movement. He was full-time director of the 1968 Billy Graham Crusade in the Sydney showground, when 455,000 attended eight rallies and 22,000 decisions were made. In 1968 he became the director of the NSW Congregational Board of Evangelism and was involved in many local church missions and youth crusades in that State. In his connexion with the Festival of Light, he arranged for a number of prominent morals campaigners and Christian celebrities to visit Australia: Mary Whitehouse (1973, 1978 and 1984); Pat Boone (1974); Malcolm Muggeridge (1976); Mother Teresa (1981). In 1981, representing the Call to Australia Party, he was elected to the Legislative Council of the NSW Parliament, with 9 per cent of the primary vote. Elaine was elected in 1988. The Festival of Light's high public profile and its resorting to political processes raised fears that Australia was turning to fundamentalism. But the Australian evangelical right has not developed the political clout of the American right institutionalised in such groups as the Moral Majority, the Christian Voice, the National Conservative Political Action Committee, and the Religious Roundtable.

Meanwhile, in Canberra, the national capital, Merv Lee (Liberal) and Gil Duthie (Labor) launched the Parliamentary Christian Fellowship in 1968 with twenty-five members. They proposed to hold a combined church service on the day Parliament opened each year, and to follow the American custom of prayer breakfasts twice a year. It was a brave move, and the nervous founders knew that it was. Arthur Calwell, the Catholic leader of the Labor Party, condemned the fellowship, and Gil Duthie, for twenty-nine years federal member for the Tasmanian seat of Wilmot, confided in his diary what he could not say in public: 'How typical of so many Labor men today. They are as cynical, as materialistic & cold as the capitalists they condemn.'[40] Duthie was a member of the New and Permanent Parliament House Committee, charged with the oversight of a new parliamentary building for the federal capital. On 2 March 1970, Duthie recorded in his diary:

> Jim Cavanagh attacked the use of the word 'chapel' in the new Parliament & got it altered to 'meditation room'. Murphy and Cavanagh, both agnostics, said some frightening things & Gough Whitlam made the cynical comment, 'Anyway, there won't be any believers left by 2000 A. D.'[41]

Twenty years later, Australia celebrated its bicentenary by opening the new Parliament House. On Monday 9 May 1988 representative religious leaders offered prayers at the opening. The brief service was an afterthought. The prior thought was to have no religious involvement. At the subsequent opening ceremony neither the Prime Minister nor the Queen, although Supreme Governor on Earth of the Church of England, had anything to say about God's role in that righteousness which exalteth a nation. The Prime Minister, Bob Hawke, the son of a Congregationalist clergyman, spoke of spirits and ghosts, but he was waxing sentimental rather than mystical. He is no high priest of the civil religion, unlike the American President who at every inauguration since George Washington's has led his people into a covenantal compact with the Deity.

Twenty thousand people came to Parliament House for the opening,[42] far short of the projected one hundred thousand. The previous Saturday there gathered on the same spot 35,000 Christians, far in excess of the numbers projected by the Prime Minister, who is reported to have said that they would not muster enough to surround a football field, let alone the grounds of the largest building in the southern hemisphere. The event, which was organised by such Charismatic groups as the Intercessors, Ministries of 10,000 Men, YWAM,[43] and the evangelical group, Fusion, testifies to the growing impact of the Charismatic movement in Australia and its integration with the mainstream churches. The crowd participated in a service of reconciliation with Aboriginal people and, linking arms, surrounded, six deep, the new sacred site with prayer. Among those who led the vast throng in prayer was Freda Whitlam,[41] sister of the prophet of Christianity's demise by the year 2000.

Australia continued to be a difficult place for conservative Christians to thrive in politics. It was not only the opposition of secularist politicians such as Wran who loved to have a dig at the Christians and remind them, whenever they made a stand for Christian principle, that the Established Church was a thing of the past. The perfectionist demands of conservative evangelicals with their keen sense of withdrawal holiness and their aversion to compromise has also made the role of the evangelical politician thankless. A great problem has been the reluctance of the evangelical pulpit to enunciate principles in other than personal morality and to give pastoral support to members of their churches who are in politics. Their fear is the charge of 'interference'. The reality is that evangelical leaders failed to get together with other Christians to express a common mind on individual items, fearing 'contamination' by non-evangelicals. The 1988 New South Wales elections were instructive. The leaders of both major parties were churchgoing Catholics. Neither in church nor school was evangelicalism producing self-denying, thoughtful, public-spirited citizens. It was a low point for evangelicals—not a Catholic plot, but an evangelical capitulation to the pursuit of private affluence.

Strengthening the World Strand

A new opportunity for evangelicals to address pressing social and political issues in a non-fundamentalist way came with the appointment of the David Penman as Archbishop of Melbourne in 1984. He was a popular modern exemplar of the evangelical synthesis of Spirit, Word and world, with a passion for the social application of the Gospel. He, together with his evangelical archdeacon, Alan Nichols, were determined to strengthen the world strand in the evangelical tapestry. Melbourne evangelicalism generally, less clerical than Sydney, is more determined to be socially relevant. In the late 1960s and 1970s Ridley College trained a large number of 'theologs', unexcited by the prospect of ordination, but very committed to the interaction of faith and society in areas such as the media, counselling for drug addicts, community counselling programmes, outdoor education, Christian approaches to the arts, and ministry to the counter-culture. Penman had been a CMS missionary in Pakistan, and he continued to combine a passion for mission with a sensitivity to multiculturalism. On his appointment as Archbishop of Melbourne, as if aware that his time was short, he made a number of dramatic changes to refocus the diocese on its mission in its social context rather than maintenance of the old structures. He created departments of multicultural ministry, of evangelism and church growth, and of youth. Though opposed by cautious traditionalists and strongly Reformed evangelicals, Penman was immensely popular with the public, particularly over his strong and courageous support for the ordination of women and for the victims of AIDS. He was an adviser to the government on public health, multiculturalism, and foreign affairs. His premature death in 1989 produced a spontaneous demonstration of community affection. His widow received over 1300 letters of condolence.[45] God moves in a mysterious way that he should allow such a rare champion of the evangelical synthesis to be removed from the scene where he was so needed.

Evangelicalism, however, continues to nurture Australians who strategise on the grand scale so that God might have the world. The Rev. Gordon Moyes, from 1978 superintendent of the Wesley Central Mission in Sydney, is a well-known example. Worship, evangelism, Christian education and social service all receive highly specialised attention at the mission, while the whole work is saturated in prayer, the evangelical heritage is preserved, and secularisation consciously resisted.[46] Less well-known is NSW Baptist education lecturer, Gordon Young, known to his acquaintances as 'the Bishop of Australia'. 'Not failure, but low aim is crime,' his mother told him.[47] He believed her, and has spent much of his life dreaming, planning and working to ensure that an evangelical presence is found in every Australian country town with more than 500 people. Precisely because the Word strand is so strong in his evangelicalism, he has not only a passion for evangelism, but a clear understanding of what his goal looks like. He has 'a grasp of where bad theology leads congregations',[48] so he wants to see at least one church in every country town where 'the whole counsel of God in His Word' is taught.[49] In 1973 he launched Partners with Local Churches, a network to achieve his goal. To help those 'in poverty, distress or loneliness' and to take advantage of the tax deductibility provision, he formed Partners in Problems. He co-operated with every organisation and individual of evangelical commitment, including Charismatics, but he was prepared to be outspoken about the problems which typically infected the evangelical body and which he identified as 'modernism, charismaticism, high Calvinism, Popery in and out of the Baptist Church, officialism in church and denomination, and modern ideas like easy divorce, especially in all church officers'.[50] He had the traditional evangelical's nervousness of reported 'second blessing' experiences. His own conversion was so glorious that he never felt the need for a second blessing, and he suspected that many who did had never been truly converted in the first place. From the instant of his sudden conversion he was given a determination 'to tell the world'.

John Curtis, a full-time lay minister in the Churches of Christ, shared the same determination. He dreamed of taking Broken Hill for Christ, which, in view of its history as a tough mining town with proud union traditions, was an ambitious dream. In 1982 he and his wife Judy sold their home and with another family bought the St Joseph's Sisters of Mercy Convent. There they housed three families, a theological college which was a branch of Cornerstone (an Australian evangelical training college operating mainly in country towns), a youth refuge, a family crisis centre, and a retreat centre for out-of-town Christian workers. To reach the rising tide of unemployed youth he purchased a double-decker bus and used it as a mobile drop-in centre. When the novelty of this had worn off, Woolworths donated their Broken Hill store to the Barrier Youth Association of which John Curtis was secretary, and it was converted to a massive games parlour. To provide money for the theological students to help pay their fees, he opened a pizza home-delivery business, and soon had the whole town converted to pizza consumption. To reach people in times of need, he bought the local funeral business. To reach people at all times of the day and night, he bought the only commercial radio station in town, which alarmed the locals until they found that he did not intend to thrust religion down their throats. He had a more subtle approach. He decided that nothing would be broadcast which was incompatible with the Christian faith. So, for example, in a town notorious for sexism, he would refuse to make any derogatory remarks, even in jest, about his wife. Only positive things would ever be said about the institution of holy matrimony. The radio station was also used to train Christian radio announcers so that they could go and do likewise. To give a job to an unemployed, bereaved man who was in danger of losing the fight with alcohol, he bought a tourist mine and put the man in as manager. His determination to meet people at their point of need from a heart full of love was wildly infectious and brought great hope to a community which felt sadly neglected by governments and industries. John Curtis, who had been a management consultant before entering the ministry, was the sort of well-rounded evangelistic entrepreneur which the evangelical synthesis of Spirit, Word and world can produce in one of conspicuous natural managerial and organisational talent.[51]

Revival: The Rivers of the Spirit Run Freely

Another whom we have identified as a powerful personification of the evangelical synthesis, Geoffrey Bingham, saw amazing scenes of revival in Pakistan in the late 1950s[52] and returned to Sydney full of the joy of the Lord. But he was not heard gladly by those whose Biblicism and experience made them nervous of anything which could be interpreted as Charismatic or sinless perfectionist. In their zeal to avoid the excesses of the past, by which some of them were damaged personally, they excluded from their understanding of pure evangelicalism any expectation of revival. Bingham, hurt, left the rather cool and unwelcoming bosom of Sydney, went to South Australia, first as principal of the Bible College of South Australia, and then as director of New Creation Ministries, where he wrote, published and taught an ever-expanding army of devoted disciples, who attended conferences and schools. Bingham also took missions, and at some of these the fire of revival fell.

In August 1969 a mission entitled Free Indeed was held at Wudinna on the Eyre peninsula in South Australia. Bingham addressed the meetings in the little Methodist church there, of which Deane Metheringham was minister. A large turn-out at the opening meeting startled the organisers and they moved to a hall, but even there many hearers had to stand outside and listen through the open windows. The addresses were Bible messages on the bondage of man to sin and Satan and the powers of darkness and of flesh and the world, and the true freedom which Christ gives from such powers. The atmosphere was one of heightened expectancy, the listening was intent, and many attended who were not thought to be at all interested in Christian things. There was a sense of the presence of God brooding over the whole geographical area. A farmer who had not been coming to the meetings, although his wife did, was out on his tractor ploughing when great conviction came upon him and he got down in the dust and gave his life to the Lord.

A woman, characterised by her husband as a chain-smoking hard-swearing harridan, gave up smoking, swearing, and anger. Many nominals, pew-sitters for years, were brought to their knees in tears and repentance, and received forgiveness, new life and unimaginable joy. Crowds of people would just sit in wonder for half an hour after the meetings were over without moving or saying a word. Many felt that it was like Pentecost, although without tongues. Over 400 people came to the last meeting, from as far away as Ceduna and Cummins. Of the final night, Bingham said:

> like a great rain of beauty and silence and joy, it just descended on the whole congregation. It was quite remarkable. I'd have called it a very gentle but a very powerful outpouring of the Holy Spirit. And I can remember the joy in the worship and the praise that night.[53]

A decade after Wudinna, Australia was visited by one of the most significant revivals in its history. This revival began among Aboriginal people in the Uniting Church in Elcho Island (now Galiwin'ku) in late 1978. According to their pastor, Djiniyini Gondarra:

> ... people were starting to feel that something strange was happening, through dreams, through being woken up at night and seeing something wonderful. Some people were just going and praying for sick people and those people were being healed. They were starting to wonder.[54]

On 14 March 1979 about thirty people gathered with Djiniyini Gondarra, who thanked those few who had been praying for renewal and he said that he too had been praying for revival. He describes what happened next:

> I asked the group to hold each other's hands and I began to pray for the people and for the church, that God would pour out His Holy

Spirit to bring healing and renewal to the hearts of men and women, and to the children. Suddenly we began to feel God's Spirit moving in our hearts and the whole form of prayer-life suddenly changed and everybody began to pray in spirit and in harmony. And there was a great noise going on in the room and we began to ask one another what was going on. Some of us said that God had now visited us and once again established His kingdom among His people.[55]

Nightly meetings were now held with upwards of 200 in attendance, some of which went on until 2 a.m. Few on the island were left untouched. On one weekend 128 either accepted Christ or rededicated their lives to him. Not only was the worship reportedly sweeter, but there was also a change in the tone of the community: less drunkenness, petrol sniffing, and fighting; greater conscientiousness in work; an increased boldness in speaking out against social injustices. Men took over leadership of the church and the singing in worship from women, an event of great significance in Aboriginal society:

It was not only in the camp but in the church and the community as a whole, in fact the relationships with the church, the council, with the departments, the foreman, the bosses, and the workmen, the family and the village life with wives, husbands and children, were affected. It just swept through as though God had turned on a tap and was cleansing out the power of darkness. All the time we could hear singing; people would go past talking about it and at night we could go to sleep hearing people still singing Christian choruses. It was just like Pentecost.[56]

Unlike most of the revivals in Australian history, the Aboriginal revival was neither localised nor short-lived. 'When we read the Scriptures,' explained Djiniyini Gondarra, 'of Peter and others when they received the power of the Spirit, they didn't stop, they went out. This was revealed to us and we started to minister to other communities.'[57] Using the facilities of the Missionary Aviation Fellowship, the Elcho Islanders spread their good news all over Arnhem Land, and north and north-western Australia. At the Anglican Roper River Mission (Ngukurr) in eastern Arnhem Land, which had been reduced to a social disaster area by the granting of a liquor licence, the revival came as a form of social salvation. Sister Edna Brooker exclaimed: 'New life has come to Ngukurr ... half the population say they have turned to Christ and the transformation from alcohol, petrol sniffing and immorality is very wonderful.'[58] At Wiluna in Western Australia crime dropped to zero, and the local publican had to put on free beer in an attempt to entice people back into his pub. In August 1981 revival came to Warburton, and some white missionaries sought ministry from Aboriginal Christians and were greatly blessed. Malcolm Champion, a Church Army evangelist and, from 1985, first Anglican Aboriginal bishop, described the coming of revival to Warburton and Meekatharra thus:

> ... God called all the Christians, and so-called Christians, together in a place called Cement Creek. There God called them to true repentance in heart and soul. The number of people there was 120. It's funny that that was the same number as in the Book of Acts. We wonder was God saying something with a sense of humour; anyway God began to work ... doing wonders and miracles, and then the rain poured down to fill Cement Creek with water and the whole 120 were baptised. It didn't rain anywhere else—just where God began this work among the people ...
>
> An arrow in the sky told them to go and preach in the town of Warburton. 3,000 people came to the Lord and then 5,000 as they went on towards Meekatharra. So this is a repeat of what happened in the Book of Acts. This is the work of the [underprivileged and powerless] people and the Holy Spirit. It was not a Convention or the Missionary way with people being ordered from here to there. You see, God used people with an open heart, people who were broken down but open to God, not people who were conformed to some other ways. This is a true story. AMEN.[59]

In 1982 the Western Australian Government was determined to hand over the old Mt Margaret mission in Western Australia to a group of Aboriginal people who practised the old tribal law, but a week before the handover was to take place, a group arrived from Warburton bringing revival with them. Practically the entire population came to put their faith in Christ. When the changeover was due to take place, the frustrated government officials were told, 'we are all Christians now'.[60] And the Aboriginal revival was not short-lived. It has continued for many years. In 1988, for example, Bishop Malcolm, following a successful teaching mission on Groote Eylandt, baptised 108 people in the Angurugu River.[61]

The Aboriginal revival must be seen as a spiritual solution to a desperate cultural and social crisis. It is one of the very few solutions which the Aboriginal people have experienced since the coming of whites. They have been suffering from what the anthropologists call 'demoralisation': a disintegrating culture, accompanied by alcohol abuse, petrol-sniffing, suicide, and violence. They have had to initiate and sustain the battle for land rights against a largely unsympathetic white population. And they have been confronted with the necessity of synthesising traditional and Christian beliefs.[62] Factors in the revival bear on all these issues critical to the survival of Aboriginal people: the assumption of control of churches by native pastors; the use of the vernacular in worship and other expressions of indigenisation such as the composition of their own songs; the charismatic element expressed in healings, exorcism, tongues, and visions; the creation of fellowship groups for ministry to one another (perhaps the chief instrument of the revival); the institutionalisation of the revival in such ceremonies as the Thanksgiving Weekend around 14 March when the revival began, for the Aborigines prefer to organise their lives around celebrations; the missionary enthusiasm to share the experience of liberation with others of their race.

It is unlikely that the Aboriginal revival would have been nearly as significant had not the Charismatic movement matured to the point that it was able to offer the Aboriginal people a whole range of methods of expressing their new-found faith in a way which they could understand. Accompanying the revival have been amazing phenomena which owe far more to the Charismatic movement than to traditional Reformed evangelicalism. John Blacket[63] reports miracles, sightings of angels, numerous visions of fire coming down from heaven igniting spotfires all over the continent, of a great river flowing from Elcho Island to towns in southern Western Australia, of signs in the sky telling the Aboriginal evangelists and their teams where to go next; he tells of many dreams in fulfilment of the prophet Joel, who prophesied that sons and daughters would prophesy, old men would dream dreams and young men would see visions, deliverances, even a resurrection or two! But these 'Charismatic' features of this revival, which had made many whites cautious at first, have come to be seen as themselves time-honoured features of Aboriginal culture. This was especially true of the visions which had preceded the revival and which continued to feature as the years passed. Visions of Christ were the most reported of all visions. In 1983 a small Aboriginal boy in kindergarten at Yarrabah, south of Cairns in Queensland, did a butterfly painting, putting paint on a piece of paper and folding it in half. When he opened it, he gazed on a remarkable likeness of Christ with crown of thorns. This was understood as a sign, and so great was the excitement among Aboriginal people that revival came to Yarrabah immediately.[64]

Djiniyini Gondarra had a remarkable vision of crows and flying foxes (which are totems of himself and his wife) and of a beautiful girl wearing lots of bangles, namely Queen Jezebel. Gondarra called out to his wife, 'Go to Jerusalem, get the blood and wash the cross.' She did so and, when she washed the cross with the blood, it turned into a flaming two-edged sword, and she thrust it through Jezebel who turned back into a flying fox and exploded. Then God said to Gondarra:

> You lay down every totem and ceremony. In each of them there is good and bad. All of them must come under my Lordship, be washed by the blood of Jesus Christ, and then you will see a new Aboriginal culture. I don't want to destroy and leave you empty. I will restore and renew what is good.[65]

It would be totally inadequate to view this experience as just another bout of Pentecostal delirium. Djiniyini's vision gave him the clear cultural message that Christianity comes not to destroy but to fulfil the aspirations of traditional Aboriginal law. The revival is thus a dramatic step by the Aboriginal people towards self-identity. Once—during the two centuries of subjugation—they were no people; now they are a people, God's people. The revival is the power by which the Aboriginal people are moving away from subjugation towards autonomy and a genuinely independent Aboriginal church. For a start, the revival itself was completely led by Aboriginal people. It was when white missionaries were away or had just left an Aboriginal community that the revival came.[66]

Revivals are often associated with the political empowerment of a social group, leading to economic progress and cultural integration.[67] Revival is the power sufficient for the indigenisation of Christianity in minority cultures, leading to the empowerment of adherents of those cultures who had hitherto been demoralised unto death. This is how anthropologist and

Uniting Church minister Robert Bos interprets the Aboriginal revival.[68] It was one of the means by which Aboriginal people were able to persevere in their campaign for land rights and for a just recompense for the land from which they had been dispossessed. On 3 June 1992, in the case of *Mabo v. State of Queensland*, the High Court of Australia buried the fiction that, at the time of white settlement, Australia was *terra nullius* (land belonging to no-one), and therefore indigenous peoples had a legal communal title to land. The States, mining and pastoral interests, howled with hysteria, but the Aboriginal people, now strengthened by revival and strongly supported by the churches, were able to persuade Australians to seek truth and justice in this issue, rather than be ruled by self-interest. The Aboriginal people, together with the churches, have been in the vanguard in the matter of land rights, but together they have changed the national mood which has become one of a desire for reconciliation between black and white and atonement for past wrongs.[69] Mabo is an achievement of the Spirit.

9. Word Rather than Peace:
The Fight over the Ordination of Women in
Australian Anglicanism, 1992

On 23 December 1991 Owen Dowling, Bishop of the Anglican Diocese of Canberra and Goulburn, announced that he intended to ordain eleven women as priests on 2 February 1992. On Christmas Eve he faxed his intention to the Archbishop of Sydney, who the same day faxed him back urging him not to proceed. It was on Christmas Eve, too, that the archbishop was invited by 'certain individuals in both Sydney and Melbourne' to be a plaintiff in a suit to the New South Wales Supreme Court to seek an injunction against Dowling. The archbishop declined the invitation, preferring to influence Dowling through his position as Metropolitan.[1] On Boxing Day, Dowling faxed his intention to proceed. On 3 January Archbishop Robinson wrote under his episcopal seal, invoking the bishop's oath of obedience to him as Metropolitan, and directing him not to proceed. Dowling replied a week later that he was not obliged to obey the archbishop's opinion. To this the archbishop replied on 24 January, pointing out that he had not asked for his opinions to be accepted, but his direction.

A Clash of World Views

The gloves were off. But it was not a two-man match. Behind the two combatants were the organisations which represented each side of the contest, including the Movement for the Ordination of Women (MOW) and the Association for the Apostolic Ministry (AAM). Behind the organisations were the convictions and world views which made this perhaps the most divisive issue which the church had confronted in its Australian history.[2] It was a dispute which caused new alignments in the church: Anglo-Catholics sided with conservative evangelicals to resist what they perceived to be a feminist onslaught, and evangelicals were divided among themselves.

It was a new and unnerving experience for Bible-believing Christians to be in such fundamental disagreement with each other. In 1985 Sydney's evangelical Anglican theologians declared the issue to be one of Biblical authority and hermeneutics. They were led by John Woodhouse and Robert Doyle of Moore Theological College, ably supported by Peter Jensen and David Peterson. Woodhouse addressed the question, how can evangelicals, who believe the Bible is the inspired Word of God, come to different opinions about the ordination of women? He argued that the problem did not lie with the Scriptural texts. Scholars were not in disagreement over their basic meaning. The problem came with the application of that meaning to the present day. It was a matter of hermeneutics, and he contended that those who favoured the ordination of women were applying the Bible to the present in a way which was inconsistent with the Bible itself. They were using the Bible in a way 'which *protects* us from our own views'.[3] In March 1988 a special conference of the Evangelical Fellowship of the Anglican Communion allowed Sydney and Melbourne evangelicals to compare their positions. It was not a happy occasion. Leon Morris, retired principal of Ridley College in Melbourne, in his paper 'Headship in the New Testament', argued that, even using the same historico-grammatical hermeneutic of the Sydney evangelicals, there was room for disagreement on the headship issue. At Ridley College, lecturer Charles Sherlock, for whom the ordination of women was a Gospel necessity rather than just an option,[4] could not identify with the Sydney scene—'I seem to be living in a different evangelical Christian world.'[5] Indeed, different evangelical worlds were emerging. The evangelicalism of Ridley College was more akin to English Anglican evangelicalism. Its theological orientation was towards the cross and the blood of Christ, whereas Moore College's was towards the Word of God. Ridley's international links were strongest with St John's Nottingham, the London Bible College, and Fuller Theological Seminary. Moore College's links were with Trinity Evangelical Divinity School in Deerfield, USA.

Identified with the pro-ordination case were a growing number of reputable evangelical scholars and clergy: Michael Green and David Watson, who were among the best-known of English evangelical clergy; J. Baldwin;[6] Ward Gasque and Gordon Fee, both Professors of New Testament at Regent College in Vancouver; Klaas Runia,[7] Professor of Practical Theology at the Reformed Seminary in Kampen, Netherlands; Colin Buchanan, principal of St John's College, Nottingham; Leon Morris,[8] principal of Ridley

College in Melbourne; Paul Jewett,[9] Fuller Theological Seminary, California; F. F. Bruce,[10] Manchester University; David Scholer, Northern Baptist Theological Seminary; I. H. Marshall, Reader in New Testament Exegesis at Aberdeen University; and even Harold Lindsell, the extremely conservative 'inerrantist' in his view of Scripture.[11] An increasing number of evangelical scholars have come to the conclusion that there is nothing in Scripture to warrant opposition to the appointment or ordination of women to the ministry of Word and Sacrament or to the office of elder. A smaller number of evangelical scholars, but they too are increasing, argue that the proper understanding of the Scriptures and the Gospel of unity and liberation makes it very important to ordain women. Some scholars argue that the Scriptures support the view that there should be full and equal partnership between men and women in ministry. The cultural argument tends to be important among such scholars. Some advise caution in pushing ahead with female ordination in cultures where women's rights are still largely unrecognised; others contend that, in societies where such rights are recognised, female ordination is essential for the prosperity of the Gospel.

Outside the church, Australians, apparently uninterested in the traditional Christian message, have been intrigued by this debate. It is a debate which touches deeply many issues of primary concern to contemporary Australians. The revolution in the social role and understanding of women is probably the biggest social issue facing our nation. A related issue is the understanding of masculinity in Australian history. If the movement for the ordination of women is likely to meet with tough opposition in the rest of the Western world, it will meet with particularly virulent opposition in Australia, where the battle between the sexes has been the most pronounced aspect of our social history.[12] A very important contribution to the debate is coming from the social sciences, which are providing the educated leaders of our society with new ways of understanding reality. Post-structuralism, the most potent methodological development in modern sociolinguistics, relativises patriarchy; it shows it to be just one political option among many, and questions its right to be accepted as Gospel in the church.

The Protagonists: Dowling and Robinson

In 1990 Owen Dowling had explained to his diocesan synod how he had come to the conclusion that he must support the ordination of women. In the late 1960s he had argued against it at a clergy conference. He won the debate, but was not convinced by his own arguments. He was beset by doubts, and came to change his mind. Now the church in which he was a bishop had declared that there is no theological objection of a kind that would prevent the ordination of women, and that there is no ground to believe that orders of deacon, priest or bishop must be male. He therefore felt conscience-bound to allow it to happen and to pursue it with vigour. Dowling angrily dismissed the argument, advanced by Dr Ian Spry, Chair of AAM, that he was prevented from ordaining women by an ancient canon of the church. In a number of areas changes of practice had occurred in the church before they were ratified by a canon of General Synod:

> The order is clear: the living experience of the church, then synodical discussion and decision-making to clear up disagreements and set uncertainties aside. The church then acts fearlessly under the Spirit, not necessarily tied by the traditions or even the written commands of Scripture. It is a church which faces the demands of the Gospel and refuses to be bound by law.[13]

No Sydney evangelical could agree with this. To set aside any written command of Scripture was quite impossible. Dowling was considered a genial and kindly man, but a quite unsafe guide to action on this or any other matter since he was not prepared to stand under the Scripture.

Unlike Dowling, Archbishop Donald Robinson never moved on the issue. He had not changed in his thinking since 1949 when he read in the *Reformed Theological Review* Donovan Mitchell's 'Women and the Ministry: Whither Exegesis?', an 'article I regard as the most important I have ever read on the topic'.[14] In an attempt to explain why New Testament scholars have failed to reach agreement on 'the mind of Christ' in this matter, Mitchell contended that scholars have dispensed with 'two instruments of thought' which Christ entrusted to the apostles, the apostolic tradition and the law or norm of nature. Robinson admitted that he had found it difficult to take seriously any case for the ordination of women which neglected to take the apostolic tradition into account. In subsequent statements of his position, he has reiterated that the case against the ordination of women rests on Scripture, tradition and nature, and there is not much evidence that anyone in Sydney has challenged his position with anywhere near the acumen that the strength of his position warrants. Outside Sydney, the position which Robinson adopted had been challenged in an arresting manner by Professor G. W. H. Lampe,[15] who characterised the tradition against female ordination as a 'peculiar kind' of tradition. It was peculiar because, while it enjoyed very wide acceptance, its foundation was uncertain. The view that female priests were contrary to the apostolic tradition and therefore an impossibility for the church was based on the mistaken belief that Scriptural authority for it was unchallengeable, compounded by the popular prejudice that women are inferior to men.

Robinson is popularly understood to believe that the exclusively male priesthood is of the essence of the Gospel. This popular misconception has probably vexed a lot of humble Christians who cannot conceive how the Gospel, by which they have been saved and which they love, could have such an unlikely element at its core. To understand Robinson's position, it is necessary to be more precise. Robinson believes that the all-male priesthood is an essential part, not of the Gospel, but of the apostolic tradition (*paradosis*), of which the Gospel is but part. This apostolic tradition has three major strands: the Gospel (e.g. I Corinthians 15.1ff.); teaching on moral conduct (e.g. I Thessalonians 4.1–8); and teaching on church order or conduct in the congregation. The proposal to ordain women violates the last, but any violation of the apostolic tradition is unacceptable because it is a violation of Scripture to obey which Anglicans are committed by their constitution as a church. This commitment is the 'only way we have of submitting to the authority of Christ over the church'.[16] Obedience to the apostolic tradition, he argued, was not something anyone should fear. The only thing we have to fear is acting contrary to the mind of Christ as revealed in Scripture. When the 1988 Lambeth Conference suggested that this tradition, which incorporates a theology of the relationship of men and women and of male leadership in church order, is open to development, Robinson dissented. It can be discarded, he claimed, but it cannot be developed:

> Unless it can be shown—and acknowledged by the consensus of Christian people—that the New Testament teaching on the relation of men and women in creation, in marriage and in the congregation has *wrongly* been understood to have been part of the apostolic paradosis, and that consequently the Church has *mistakenly* included it in its on-going tradition ever since, the ordination of women to the priesthood and episcopate today must be regarded as a violation of the charter of our faith as a church.[17]

Archbishop Robinson's opposition to the ordination of women was so intransigent that wondering journalists sought the reason. He was able to withstand the feminist push, he maintained, by separating the principle from the personal. Though he moved to tears women who supported the ordination of women, he himself was unmoved by those tears. His integrity, made up of fairmindedness combined with a capacity to lift the debate above the personal and never to bear a grudge, became legendary and won him admiration from both sides. But the assessment of his role in the struggle has not been entirely complimentary. He has been accused of using whatever power he possesses to maintain his position, apparently without regard to the cost.[18] Surrounded by conservatives, he did not hear much about the cost anyway, and was heard to say such things as he did not know of any women who had left the church over the issue. He was not able to continue to make that claim, however. One who wrote to him on 21 March 1992 informing him of her decision on the grounds of conscience to leave the Anglican Church was Patricia Hayward, convenor of Sydney MOW. To her the archbishop replied:

> ... on both sides there are those who believe themselves to be following obedience to God as they understand it. This may be, in one sense, the most difficult part of the dilemma.
>
> I regret to read of the clear sense of hurt and dismay which is yours. I would ask you to join your prayers with mine that God will bring us to a just and peaceable outcome of our present troubles and that we may be brought to that unity of mind and heart which all agree is God's intention for his people.[19]

The Pressure Groups: MOW and AAM

The Movement for the Ordination of Women had been established in 1983 by Dr Patricia Brennan. To Monica Furlong, the English author, who visited Australia for MOW in 1984, 'it was the adamant, wounding kind of opposition within the Sydney diocese that had got MOW started there, mainly by women from Evangelical backgrounds'.[20] In April 1983 Brennan worked with a prominent diocesan leader on a committee considering female priesthood, and she presented him with the accounts of eighteen females who were finding the church's stance on feminism problematical.

Within two days, she asserts, he returned the accounts and declined to talk to her about the issue. This galvanised her in her determination to form MOW. 'He created MOW,' she now asserts provocatively.[21] History cannot accord him that honour, of course: surely MOW would have been formed anyway. But the scene was set for a struggle within the evangelical fellowship itself.

Brennan had worked as a missionary doctor in Nigeria with a conservative evangelical missionary society, the Sudan Interior Mission, serving in mission hospitals and for a number of aid agencies, such as the Ethiopian Famine Relief Fund. She was national president of MOW from 1985 until 1989, and was a foundation member of the General Synod Women's Commission. She increased her profile as presenter of the ABC TV social issues programmes, 'Brennan's Way' (1986) and 'Brennan' (1987). In 1993 she was awarded the Australia Medal for her 'distinctive and pioneering role in the struggle by women for equality within the Christian Churches in Australia and beyond'.[22] MOW was joined by tertiary-educated and professional women from all denominations. It has been a singularly effective organisation, never large in numerical support or in financial resources, but with great resources of determination and creativity. It has been dangerously underestimated by its opponents, who have looked down on its members as the 'ratbag fringe'. In fact, it has understood and tapped the tremendous support of the Australian population for sexual equality, and has used the media to brilliant effect. It is interesting that it started as an evangelical group in Sydney, but in meeting the needs of the Australia-wide church and mixing with women of different traditions within the church, it found a means of promoting a tolerance not generally found among males within the church. MOW has actually been a positive force in the uniting of the Anglican Church of Australia, but, because it was an international and ecumenical movement as well as a feminist one, it was far too rich a blend for the conservative evangelical palate. In the belief that alignment with MOW was damaging, some evangelicals who supported the ordination of women pulled back and formed Men, Women and God which argued the case for ordination of women on Biblical grounds.

In March 1989 the various anti-ordination groups formed an Australian branch of the Association for the Apostolic Ministry, an international body which Archbishop Robinson of Sydney co-chaired with the Bishop of London, Graham Leonard. The Chair of the Australian branch of AAM was

Dr Ian C. F. Spry, a senior Melbourne QC, 'brilliant, kind, but notoriously hard on people with whom he disagrees'.[23] By August 1989 twelve bishops had joined AAM Australia, and its leadership, heartened by news from England that the movement for the ordination of women was losing ground, expressed a determination to oppose the 'essentially secular and largely feminist movement for the ordination of women as priests and bishops'.[24] AAM regretted the weakness under pressure evinced by Anglican leadership for some time, and reminded bishops of their primary responsibility, which was to preserve the tradition of the church. The clergy, too, were a bunch of wimps who were influenced by their wives who had been infected with feminism. The dominance of clergy by their feminist wives was labelled 'the Mrs Proudie factor', a reference to the harridan of Trollope's *Barchester Towers*.[25] By September 1989 the Australian membership of AAM stood at 2000, with fourteen bishops. It was a group which looked to the Appellate Tribunal to stop the rampaging pro-ordination bishops, and then, should this fail, the civil courts. That the unthinkable should happen, and Christians should find themselves attempting to resolve the issue in civil courts, was never unthinkable to AAM under the redoubtable Ian Spry, QC.

The First Court Hearings

Dr Laurie Scandrett, a Sydney layman, and two clergymen, Dalba Primmer from Canberra and Goulburn Diocese and David Robarts from Melbourne, on 16 January 1992 commenced proceedings in the New South Wales Supreme Court to obtain a restraining order on the grounds that Dowling could not lawfully ordain women without a General Synod canon. They then asked Dowling to hold off the ordination until the matter had been heard. Dowling refused to give such an undertaking, so the plaintiffs applied for an injunction preventing Dowling from proceeding before the matter was determined. On 28 January, Mr Justice Rogers dismissed the application. The plaintiffs then appealed to the Supreme Court of New South Wales Court of Appeal. On 31 January, Justices Gleeson, Samuels, and Meagher upheld the appeal, and Dowling was restrained from the ordination pending the final determination of the proceedings.[26] Exasperated, he denounced 'the outlook and attitudes of the controlling faction in the Diocese of Sydney, the most conservative diocese in the whole of the worldwide Anglican communion ... who turn questionable tradition into immutable law'. The Bishop of Newcastle condemned events in the New South Wales Supreme Court when 'the cold, clammy hand of legalism was placed on the heart of the church'. The Sydney legalists were characterised as 'a brood of vipers' who engage in 'legalistic filibustering'.[27] To the charge that the defenders of Biblical inspiration were themselves refusing to stand under the authority of Scripture in taking their fellow believers to court, the Archbishop of Sydney expressed his opinion that I Corinthians 6 did not apply in this case.[28]

Meanwhile, the eleven women deacons whose hopes of ordination had been blasted at the eleventh hour, were comforted by the ministry of the Rev. Alison Cheek, a close friend of Brennan. An Australian by birth, she is now on the faculty of Harvard University, and one of the Philadelphia Eleven ordained to the priesthood by three retired Episcopal bishops in 1974. She had flown from America to attend the Goulburn celebration. The resort to the courts and the stopping of the ordination created martyrs, of course, and added emotional and popular support to the women's cause. The Goulburn un-ordination, or non-ordination as it became known, probably did more for the women's cause by being stopped than it did by proceeding. One of the frustrated deacons, Ruth Mills, a chaplain at Canberra's Calvary Hospital, said:

> I hadn't accounted for how the congregation would lift me. Life will never be the same; if anything I feel I have a stronger fire in my belly and, as they say, I won't let the bastards get me down.[29]

The Reformed Evangelical Protestant Association

The emotions unleashed by the resort to the civil courts threatened not only the unity of the Anglican Church in Australia, but also the residual unity of evangelicalism. Rival pressure groups sprang up overnight. REPA was formed at two meetings on 7 and 21 February 1992 by eighteen clergymen. The occasion was the constitutional crisis provoked by the ordination of women, but the stated real purpose was to remedy the malaise which had come over the church's evangelistic outreach,[30] and to allow the Gospel to do its work of 'framing, shaping and changing our society'.[31] Its name was devised by the Rev. Jim Ramsay, rector of Liverpool, on the spur of the moment as the founders needed a name under which to open a bank account.

Ramsay came up with Reformed Evangelical Protestant Association or REPA. The name was unashamedly theological, and the determination of the founders was to explore and implement changes flowing from that stance. Its opponents branded it as 'fundamentalist' and 'the Opus Dei of the Evangelical World'.

Among the REPA eighteen, one who most earnestly and insistently called the evangelicals to the barricades was that redoubtable opponent of female ordination, John Woodhouse, by now rector of Christ Church, St Ives. He had longed for the 'full flowering of a new, biblically literate but socially relevant theology', but that possibility had receded. Instead, the distressing reality was 'a retreat from the ideas marketplace and the secular media; and a loss of spiritual energy, originality or creativity'. He pleaded for new leaders with new ideas, and was to emerge early in 1993 as the chief architect of the move to have Phillip Jensen, the main mover and shaker behind REPA, elected Archbishop of Sydney.

Phillip Jensen presides over one of the most dynamic ministries in Sydney. He has taught the Bible over the years to thousands of students of the University of New South Wales; he employs up to thirty full-time staff; his church is attended by over 1000 every week; he operates a publishing arm which produces tough-minded, Biblically based material; and he sends one-quarter of all candidates to theological college. He is not only an inspiring Bible teacher, but he is also an adroit strategist and he saw that the crisis within the Anglican Church over the ordination of women was a great and perhaps once-only opportunity to reform Anglicanism along lines more consistent with the evangelical Gospel. He met with the Primate, Archbishop Keith Rayner, and with Bishop Dowling. He suggested that it might be appropriate for the Sydney evangelicals to make concessions in return for relief from some traditions which they found irksome. The Primate, however, was not of the opinion that any compromise was needed to resolve the constitutional dilemma, and he stated his conviction that when it came to the crunch, churchgoers in Sydney would be Anglicans first and conservative evangelicals second.

The Perth Ordination

In January 1992 Archbishop Carnley of Perth announced that he intended to ordain ten women to the priesthood on 7 March. An attempt by four plaintiffs, including Laurie Scandrett, to restrain the archbishop failed, and Carnley, variously dubbed 'the episcopalian cowboy' and 'the Gucci bishop', carried out the historic ordination. He called it a 'day of liberation and expanding horizons'. In his sermon, with the help of an allusion to wallpaper from the writings of Charlotte Perkins Gilman, a nineteenth-century American feminist, he told the overflowing congregation: 'Today we are peeling away the sickly yellow, faded, silverfish-ridden wallpaper with whom the church has surrounded itself and imprisoned women for centuries past in its benign and perhaps well-meaning determination to confine them by role.'[32] At the MOW annual meeting on 15 March 1992, Patricia Brennan reported that, at the ordination in Perth, Archbishop Carnley declared that 'None of my deacons had anything to do with MOW.'[33] Carnley's deacons may have had little to do with MOW, but MOW was not reluctant to support him, at least privately. John Pomeroy, a committee member of Sydney MOW, who had been a supporter of female ordination for more than two decades, faxed the archbishop before and after the Perth ordination. His first fax said: 'Congratulations on your decision to proceed and to join John Bunyan if necessary … It is not so much "custard" on the part of the opposition, merely constitutional misogyny!' And his second: 'Marvellous! wonderful! The Midianites are in disarray.'[34]

It is clear from the MOW correspondence file, following the Perth ordinations, that many of Carnley's deacons greatly appreciated the support which members of MOW had given them. The sisterhood of suffering was becoming a sisterhood of celebration. As one enthused: 'Wot a day! Wot a life! Felt the presence of you all—such a wave of wonder and joy!'[35] The symbolic significance of Carnley's step can hardly be over-estimated. It breached the dyke holding back the rising tide of support for female ordination; it was taken by the media as the event for which they had been clamouring; and, precisely because it snubbed its nose at the cumbersome procedures of the legalists, it gave heart to supporters who were longing for a bishop to take on the establishment. One small step for Carnley was a giant leap for womankind. After Carnley there was no going back.[36]

Easter 1992

Further strains were imposed on the Diocese of Sydney on Good Friday (17 April) 1992 with the publication of an article in the *Sydney Morning Herald* representing a leading clergyman, Bruce Ballantine-Jones, as calling for the diocese to secede from the national church. He contended that the real issue was the 'drift away from biblical authority' and that female ordination was a catalyst which would lead to the constitutional reform of the church which, in turn, would provoke the Sydney Anglicans to separate from compromised sections of the Anglican Church of Australia.[37] The next day the *Herald* was full of talk of secession. Ballantine-Jones later claimed that he had put forward three options to the *Herald*, of which secession was only one; and that he had not been reported fully. As if all the talk of secession were not sufficient pain, the media pushed the issue of sexual abuse by clergy. On Easter Day itself, the archbishop found himself being interviewed on this unsavoury topic. Some misguided members of Standing Committee vented their frustration on the Anglican Information Office at its failure to control the media. It was an almighty and unholy row, but Ballantine-Jones, with the help of a lesson from history, warned that the contenders were still but sparring:

> Between September 1939 and May 1940, before they started fighting World War II, there was a phoney war period. That's what's happening now. We are in the hiatus stage and nothing is going to happen until General Synod in July.[38]

The Parramatta Conference

At the Sydney Diocesan Synod in October 1991, a motion by the Rev. Tim Harris to hold a conference the following year on the ordination of women had been passed without debate. On 27 June 1992 a diocesan conference, with speakers 'generally recognised as being within the evangelical tradition of the Anglican Church of Australia',[39] was held at St John's, Parramatta.[40] It was chaired by Bishop Harry Goodhew, now Archbishop of Sydney; the speakers included Chris Forbes and Kevin Giles, who gave the case for Biblical equality, and David Peterson and Glenn Davies, who presented the traditionalist case. The conference caused much excitement. The anti-ordination camp were judged to have been defeated on the day, but then the majority who attended were pro-ordination. Kevin Giles was reported to have spoken with too much heat and to have gone too far, but that is a matter of judgment, and others thought he was perfectly correct. This last assessment was an interesting pointer to the changing state of evangelical opinion on this subject which was the very subject of Giles' address to the conference:

> The Sydney arguments against the ordination of women … are just like the Emperor's clothes. Everyone is agreed … that there is a very strong case for the position taken, but the reality is the reverse. At no point can the case stand examination. It is a collection of texts and arguments which appear to prove what those who quote them say, but on examination each one of them is bankrupt … what you have to understand is that outside of Sydney most mainstream evangelicals—but not all—have changed their minds. They have come to see that the old theology, used to subordinate women, simply does not make sense in the culture in which we find ourselves, it unfairly discriminates against women and it sets scripture at conflict with itself. What happened is that older theologians, in the early stage of this debate, began with their own cultural assumptions about women, they thought these were reflected in I Tim 2.10–14 and then they read the rest of the New Testament through these tinted spectacles. Gradually younger theologians came to see what had taken place and started reformulating the questions and the answers. A revolution in theological thought about the status and contribution of women has taken place, and evangelical thinkers on the world scene have been right at the forefront in this process. Because Sydney keeps itself apart and does not interact in any vital way with progressive evangelical opinion, a time warp has occurred.[41]

The Parramatta conference was attended by over 370 people, who in the evaluation gave it overwhelmingly a 'very worthwhile' endorsement. The report of the synod committee who organised the conference claimed to be written 'firmly and unashamedly from an evangelical perspective'.[42] The issue was not whether the authority of Scripture should be accepted—it was accepted by all parties. The issue was the interpretation and application of Scripture in this complex area. Differences, then, between evangelicals are to be attributed to differences in exegesis (the understanding of Scripture in its original context) and in hermeneutics (the way the results of the exegesis are to be applied in today's world). The pro-ordination forces were heartened by the conference, and indeed the report is a worthy document which demonstrates, unlike any previous synod document, the strength of the pro-ordination case from a Biblical viewpoint.

The Court Judgment

The impression that the tide was beginning to flow in favour of female ordination was reinforced by the secular court. In the week that followed Easter the adjourned *Scandrett & Ors v. Dowling & Ors* case was heard before Justices D. L. Mahoney, L. J. Priestley, and R. M. Hope. Patricia Hayward, convenor of Sydney MOW, reflected with weary indignation on the fact that this case 'arbitrating on the calling by God of women' was brought by three men and heard by three men with the assistance of five male barristers.[43] The judgment was delivered on 3 July 1992 in a historic document of 167 pages. The leading judgment was the 106-page judgment of Justice Priestley, with which Justice Hope concurred. Priestley had borrowed books from Moore College in the process of reaching his verdict, and the freshness of his findings is underscored by the fact that he had to cut open the pages of the borrowed books.

The judgment went against the plaintiffs. The judges ruled that the NSW Anglican Church of Australia Constitution Act of 1961 does not have binding force at general law except in regard to matters of church property, and that from the time of the institution of legislation in New South Wales, church law was not State law. The 1866 constitution and the constitutions of 1902 and 1961 regulated the government of the church by consensual compact in every matter except property. But the binding effect of the consensual compact is not the sanction of secular courts. Any rules of the church which might forbid the ordination of women are not legally binding, for only rules on property matters are potentially legally binding. No property issue was at stake, and therefore the judges dismissed the proceedings. The plaintiffs were to pay the costs.[44]

The Archbishop of Sydney was 'greatly' puzzled by two aspects of the Appeal Court's judgment:

> They are why the Court should have concluded, first, that the question of the ordination of priests was not a matter related to church property, and, secondly, that the consensual compact binding Angli-

cans together and embodied in its written Constitution should not
have the effect of a common law contract like other public agreements
binding citizens together.[45]

It is clear that the archbishop disagreed with the court ruling and was most
uncomfortable with the view that the whole matter was one of 'imponder-
ables', of 'religious, spiritual and mystical ideas' or 'religious dogma' and
therefore not justiciable. It must be said, however, that the archbishop's
view of the justiciability of matters arising from the consensual compact was
never the will of the Diocese of Sydney, let alone the law of the land. The
view of the State Solicitor General, Keith Mason, who had represented
Bishop Dowling at the hearing, is that the result was not surprising. The
court was simply saying that church members must rely on their own procedures to settle disputes. To Keith Mason's mind, the decision was not
only legally consistent, but it was also theologically correct. He observed
that it was ironical that the state (through Priestley JA) should remind the
church that its unity was to be preserved in love and that differences were to
be resolved by a spiritual, rather than a legal, bond.[46]

General Synod

From 6 to 10 July, the General Synod met in Sydney. The Archbishop of
Brisbane proposed a canon to remove any English law which might prevent
women from being ordained. It was known as the Phillimore canon.[47]
Archbishop Donald Robinson declared that the bill was morally and theologically wrong, and pleaded with delegates, 'Go back! You are going the
wrong way!' The motion was passed and was sent to the diocesan synods for
comment. A second proposal was to shift from the General Synod to the
diocesan synods responsibility for their own 'ritual, ceremony and discipline'. This would have allowed Sydney to free itself at last from those tram-
mels of the Australian church which seemed to owe nothing to the Gospel
or the Scriptures. In the third reading, however, the words 'ritual' and 'ceremony' were deleted. This was designed to give dioceses the power to
either accept or reject the ordination of women, which was seen as a matter
of discipline, but to disallow other changes. The Sydney delegates felt that
the General Synod was abusing its power in so rejecting their wishes, and
moved smartly at subsequent meetings of Standing Committee to cut back

on its financial support for the General Synod. They were not the only ones distressed by the synod. Because the two motions bearing on the ordination of women were not to become effective immediately, Susan Glover, a long-time member of MOW, walked out of the public gallery and out of the church, never to return. Patricia Hayward, convenor of MOW (Sydney), cannot recall the scene without tears.

The English Decision

On 11 November 1992 the General Synod of the Church of England in England met in London to vote on the ordination of women. The lobbyists had done their work, and one thing was known in advance: it was going to be a close thing. The sick and elderly were encouraged to vote at all costs, and a sick bed and first aid were in readiness. Synod members looking for last-minute wisdom found plenty of it that morning in the letters to the editor of the *Times*. From St Andrew's House, Sydney Square, the Archbishop of Sydney wrote:

> As a member of the Anglican Church of Australia which is derived from the Church of England and whose constitution 'retains and approves the doctrine and principles of the Church of England', I take the liberty of pointing out that, should the Church of England admit women to the order of priests, it will place itself out of communion (or into 'impaired' communion) with dioceses such as my own which adhere to the present law of the Church of England in regard to apostolic and catholic order.

Robinson was to find the English as recalcitrant as the Bishop of Canberra and Goulburn, however, and the required two-thirds majority in each of the church's three houses was finally achieved: House of Bishops 75 per cent; House of Clergy 70.5 per cent; House of Laity 67.3 per cent. For twenty-five years the church had debated the issue.[48] One Sydney rector was probably not exaggerating when he wrote to his flock:

> No single issue in the life of the English Church has been subject to such intense scrutiny theologically, sociologically and perhaps biologically since the time of the Reformation. The Scriptures have been carefully weighed and the basis of the Apostolic Tradition considered.

No one can say the subject of Women as Priests has not been thoroughly aired in the English Church.[49]

The Queen, it was rumoured,[50] was not amused and added the outcome to her catalogue of woes which bedevilled her *annus horribilis*. In the Anglo-Catholic church of St Barnabas, Tunbridge Wells, Father Michael Nicholls was heard to declare, 'Next to this, the Reformation is *nothing*.'[51] In Australia, the English decision came as a shock to AAM, which all along had predicted that the pro-ordination case would be defeated in 1992 when the matter was to be decided once and for all.[52] In Auckland, New Zealand, news of the English decision prompted the writing of an uninspired:

> Praise my soul the MOW,
> > To your doors our tribute bring
> Ransomed, healed, restored to favour,
> > Who with us their praise should sing?
> Women! Women! Women! Women!
> Women priests are just the thing.[53]

Tearful Victory

On 21 November 1992 the General Synod of the Anglican Church of Australia met in Sydney. In his presidential address, the Primate reminded members that the dioceses in favour of the ordination of women had acted with remarkable restraint and to deny them now the opportunity to proceed as they had wished for so long would stretch their goodwill to breaking point. He added that the overwhelming support of church members for the ordination of women was now evident, and that the Church of England and the Church of the Province of South Africa had both legislated to ordain women. It was not an impartial address and it distressed opponents of the ordination of women, but the Primate made it clear that he had had enough. He concluded:

> This question has been before us for almost twenty years. It has rightly claimed our attention, because it is an issue with profound human as well as ecclesiastical implications. But we have been distracted long enough from tackling other parts of our Christian mission. The time has come to resolve this matter and move ahead.[54]

Some Sydney delegates sought to delay the inevitable, thus causing agony to MOW supporters, who sat through the proceedings in growing despair. At afternoon tea with the matter still not resolved, one of the Sydney bishops is reputed to have drawn aside the architect of the delay in proceedings and suggested that he might desist. The result was announced at ten minutes to 5 p.m. The synod resolved by just two votes to ordain women as priests.[55] It was the crossing of the Rubicon. As Bishop Paul Barnett had said in the preceding debate, the canon if passed would not be reversed. There would be no going back as the Presbyterians had done, inviting a maximum of ridicule and a minimum of understanding.

In the silence which followed the historic decision, Charles Sherlock from Melbourne wept. It was not for himself, as he explained to one who sought to comfort him, for he was a committed supporter of the movement for the ordination of women. He wept for the Archbishop of Sydney. To Donald Robinson himself, who also sought to comfort him, he explained that if the vote had not gone as it had, he would not have known how to comfort his wife, but because it had gone as it had he did not know how to comfort the archbishop, for whom he had always had a special affection. It was an incident which perfectly encapsulated the pain which the decision had to inflict, whichever way it went.

At all but two of the ordination ceremonies which followed quickly upon the decision of General Synod, protests were mounted. At Adelaide, where the first ordination after the passage of the clarification canon took place, a retired Bishop of Adelaide, Lionel Renfrey, a veteran in his opposition to female ordination, declared that the ordination was contrary to Scripture and tradition. Archbishop George thanked the bishop but announced his intention to proceed. During the applause which greeted the archbishop's words, Ms Elizabeth Hammond stepped forward and, in a voice which sent shivers down the spine, cried out three times, 'Cursed be the man who ordains women to the priesthood.' The archbishop was prepared to wear the curse, and the ordinations proceeded. In 1992, ninety women were ordained to the priesthood in the Anglican Church of Australia.

The year 1992 was a great one for Sydney MOW, of course. Though alienated from the powerbrokers of the diocese, it had fought a good fight with a relatively low membership, and with few hands-on workers. Unlike its vexed opponents, however, MOW did receive a lot of support from the media. Patricia Hayward, convenor of Sydney MOW, for example, in 1992 gave seventeen press conferences. But still Sydney had no women priests. On the election of Harry Goodhew as Archbishop of Sydney (1 April 1993), Colleen O'Reilly, the deputy Chair of Anglicans Together, wrote to Patricia Hayward, counselling patience and moderation:

> I would hope that the next few years see trust replace suspicion and that we can learn to live with mutual regard of one another even as we hold differing views and practices in our common life in Christ Jesus ... The morning after the Election Synod I feel quietly confident that we have a new Archbishop for a new day in the Church in Sydney and I pray that we can all learn new and mature ways to work together for the mission of the Church.[56]

Archbishop Goodhew indeed came to office with the prayers of Sydney Anglicans that he would be instrumental in quickly healing the divisions within the diocese. Those prayers were not to be answered in the affirmative. Divisions within evangelical ranks between those who may be labelled the Reformed evangelical radicals on the one hand and the Anglican evangelical traditionalists on the other were too deep to heal quickly. As John Woodhouse had acknowledged almost a decade earlier, the time had passed when evangelicals could be described as a monochrome community, if they ever had been. Evangelicals were now deeply divided over an increasing range of issues: the Charismatic movement, the Gospel's social mandate, nuclear disarmament, the roles of men and women in family and church, creation and evolution.[57] When those matters are allowed to occupy centre stage, and when matters are settled through the political processes of synodical government, it is difficult to envisage how unity can be brought back to Anglican evangelicalism. The Word alone is not the answer. The interpretation and use of Scripture has never since the Reformation been a road to unity for Protestants: there has always been dispute on those matters. What gave evangelicalism its identity and its solidarity as a movement over a long period of time and over a large part of the world was the experience of Jesus Christ as Saviour and Lord, which all shared in response to the proclamation of the Gospel, and the work of evangelism, which all shared in obedience to that Gospel. When evangelicals insist in putting Christ, his Gospel, and his mission at centre stage, they will again enjoy the creative synthesis of Spirit, Word and world which they are currently in great danger of losing.

Conclusion

Throughout almost two hundred years the mission of Australian evangelical Christianity has been to preserve society by reforming it along Biblical lines, and to bring its members to faith in Christ through the proclamation of the Gospel. The argument of this book is that the movement's effectiveness in that mission has been dependent on how successful it has been in maintaining the evangelical synthesis of Spirit, Word and world. In synthesis, evangelical spirituality has nourished engagement with the social as well as the spiritual needs of many Australians. Outside the synthesis, evangelical spirituality has fostered a world-denying pietism which has produced revivalism more often than revival. Occasionally (chapter 5) it has produced a world-renouncing perfectionism which has ironically ended in powerlessness to resist worldliness. In synthesis, the evangelical commitment to the Word of God has resulted in prophetic prescriptions for personal salvation and social reform. Outside the synthesis, it has been used as a weapon to bludgeon friends too often perceived as opponents. Synthesised with Spirit and Word, evangelical social action has been sustained and committed. On its own, it has been desultory and ill-informed.

Australian society has been a challenging context for the evangelical movement. Its materialism has challenged evangelical spirituality; its secularity has disputed the claims of the Word and the lordship of Jesus Christ; and its own reformist movements have sought inspiration from sources outside the Bible. Surrounded by such great temptations, Australian evangelicals have yielded too easily and too often to the options of private religion, personal convictions, and the face-saving tolerance which passes for charity. Yet, just as many an Australian heart has been softened by the love of God revealed in the Gospel, so this domain of mammon has not always been impervious to the evangelical Gospel.

In three major areas the evangelical movement seems to have made a positive contribution to the creation of Australian society and culture. First, throughout much of the nineteenth century it made a sustained and possibly vital contribution to the development of Australian nationhood. It was a movement which was unembarrassed about co-operating with people of all creeds and none whenever the cause was right. Political liberalism and philosophical utilitarianism, which are traditionally credited with the development of the progressive, democratic nation which Australia has become, were movements probably more enthusiastically endorsed by evangelicals than by any other group. Particularly in the area of education, the evangelicals came to an agreement with colonial legislatures which significantly shaped the young nation. The churches imparted their denominational and doctrinal expressions of Christianity to the Australian people through schools, missions, churches, Sunday schools, the media, and whatever other means they could devise, while the state through its school systems gave to its citizens an expression of Christianity which was civic, general and practical.

Secularisation has meant that the churches can no longer rely on the state to impart any expression of Christianity. Yet the state still depends on the churches to supplement both its educational and welfare systems. The involvement of the churches in social welfare has been extended and streamlined in the past four decades. The churches of the 1990s find themselves far better equipped to assist the needy than they were during the Great Depression of the 1930s. Churches, conservative as well as liberal, are increasingly conscious of their need to engage with the community of which they are part. Australian conservative Christians are now less philistine in their attitude to artistic and intellectual pursuits. Throughout our history the average 'ocker' is supposed to have been hostile to religion, art, and academia. Yet, strangely, only recently have all three recognised that they have this problem in common. But, leaving the worlds of art and academia and welfare aside, it is not as easy to demonstrate the formative impact of evangelicalism on Australian culture and society in the present century as it is for the nineteenth. It proved possible in this study to organise the material around the world theme only for the nineteenth century. Then evangelicals focused on those to whom they were taking the Gospel. Since then, evangelicals have become noticeably narrower and have become more easily preoccupied with matters of the Spirit or of the Word. In the twentieth century, in other words, evangelicals have become far more concerned with each other. In so far as it is possible to learn from history, it would be good if evangelicals could regain the habit of thinking about those to whom they are to minister, as much as about those who are engaged in a similar task.

A second major area in which the evangelical movement has made a positive contribution to Australian national development is through its insistence on the centrality of the Word of God, the Bible, as the only authoritative source of revelation about the saving purpose of God. Too often throughout Australia's history, a robust theology based on the Bible has been absent even from evangelical churches. Too often weakness in Bible-based theology has allowed Christianity to accept as part of the Gospel some value which was really class- or culture-based. The most obvious example—although, as we have seen (chapter 2), it requires qualification—is the endorsement by the churches in the nineteenth century of prevailing views of morality. The Gospel is not moralism, and the absence of sound Biblical theology has deprived evangelicalism of a strong prophetic role in Australia's history. Still, it is the distinctive glory of the evangelical churches, to which Catholic, liberal or Charismatic churches cannot lay claim, that it has insisted on seeking God's incontrovertible will for our society and the Australian people through the Bible alone.

The third major contribution of evangelicalism to Australia's history has been a spiritual one. Spiritual hunger, which Charismatic churches have sought to satisfy in recent decades so conspicuously, has been a constant feature of Australian history. The desire for revival has been evident throughout our history. Revival itself has been a surprisingly frequent experience of Australian Christians, and occasionally, as with Aboriginal Christians, has been the means of giving a place and hope to marginalised segments of the population.

In each of these three areas of contribution to the shaping of the Australian nation, there have been major problems as well as gains. As far as the world is concerned, evangelicals in Australia have found it very difficult to steer between the twin dangers of sleeping with the enemy and failing to show the enemy that they are loved at all. Evangelicals have found it very difficult to give due weight to the Word of God and not exclude other elements essential to healthy evangelicalism, such as the spiritual disciplines and concern for the church's mission to the needy. They have found it difficult to have a healthy longing for revival and the life of the Spirit, and to avoid pathological excesses. The very identification of these difficulties, however, may point the way ahead for the evangelical movement in Australia. First, it has to regain the commitment of the first evangelicals to the mission which comes from the Gospel. This mission is concerned with reforming the world and with the salvation of individuals. Jesus himself taught that he died, not for the church, but for the world, and that Christians must love and not ignore their enemies. Second, it has to sustain its commitment to a thoroughly Biblical theology or all is lost, but it has to do this in such a way as not to make enemies of friends and so divide and destroy the movement. Third, to be truly evangelical it has to foster holy living and prayer for the revival of the churches, but it has to avoid the errors of perfectionism, the heresy of laying claim to special revelations from the Holy Spirit, and the destructive and ultimately disappointing manipulations of revivalism.

As Christianity enters its third century in Australia and on the eve of its third millennium in the world, the evangelical movement retains much of its vitality, although its three strands are only loosely bound together. There is every danger that the synthesis which gave the movement so much of its vigour historically will disintegrate. Supporters of the Word strand are so trigger-happy in their great commitment to defending the faith against a range of enemies (ritualism, liberalism, secularism, humanism, feminism, charismaticism, mysticism, ecclesiasticism) that they sometimes shoot their own allies (from the Spirit strand) and even each other, on the suspicion that they are really wolves dressed in the finest merino. The casualties on the battlefield of Australian evangelicalism have often been shot by their own troops. Many of the Spirit strand, like their forebears, the European Pietists of the seventeenth and eighteenth centuries, have wearied of confessional rivalries and theological disputation, and have withdrawn into pentecostal denominations no longer interested in being labelled 'evangelical'. And many others, whose worlds have been shaped increasingly by feminism and liberalism, have also taken their leave, unable to find room in the world constructed by the current forces which make up the evangelical movement. The answer seems to lie not in emphasising any of the three elements in the evangelical synthesis—not Spirit, Word, or world—but putting at centre stage the one to whom each of the three elements points, namely Christ and his Gospel. Professor Herbert Butterfield ended his classic book, *Christianity and History*, with the memorable words, 'Hold to Christ, and for the rest be totally uncommitted.'[1] I am not so bold nor so wise, so I would want to say by way of conclusion, 'Hold fast to Christ, and do not be overly committed to your own understanding of the rest.'

Notes

Preface

1 Murray A. Pura and Donald M. Lewis, 'On Spiritual Symmetry: The Christian Devotion of William Wilberforce,' in J. I. Packer and Loren Wilkinson (eds), *Alive to God: Studies in Spirituality*, IVP, Downers Grove, 1992, pp. 176–89.

2 D.W. Bebbington, *Evangelicalism in Modern Britain: A History from the 1730s to the 1980s*, Unwin Hyman, London, 1989.

3 Bruce Mansfield, 'Thinking about Australian Religious History,' in Robert S. M. Withycombe (ed.), *Australian and New Zealand Religious History, 1789–1988*, ANZATS and STS, Canberra, 1988, p. 3.

4 W. R. Ward, *The Protestant Evangelical Awakening*, Cambridge UP, Cambridge, 1992, ch. 1.

5 Thomas Haweis' commitment to missions led to the sending of many evangelicals to the South Seas. His papers are deposited in the Mitchell Library in Sydney.

6 See Stuart Piggin, 'Jonathan Edwards and the Revival Chronicles of the 1740s', *Lucas: An Evangelical History Review*, 15, June 1993, pp. 14–20. The most extensive study of church history from an evangelical perspective was Joseph Milner's *History of the Church of Christ* in five volumes (1794–1809) which was probably an evangelical answer to Edward Gibbon's *Decline and Fall of the Roman Empire* (1776-88).

7 James Colwell, *The Illustrated History of Methodism: Australia 1812-1855; New South Wales and Polynesia 1856–1902*, Sydney, 1904; Don Wright and Eric Clancy, *The Methodists: A History of Methodism in New South Wales*, Allen & Unwin, Sydney, 1993; Arnold Hunt, *This Side of Heaven: A History of Methodism in South Australia*, Lutheran Publishing House, Adelaide, 1985.

8 Among important, if preliminary, surveys of Australian religious history which appeared in 1988 were Iain Murray, *Australian Christian Life from 1788*, Banner of Truth Trust, Edinburgh, and Ian Breward, *Australia: 'The Most Godless Place under Heaven'?*, Beacon Hill, Melbourne. Roger C. Thompson, *Religion in Australia*, Oxford UP, Melbourne, 1994, is a fine survey of the literature, although it is narrower than Breward's surveys, focusing on the impact of Christianity on political and social issues.

9   Published in *Understanding our Christian Heritage*, A Journal of the Christian
    History Research Institute, Orange, NSW, 1987.

10 Christian Research Institute, Orange, NSW.

11 For a list of Cole's extensive publications, see Keith Cole, *But I Will Be with You:
    An Autobiography*, Keith Cole Publications, Bendigo, 1988, pp. 217–23.

12 For some examples, see the bibliography at the end of this book.

13 Patrick O'Farrell, *The Catholic Church and Community in Australia: A History*,
    Nelson, Melbourne, 1977 (revised 1985 and 1992); Edmund Campion,
    Rockchoppers: Growing Up Catholic in Australia, Penguin, Ringwood, Vic., 1982,
    and *Australian Catholics*, Viking, Melbourne, 1987; Paul Collins, *Mixed Blessings:
    John Paul II and the Church of the Eighties*, Penguin, Ringwood, Vic., 1986.

14 D. Hilliard, 'The Anglo-Catholic Tradition in Australian Anglicanism', in
    Mark Hutchinson and Edmund Campion (eds), *Re-Visioning Australian Colonial
    Christianity*, CSAC, Sydney, 1994, ch. 9. See also Brian Porter (ed.), *Colonial
    Tractarians*, Joint Board of Christian Education, Melbourne, 1989.

Chapter 1   Going into All the World, 1788–1835

1   Jonathan Edwards (1724), *Apocalyptic Writings,* ed. Stephen J. Stein, Yale UP,
    New Haven, 1977, p. 143.

2   Quoted in J. Owen, *History of the British and Foreign Bible Society*, London,
    1816–20, vol. 2, p. 310.

3   Penny Carson, 'Evangelicals and India', PhD thesis, University of London,
    1988, p. 17.

4   Henry Venn, *Memoir of Henry Venn,* London, 1834, p. 446f.

5   See Ged Martin (ed.), *The Founding of Australia: The Argument about Australia's
    Origins,* Hale & Iremonger, Sydney 1978; reprinted 1980.

6   Robert J. King, *The Secret History of the Convict Colony: Alexandro Malaspina's
    Settlement in New South Wales,* Allen & Unwin, Sydney, 1990, p. 95. The
    reference is to p. 103 of Tench's journal. See Watkin Tench, *Sydney's First Four
    Years* (1793), Sydney, 1961.

7   Quoted in Martin Southwood, *John Howard: Prison Reformer*, Independent
    Press, London, 1958, p. 69.

8   J. D. Walsh, 'The Magdalene Evangelicals', *Church Quarterly Review,*
    October–December 1958, pp. 499–511.

9   A. M. Wilberforce (ed.), *Private Papers of William Wilberforce,* London, 1897,
    vol. 1, p. 15; cited in Neil K. Macintosh, *Richard Johnson, Chaplain to the Colony
    of New South Wales: His Life and Times, 1755–1827*, Library of Australian
    History, Sydney, 1978, p. 25.

10 R. I. and S. Wilberforce, *Correspondence of William Wilberforce,* London, 1840,
    vol. 1, p. 15.

11 *Memoir of the Rev. Josiah Pratt, by his Sons*, London, 1849, p. 463.

12 1792, facsimile, Carey Kingsgate Press, London, 1961, p. 51.

13 Niel Gunson, *Messengers of Grace: Evangelical Missionaries in the South Seas, 1797–1860*, Oxford UP, Melbourne, 1978.

14 S. Judd and K. Cable, *Sydney Anglicans*, Anglican Information Office, Sydney, 1987, p. 6.

15 J. D. Bollen, 'A Time of Small Things—The Methodist Mission in New South Wales', *Journal of Religious History,* 7.3, June 1973, pp. 225–47.

16 Butterworth to Marsden, 10 January 1815, Marsden Papers, vol. 1, Mitchell Library.

17 See review of Collins, *Account of the English Colony in New South Wales*, 1804, in *The Eclectic Review* for August 1805 (extract in the Bonwick Transcripts).

18 Newton to Johnson, 10 March 1791, *Historical Records of New South Wales* (hereafter *HRNSW*), vol. 2, p. 445.

19 Humphrey McQueen, *A New Britannia,* Penguin, Ringwood, Vic., 1970.

20 L. C. Robson, *The Convict Settlers of Australia,* Melbourne UP, Carlton, 1965.

21 M. B. and C. B. Schedvin, 'The Nomadic Tribes of Urban Britain: A Prelude to Botany Bay', *Historical Studies: Australia and New Zealand*, 18, 1978, pp. 254–76.

22 B. Wilson, *Can God Survive in Australia?* Albatross, Sydney, 1983.

23 Johnson to Fricker, 18 March 1791, in G. Mackaness (ed.), *Some Letters of the Rev. Richard Johnson,* Part 1, D. S. Ford, Sydney 1954, p. 36.

24 Johnson to Hunter, 5 July 1798, *Historical Records of Australia*, I, ii, pp. 178–82.

25 Johnson to Fricker, 4 October 1791, in Mackaness, *Some Letters*, pp. 39–42.

26 James Bonwick, *Australia's First Preacher: The Rev. Richard Johnson, First Chaplain of New South Wales*, London, 1898, p. 41.

27 Bonwick, *Australia's First Preacher*, p. 67.

28 Newton to Johnson, 29 March 1794, *HRNSW*, vol. 2, p. 196.

29 Macintosh, *Richard Johnson*, p. 51.

30 Johnson to Fricker, 4 October 1791, Johnson Letters, MS Aj1, Mitchell Library.

31 David Collins, *An Account of the English Colony in New South Wales*, London, 1798, vol. 1, p. 100.

32 Letter from an unnamed convict to Thomas Olds, 29 December 1790, *HRNSW*, vol. 2, p. 758.

33 Portia Robinson, *The Hatch and Brood of Time: A Study of the First Generation of Native-born White Australians 1788–1828*, Oxford UP, Melbourne, 1985, p. 281f.

34 Macintosh, *Richard Johnson*, p. 54f.

35 '... the indifference and hostility encountered by religion in the Australian colonies was at least as much an imported attitude, a part of the usual migrant baggage, as it was a local-grown product.' P. J. O'Farrell, *Letters from Irish Australia, 1825–1929,* UNSW Press, Kensington, 1984, p. 22.

36 '[Marsden's] sentences are not only, in fact, more severe than those of the other magistrates, but ... the general opinion of the colony is, that his

character, as displayed in the administration of the penal law in New South Wales, is stamped with severity': Bigge, *Report*, vol. 1, p. 84.

37 Allan M. Grocott, *Convicts, Clergymen and Churches: Attitudes of Convicts and Ex-convicts towards the Churches and Clergy in New South Wales from 1788 to 1851*, Sydney UP, Sydney, 1980, pp. 116, 230–4, 284.

38 Alexander Strachan, *The Life of the Rev. Samuel Leigh, Missionary to the Settlers and Savages of Australia and New Zealand, with a History of the Origin and Progress of the Missions in those Colonies*, London, 1870, p. 84.

39 Quoted in George Nadel, *Australia's Colonial Culture,* Harvard UP, Cambridge, Mass., 1957, p. 241.

40 Arthur Skevington Wood, *Thomas Haweis, 1743–1820*, Society for Promoting Christian Knowledge, London, 1957, p. 265f.

41 A. T. Yarwood, *Samuel Marsden: The Great Survivor*, Melbourne UP, Carlton, 1977, p. 127; S. M. Johnstone, *A History of the Church Missionary Society in Australia and Tasmania*, CMS, Sydney, 1925, p. 97.

42 Johnstone, *A History*, p. 143.

43 Quoted in *Australian Dictionary of Biography* (hereafter *ADB*), vol. 2, entry on Walter Lawry.

44 Margaret Reeson, *Currency Lass*, Albatross, Sutherland, 1985, p. 99.

45 Quoted in Reeson, *Currency Lass,* p. 206.

46 On marriage and family life in early colonial Australia, see Katrina Alford, *Production or Reproduction? An Economic History of Women in Australia*, Oxford UP, Melbourne, 1984, chs 1–3.

47 Quoted in Yarwood, *Samuel Marsden*, p. 93.

48 R. Johnson to J. Hardcastle, 26 August 1799, *Evangelical Magazine,* 1800, p. 298.

49 R. Johnson to J. Hardcastle, 18 October 1799, *Evangelical Magazine,* 1800, p. 302.

50 W. N. Gunson, 'The Contribution of the Calvinistic Methodist Movement to the Church History of Australia', *Church Heritage,* 4.1, March 1985, pp. 28–59.

51 Marsden, 4 August 1821, Bonwick Transcripts, III, No.181, Mitchell Library.

52 Yarwood, *Samuel Marsden*, p. 73.

53 Bowden to WMMS 20 July 1812, quoted in James Colwell, *The Illustrated History of Methodism*, Sydney, 1904, pp. 36–9.

54 Diary of Walter Lawry, 11 August 1819, p. 30, Mitchell Library.

55 Don Wright and Eric G. Clancy, *The Methodists: A History of Methodism in New South Wales*, Allen & Unwin, Sydney 1993, p. 11.

56 Quoted in Wright and Clancy, *The Methodists*, p. 17.

57 An evangelical prison reformer who favoured more religion coupled with solitary confinement.

58 John H. Harris, 'Two Hundred Years of the Church and Aboriginals,' *Church Scene*, 11 December 1987, p. 6f.

59 Harris, 'Two Hundred Years', p. 6f.

60 G. G. Findlay and W. W. Holdsworth, *The History of the Wesleyan Methodist Missionary Society*, vol. III, Epworth Press, London, 1921, p. 151.

61 John Harris, *One Blood*, Albatross, Sydney, 1990, p. 236.

62 Niel Gunson (ed.), *Australian Reminiscences and Papers of L. E. Threlkeld*, Australian Institute of Aboriginal Studies, Canberra, 1974.

63 *Annual Report of the Mission to the Aborigines, Lake Macquarie*, 1841, quoted in Gunson (ed.), *Reminiscences of Threlkeld*, vol. 1, pp. 168–70.

64 Barbara Thiering, *God's Experiment—Australian Religion*, Murdoch University, 1982.

65 S. Judd and K. Cable, *Sydney Anglicans*, Anglican Information Office, Sydney, 1987, p. 14.

Chapter 2   Identifying with the Liberal World, 1836–1870

1 Alan Atkinson and Marian Aveling (eds), *Australians 1838*, Fairfax, Syme & Weldon, Sydney, 1987, p. 331.

2 Allan M. Grocott, *Convicts, Clergymen and Churches*, Sydney UP, Sydney, 1980, p. 259.

3 Atkinson and Aveling, *Australians 1838*, p. 330.

4 *ADB* entry.

5 Quoted in J. S. Gregory, *Church and State,* Cassell, Sydney, 1973, p. 14.

6 Gregory, *Church and State*, p. 17.

7 Tasmania had been separated from New South Wales in 1825, and Western Australia was settled in 1827.

8 *The Port Phillip Patriot*, Melbourne, 9 December 1839.

9 David Mackenzie, *The Emigrant's Guide*, London, 1845, pp. 30, 51; cited in Russel Ward, *The Australian Legend*, Oxford UP, Melbourne, 1958, 1980, p. 91f

10 Cited in Ward, *The Australian Legend*, p. 92.

11 Ward, *The Australian Legend*, p. 92.

12 Douglas Pike, *Paradise of Dissent*, Melbourne UP, Carlton, 1967.

13 Quoted in Pike, *Paradise of Dissent*, p. 127.

14 W. N. Gunson, 'The Nundah Missionaries', *Royal Historical Society of Queensland Journal*, 6.3, 1960–61, pp. 511–39.

15 Leslie James Ball, 'Queensland Baptists in the Nineteenth Century: The Historical Development of a Denominational Identity', PhD thesis, University of Queensland, 1994, p. 74f.

16 *ADB*.

17 Rod Kirkpatrick, *Sworn to No Master; A History of the Provincial Press in Queensland to 1930*, DDIAE Press, Toowoomba, 1984, p. 13.

18 J. D. Lang was obsessed with the need for a white Protestant citadel in the South Seas.

19 Pike, *Paradise of Dissent*, documents the nonconformist role in the establishment of civil liberties in South Australia.

20 George Shaw, 'Judeo-Christianity and the Mid-Nineteenth Century Colonial
Civil Order', in Mark Hutchinson and Edmund Campion (eds), *Re-Visioning
Australian Colonial Christianity: New Essays in the Australian Christian Experience,
1788–1900*, CSAC, Sydney, 1994, p. 37.

21 Shaw in Hutchinson and Campion, *Re-Visioning*, p. 37.

22 Ian Gillman, *Many Faiths, One Nation*, Collins, Sydney, 1988, pp. 33–5.

23 S. Piggin, *Making Evangelical Missionaries*, Sutton Courtenay Press, Appleford,
Oxford, 1984, pp. 40–4,129–32; Boyd Hilton, *The Age of Atonement: The
Influence of Evangelicalism on Social and Economic Thought, 1795–1865*, Oxford
UP, Oxford, 1988, p. 379.

24 S. Piggin, 'Towards a Bicentennial History of Australian Evangelicalism',
Journal of Religious History, 15.1, June 1988, pp. 20–37; R. Ely, 'The Forgotten
Nationalism: Australian Civic Protestantism in the Second World War',
Journal of Australian Studies, 20, May 1987, pp. 59–67.

25 Michael Hogan, *The Sectarian Strand: Religion in Australian History*, Penguin,
Ringwood, Vic., 1987, p. 8.

26 Hogan, *The Sectarian Strand*, p. 6.

27 Quoted in S. Piggin, *Faith of Steel*, University of Wollongong, Wollongong,
1984, p. 77.

28 Piggin, *Faith of Steel*, p. 77.

29 Patrick John O'Leary, 'Queensland Baptists: The Development of Baptist
Evangelicalism, 1846–1926', MA thesis, University of Queensland, 1991, p.
16f.; Ball, 'Queensland Baptists', p. 77.

30 *Moreton Bay Courier*, 27 January 1849.

31 Alexander Hay, *Jubilee Memorial of the Presbyterian Church of Queensland*,
Brisbane, 1900, p. 5.

32 J. D. Bollen, *Australian Baptists: A Religious Minority*, Baptist Historical Society,
London, 1975, pp. 8–12.

33 Bollen, *Australian Baptists*, p. 28.

34 The main clue to Lowe's involvement is in Mrs Barker's letters, which reveal
that the Barkers had close and friendly contact with Lowe.

35 S. Judd and K. Cable, *Sydney Anglicans*, Anglican Information Office, Sydney,
1987, p. 69.

36 *The Australian Churchman*, 14 December 1867.

37 'Barker saw Australia as a mission field which required parish clergy to be able
evangelical missionaries.' Judd and Cable, *Sydney Anglicans*, p. 42.

38 E. D. Daw, 'Hulton Smyth King: The Curate of Fenagh and Wells', *Church of
England Historical Society Journal*, 15.4, December 1970, pp. 94–99.

39 Judd and Cable, *Sydney Anglicans*, p. 92.

40 Daw, 'Hulton Smyth King', p. 94

41 Judd and Cable, *Sydney Anglicans*, p. 75.

42 A. de Q. Robin, *Charles Perry, Bishop of Melbourne: The Challenges of a Colonial Episcopate, 1847–76*, UWA Press, Nedlands, 1967, pp. 128–30.

43 M. Loane, *Hewn from the Rock,* Anglican Information Office, Sydney, 1976, p. 112.

44 On revival in Australian Christianity, see Mark Hutchinson and Stuart Piggin (eds), *Reviving Australia: Essays on the History and Experience of Revival and Revivalism in Australian Christianity*, CSAC, Sydney, 1994.

45 Quoted in Iain Murray, *Australian Christian Life from 1788*, Banner of Truth Trust, Edinburgh, 1987, p. 226.

46 Murray, *Australian Christian Life,* p. 229.

47 Murray, *Australian Christian Life,* p. 236.

48 Don Wright and Eric Clancy, *The Methodists: A History of Methodism in New South Wales*, Allen & Unwin, Sydney, 1993.

49 Grocott, *Convicts, Clergymen, and Churches*, p. 102.

50 'History of Hobart Circuit', *The Spectator*, 13–24, 1900–01; J. Edwin Orr, *Evangelical Awakenings in the South Seas*, Bethany Fellowship, Minneapolis, 1976, p. 53.

51 *Minutes of the Conference of the Australasian Methodist Church*, 1863 and 1864, Uniting Church Archives.

52 Dean Drayton, *Five Generations: Evangelism in South Australia*, South Australian Synod, Uniting Church in Australia, 1980, p. 3.

53 W. L. Blamires and John B. Smith, *The Early Story of the Wesleyan Methodist Church in Victoria*, Melbourne, 1886, p. 315.

54 John Watsford, *Glorious Gospel Triumphs*, Charles H. Kelly, London, 1900, p. 22.

55 Arnold Hunt, 'The Moonta Revival of 1875', cassette produced by New Creation Publications, Blackwood, SA.

56 Blamires and Smith, *Wesleyan Methodist Church*, p. 90. For 'Bochim', see Judges 2.1, 5.

57 J. Edwin Orr, 'Evangelical Revival in Australia in the Mid-nineteenth Century', lecture, Pasadena, 1968.

58 *Wesleyan Chronicle*, 22 May 1959, p. 157.

59 Orr, *Evangelical Awakenings in the South Seas*, pp. 52, 55.

60 J. Campbell Robinson, quoted in Murray, *Australian Christian Life*, p. 267; Rowland S. Ward, *The Bush Still Burns: The Presbyterian and Reformed Faith in Australia, 1788–1988*, published by the author, Wantirna, Vic., 1989, pp. 128ff.; Barry J. Bridges, *Ministers, Licentiates and Catechists of the Presbyterian Churches in New South Wales to 1865*, Rowland S. Ward, 1989, p. 100.

61 See Rowland Ward, 'Spiritual Awakenings in Scottish Gaelic Communities in Australia, 1837–1870', in Hutchinson and Piggin, *Reviving Australia,* pp. 75–96.

62 John Ramsland, *The Struggle against Isolation: A History of the Manning Valley*, Library of Australian History, Greater Taree City Council, NSW, 1987, p. 130.

63 Stanley to Gipps, 20 December 1842, *Historical Records of Australia*, I.xxii, p. 437.

64 Quoted in Jean Woolmington, 'Missionary Attitudes to the Baptism of Australian Aborigines before 1850', *Journal of Religious History*, 13.3, 1985, pp. 283–93.

65 Marsden to Josiah Pratt, the CMS secretary, 24 February 1819, in J. R. Elder (ed.), *The Letters and Journals of Samuel Marsden, 1765–1838*, Otago University Council, Dunedin, 1932, p. 231f.

66 John Harris, *One Blood*, Albatross, Sydney, 1990, pp. 73–7.

67 James Dredge, *Brief Notices of the Aborigines of New South Wales*, James Harrison, Geelong, 1845.

68 D. W. A. Baker, *Days of Wrath: A Life of John Dunmore Lang*, Melbourne UP, Carlton, 1985, p. 114.

69 Harris, 'Two Hundred Years of the Church and Aboriginals,' *Church Scene*, 11 December 1987, p. 6f.

70 Watsford, *Glorious Gospel Triumphs*, p. 54.

71 Quoted in Peter Barnes, '"The Iona of the New Hebrides": The Coming of Christianity to Aneityum, 1848–1876', MA thesis, University of Sydney, 1985, p. 72.

72 Barnes, 'Aneityum', p. 5.

Chapter 3   The Spirit and Protestant Culture, 1870–1913

1 A. Trollope, *Australia* (1873), UQP, St Lucia, 1967, p. 240.

2 J. S. Gregory, *Church and State*, Cassell, Sydney, 1973.

3 Dean Drayton, *Five Generations: Evangelism in South Australia*, South Australian Synod, Uniting Church in Australia, 1980, p. 10.

4 R. Ely, 'Protestantism in Australian History: An Interpretative Sketch', *Lucas*, 5, March 1989, p. 15.

5 J. D. Bollen, *Religion in Australian Society*, Leigh College, Sydney, 1973, p. 53.

6 Henry Lawson, 'The Song of the Heathen', in C. Roderick (ed.), *Collected Verse of Henry Lawson*, Angus & Robertson, Sydney, 1967–69, vol. 3, p. 64.

7 S. Piggin, *Faith of Steel*, University of Wollongong, Wollongong, 1984, p. 169.

8 R. D. Linder, 'Australian Evangelicals in Politics in the Victorian Age: The Cases of J. D. Lang, W. G. Spence, and J. S. T. McGowen', *Lucas*, 13, July 1992, pp. 34–60.

9 I read this in the *South Coast Times*, c. 1900, and committed it to memory.

10 Henry Lawson, *Prose Works of Henry Lawson*, Angus & Robertson, Sydney, 1948, p. 683.

11 'The Shearers', *Collected Verse of Henry Lawson*, vol. 2, p. 12.

12 T. Inglis Moore, 'The Meanings of Mateship', *Meanjin Quarterly*, March 1965, pp. 45–54.

13 W. G. Spence, *Australia's Awakening*, Sydney, 1908, p. 78.

14 Rod Quinn, 'The House of the Commonwealth', newspaper cuttings, Mitchell Library, MS QA 821/5.

15 'In the Street', *Collected Verse of Henry Lawson*, vol. 1, p. 273f.

16 Victor Daley, 'The Sorrowful One', in M. Holburn and M. Pizer (eds), *Creeve Roe*, Pinchgut Press, Sydney, 1947, p. 78. On the relationship between Christianity, mateship and unionism, see the excellent MA thesis by Marion Zaunbrecher, 'Religious Attitudes in Australian Literature of the 1890s', University of Wollongong, 1979.

17 So argues Alan Dunstan in his forthcoming thesis on the origins of the New South Wales Labor Party, Macquarie University.

18 See Bede Nairn, *Civilising Capitalism: The Labour Movement in New South Wales, 1870–1900*, ANU Press, Canberra, 1973.

19 *Divided Heart: The Memoirs of Catherine B. Mackerras*, Little Hills Press, 1991, pp. 61, 109.

20 P. Ford, *Cardinal Moran and the ALP*, Melbourne UP, Carlton, 1966, p. 108n.

21 D. Longo, 'Attitudes of Church to Working Class and of Working Class to the Church, 1848–1891', BA hons thesis, University of Adelaide, 1979.

22 Oswald Pryor, *Australia's Little Cornwall*, Rigby, Adelaide, 1962, reprinted 1980, p. 101.

23 K. S. Latourette, *A History of the Expansion of Christianity*, vol. 5, Harper, New York, 1943, p. 176.

24 *The Katoomba Convention*, 1912, p. 11.

25 *The Christian*, 14 April 1871.

26 Michael Chavura, 'A History of Calvinism in the Baptist Churches of New South Wales, 1831–1914', PhD thesis, Macquarie University, 1994, pp. 414–23.

27 D. Hulme-Moir, *The Edge of Time*, Christian Outreach Book Service, Newtown, NSW, 1988, has extracts from her diaries.

28 J. Edwin Orr, *Evangelical Awakenings in the South Seas*, Bethany Fellowship, Minneapolis, 1976, p. 44.

29 W. Warren, 'The Genesis of the Australian Revival', *The Missionary Review of the World*, 26, March 1903, p. 202f.

30 Helen Alexander, *Charles M. Alexander*, London, n.d., p. 153.

31 Darrell Paproth, 'Revivalism in Melbourne from Federation to World War I: The Torrey–Alexander–Chapman Campaigns', in Mark Hutchinson and Stuart Piggin (eds), *Reviving Australia: Essays on the History and Experience of Revival and Revivalism in Australian Christianity*, CSAC, Sydney, 1994, pp. 143–69.

32 R. A. Torrey, *The Power of Prayer and the Prayer of Power*, 1924, Zondervan, Grand Rapids, Michigan, 1971, p. 48f.

33 Alan F. Dyer, *God Was Their Rock,* Pioneer Publishers, Sheffield, Tas., 1974, p. 6.

34 Dyer, *God Was Their Rock*, p. 8.

35 Dyer, *God Was Their Rock*, p. 16, taken from the official Lands Dept maps.

36 James Colwell, *The Illustrated History of Methodism*, Sydney, 1904, p. 460.

37 Colwell, *Illustrated History of Methodism,* p. 630; Piggin, *Faith of Steel*, pp. 135–41.

38 E. T. Rien, *A Challenge to Holiness*, Wyee, n.d.; A. D. Deane, 'The Contribution of the New Evangelical Movements of the late Nineteenth Century to Evangelical Enterprise in Australia, 1870–1920', MA thesis, University of Sydney, 1983, p. 37f.

39 Barry Chant, 'Wesleyan Revivalism and the Rise of Australian Pentecostalism', in Hutchinson and Piggin (eds), *Reviving Australia*, pp. 97–122.

40 Donald W. Dayton, *Theological Roots of Pentecostalism*, Scarecrow Press, NJ, 1987, p. 174.

41 Barry Chant, *Heart of Fire: The Story of Australian Pentecostalism*, Adelaide, 1973, p. 35.

42 Stuart Piggin, *Making Evangelical Missionaries, 1789–1858*, Sutton Courtenay Press, Appleford, Oxford, 1984, pp. 133–5.

43 Retta Long, *Providential Channels*, Aborigines Inland Mission, Sydney, 1935, p. 19.

44 John Harris, *One Blood*, Albatross, Sydney, 1990, pp. 553–69.

45 On Christian missions to the Chinese in late nineteenth-century Sydney, see Geoff Huard, 'Ministry to the Chinese in Sydney between 1855 and 1900 by the Anglican and Presbyterian Churches Compared and Contrasted', Doctor of Ministry essay, Northern Baptist Theological Seminary, Sydney, 1992; Ruth Teale, 'Soo Hoo Ten', *ADB*; Judd and Cable, *Sydney Anglicans*, p. 149f.; S. M. Johnstone, *A History of the Church Missionary Society in Australia and Tasmania*, CMS, Sydney, 1926, pp. 284–99.

46 *South Sea Evangelical Mission: Not in Vain: In Memoriam Florence S. H. Young*, 79, July–August 1940, p. 2.

47 F. S. H. Young, *Pearls from the Pacific*, Marshall Brothers, London and Edinburgh, n.d., p. 52.

48 Young, *Pearls from the Pacific*, p. 103.

49 Alison Griffiths, *Fire in the Islands*, Harold Shaw, Wheaton, Ill., 1977, p. 22.

50 Young, *Pearls from the Pacific*, pp. 160–76.

51 F. Hibberd, 'Federation and our Missions', *The Baptist,* 15 October 1903, p. 4; Baptist Union of NSW, Minute Book, 1871; Alan C. Prior, 'Missionary Service Overseas', *Some Fell on Good Ground*, Baptist Union of New South Wales, Sydney, 1966, pp. 187–97; G. B. Ball, 'The Australian Baptist Mission and its Impact in Bengal', MA thesis, Flinders University, 1978. The official history of the Australian Baptist Missionary Society is J. Redman, *The Light Shines On: The Story of the Missionary Outreach of the Baptist People of Australia 1882–1982*, Australian BMS, Hawthorn, Vic., 1982.

52 Silas Mead, 'Home Problems in Relation to Indian Baptist Missions,' *First Australasian Baptist Congress,* Sydney, 1908, p. 123. See also the address at the

congress by S. Pearce Carey, 'The Steady March of Jesus to the Conquest of the World'; and A. Christopher Smith, 'The Spirit and Letter of Carey's Catalytic Watchword: A Study in the Transmission of Baptist Tradition', *Baptist Quarterly*, XXXIII.5, 1990, pp. 226–37.

53 Leslie James Ball, 'Queensland Baptists in the Nineteenth Century: The Historical Development of a Denominational Identity', PhD thesis, University of Queensland, 1994, p. 174f.

54 D. F. Mitchell, *Ellen Arnold, Pioneer and Pathfinder,* Baptist Publications, Adelaide, 1932; *The Missionary Heritage of Australian Baptists,* Australian Baptist Foreign Missions, Glebe, NSW, n.d.

55 Not to be confused with the 1891 Anglo-Catholic mission of the same name.

56 K. J. Newton, 'A History of the Brethren in Australia with Particular Reference to the Open Brethren', PhD thesis, Fuller Theological Seminary, 1990, p. 34.

57 Personal diary of Mrs J. J. Kitchen, in the possession of Connie Kitchen.

58 Marcus Loane, *The Story of the China Inland Mission in Australia and New Zealand*, CIM and Overseas Missionary Fellowship, Sydney, 1965.

59 Keith Cole (ed.), *Letters from China, 1893–1895: The Story of the Sister Martyrs of Ku Cheng*, St Hilary's Anglican Church, Kew, Vic., 1988.

60 Marcus Loane, 'The Keswick Convention and the Missionary Movement', *Southern Cross Booklet*, No.3, n.d., p. viii.

61 Quoted in James and Marti Hefley, *By Their Blood: Christian Martyrs of the Twentieth Century*, Baker Book House, Grand Rapids, Michigan, 1979, p. 24. See Marshall Broomhall (ed.), *Last Letters and Further Records of Martyred Missionaries of the China Inland Mission*, London, 1901.

62 David Hilliard, *God's Gentlemen: A History of the Melanesian Mission*, UQP, St Lucia, 1978.

63 Darrell Whiteman, *Melanesians and Missionaries: An Ethnohistorical Study of Social and Religious Change in the Southwest Pacific*, William Carey Library, Pasadena, 1983.

64 James Grant, 'The Diocese of Melbourne (and Victoria)', in Brian Porter (ed.), *Colonial Tractarians,* Joint Board of Christian Education, Melbourne, 1989, p. 73; David Wetherell, *Reluctant Mission: The Anglican Church in Papua New Guinea, 1891–1942*, UQP, St Lucia, 1977; Dorothea Tomkins and Brian Hughes, *The Road from Gona,* Angus & Robertson, Sydney, 1969; David Wetherell (ed.), *The New Guinea Diaries of Philip Strong, 1936–1945*, Macmillan, South Melbourne, 1981.

65 E. Jones, *Florence Buchanan: The Little Deaconess of the South Seas*, SPG, London, 1921; John Bayton, *Cross over Carpentaria*, W. R. Smith & Paterson, Brisbane, 1965; E. C. Rowland, *The Tropics for Christ*, Townsville, 1960; Barbara Darling, 'Some Leading Women in the History of the Anglican Church in Australia', in R. S. M. Withycombe (ed.), *Australian and New Zealand Religious History, 1788–1988*, ANZATS and STS, Canberra, 1988, pp. 147–56.

66 Jill Roe, 'Challenge and Response: Religious Life in Melbourne, 1876–86', *Journal of Religious History*, 5.2, December 1968, p. 160.

67 *Victorian Review*, October 1880. On this anti-Christian journal, see Roe, 'Challenge and Response', p. 149f.

68 On Strong, see Susan Emilsen, *A Whiff of Heresy: Samuel Angus and the Presbyterian Church in New South Wales*, UNSW Press, Kensington, 1991; Rowland Ward, *The Bush still Burns: The Presbyterian and Reformed Faith in Australia, 1788–1988*, published by the author, Wantirna, Vic., 1989, pp. 250–69; C. R. Badger, *The Reverend Charles Strong and the Australian Church*, Abacada, Melbourne, 1971; R. B. Walker, 'Presbyterian Church and People in the Colony of New South Wales in the Late Nineteenth Century', *Journal of Religious History*, 2.1, 1969, pp. 49–65; Don Chambers, *Theological Teaching and Thought in the Theological Hall of the Presbyterian Church of Victoria, 1865-1906*, Theological Hall, Ormond College, Parkville, Vic., 1967.

69 Chambers, *Theological Teaching*, p. 18.

70 Minutes of the Presbytery of Melbourne, p. 546f.

71 Badger, *The Reverend Charles Strong*, p. 104.

72 Ernest Bacon, *Spurgeon: Heir to the Puritans*, Allen & Unwin, London, 1967, p. 136.

73 Michael Chavura, 'Calvinism and the Spurgeonic Tradition among the Baptists of New South Wales—The Downgrade Controversy', in Mark Hutchinson and Edmund Campion (eds), *Re-Visioning Australian Colonial Christianity: New Essays in the Australian Christian Experience, 1788–1900*, CSAC, Sydney, 1994, pp. 111–30.

74 *Brisbane Courier*, 14 November 1887.

75 *Brisbane Courier*, 21 November 1887.

76 William James Lawton, *The Better Times to Be: Utopian Attitudes to Society among Sydney Anglicans, 1885 to 1914*, UNSW Press, Kensington, 1990, ch. 2.

77 Len Abbott to Margaret Lamb, 11 October 1990. Bishop James Grant is of the opinion that this story is in the same genre as his reported prayer, 'Lord, don't let anything happen today.'

78 Barbara Darling, 'Goe', in Brian Dickey. (ed.), *Australian Dictionary of Evangelical Biography*, Evangelical History Association, Sydney, 1994 (hereafter *ADEB*).

79 Canon Len Abbott, 'Berry', in *ADEB*.

80 Porter, *Colonial Tractarians*, p. 73.

81 Judd and Cable, *Sydney Anglicans*, p. 150.

82 Minutes of the Melbourne Gospel Crusade in the possession of David Renshaw.

Chapter 4　The Word Challenged, 1914–1932

1 For example, Begbies, Kitchens, Youngs, Decks, Grants, Langford-Smiths, Knoxs, Shorts.

2 'Growing up with Reverend Father', *Good Weekend*, 13 February 1988, pp. 24–6.

3 He lists A. D. Hope; Bob Hawke; David Abba, executive director of the Sydney Chamber of Commerce; Evan Walker, former Victorian Minister for Agriculture; Geoffrey Blainey; John Button; Keith Hancock; Keith Murdoch; Manning Clark; Meredith Burgmann; Patrick McCaughey, art gallery director; Paul Hasluck; and Trevor Morling. Rupert Murdoch is the grandson of a Presbyterian minister, and his values of enterprise, hard work, and democracy may reflect the cultural Calvinism of Presbyterian Scotland.

4 From Archbishop Wright's speech as reported in the annual report of the Mothers' Union for 1919–20. Quoted in Ruth I. Sturmey, 'Women and the Anglican Church in Australia: Theology and Social Change', PhD thesis, University of Sydney, 1989, p. 147.

5 K. Reiger, *The Disenchantment of the Home*, Oxford UP, 1985, pp. 68–70.

6 N. Tress, *Caught for Life. A Story of the Anglican Deaconess Order in Australia*, Mission Publications, New South Wales, 1933; Dorothy Harris, *God's Patience*, Book Printer, Maryborough, Vic., 1990; and G. H. Cranswick, *The Ministry of Women. Official Report of the Ninth Australian Church Congress*, Diocesan Registry, Melbourne, 1925.

7 M. Knauerhase, *Winifred*, Lutheran Publishing House, Adelaide, 1978.

8 Methodist Overseas Mission Board, Report in Minutes of 4 October 1918, Box 206, p. 130f, Uniting Church Archives.

9 K. Cole, *Oenpelli Pioneer: A Biography of the Founder of the Oenpelli Mission, the Rev. Alfred John Dyer*, Church Missionary Historical Publications, Melbourne, 1972.

10 See L. M. Abbott, 'Irwin, Frederick Chidley', in *ADEB*.

11 Donald Anderson, 'Defending an Evangelical Society and an Evangelical Diocese: Sydney James Kirkby, 1879–1935', MA thesis, University of Wollongong, 1985; T. E. Jones, *'These Twenty Years': A Record of the Work of the Bush Church Aid Society for Australia and Tasmania*, BCA, Sydney, 1939; Helen Caterer, *Australians Outback: 60 Years of Bush Church Aid*, Anglican Information Office, Sydney, 1981; L. Daniels, *Far West*, The Church of England Information Trust, Sydney, 1959.

12 Michael McKernan, *Australian Churches at War*, Catholic Theological Faculty and Australian War Memorial, Sydney and Canberra, 1980, ch. 8.

13 Susan Westwood, 'A Study of the Attitudes and Activities of the Church of England in the Illawarra during the First World War', BA hons thesis, University of Wollongong, 1980, pp. 101–7.

14 John Moses, 'The First World War as Holy War in German and Australian Perspective', *Colloquium*, 26.1, 1994, p. 48.

15 John Moses, 'Anzac Day as Religious Revivalism: The Politics of Faith in Brisbane, 1916–1939', in Mark Hutchinson and Stuart Piggin (eds), *Reviving Australia: Essays on the History and Experience of Revival and Revivalism in Australian Christianity*, CSAC, Sydney, 1994, pp. 170–84.

16 *South Coast Times*, 3 May 1918.

17 *Australian Baptist*, 23 April 1918.

18 *South Coast Times*, 28 May 1915.

19 Paul White, *Alias Jungle Doctor: An Autobiography*, Paternoster, Exeter, 1977, p. 43.

20 *Australian Baptist*, 12 February 1918.

21 Stuart Piggin, *Faith of Steel*, University of Wollongong, Wollongong, 1984, p. 172.

22 McKernan, *Australian Churches at War*, p. 2.

23 *Illawarra Mercury*, 6 July 1915.

24 Lionel B. Fletcher, *Mighty Moments*, Religious Tract Society, London, n.d., p. 16. This book was dedicated to Ross Thomas, 'who introduced me to the Petersham Conference where I made the greatest discovery of my Christian life—that the fullness of the Holy Ghost is for Christians to-day, as much as for the disciples of old.'

25 Fletcher, *Mighty Moments*, p. 21.

26 Moses, 'Anzac Day as Religious Revivalism'.

27 Don Wright and Eric Clancy, *The Methodists: A History of Methodism in New South Wales,* Allen & Unwin, Sydney, 1993, p. 134.

28 Janet West, *Innings of Grace: A Life of Bishop W. G. Hilliard*, Trinity Grammar School, Sydney, 1987, p. 33.

29 S. Judd and K. Cable, *Sydney Anglicans*, Anglican Information Office, Sydney, 1987, p. 240f.

30 Donald George Anderson, 'The Bishop's Society, 1856 to 1958: A History of the Sydney Anglican Home Mission Society', PhD thesis, University of Wollongong, 1990, p. 315.

31 Don Wright, *Mantle of Christ: A History of the Sydney Central Methodist Mission*, UQP, St Lucia, 1983, p. 140.

32 Ian Breward, *A History of the Australian Churches*, Allen & Unwin, Sydney, 1993, p. 126.

33 Barbara Bolton, *Booth's Drum: The Salvation Army in Australia, 1880–1980*, Hodder & Stoughton, Sydney, 1980, p. 132.

34 Henry Gariepy, *General of God's Army: The Authorized Biography of General Eva Burrows*, Victor Books, Wheaton, Ill., 1993, p. 24.

35 J. Mansfield, 'The Social Gospel and the Church of England in New South Wales in the 1930s', *Journal of Religious History*, 13.4, December 1985, pp. 411–33; Peter Hempenstall, *The Meddlesome Priest: A Life of Ernest Burgmann*, Allen & Unwin, Sydney, 1993, pp. 196–201.

36 Bob James, '"Lots of Religion and Freemasonry": The Politics of Revivalism during the 1930s Depression on the Northern Coalfields', in Hutchinson & Piggin (eds), *Reviving Australia*, pp. 233–48.

37 *ADEB.*

38 W. S. Clack (ed.), *We Will Go: The History of 70 Years Training Men and Women for World Missionary Ministry,* Bible College of Victoria, Melbourne, 1990.

39 *The Melbourne Bible Institute, Interdenominational, Evangelical, Biblical, Missionary: Sixth Annual Report, 1925–6,* p. 3.

40 Parker, David, 'The Bible College Movement in Australia', paper presented at the 9th conference of the South Pacific Association of Bible Colleges, August 1980, p. 4.

41 Parker, 'The Bible College Movement', p. 7.

42 Susan E. Emilsen, *A Whiff of Heresy: Samuel Angus and the Presbyterian Church in New South Wales,* UNSW Press, Kensington, 1991.

43 Rowland S. Ward, *The Bush Still Burns: The Presbyterian and Reformed Faith in Australia, 1788–1988,* published by the author, Wantirna, Vic., 1989, p. 313.

44 Samuel Angus, *Truth and Tradition,* Angus & Robertson, Sydney, 1934.

45 Winifred L. Ward, 'Aspects of Secularised Religion within the Tradition of New South Wales Methodism since 1930', PhD thesis, University of Wollongong, 1988.

46 Quoted in E. R. Rogers, '"Our Beloved Principal": The Rev. G. H. Morling, O. B. E., M. A', manuscript, n.d., p. 29.

47 Rogers, '"Our Beloved Principal"', p. 109.

48 Rogers, '"Our Beloved Principal"', p. 131.

49 Dr Paul White, interviewed by Margaret Lamb, 3 March 1986, CSAC.

50 M. Bottomley, interviewed by Margaret Rush, 30 November 1992, CSAC.

51 Minutes of the SUEU, 10 and 27 June 1935, CSAC Archives.

52 J. D. Bollen, *Australian Baptists: A Religious Minority,* Baptist Historical Society, London, 1975, p. 44.

53 Bollen, *Australian Baptists,* pp. 53 n.214, 56 n.245.

54 Michael Petras, *Extension or Extinction: Baptist Growth in New South Wales,* Baptist Historical Society, Eastwood, 1983, pp. 10, 11, 39; A. C. Prior, *Some Fell on Good Ground: A History of the Beginnings and Development of the Baptist Church in New South Wales, Australia, 1831–1965,* Sydney, 1966, ch.14.

55 Rogers, '"Our Beloved Principal"', pp. 134, 164, 174.

56 Will F. Renshaw, *Some Melbourne Notes and Comments,* 8, 1 August 1994, p. 4.

57 S. Piggin, *Making Evangelical Missionaries,* Sutton Courtenay Press, Appleford, Oxford, 1984, pp. 70, 169f.

58 Rogers, '"Our Beloved Principal"', p. 16. See also pp. 49, 52 and 97.

59 J. Thomson, interviewed by R. D. Linder, 28 August 1987, CSAC.

60 See chapter 5.

61 Bollen, *Australian Baptists,* p. 33.

62 'Edwin Lee Neil: An Appreciation', typescript, n.d.

63 Chiefly instrumental in his conversion was Brewster Adams, an American preacher. See Ambrose Pratt, *Sidney Myer: A Biography,* Quartet, Melbourne, 1978, p. 112.

64 Dallas Clarnette, *50 Years on Fire for God: The Story of Walter Betts,* People's Church, Kew, 1967.

65 Shirley Lees, *Drunk before Dawn,* Overseas Missionary Fellowship, Sevenoaks, 1979; John and Moyra Prince, *No Fading Vision: The First 50 Years of A. P. C. M.*, Asia Pacific Christian Mission, no place, 1981.

66 Quoted in G. Cutler, *The Torch,* no publisher, Lilydale, Vic., 1976, p. 7.

67 Len Abbott to Margaret Lamb, 11 October 1990.

68 Len Abbott to Margaret Lamb, 11 October 1990.

69 Leonard Buck to Margaret Lamb, 14 December 1990.

70 Allan Tinsley, interviewed in Adelaide by R. D. Linder, 22 September 1987, CSAC.

71 Rogers, '"Our Beloved Principal"', pp. 77, 114. *The Quest for Serenity* was republished in Dallas in 1989.

72 Morling told H. Watkin-Smith he would be quite happy to be a Quaker (comment made at the annual general meeting of the Baptist Historical Society, 17 April 1990).

73 Quoted in Rogers, '"Our Beloved Principal"', p. 9. On the development of the understanding of this element in vital evangelical Christianity, see D. M. Lloyd-Jones, *Romans: An Exposition of Chapter 8: 5–17: The Sons of God,* Banner of Truth Trust, Edinburgh, 1974, ch.27.

74 Rogers, '"Our Beloved Principal"', p. 154.

75 Rogers, '"Our Beloved Principal"', p. 59.

76 Rogers, '"Our Beloved Principal"', pp. 69,89.

77 See I. Jagelman, 'The Role of the Historian/Teacher in Contemporary Pentecostalism', *Barsabbas*, 4, November 1993.

78 Barry Chant, *Heart of Fire: The Story of Australian Pentecostalism*, House of Tabor, Adelaide, 1973, revised 1984, p. 91.

79 Chant, *Heart of Fire*, p. 93.

80 Vinson Synan, 'Fundamentalism', in *Dictionary of Pentecostal and Charismatic Movements*, ed. S. Burgess, G. B. McGee and P. H. Alexander, Regency Zondervan, Grand Rapids, Michigan, 1991.

81 See also J. M. Hickson, *The Revival of the Gifts of Healing, Some of the Practical Difficulties which Hinder the Revival of Spiritual Healing*, Church Stores, Sydney, 1910.

82 *The Anglican*, 14 November 1952.

Chapter 5 *Holiness above the Word*

1 David Millikan, *Imperfect Company: Power and Control in an Australian Christian Cult*, Heinemann, Sydney, 1991, p. 175.

2 D. Jenkyns, 'Sinless Perfection and After: The Religion of Tinker Tailor at Hunter's Hill', *Nation*, 7 October 1961, p. 9f.

3 R. A. Knox, *Enthusiasm*, Clarendon Press, Oxford, 1950.

4 D. M. Lloyd-Jones, *The Puritans*, Banner of Truth Trust, Edinburgh, 1987, p. 321.

5 Interview with D. B. Knox, 17 June 1988, CSAC.

6 See above, chapter 3.

7 D. Parker, 'Fundamentalism and Conservative Protestantism in Australia 1920–1980', PhD thesis, University of Queensland, 1982, p. 478.

8 Win Dunkley, 'Some Comments on EU in the 1930s', typescript, 27 February 1990.

9 Alister, Murray, Helen, Margaret (who died as a child), Brian, John.

10 Interview with A. W. Prescott, 23 December 1987, CSAC.

11 Dunkley, 'Some Comments on EU in the 1930s'.

12 On the Brysons, see Bruce Stuart Bryson, *My Father's House: The Bryson Story of Life on Four Continents*, published by the author, Adelaide, 1993.

13 Phillip J. Heath, *Trinity: The Daring of your Name*, Allen & Unwin, Sydney, 1990, p. 117.

14 See chapter 4 above.

15 SUEU Minute Book, 19 February 1935 to 23 September 1942, p. 24, CSAC Archives.

16 John and Moyra Prince, *Out of the Tower*, Anzea, Sydney, 1987, p. 16.

17 Millikan, *Imperfect Company*, p. 174.

18 E. W. Gosden, *Thank You, Lord! The Eightieth Anniversary of the Japan Evangelistic Band, 1903–1983*, Japan Evangelistic Band, London, 1982, p. 82.

19 *The Edifier*, 10 June 1938. Alan's brother-in-law, and co-worker in the Solomons, Ken Griffiths, denied that this was, or that Alan had ever claimed it was, sinless perfectionism. Ronald Grant always insisted that his teaching subscribed to the 13th chapter of the *Westminster Confession*, 'Of Sanctification': Mary Grant to author, 27 August 1993.

20 Interview with Len Buck, 15 November 1986, CSAC.

21 D. L. Hilliard, 'Protestant Missions in the Solomon Islands', PhD thesis, ANU, 1966, vol. 2, p. 406.

22 See David Hilliard, 'The South Sea Evangelical Mission in The Solomon Islands: The Foundation Years', *Journal of Pacific History*, 4, 1969, pp. 41–64.

23 See chapter 3.

24 See chapter 4.

25 Darrell Neil Paproth, 'C. H. Nash and his Influence', PhD thesis, Deakin University, 1993.

26 Quoted in David Chambers, *Tempest-Tossed: The Life and Teaching of the Rev. C. H. Nash, M. A.*, Church Press Publications, Melbourne, 1959, p. 139f.

27 Alice Smith was the leader of the perfectionists among women at Sydney University. She was an immensely popular girl and very charming—'a lovely Christian' according to Bruce Bryson (interview, 15 December 1988). She had been EU women's secretary in the early 1930s. A Presbyterian, she had been active in Presbyterian Fellowship Union camps.

28 Interview with Bruce Bryson, 15 December 1988, CSAC.

29 Win Dunkley to Margaret Lamb, 12 August 1990.

30 On the Oxford Group, see David Bebbington, *Evangelicalism in Modern Britain*, Unwin Hyman, London, 1989, pp. 235–40.

31 Interview with Dr R. Winton, 25 August 1987.

32 Dunkley, 'Some Comments on EU'.

33 Interview with Ian Holt, 9 March 1987, CSAC.

34 Holt fell under suspicion for his connection with the Agnews. The Scripture Union appointed an Englishman, the Rev. Ron Bevington, as its secretary. On his arrival in Port Melbourne, Ian Holt collected him from the boat. It was plain that sinless perfectionism was on his mind for he lost no time in quizzing Holt:

    'Oh, you know the SP business?'

    'Yes.'

    'Do you know the latest recruit?'

    'No.'

    'Oh, it's you.'

    'Where did they get that idea?'

    'You were at the houseparty [at Mrs Agnew's]?'

    'Yes, but I told Mrs. Agnew that there was nothing new in what she was teaching. Get back to Sydney and tell them I'm not a recruit.' (Interview with Ian Holt, 9 March 1987.)

35 Interview with Ian Holt, 9 March 1987, CSAC.

36 Interview with A. W. Prescott, 23 December 1987, CSAC.

37 Somerlad was a Methodist and an evangelical. His father was a member of the State Parliament.

38 See chapter 6.

39 Interview with Ian Holt, 9 March 1987, CSAC.

40 SUEU Minute Book, 18 September 1940.

41 SUEU Minute Book, 25 September 1940.

42 Dunkley, 'Some Comments on EU'.

43 Dunkley, 'Some Comments on EU'.

44 A. Bryson to Margaret Lamb, 12 December 1989.

45 Prince, *Out of the Tower*, p. 20.

46 Interview with A. Prescott, 23 December 1987, CSAC.

47 Interview with Ian Holt, 9 March 1987, CSAC.

48 Interview with A. Bryson, 15 November 1986, CSAC.

49 Interview with A. Bryson, 15 November 1986, CSAC.

50 A study of the cult to the present day is found in Millikan, *Imperfect Company*.

51 Interview with Tony McCarthy, 26 June 1986, CSAC.

52 One wonders if there are not deeper religious overtones in the habitation of a castle. Is it thought of, for example, as the mystical Monsalvat where the Templars kept the holy grail?

53 Millikan, *Imperfect Company*.

54 A. A. Bonar, *Memoir and Remains of Robert Murray McCheyne* (1844), Banner of Truth Trust, Edinburgh, 1966, p. 159.

55 T. C. Hammond, *The Way of Holiness*, S. John Bacon, Melbourne, 1952.

56 See chapters 6 and 8.

Chapter 6 Word and Spirit, 1933–1959

1 See G. Marsden, *Reforming Fundamentalism: Fuller Seminary and the New Evangelicalism*, Eerdmans, Grand Rapids, Michigan, 1987.

2 Marcus L. Loane, *Archbishop Mowll*, Hodder & Stoughton, London, 1960, p. 190.

3 Mowll's Bible is in the CSAC Archives.

4 Robert Banks, 'Fifty Years of Theology in Australia, 1915–1965, Part One', *Colloquium*, 9.1, 1976, p. 40.

5 Warren Nelson, *T. C. Hammond: Irish Christian,* Banner of Truth Trust, Edinburgh, 1994.

6 S. Judd and K. Cable, *Sydney Anglicans*, Anglican Information Office, Sydney, 1987, p. 251.

7 Programme of *A Pageant of Early Church History,* Town Hall, Sydney, 20–22 May 1937, p. 42, CSAC Archives.

8 Quoted in S. Piggin, *Helpmeets and Heroines: Women and the History of Australian Evangelicalism*, The Mothers' Union, Figtree, 1988, p. 30.

9 *Sydney Diocesan Magazine*, 10.12, February 1958, pp. 190–207.

10 Sydney Showground, 10 May 1959, Film CN 113, F 153, Billy Graham Center Archives.

11 Roslyn Otzen, *Whitley: The Baptist College of Victoria*, Hyland House, Melbourne, 1991, pp. 68–70.

12 T. C. Hammond, *Reasoning Faith: An Introduction to Christian Apologetics*, IVF, London, 1943, p. 80.

13 David Parker, 'Theological and Bible College Education in Australia', *Journal of Christian Education*, Papers 86, July 1986, p. 8.

14 A. de Q. Robin, 'Theology and Theological Training in Australia: An Outline Historical Survey', *Journal of the Royal Australian Historical Society*, 54.4, 1968, pp. 356–67.

15 Gabriel Hebert, *Fundamentalism and the Church of God*, SCM, London, 1957, p. 10.

16 Alan Cole, 'Gabriel Hebert on "Fundamentalism and the Church of God"', *Reformed Theological Review*, XVII.1, February 1958, p. 12.

17 J. W. Deenick (ed.), *A Church en Route: 40 Years Reformed Churches of Australia,* Reformed Churches Publishing House, Geelong, 1991, p. 178.

18 Rowland Ward, *The Bush Still Burns: The Presbyterian and Reformed Faith in Australia, 1788–1988*, published by the author, Wantirna, Vic., 1989, p. 379.

19 Klaas Runia, *Reformed Dogmatics: Its Essence and Method*, Reformed Theological College, Geelong, 1957, p. 29.

20 Editorial, *Journal of Christian Education*, 1.1, June 1958, p. 3.

21 Stuart Piggin, *Making Evangelical Missionaries*, Sutton Courtenay Press, Appleford, Oxford, 1984, pp. 29–47.

22 A. J. Dyer, *Unarmed Combat: An Australian Missionary Adventure,* no publisher, n.d. [c.1954?], p. 56.

23 Quoted in Dyer, *Unarmed Combat*, p. 14.

24 Dyer, *Unarmed Combat,* p. 67.

25 On the peace expedition, see Dyer, *Unarmed Combat*; John Harris, *One Blood*, Albatross, Sydney, 1990; Keith Cole, *Oenpelli Pioneer: A Biography of the Rev. Alfred John Dyer*, Church Missionary Historical Publications, Melbourne, 1972.

26 Harris, *One Blood*, p. 763.

27 *Aboriginal Welfare: Initial Conference of Commonwealth and State Aboriginal Authorities*, Canberra, 1937, p. 3.

28 Keith Cole, *'But I Will Be with You': An Autobiography*, Keith Cole Publications, Bendigo, 1988, p. 157.

29 Nash, 'Edwin Lee Neil: An Appreciation', typescript, n.d.

30 Recollections of Charles Sandland in a letter to the author, 17 September 1994.

31 D. N. Paproth, 'C. H. Nash and his Influence', PhD thesis, Deakin University, 1993, pp. 164, 174, 180.

32 'The Old Order Changes', *Keswick Quarterly*, February 1948, p. 23.

33 *Keswick Quarterly*, February 1948, p. 49.

34 Ralph Davis, interviewed by Margaret Lamb, 17 May 1988, CSAC.

35 Typescript written by R. C. Davis about 1990 and sent to the author by Gerald Charles Davis, 7 April 1994.

36 L. Buck, interviewed by Margaret Lamb, 15 November 1986, CSAC.

37 C. Sandland, interviewed by Margaret Lamb, 20 March 1987, CSAC.

38 J. Oswald Sanders, *Planting Men in Melanesia: The First Decade of Development of the Christian Leaders' Training College of Papua New Guinea*, Christian Leaders' Training College of PNG, Mt Hagen, 1978.

39 Vic Ambrose, *Balus Bilong Mipela: The Story of the Missionary Aviation Fellowship, Australia and New Zealand*, MAF, Melbourne, 1987.

40 Steer Inc.'s aim is to raise money for missions from farming. It was incorporated in 1962, and by 1994 had directed $14 million to missions.

41 Including Asia Pacific Christian Mission (was Unevangelised Field Mission), Australian Institute of Archaeology, Bible Society, Care, Children's Special Service Mission, China Inland Mission, Church Missionary Society, Crusaders, Egypt General Mission, Evangelical Union, Evangelisation Society of Australia, God's Squad, Melbourne City Mission, Mission to the Lepers, Scripture Union, SIL/WBT.

42 Alan Kerr, interviewed by Stuart Piggin, 22 February 1989.

43 Will F. Renshaw to the author, 19 August 1994.

44 Charles G. Sandland, 'A Ninety-Year-Old's Memories of the Background and Early Years of Campaigners for Christ', typescript, 19 July 1993.

45 Paproth, 'C. H. Nash and his Influence', p. 378.

46 Will F. Renshaw, 'H. P. Smith', in *ADEB*.

47 Ezekiel 47.1–12.

48 Peter Morgan (pentecostal Aboriginal Pastor), address given at the National Praise and Worship Conference, Lighthouse Christian Centre, Wollongong, 28 September 1993.

49 G. Bingham, interviewed by Ian Pennicook, 9, 10 July 1986, CSAC.

50 Quoted in S. Piggin, *The Fruitful Figtree, A History of All Saints Anglican Church Figtree, 1888–1983*, Figtree, NSW, 1983, p. 43.

51 Tony Tress, interviewed by S. Piggin, 15 June 1986, CSAC.

52 W. W. Phillips, 'Religion', in W. Vamplew (ed.), *Australians: Historical Statistics*, Fairfax, Syme & Weldon, Sydney, 1987, pp. 428–35.

53 Richard Prideaux, response to Perry Lecture given by S. Piggin on 19 October 1990.

54 Peter Adam to the author, 2 May 1990.

55 Alan Walker, *The Whole Gospel for the Whole World*, Marshall, Morgan & Scott, London, 1958, pp. 117–28; Rex Mathias, *Mission to the Nation*, Joint Board of Christian Education, Melbourne, 1986; Samantha Frappell, 'Post-War Revivalism in Australia: The Mission to the Nation, 1953–1957', in Mark Hutchinson and Stuart Piggin (eds), *Reviving Australia*, CSAC, Sydney, 1994, pp. 249–61.

56 D. Wright, *The Mantle of Christ: A History of the Sydney Central Methodist Mission*, UQP, St Lucia, 1984, p. x.

Chapter 7   The Evangelical Synthesis Attained

1 The chief published source on the 1959 crusades in Australia is S. B. Babbage and I. Siggins, *Light Beneath the Cross: The Story of Billy Graham's Crusade in Australia*, The World's Work, Kingswood and Melbourne, 1960.

2 Gordon Powell, 'Six Months after Billy Graham, An Address delivered at the University of Sydney on October 8, 1959', Billy Graham Evangelistic Association, 1960 (unpaginated).

3 Powell, 'Six Months after Billy Graham'.

4 M. Loane, 'Billy Graham: God's Man for this Century!', *Decision*, May 1984, p. 17f.

5 N. W. Wallis, *The Warhorse: The Life and Work of Rev. Dr. Harold J. Whitney*, Mission Publications of Australia, Lawson, NSW, 1986, p. 82.

6 H. J. Whitney, *Pilgrimage with a Purpose*, Mission Publications of Australia, Lawson, NSW, 1988, p. 31f.

7 *Christianity Today,* February 1980. For a more ferocious assertion of the same point, see J. Pollock, *Billy Graham, The Authorised Biography,* Hodder & Stoughton, London, 1966, p. 211.

8 June Cox, testimony, November 1961, Billy Graham Archives (hereafter BGA), CN 245, 2, 2.

9 Deane E. Meatheringham, statement, BGA, CN 245, 14, 23.

10 Crusade Procedure Book, Melbourne, 1959 (hereafter CPB).

11 *The Distinguishing Marks of a Work of the Spirit of God*, in C. C. Goen (ed.), *Jonathan Edwards: The Great Awakening*, Yale UP, New Haven, 1972, p. 230.

12 Quoted in 'Billy Graham in Australia', *Current Affairs Bulletin*, 24.4, 22 June 1959, p. 53.

13 Quoted in 'Billy Graham in Australia', p. 53f.

14 CN 245, 18, 9, BGA.

15 CPB, 4 March 1959.

16 Australian readers will find it difficult to forgive the error of Graham's latest biographer when he says that the 143,000 obliterated by 27,000 'previous highs recorded during soccer finals and the 1956 Olympics' (William Martin, *A Prophet with Honor: The Billy Graham Story,* William Morrow & Co., New York, 1991, p. 254). The finals were in Australian Rules football, which is far more of a religion in Australia than soccer, and, I pray, always will be.

17 F 130, 15 March 1959, BGA.

18 Film 124, 18 February 1959, BGA.

19 See Stuart Piggin, 'Towards a Theoretical Understanding of Revival', in Mark Hutchinson and Stuart Piggin (eds), *Reviving Australia*, CSAC, Sydney, 1994, pp. 6, 13–33.

20 Roger Finke and Rodney Stark, *The Churching of America, 1776–1990*, Rutgers UP, New Brunswick, 1992, p. 238.

21 William G. McLoughlin, *Revivals, Awakenings and Reform*, University of Chicago Press, Chicago, 1978; J. F. Wilson, 'Perspectives on the Historiography of Religious Awakenings', *Sociological Analysis,* 44, 1983, pp. 117–20; R. C. Gordon-McCutchan, 'Great Awakenings', *Sociological Analysis*, 44, 1983, pp. 83–95.

22 R. C. Gordon-McCutchan, 'The Irony of Evangelical History', *Journal for the Scientific Study of Religion*, 20, 1981, pp. 309–26.

23 Michael J. Crawford, *Seasons of Grace, Colonial New England's Revival Tradition in Its British Context,* Oxford UP, New York, 1991, p. 7.

24 This catalogue of the mundane factors is found in K. S. Inglis, 'Sydney, Meet Mr. Graham', *Nation*, 11 April 1959, p. 14.

25 S. B. Babbage, *A Merciful Providence*, Albatross, Sydney, forthcoming.

26 Bill Lawton, 'The Winter of Our Days: The Anglican Diocese of Sydney 1950–1960', *Lucas,* 9, July 1990, pp. 11–32.

27 Bill Lawton, '"That Woman Jezebel"—Moore College after 25 Years', The Moore College Library Lecture, 1981, pp. 14–17.

28 Lawton, '"That Woman Jezebel"', p. 30.

29 See chapter 8.

30 On this point, Dr Bill Lawton made the interesting observation to the author that Billy Graham killed Keswick piety in Sydney and replaced it with an altogether healthier spirituality.

31 Bruce Ogden, Chair of the Arrangements Committee, informed the author that at the Sydney Showground Gerry Beavan requested him to build the platform facing only about one-third of the available seating. Thinking that the need would be greater than that, Ogden had wheels built on the platform so that its direction could be changed if required!

32 'Times Square Story', Film CN 54 F 149, BGA.

33 John Pollock, *Crusades: 20 Years with Billy Graham*, World Wide Publications, Minneapolis, 1969, p. 186; Martin, *Prophet with Honor*, p. 252.

34 CPB.

35 Pollock, *Crusades*, p. 187.

36 Pollock, *Crusades*, p. 187.

37 'For thus saith the high and lofty One that inhabiteth eternity, whose name is Holy; I dwell in the high and holy place, with him also that is of a contrite and humble spirit, to revive the spirit of the humble, and to revive the heart of the contrite ones.'

38 *Age*, 14 February 1959.

39 *Diocesan Magazine*, 9.12, May–June 1956, p. 176.

40 Quoted in 'Billy Graham in Australia', p. 55.

41 F. Butler, 'Billy Graham and the End of Evangelical Unity', PhD thesis, Florida, 1976.

42 CPB, Sydney executive minutes, 12 November 1958.

43 Pentecostalism still did well out of the 1959 crusades. Among those then converted was Clark Taylor, later senior pastor of the Brisbane Christian Outreach Centre, one of Australia's most successful church planters. Clark Taylor, interviewed by R. D. Linder, 29 May 1987, CSAC.

44 Dr James Ridgeway, interviewed by R. D. Linder, 26 August 1987.

45 Marcus Loane, 'How Anglican and Episcopal Churches Co-operate and Benefit through the Billy Graham Crusades', manuscript, BGA.

46 Harold Whitney, *Tell Australia*, W. R. Smith & Paterson, Brisbane, 1957, pp. 59–62.

47 Interviewed by M. Lamb and S. Piggin, 22 February 1989, CSAC.

48 Quoted in 'Billy Graham in Australia', p. 56.

49 Minutes of the Executive, 12 November 1958, CPB, Sydney.

50 Gordon Powell to the author, 28 January 1989; Gordon Powell to Billy Graham, 26 August 1964, CN 245, 2, 2, BGA.

51 Quoted in 'Billy Graham in Australia', p. 57.

52 *Sydney Morning Herald*, 2 May 1959; see also 'Billy Graham in Australia', p. 57.

53 Film 127, 28 February 1959, BGA.

54 Film CN 113, F 153, 10 May 1959, BGA.

55 Kerle and Gilchrist, circular letter, 1 June 1967, CN 12, box 14, folder 25, BGA.

56 Butler, 'Billy Graham'.

57 Richard M. Nixon, Pre-presidential Papers, Federal Records Center, Laguna Niguel, California.

58 *Daily Herald*, 12 June 1959.

59 Film F 124, BGA.

60 Inglis, 'Sydney, Meet Mr. Graham', p. 14.

61 Film F 130, BGA.

62 *Crusade Bulletin*, March 1959.

63 CPB.

64 CPB, Sydney executive minutes, 25 March 1959.

65 From the foreword by Warren W. Wiersbe, in *A Frank Boreham Treasury*, compiled by Peter F. Gunther, Moody Press, Chicago, 1984, p. vii.

66 CN 245, 2,2, BGA.

67 30 July 1962, CN 19, box 5, folder 47, BGA.

68 'Never before in Human History', *Decision*, May 1984, p. 20.

69 Based on W. Vamplew, *Australians: Historical Statistics*, Fairfax, Syme & Weldon, Sydney, pp. 428–31.

70 F. Alleyne and H. Fallding, 'Decisions at the Graham Crusade in Sydney: A Statistical Analysis', *Journal of Christian Education*, 3.1, July 1960, p. 39.

71 Alleyne and Fallding, 'Decisions at the Graham Crusade', pp. 37, 39n.5.

72 'Billy Graham in Australia', p. 56.

73 G. Bingham to Berryman, 12 October 1972, CN 245, 14, 23, BGA.

74 Bill Lawton, '"That Woman Jezebel"', pp. 22, 32; S. Judd and K. Cable, *Sydney Anglicans*, Anglican Information Office, Sydney, 1984, p. 302.

75 Mary Andrews to the author, 5 May 1989.

76 Irene Jeffreys, interviewed by R. D. Linder, 22 September 1987, CSAC.

77 A. J. Dain to Berryman, 28 September 1972, CN 245, 14, 23, BGA.

78 John and Moyra Prince, *Tuned in to Change: A History of the Australian Scripture Union 1880–1980*, Scripture Union of Australia, Sydney, 1979, p. 166.

79 Arthur Deane to the author, 16 April 1993.

80 CPB.

81 *Report of the Billy Graham Crusades in Australia and New Zealand*, 1959 (unpaginated).

82 Quoted in S. Piggin, *Faith of Steel*, University of Wollongong, Wollongong, 1984, p. 242.

83 Alleyne and Fallding, 'Decisions at the Graham Crusade', pp. 34–9.

84 S. K. Mukherjee, *Crime Trends in Twentieth Century Australia*, Australian Institute of Criminology and Allen & Unwin, Sydney, 1981, pp. 82–4. Drunkenness offences in Australia peaked in 1951 and then declined throughout the 1950s and 1960s.

85 *Sunday Mirror*, 17 May 1959.

86 Telephone conversation with Mr and Mrs A. E. Debenham, 18 May 1989.

87 *Decision*, June 1962, p. 13.

88 The population increased by a steady rate of about 200,000 per year throughout the 1950s. See *Demography, 1965*, Bulletin No.83, Commonwealth Bureau of Census and Statistics, Canberra, 1966, p. 4.

89 See S. Mukherjee *et al.*, *Source Book of Australian Criminal and Social Statistics, 1900–1980*, Australian Institute of Criminology, Canberra, 1981.

90 *Demography*, p. 80.

Chapter 8   Word or Spirit, 1960–1994

1 Hans J. J. Mol, *Religion in Australia: A Sociological Investigation*, Nelson, Melbourne, 1971, p. 302.

2 W. W. Phillips, 'Religion', in W. Vamplew (ed.), *Australians: Historical Statistics*, Fairfax, Syme & Weldon, Sydney, 1987.

3 R. J. Neuhaus (ed.), *Unsecular America*, Eerdmans, Grand Rapids, Michigan, 1986, p. 21.

4 Mol, *Religion in Australia*, p. 41.

5 See Robert Humphreys and Rowland Ward, *Religious Bodies in Australia*, published by the authors, Melbourne, 1988.

6 D. W. B. Robinson, Presidential Address, *Yearbook of the Diocese of Sydney, 1990*, p. 234.

7 Barbara Thiering, *Jesus the Man: A New Interpretation from the Dead Sea Scrolls*, Doubleday, Sydney, 1992.

8 J.S. Spong, *Born of Woman: A Bishop Rethinks the Birth of Jesus*, Harper, San Francisco, 1992; *Living in Sin: A Bishop Rethinks Human Sexuality*, Harper, San Francisco, 1988; *Resurrection—Myth or Reality?*, Harper, San Francisco, 1994. See also Paul Barnett *et al.*, *Resurrection: Truth and Reality*, Aquila, Sydney, 1994.

9 J. H. S. Kent, *The End of the Line?*, SCM Press, London, 1982, p. 103f.

10 Iain H. Murray, *David Martyn Lloyd-Jones: The Fight of Faith*, Banner of Truth Trust, Edinburgh, 1990, p. 486.

11 The address, 'Evangelical Unity: An Appeal', is published in D. M. Lloyd-Jones, *Knowing the Times*, Banner of Truth Trust, Edinburgh, 1989, pp. 246–57; see also Murray, *David Martyn Lloyd-Jones*, ch. 25.

12 *Report of the Committee on the Future of Tertiary Education in Australia*, Government Printer, Melbourne, 1964–65, vol. 2, p. 143.

13 Rex Davis (ed.), *The Morpeth Papers: A Conference on Theological Education*, Diocese of Newcastle, Morpeth, 1966, p. 29.

14 Keith Cole, *'But I Will Be with You': An Autobiography*, Keith Cole Publications, Bendigo, 1988, pp. 156–78.

15 John J. Harding, 'The Reformed Faith Today', *The Times,* 5 December 1988.

16 Rowland Ward, *The Bush Still Burns: The Presbyterian and Reformed Faith in Australia, 1788–1988*, published by the author, Wantirna, Vic., 1989, pp. 389–91.

17 Ward, *The Bush Still Burns*, pp. 391–401.

18 The teaching of American revivalist, Charles Finney, that whether or not a person turns to God is a matter of human will rather than divine election.

19 21 March 1968, CN 245, 7, 16, no.12, BGA.

20 26 April 1968, CN 245, 7, 16, BGA.

21 *Victorian Crusade Bulletin*, January 1969.

22 Undated, CN 245, 7, 16, no.12, no.9, BGA.

23 272, May 1986, p. 1.

24 M. Himbury, interviewed by R. D. Linder, 25 August 1987, CSAC.

25 On David Broughton Knox, see Peter T. O'Brien and David G. Peterson (eds), *God Who is Rich in Mercy,* Lancer, Homebush West, NSW, 1986; Marcus L. Loane and Peter F. Jensen, *Broughton Knox, Principal of Moore College, 1959–1985*, Moore Theological College, Newtown, 1994.

26 D. B. Knox, *The Doctrine of Faith in the Reign of Henry VIII*, James Clarke & Co, London, 1961, p. 274.

27 'The Authority of Holy Scripture', in D. B. Knox, *Thirty-Nine Articles,* Anglican Information Office, Sydney, 1976, pp. 15–20.

28 *Reformed Theological Review*, February 1960, 19.1, pp. 1–9.

29 D. B. Knox, 'Propositional Revelation the Only Revelation', *Reformed Theological Review*, February 1960, 19.1, p. 6.

30 By inerrancy, Knox meant not so much in a historical or scientific sense, but in its capacity to inculcate infallibly and authoritatively the truth about and from God pertaining to faith and morals.

31 D. B. Knox, 2CH radio broadcasts: *The Holy Catholic Church*, 13 October 1963; *Christian Denominations*, 7 October 1963; *The Spirit, the Church, and the Denomination*, 7 March 1976; *Denomination as a God*, 25 January 1981; and 'What the Church Is', *The Briefing*, 15.

32 The subject of the nature of the church was on the agenda of the World Council of Churches assemblies in 1948, 1954 and 1961 and on the agenda of the National Conference of Australian Churches in Melbourne in 1960.

33 D. W. B. Robinson, 'The Church Universal and its Earthly Form', parts 1 and 2, *Australian Church Record*, 2, 16 February 1956; 'The Church in the New Testament', *St Mark's Review*, 17, August 1959; 'The Doctrine of the Church and Its Implications for Evangelism', *Interchange*, 1974; 'The Church Revisited: An Autobiographical Fragment', *Reformed Theological Review*, 1, January–April 1989; G. Cole, 'The Doctrine of the Church: Towards Conceptual Clarification', in B. G. Webb (ed.), *Church, Worship, and the Local Congregation*, Lancer, Homebush West, NSW, 1987, pp. 3–18.

34 *Looking into the Parish*, Anglican Information Office, Sydney, 1972.

35 See *Southern Cross*, November 1971, p. 11.

36 Robert J. Banks, 'The Theology of D. B. Knox, a Preliminary Estimate', in O'Brien and Peterson (eds), *God Who is Rich in Mercy*, pp. 391–2.

37 Anecdote reported to the author by L. Lyons, 21 January 1994.

38 David Parker, 'Fundamentalism and Conservative Protestantism in Australia 1920–1980', PhD thesis, University of Queensland, 1982, p. 619f.

39 Roger C. Thompson, *Religion in Australia*, Oxford UP, Melbourne, 1994, p. 116.

40 Gil Duthie, *I Had 50,000 Bosses: Memoirs of a Labor Backbencher, 1946–1975*, Angus & Robertson, Sydney, 1984, p. 241.

41 Duthie, *50,000 Bosses*, p. 241f.

42 Estimates vary: one put it as low as 6000.

43 Youth With a Mission.

44 Anne Nanscawen, *With One Accord: The Beginning of an Aussie Awakening*, Anzea, Sydney, 1989, p. 124f.

45 Alan Nichols, *David Penman*, Albatross, Sydney, 1991.

46 Don Wright, *The Mantle of Christ: A History of the Sydney Central Methodist Mission*, UQP, St Lucia, 1983, pp. 225–9.

47 Mervyn Keith Olsen, 'One Consuming Passion—To Tell the World: An Assessment of the Life and Ministry of Leslie Gordon Young', dissertation, Baptist Theological College of Queensland, Brisbane, 1986, p. 146.

48 Olsen, 'One Consuming Passion', p. 100.

49 Olsen, 'One Consuming Passion', p. 125.

50 Olsen, 'One Consuming Passion', p. 125f.

51 *New Life*, 26 April 1984.

52 Bingham is the author of more than 200 books. His best account of the Pakistan revivals is in his *Twice-Conquering Love,* New Creation, Blackwood, SA, 1992.

53 Quoted in Trevor Faggotter, 'Revival Fire at Wudinna', *Renewal Journal,* 4, 1994, p. 50.

54 Terry Djiniyini, cited in Max Hart, *A Story of Fire: Aboriginal Christianity*, New Creation, Blackwood, SA, 1988, p. 49f.

55 Cited in Jeanette Boyd, 'The Arnhem Land Revival of 1979: An Australian Aboriginal Religious Movement', unpublished paper, October 1986.

56 Hart, *A Story of Fire*, p. 50f.

57 Quoted in Hart, *A Story of Fire*, p. 51.

58 Quoted in Boyd, 'The Arnhem Land Revival'.

59 'Minjung in Australia', *South Pacific Journal of Mission Studies*, 1.1, July 1989, p. 8f.

60 Ian Lindsay, *Fire in the Spinifex,* United Aborigines Mission, Box Hill, Vic., 1986, p. 18; on the Mt Margaret Revival, see Stewart Gill, '"Revival Days at Mt Margaret": The UAM and the 1982 Revival', in Mark Hutchinson and Stuart Piggin (eds), *Reviving Australia*, CSAC, Sydney, 1994, pp. 275–90.

61 John Harris, *One Blood*, Albatross, Sydney, 1990, p. 852.

62 For an analysis of the continuities of the revival with traditional Aboriginal customs, see Robert Bos, 'The Dreaming and Social Change in Arnhem Land', in T. Swain and D. B. Rose (eds), *Aboriginal Australians and Christian Missions*, Australian Association for the Study of Religions, Adelaide, 1988, pp. 422–37.

63 John Blacket, '"I Will Renew the Land": Island on Fire', MS history of the Aboriginal revival, 18 May 1993; see also his '"Rainbow or the Serpent?" Observing the Arnhem Land Aboriginal Revival, 1979 and Now', in Hutchinson and Piggin (eds), *Reviving Australia*, pp. 291–301.

64 Harris, *One Blood*, facing p. 783 and p. 850.

65 Blacket, '"I Will Renew the Land"'.

66 The arrival of revival when the minister has gone is a time-honoured feature of revivals. In the eighteenth century Jonathan Edwards preached his great sermon 'Sinners in the Hands of an Angry God' to his own congregation who were only mildly ruffled, but when he preached it in a nearby town, the lid blew off. In the nineteenth century, Robert Murray McCheyne, a Scottish preacher, was overseas on a holiday, when revival swept through his church in Dundee in 1839.

67 Richard Carwardine, 'The Second Great Awakening in Comparative Perspective: Revivals and Culture in the United States and Britain', in Edith L. Blumhofer and Randall Balmer, *Modern Christian Revivals*, University of Illinois Press, Urbana, 1993, p. 84.

68 Robert Bos, 'The Dreaming and Social Change in Arnhem Land,' in Swain and Rose (eds), *Aboriginal Australians and Christian Missions*, pp. 422–37.

69 See, for example, *Social Issues Update*, The occasional newsletter of the Social Issues Committee, 3.2, October 1993, Anglican Diocese of Sydney.

Chapter 9   *Word Rather than Peace*

1 Statement of the archbishop to Standing Committee, 3 February 1992.

2 For a comprehensive study of the movement before 1990, see Muriel Porter, *Women in the Church: The Great Ordination Debate in Australia,* Penguin, Ringwood, Vic., 1989.

3 John Woodhouse, 'The Use of the Bible in Modern Controversies; A Watershed among Evangelicals?', in B. G. Webb (ed.), *Personhood, Sexuality, and Christian Ministry*, Explorations: Moore Papers No. 1, Sydney, 1986, pp. 4–14.

4 Muriel Porter, *Women in the Church*, p. 79.

5 Quoted by Ruth I. Sturmey, 'Women and the Anglican Church in Australia: Theology and Social Change', PhD thesis, University of Sydney, 1989, p. 214.

6 'Women's Ministry: A New Look at the Biblical Texts', in Shirley Lees (ed.), *The Role of Women* (When Christians Disagree series), IVP, England, 1984.

7 Klaas Runia, *The Sermon under Attack*, Paternoster, Exeter, 1983 (1980 Moore College lectures).

8 Leon Morris, 'The Ministry of Women', in Morris *et al.*, *A Woman's Place*, Anglican Information Office, Sydney, 1976; *Southern Cross,* April 1985.

9 Paul Jewett's *Man as Male and Female,* Eerdmans, Grand Rapids, Michigan, 1975, was considered too liberal by conservatives and fundamentalists. See for example Robert Forsyth, 'Getting There Is Half the Fun: An Approach to Women's Ordination', *Australian Church Record*, 11 March 1985, p. 6. Jewett was charged with heresy, but he believed it was very important to go through the trial to demonstrate that an evangelical could hold such a view.

10 F. F. Bruce, 'Women in the Church: A Biblical Survey', paper presented to *The Christian Brethren Research Fellowship Journal*, No. 23.

11 Harold Lindsell, *The World, the Flesh and the Devil*, Canon Press, Washington, 1973.

12 Stuart Piggin, 'From Independence to Domesticity: Masculinity in Australian History and the Female Ordination Debate', in Mark Hutchinson and Edmund Campion (eds), *Long Patient Struggle: Essays on Women and Gender in Australian Christianity*, CSAC, Sydney, 1994, pp. 151–60.

13 Dowling, Presidential Address, 1990, p. 27.

14 *Southern Cross,* March 1985, p. 7.

15 G. W. H. Lampe, 'Church Tradition and the Ordination of Women', *Expository Times*, LXXVI.4, January 1965, pp. 123–5.

16 *Southern Cross,* March 1985, p. 7.

17 D. W. B. Robinson, 'Scripture, Apostolic Tradition and the Ordination of Women', *AAM Australia Newsletter*, November 1990.

18 Louise Williams, 'A Hard Man of God', *Sydney Morning Herald*, 12 December 1992.

19 Donald Robinson to Patricia Hayward, 13 April 1992, MOW Papers.

20 'Furlong catalyst for MOW in Australia', *MOW Newsletter*, August 1984, p. 4.

21 Telephone conversation with the author, 29 October 1993.

22 Application for an award in the Order of Australia, Patricia Brennan, The Movement for the Ordination of Women (National) Inc. Thirty-two referees were listed in this application, including Veronica Brady, Quentin Bryce, Owen Dowling, Elizabeth Evatt, Rowena Harris, Irene Jeffreys, Susan Ryan, Elisabeth Schussler-Fiorenza, Jocelyn Scutt, Ruth Shatford, Jean Skuse, Marie Tulip, and Freda Whitlam.

23 Patricia Brennan, 'Five Men on a Shaky Bridge', *The Bulletin,* 21 April 1992, p. 38.

24 *AAM Australia Newsletter,* August 1989.

25 *AAM Australia Newsletter,* December 1989.

26 *Scandrett v. Dowling and Ors*, Friday 31 January 1992.

27 *Church Scene*, 7 February 1992, p. 17.

28 His letter to the clergy of 5 February 1992.

29 *Sydney Morning Herald*, 3 February 1992.

30 Letter signed by Phillip Jensen, 25 March 1992.

31 'The Reforming Process', REPA brochure.

32 ABC telecast, 7 March 1992.

33 *MOW Newsletter*, April 1992.

34 MOW Papers, 5, 8 March 1993.

35 Jennifer Hall to Sydney MOWers, MOW Papers, April 1992.

36 Muriel Porter, 'The End of the "Great Debate": The 1992 General Synod Decision on Women Priests', in Hutchinson and Campion (eds), *Long Patient Struggle*, p. 170.

37 Editorial, 'On the brink of a schism', *Sydney Morning Herald*, 18 April 1992.

38 *Daily Telegraph Mirror*, 18 April 1992, p. 30.

39 10/91 Ordination of Women to the Priesthood: A Report to Synod.

40 A transcript of the proceedings has been published, entitled *Women in Ministry Conference*.

41 Kevin Giles, 'Subordinated Arguments', typescript.

42 10/91 Ordination of Women to the Priesthood: A Report to Synod.

43 Convenor's Report to Sydney MOW, 18 April 1993.

44 *Scandrett & Ors v. Dowling & Ors*, 3 July 1992, Supreme Court of New South Wales Court of Appeal.

45 D. W. B. Robinson, 'Presidential Address to Synod', 12 October 1992, Diocese of Sydney, 1992, p. 7.

46 Keith Mason, 'The Final Judgment in Scandrett v. Dowling: Its Impact beyond Women's Ordination', typescript, August 1992, written for *Southern Cross*, but stopped from publication.

47 A prominent nineteenth-century lawyer, Phillimore, wrote in his *Ecclesiastical Law of the Church of England* (1873): 'There are two classes of persons absolutely incapable of ordination; namely, unbaptised persons and women. Ordination of such persons is wholly inoperative. The former, because baptism is the condition of belonging to the Church at all. The latter, because by nature, Holy Scripture and Catholic usage they are disqualified.'

48 The *Report of the Archbishop's Commission on Women and Holy Orders* was presented to the General Synod in 1967.

49 John Holle, 'The C of E votes for Women Priests', *Sunday News*, 15 November 1992, St Paul's, Burwood, NSW.

50 *Spectator*, 21 November 1992, p. 8.

51 *Spectator*, 21 November 1992, p. 2.

52 *AAM Australia Newsletter*, November 1990.

53 *Women's Resource Centre*, Auckland Diocese, November–December 1992.

54 Keith Rayner, Supplementary Presidential Address, 21 November 1992.
55 The voting was: House of Laity (99 members), 69 for and 30 against; House of Clergy (99 members), 67 for and 32 against; House of Bishops (22 members), 16 for and 4 against, 2 informal.
56 MOW Papers, 5 April 1993.
57 John Woodhouse, 'The Use of the Bible' p. 4.

Conclusion

1 Herbert Butterfield, *Christianity and History*, Fontana, London, 1957, p. 189.

Bibliography

Much of the unpublished material cited in this book is held at the Centre for the Study of Australian Christianity (CSAC), Robert Menzies College, Macquarie University. The centre has also recorded more than 300 interviews with prominent Australian evangelicals. They were used extensively in the present work.

Unpublished Manuscripts and Archival Sources

Billy Graham Evangelistic Association, Records of Australian Crusades, Billy Graham Center Archives, Wheaton, Illinois: Papers CN12, 16, 19, 245, 87042, 87142; Audio tapes CN24, 25; Films and video tapes CN54, 113, 214; F124–130, 149, 153.

Bonwick Transcripts. Mitchell Library, A2000–2003.

Dunkley, Win, 'Some Comments on EU in the 1930s', typescript, 27 February 1990. CSAC Archives.

Giles, Kevin, 'Subordinated Arguments', paper read at the Women in Ministry Conference, on 27 June 1992, Parramatta. CSAC Archives. The material here quoted is not found in the transcript of proceedings listed below under 'Women in Ministry Conference'.

Johnson, Richard, Letters to Fricker. Mitchell Library, MS Aj1.

Kitchen, J. J., Diary. In possession of Marjorie Kitchen.

Lamb, Margaret, Correspondence, 1986–90. CSAC Archives.

Loane, Marcus, 'How Anglican and Episcopal Churches co-operate and benefit through the Billy Graham Crusades', manuscript, Billy Graham Archives.

Marsden, Samuel, Papers. Mitchell Library, A1992–1999.

Mason, Keith, 'The Final Judgment in Scandrett v Dowling: Its Impact beyond women's ordination', typescript, August 1992, written for *Southern Cross*, but stopped from publication. CSAC Archives.

Melbourne Gospel Crusade, Minutes. In possession of David Renshaw.

Methodist Overseas Mission Board, Minutes, 1918. Uniting Church Archives, Box 206.

Morgan, Peter, Address given at the National Praise and Worship Conference, Lighthouse Christian Centre Wollongong, 28 September 1993. Part transcript, CSAC Archives.

Movement for the Ordination of Women, Papers, 1992–93. In the possession of Patricia Haywood, Sydney.

Nash, C. H. 'Edwin Lee Neil: An Appreciation', typescript, n.d. probably 1934. CSAC Archives.

Quinn, Rod, Newspaper Cuttings. Mitchell Library, QA 821/5.

Rogers, E. R. '"Our Beloved Principal": The Rev. G. H. Morling, O.B.E., M.A.', n.d. In possession of Justice Trevor Morling.

Sandland, Charles G., 'A Ninety-Year Old's Memories of the Background and Early Years of Campaigners for Christ', 19 July 1993. CSAC Archives.

Sydney University Evangelical Union, Minute Books. CSAC Archives.

'Women in Ministry Conference', Diocesan Conference on Women in Ministry, 27 June 1992, St John's Parramatta Parish Hall. CSAC Archives.

Newspapers, Magazines and Periodicals

The Age
The Anglican
Australian Baptist
Australian Church Record
The Baptist
The Briefing
The Bulletin
Church Scene
Decision
The Edifier
Interchange
Journal of Christian Education
Keswick Quarterly
Nation, 1961
New Life
Not in Vain (South Sea Evangelical Mission)
Reformed Theological Review
St Mark's Review
Social Issues Update
South Coast Times
Sunday Mirror
Sydney Morning Herald

Books, Articles and Theses

Aboriginal Welfare: Initial Conference of Commonwealth and State Aboriginal Authorities, Canberra, 1937.

Alexander, Helen, *Charles M. Alexander*, London, n.d.

Alford, Katrina, *Production or Reproduction? An Economic History of Women in Australia*, Oxford UP, Melbourne, 1984.

Alleyne, F., and Fallding, H., 'Decisions at the Graham Crusade in Sydney: A Statistical Analysis', *Journal of Christian Education*, 3.1, July 1960, pp. 32–41.

Ambrose, Vic, *Balus Bilong Mipela: The Story of the Missionary Aviation Fellowship, Australia and New Zealand*, MAF, Melbourne, 1987.

Anderson, Donald George, 'Defending an Evangelical Society and an Evangelical Diocese, Sydney James Kirkby, 1879–1935', MA thesis, University of Wollongong, 1985.

—— 'The Bishop's Society, 1856 to 1958: A History of the Sydney Anglican Home Mission Society', PhD thesis, University of Wollongong, 1990.

Angus, Samuel, *Truth and Tradition*, Angus & Robertson, Sydney, 1934.

Atkinson, Alan, and Aveling, Marian (eds), *Australians 1838*, Fairfax, Syme & Weldon, Sydney, 1987.

Babbage, S. B., *A Merciful Providence*, Albatrosss, Sydney, forthcoming.

—— and Siggins, I., *Light Beneath the Cross: The Story of Billy Graham's Crusade in Australia*, The World's Work, Kingswood and Melbourne, 1960.

Bacon, Ernest, *Spurgeon: Heir to the Puritans*, Allen & Unwin, London, 1967.

Badger, C. R., *The Reverend Charles Strong and the Australian Church*, Abacada, Melbourne, 1971.

Baker, D. W. A., *Days of Wrath: A Life of John Dunmore Lang*, Melbourne UP, Carlton, 1985.

Ball, G. B., 'The Australian Baptist Mission and its Impact in Bengal', MA thesis, Flinders University, 1978.

Ball, Leslie James, 'Queensland Baptists in the Nineteenth Century: The Historical Development of a Denominational Identity', PhD thesis, University of Queensland, 1994.

Banks, Robert J., 'Fifty Years of Theology in Australia, 1915–1965, Part One', *Colloquium*, 9.1, October 1976, pp. 36–42; 'Fifty Years of Theology in Australia, 1915–1965, Part Two', *Colloquium*, 9.2, May 1977, pp. 7–16.

—— 'The Theology of D. B. Knox, a Preliminary Estimate', in Peter T. O'Brien and David G. Peterson (eds), *God Who is Rich in Mercy*, Lancer, Homebush West, NSW, 1986.

Barnes, Peter, '"The Iona of the New Hebrides": The Coming of Christianity to Aneityum, 1848–1876', MA thesis, University of Sydney, 1985.

Barnett, Paul, *et. al.*, *Resurrection: Truth and Reality*, Aquila, Sydney, 1994.

Barrett, John, *That Better Country: The Religious Aspect of Life in Eastern Australia*, Melbourne UP, Carlton, 1966.

Bayton, John, *Cross over Carpentaria*, W. R. Smith & Paterson, Brisbane, 1965.

Bebbington, D. W., *Evangelicalism in Modern Britain: A History from the 1730s to the 1980s*, Unwin Hyman, London, 1989.

Bigge, J. T., *Report on the State of the Colony of New South Wales*, 1922.

Bingham, Geoffrey, *Twice-Conquering Love*, New Creation, Blackwood, SA, 1992.

Black, Alan W. (ed.), *Religion in Australia*, Allen & Unwin, Sydney, 1991.

Blacket, John, '"Rainbow or the Serpent?" Observing the Arnhem Land Aboriginal Revival, 1979 and Now', in Mark Hutchinson and Stuart Piggin (eds), *Reviving Australia*, CSAC, Sydney, 1994, pp. 291–301.

—— '"I Will Renew the Land": Island on Fire', manuscript history of the Aboriginal Revival, 18 May 1993.

Blacklock, Merv, *et al.*, 'Minjung in Australia', *South Pacific Journal of Mission Studies*, 1.1, July 1989, pp. 8–10.

Blamires, W. L., and Smith, John B., *The Early Story of the Wesleyan Methodist Church in Victoria: A Jubilee Volume*, Melbourne, 1886.

Blumhofer, Edith L., and Balmer, Randall, *Modern Christian Revivals*, University of Illinois Press, Urbana, 1993.

Bollen, J. D., *Australian Baptists: A Religious Minority*, Baptist Historical Society, London, 1975.

—— 'A Time of Small Things—The Methodist Mission in New South Wales', *Journal of Religious History*, 7.3, June 1973, pp. 225–47.

—— *Religion in Australian Society*, Leigh College, Sydney, 1973.

—— *Protestantism and Social Reform in New South Wales, 1890–1910*, Melbourne UP, Carlton, 1972.

—— *et al.*, 'Australian Religious History, 1960–80', *Journal of Religious History*, 11.1, June 1980, pp. 8–44.

Bolton, Barbara, *Booth's Drum: The Salvation Army in Australia, 1880–1980*, Hodder & Stoughton, Sydney, 1980.

Bonar, A. A., *Memoir and Remains of Robert Murray McCheyne* (1844), Banner of Truth Trust, Edinburgh, 1966.

Bonwick, James, *Australia's First Preacher: The Rev. Richard Johnson, First Chaplain of New South Wales*, London, 1898.

—— *Curious Facts of Old Colonial Days*, London, 1870.

Bos, Robert, 'The Dreaming and Social Change in Arnhem Land', in T. Swain and D. B. Rose, *Aboriginal Australians and Christian Missions*, Australian Association for the Study of Religions, Adelaide, 1988, pp. 422–37.

Bouma, Gary D., and Dixon, Beverly R., *The Religious Factor in Australian Life*, MARC, Australia, 1986.

Boyd, Jeanette, 'The Arnhem Land Revival of 1979: An Australian Aboriginal Religious Movement', unpublished paper, October 1986.

Brady, Veronica, *A Crucible of Prophets: Australians and the Question of God*, Theological Explorations, Sydney, 1981.

Brennan, Patricia, 'Five Men on a Shaky Bridge', *Bulletin*, 21 April 1992, pp. 36–9.

Breward, Ian, *A History of the Australian Churches*, Allen & Unwin, Sydney, 1993.

—— *Australia: 'The Most Godless Place under Heaven'?*, Beacon Hill, Melbourne, 1988.

Bridges, Barry J., *Ministers, Licentiates and Catechists of the Presbyterian Churches in New South Wales to 1865*, Rowland S. Ward, Melbourne, 1989.

Broomhall, Marshall (ed.), *Last Letters and Further Records of Martyred Missionaries of the China Inland Mission*, London, 1901.

Bruce, F. F., 'Women in the Church: A Biblical Survey,' Paper presented to *The Christian Brethren Research Fellowship Journal*, No. 23, 1972.

Bryson, Bruce Stuart, *My Father's House: The Bryson Story of Life on Four Continents*, published by the author, Adelaide, 1993.

Burgess, S., McGee, G. B., and Alexander, P. H. (eds), *Dictionary of Pentecostal and Charismatic Movements*, Regency Zondervan, Grand Rapids, Michigan, 1991.

Burgmann, Verity, and Lee, Jenny, *Making a Life: A People's History of Australia since 1788*, McPhee Gribble and Penguin, Melbourne, 1988.

Butler, F., 'Billy Graham and the End of Evangelical Unity', PhD thesis, Florida, 1976.

Campion, Edmund, *Australian Catholics*, Viking, Melbourne, 1987.

—— *Rockchoppers: Growing Up Catholic in Australia*, Penguin, Ringwood, Vic., 1982.

Carey, William, *Enquiry into the Obligations of Christians to Use Means for the Conversion of the Heathens*, 1792; facsimile, Carey Kingsgate, London, 1961.

Carson, Penny, 'Evangelicals and India', PhD thesis, University of London, 1988.

Caterer, Helen, *Australians Outback: 60 Years of Bush Church Aid*, Anglican Information Office, Sydney, 1981.

Chambers, David, *Tempest-Tossed: The Life and Teaching of the Rev. C. H. Nash, M.A.*, Church Press Publications, Melbourne, 1959.

Chambers, Don, *Theological Teaching and Thought in the Theological Hall of the Presbyterian Church of Victoria, 1865–1906*, Theological Hall, Ormond College, Parkville, 1967.

Chant, Barry, 'Wesleyan Revivalism and the Rise of Australian Pentecostalism', in Mark Hutchinson and Stuart Piggin (eds), *Reviving Australia*, CSAC, Sydney, 1994, pp. 97–122.

—— *Heart of Fire: The Story of Australian Pentecostalism*, Adelaide, House of Tabor, 1973; revised edition, 1984.

Chavura, Michael, 'Calvinism and the Spurgeonic Tradition among the Baptists of New South Wales: The Downgrade Controversy', in Mark Hutchinson and Edmund Campion (eds), *Re-Visioning Australian Colonial Christianity: New Essays in the Australian Christian Experience, 1788–1900*, CSAC, Sydney, 1994, pp. 111–30.

—— 'A History of Calvinism in the Baptist Churches of New South Wales, 1831–1914', PhD thesis, Macquarie University, 1994.

Clack, W. S. (ed.), *We Will Go: The History of 70 Years Training Men and Women for World Missionary Ministry*, Bible College of Victoria, Melbourne, 1990.

Clark, C. M. H., *A History of Australia*, MUP, Melbourne, 6 vols, 1962–87.

Clark, M., 'Faith', in P. Coleman (ed.), *Australian Civilisation*, Cheshire, Melbourne, 1962.

Clarnette, Dallas, *50 Years on Fire for God: The Story of Walter Betts*, People's Church, Kew, 1967.

Clyde, Laurel, *In a Strange Land: A History of the Anglican Diocese of Riverina*, Hawthorn Press, Melbourne, 1979.

Cole, Alan, 'Gabriel Hebert on "Fundamentalism and the Church of God"', *Reformed Theological Review*, XVII.1, February 1958, pp. 11–21.

Cole, G., 'The Doctrine of the Church: Towards Conceptual Clarification', in B. G. Webb (ed.), *Church, Worship, and the Local Congregation*, Lancer, Homebush West, NSW, 1987, pp. 3–18.

Cole, Keith, *'But I Will Be with You': An Autobiography*, Keith Cole Publications, Bendigo, 1988.

—— *Oenpelli Pioneer: A Biography of the Rev. Alfred John Dyer*, Church Missionary Historical Publications, Melbourne, 1972.

—— *A History of the Church Missionary Society of Australia*, Church Missionary Historical Publications, Melbourne, 1971.

—— (ed.), *Letters from China, 1893–1895: The Story of the Sister Martyrs of Ku Cheng*, St Hilary's Anglican Church, Kew, Vic., 1988.

Collins, David, *An Account of the English Colony in New South Wales*, London, 1798.

Collins, Paul, *Mixed Blessings: John Paul II and the Church of the Eighties*, Penguin, Ringwood, Vic., 1986.

Colwell, James, *The Illustrated History of Methodism*, Sydney, 1904.

Cranswick, G. H., *The Ministry of Women. Official Report of the Ninth Australian Church Congress*, Diocesan Registry, Melbourne, 1925.

Crawford, Michael J., *Seasons of Grace, Colonial New England's Revival Tradition in Its British Context*, Oxford UP, New York, 1991.

Cutler, G., *The Torch*, no publisher, Lilydale, 1976.

Daniels, L., *Far West*, Church of England Information Trust, Sydney, 1959.

Darling, Barbara, 'Some Leading Women in the History of the Anglican Church in Australia', in R. S. M. Withycombe (ed.), *Australian and New Zealand Religious History, 1788–1988: A Collection of Papers and Addresses*, ANZATS and STS, Canberra, 1988, pp. 147–56.

Davis, Rex (ed.), *The Morpeth Papers: A Conference on Theological Education*, Diocese of Newcastle, Morpeth, NSW, 1966.

Daw, E.D., 'Hulton Smyth King: The Curate of Fenagh and Wells,' *Church of England Historical Society Journal*, 15.4, December 1970, pp. 94–9.

Dayton, Donald W., *Theological Roots of Pentecostalism,* Scarecrow Press, NJ, 1987.

Deane, A. D., 'The Contribution of the New Evangelical Movements of the Late Nineteenth Century to Evangelical Enterprise in Australia, 1870–1920', MA thesis, University of Sydney, 1983.

Deenick, J. W. (ed.), *A Church en Route: 40 Years Reformed Churches of Australia*, Reformed Churches Publishing House, Geelong, 1991.

Dempsey, K., *Conflict and Decline: Ministers and Laymen in an Australian Country Town*, Methuen, Australia, 1983.

Dickey, Brian, *Holy Trinity, Adelaide, 1836–1988*, Trinity Church Trust, Adelaide, 1988.

—— (ed.), *Australian Dictionary of Evangelical Biography*, Evangelical History Association, Sydney, 1994.

Drayton, Dean, *Five Generations: Evangelism in South Australia*, South Australian Synod, Uniting Church in Australia, 1980.

Dredge, James, *Brief Notices of the Aborigines of New South Wales*, James Harrison, Geelong, 1845.

Duthie, Gil, *I Had 50,000 Bosses: Memoirs of a Labor Backbencher, 1946–1975*, Angus & Robertson, Sydney, 1984.

Dyer, A. J., *Unarmed Combat: An Australian Missionary Adventure*, no publisher, no date [c.1954?].

Dyer, Alan F., *God Was Their Rock*, Pioneer Publishers, Sheffield, Tas., 1974.

Edwards, Jonathan, *Apocalyptic Writings*, ed. by Stephen J. Stein, Yale UP, New Haven, 1977.

—— *The Great Awakening*, ed. by C. C. Goen, Yale UP, New Haven, 1972. Includes *The Distinguishing Marks of a Work of the Spirit of God* (1741).

Elder, J. R. (ed.), *The Letters and Journals of Samuel Marsden, 1765–1838*, Otago University Council, Dunedin, 1932.

Ely, R., 'Protestantism in Australian History: An Interpretative Sketch', *Lucas*, 5, March 1989, pp. 11–20.

—— 'The Forgotten Nationalism: Australian Civic Protestantism in the Second World War', *Journal of Australian Studies*, 20, May 1987, pp. 59–67.

Emilsen, Susan E., *A Whiff of Heresy: Samuel Angus and the Presbyterian Church in New South Wales*, UNSW Press, Kensington, 1991.

Faggotter, Trevor, 'Revival Fire at Wudinna', *Renewal Journal*, 4, 1994, pp. 43–52.

Findlay, G. G., and Holdsworth, W. W., *The History of the Wesleyan Methodist Missionary Society*, vol. III, Epworth Press, London, 1921.

Finke, Roger, and Stark, Rodney, *The Churching of America, 1776–1990*, Rutgers UP, New Brunswick, 1992.

First Australasian Baptist Congress, Sydney, 1908.

Fletcher, Lionel B., *Mighty Moments*, Religious Tract Society, London, n.d.

Ford, P., *Cardinal Moran and the ALP*, Melbourne UP, Carlton, 1966.

Forsyth, Robert , 'Getting There is Half the Fun: An Approach to Women's Ordination', *Australian Church Record*, 11 March 1985, p. 6.

Frappell, Ruth M., 'The Anglican Ministry to the Unsettled Rural Districts of Australia, c. 1890 to 1940', PhD thesis, University of Sydney, 1991.

Frappell, Samantha, 'Post-War Revivalism in Australia: The Mission to the Nation, 1953–1957', in Mark Hutchinson and Stuart Piggin (eds), *Reviving Australia*, CSAC, Sydney, 1994, pp. 249–61.

Gariepy, Henry, *General of God's Army: The Authorized Biography of General Eva Burrows*, Victor, Wheaton, Ill., 1993.

Gill, Stewart, '"Revival Days at Mt Margaret": The UAM and the 1982 Revival', in Mark Hutchinson and Stuart Piggin (eds), *Reviving Australia*, CSAC, Sydney, 1994, pp. 275–90.

Gillman, Ian, *Many Faiths, One Nation*, Collins, Sydney, 1988.

Gordon-McCutchan, R. C., 'Great Awakenings', *Sociological Analysis*, 44, 1983, pp. 83–95.

—— 'The Irony of Evangelical History', *Journal for the Scientific Study of Religion*, 20, 1981, pp. 309–26.

Gosden, E. W., *Thank You, Lord! The Eightieth Anniversary of the Japan Evangelistic Band, 1903–1983*, Japan Evangelistic Band, London, 1982.

Gregory, J. S., *Church and State*, Cassell, Sydney, 1973.

Griffiths, Alison, *Fire in the Islands*, Harold Shaw, Wheaton, Ill., 1977.

Grocott, Allan M., *Convicts, Clergymen and Churches: Attitudes of Convicts and Ex-convicts towards the Churches and Clergy in New South Wales from 1788 to 1851*, Sydney UP, Sydney, 1980.

Gunson, Niel, *Messengers of Grace: Evangelical Missionaries in the South Seas, 1797–1860*, Oxford UP, Melbourne, 1978.

—— (ed.), *Australian Reminiscences and Papers of L. E. Threlkeld*, 2 vols, Australian Institute of Aboriginal Studies, Canberra, 1974.

Gunson, W. N., 'The Contribution of the Calvinistic Methodist Movement to the Church History of Australia', *Church Heritage*, 4.1, March 1985, pp. 28–59.

—— 'The Nundah Missionaries', *Royal Historical Society of Queensland Journal*, 6.3, 1960–61, pp. 511–39.

Gunther, Peter F. (ed.), *A Frank Boreham Treasury*, compiled by Moody Press, Chicago, 1984.

Hammond, T. C., *In Understanding Be Men*, 6th edition, IVF, London, 1968.

—— *The Way of Holiness*, S. John Bacon, Melbourne, 1952.

—— *Reasoning Faith: An Introduction to Christian Apologetics,* IVF, London, 1943.

Harding, John J., 'The Reformed Faith Today,' *The Times*, 5 December 1988.

Harris, Dorothy, *God's Patience*, The Book Printer, Maryborough, Vic., 1990.

Harris, John, *One Blood*, Albatross, Sydney, 1990.

Harris, John H. 'Two Hundred Years of the Church and Aboriginals,' *Church Scene*, 11 December 1987, p. 6f.

Hart, Max, *A Story of Fire: Aboriginal Christianity*, New Creation Publications, Blackwood, SA, 1988.

Hay, Alexander, *Jubilee Memorial of the Presbyterian Church of Queensland*, Brisbane, 1900.

Heath, Phillip J., *Trinity: The Daring of Your Name*, Allen & Unwin, Sydney, 1990.

Hebert, Gabriel, *Fundamentalism and the Church of God*, SCM, London, 1957.

Hefley, James and Marti, *By their Blood: Christian Martyrs of the Twentieth Century*, Baker Book House, Grand Rapids, Michigan, 1979.

Hempenstall, Peter, *The Meddlesome Priest: A Life of Ernest Burgmann*, Allen & Unwin, Sydney 1993.

Hickson, J. M., *The Revival of the Gifts of Healing, Some of the Practical Difficulties which Hinder the Revival of Spiritual Healing*, Church Stores, Sydney, 1910.

Hilliard, David, *Popular Revivalism in South Australia*, Uniting Church Historical Society, South Australia, 1982.

—— 'The South Sea Evangelical Mission in the Solomon Islands: The Foundation Years', *Journal of Pacific History*, 4, 1969, pp. 41–64.

—— *God's Gentlemen: A History of the Melanesian Mission*, UQP, St Lucia, 1978.

—— 'Protestant Missions in the Solomon Islands', PhD thesis, ANU, 1966.

Hilton, Boyd, *The Age of Atonement: The Influence of Evangelicalism on Social and Economic Thought, 1795–1865*, Oxford UP, Oxford, 1988.

Hogan, Michael, *The Sectarian Strand: Religion in Australian History*, Penguin, Ringwood, Vic., 1987.

Holburn, M., and Pizer, M. (eds), *Creeve Roe*, Pinchgut Press, Sydney, 1947.

Holle, John, 'The C of E Votes for Women Priests', *Sunday News*, St Paul's, Burwood, NSW, parish magazine, 15 November 1992.

Huard, Geoff, 'Ministry to the Chinese in Sydney between 1855 and 1900 by the Anglican and Presbyterian Churches Compared and Contrasted', Doctor of Ministry essay, Northern Baptist Theological Seminary, Sydney, 1992.

Hughes, Philip, *Religion: A View from the Australian Census*, Christian Research Association, Melbourne, 1993.

Hulme-Moir, D., *The Edge of Time*, Christian Outreach Book Service, Newtown, NSW, 1988.

Humphreys, Robert, and Ward, Rowland, *Religious Bodies in Australia*, published by the authors, Melbourne, 1988.

Hunt, Arnold, *This Side of Heaven: A History of Methodism in South Australia*, Lutheran Publishing House, Adelaide, 1985.

—— 'The Moonta Revival of 1875', cassette produced by New Creation Publications, Blackwood, SA, n.d.

Hutchinson, Mark, 'Manning Clark and the Limits of Prophet-ability', *Lucas*, 4, September 1988, pp. 28–36.

Hutchinson, Mark, and Campion, Edmund (eds), *Long Patient Struggle: Essays on Women and Gender in Australian Christianity*, CSAC, Sydney, 1994.

—— (eds), *Re-Visioning Australian Colonial Christianity: New Essays in the Australian Christian Experience, 1788–1900*, CSAC, Sydney, 1994.

Hutchinson, Mark, and Piggin, Stuart (eds), *Reviving Australia: Essays on the History and Experience of Revival and Revivalism in Australian Christianity*, CSAC, Sydney, 1994.

Inglis, K. S., 'Catholic Historiography in Australia', *Historical Studies*, 8.31, November 1958, pp. 233–53.

Jackson, H. R., *Churches and People in Australia and New Zealand, 1860–1930*, Allen & Unwin, Sydney, 1987.

Jagelman, Ian, 'The Role of the Historian/Teacher in Contemporary Pentecostalism', *Barsabbas*, 4, November 1993.

James, Bob, '"Lots of Religion and Freemasonry": The Politics of Revivalism during the 1930s Depression on the Northern Coalfields', in Mark Hutchinson and Stuart Piggin (eds), *Reviving Australia: Essays on the History and Experience of Revival and Revivalism in Australian Christianity*, CSAC, Sydney, 1994, pp. 233–48.

Jenkyns, D., 'Sinless Perfection and After: The Religion of Tinker Tailor at Hunter's Hill', *Nation*, 7 October 1961, p. 9f.

Jewett, Paul, *Man as Male and Female*, Eerdmans, Grand Rapids, Michigan, 1975.

Johnstone, S. M., *A History of the Church Missionary Society in Australia and Tasmania*, CMS, Sydney, 1925.

Jones, E., *Florence Buchanan: The Little Deaconess of the South Seas*, SPG, London, 1921.

Jones, T. E., *'These Twenty Years': A Record of the Work of the Bush Church Aid Society for Australia and Tasmania*, BCA, Sydney, 1939.

Judd, S., and Cable, K., *Sydney Anglicans*, Anglican Information Office, Sydney, 1987.

Kaldor, Peter, *Winds of Change*, Anzea, Sydney, 1994.

—— *First Look in the Mirror: Initial Findings of the National Church Life Survey*, Lancer, Homebush West, NSW, 1992.

—— *Who Goes Where? Who Doesn't Care?* Lancer, Homebush, NSW, 1987.

Kent, J. H. S., *The End of the Line?*, SCM, London, 1982.

King, Robert J., *The Secret History of the Convict Colony: Alexandro Malaspina's Settlement in New South Wales*, Allen & Unwin, Sydney, 1990.

Kirkpatrick, Rod, *Sworn to No Master; A History of the Provincial Press in Queensland to 1930*, Toowoomba, DDIAE Press, 1984.

Knauerhase, M., *Winifred*, Lutheran Publishing House, Adelaide, 1978.

Knox, D. B., 'What the Church Is', *The Briefing*, 15, 15 November 1988, p. 3f.

—— *Thirty-Nine Articles*, Anglican Information Office, Sydney, 1976.

—— *The Doctrine of Faith in the Reign of Henry VIII*, James Clarke & Co., London, 1961.

—— 'Propositional Revelation the only Revelation,' *Reformed Theological Review*, 19.1, February 1960, pp. 1–9.

Knox, R. A., *Enthusiasm*, Clarendon Press, Oxford, 1950, revised edition 1962.

Kotlowski, Elizabeth, *Southland of the Holy Spirit: A Christian History of Australia*, Christian Research Institute, Orange, NSW, 1994.

Lampe, G. W. H., 'Church Tradition and the Ordination of Women', *Expository Times*, LXXVI.4, January 1965, pp. 123–5.

Latourette, K. S., *A History of the Expansion of Christianity*, vol. 5, Harper, New York, 1943.

Lawson, Henry, *Prose Works of Henry Lawson*, Angus & Robertson, Sydney, 1948.

Lawton, William James (Bill), 'The Winter of our Days: The Anglican Diocese of Sydney, 1950–1960', *Lucas*, 9, July 1990, pp. 11–32.

—— *The Better Times to Be: Utopian Attitudes to Society among Sydney Anglicans, 1885 to 1914*, UNSW Press, Kensington, 1990.

—— '"That Woman Jezebel"—Moore College after 25 Years', Moore College Library Lecture, 1981.

Lees, Shirley, *Drunk before Dawn*, Overseas Missionary Fellowship, Sevenoaks, 1979.

Lillyman, John, 'Taylor of Down Under: The Life Story of an Australian Evangelist', MA thesis, Wheaton, Ill., 1994.

Linder, R. D., 'Australian Evangelicals in Politics in the Victorian Age: The Cases of J. D. Lang, W. G. Spence, and J. S. T. McGowen', *Lucas*, 13, July 1992, pp. 34–60.

Lindsay, Ian, *Fire in the Spinifex*, United Aborigines Mission, Box Hill, Vic., 1986.

Lindsell, Harold, *The World, the Flesh and the Devil*, Canon Press, Washington, 1973.

Lloyd-Jones, D. M., *Knowing the Times*, Banner of Truth Trust, Edinburgh, 1989.

—— *The Puritans*, Banner of Truth Trust, Edinburgh, 1987.

—— *Romans: An Exposition of Chapter 8:5–17: The Sons of God*, Banner of Truth Trust, Edinburgh, 1974.

Loane, Marcus, 'Billy Graham: God's Man for this Century!', *Decision*, May 1984.

—— *Hewn from the Rock*, Anglican Information Office, Sydney, 1976.

—— *Mark These Men: A Brief Account of Some Evangelical Clergy in the Diocese of Sydney Who Were in Association with Archbishop Mowll*, Acorn Press, Canberra, 1985.

—— 'Portrait of an Evangelical', *Australian Evangelical*, July–August 1973, pp. 5–6.

—— *The Story of the China Inland Mission in Australia and New Zealand*, China Inland Mission and Overseas Missionary Fellowship, Sydney, 1965.

—— 'The Keswick Convention and the Missionary Movement', *Southern Cross Booklet*, No.3, n.d.

—— *These Happy Warriors: Friends and Contemporaries*, New Creation, Blackwood, SA, 1988.

—— *Men to Remember*, Acorn Press, Canberra, c. 1987.

—— *Makers of our Heritage: A Study of Four Evangelical Leaders*, Hodder & Stoughton, London, 1967.

—— *Archbishop Mowll: The Biography of H. W. K. Mowll*, Hodder & Stoughton, London, 1960.

—— *A Centenary History of Moore Theological College*, Angus & Robertson, Sydney, 1955.

—— and Jensen, Peter F., *Broughton Knox, Principal of Moore College, 1959–1985*, Moore Theological College, Newtown, 1994.

Long, Retta, *Providential Channels*, Aborigines Inland Mission, Sydney, 1935.

Longo, D., 'Attitudes of Church to Working Class and of Working Class to the Church, between 1848 and 1891', BA hons thesis, University of Adelaide, 1979.

Macintosh, Neil K., *Richard Johnson, Chaplain to the Colony of New South Wales: His Life and Times, 1755–1827*, Library of Australian History, Sydney, 1978.

Mackaness, G. (ed.), *Some Letters of the Rev. Richard Johnson*, Part 1, D. S. Ford, Sydney, 1954.

Mackerras, Catherine B., *Divided Heart: The Memoirs of Catherine B. Mackerras*, Little Hills Press, 1991.

Mansfield, Bruce, 'Thinking about Australian Religious History', in Robert S. M. Withycombe (ed.), *Australian and New Zealand Religious History, 1788–1988: A Collection of Papers and Addresses*, ANZATS and STS, Canberra, 1988, pp. 3–18.

Mansfield, J., 'The Social Gospel and the Church of England in New South Wales in the 1930s', *Journal of Religious History*, 13.4, December 1985, pp. 411–33.

Marsden, G., *Reforming Fundamentalism: Fuller Seminary and the New Evangelicalism*, Eerdmans, Grand Rapids, Michigan, 1987.

Martin, Ged (ed.), *The Founding of Australia: The Argument about Australia's Origins*, Hale & Iremonger, Sydney 1978; 1980.

Martin, William, *A Prophet with Honor: The Billy Graham Story*, William Morrow & Co., New York, 1991.

Mathias, Rex, *Mission to the Nation*, Joint Board of Christian Education, Melbourne, 1986.

McKernan, Michael, *Australian Churches at War*, Catholic Theological Faculty and Australian War Memorial, Sydney and Canberra, 1980.

McLennan, Graham, *Understanding our Christian Heritage*, Christian History Research Institute, Orange, New South Wales, 1987.

McLeod, A. L., *The Pattern of Australian Culture*, Cornell University Press, Ithaca, NY, 1963.

McLoughlin, William G., *Revivals, Awakenings and Reform*, University of Chicago Press, Chicago, 1978.

McQueen, Humphrey, *A New Britannia*, Penguin, Ringwood, Vic., 1970.

The Melbourne Bible Institute, Interdenominational, Evangelical, Biblical, Missionary: Sixth Annual Report, 1925–6.

Millikan, David, *Imperfect Company: Power and Control in an Australian Christian Cult*, Heinemann, Sydney, 1991.

The Missionary Heritage of Australian Baptists, Australian Baptist Foreign Missions, Glebe, NSW, n.d.

Mitchell, D. F., *Ellen Arnold, Pioneer and Pathfinder*, Baptist Publications, Adelaide, 1932.

Mol, Hans, *The Faith of Australians*, Allen & Unwin, Sydney, 1985.

—— *Religion in Australia: A Sociological Investigation*, Nelson, Melbourne, 1971.

Moore, T. Inglis, 'The Meanings of Mateship', *Meanjin Quarterly*, March 1965, pp. 45–54.

Morris, Leon, *et al.*, *A Woman's Place*, Anglican Information Office, Sydney, 1976.

Moses, John, 'Anzac Day as Religious Revivalism: The Politics of Faith in Brisbane, 1916–1939', in Mark Hutchinson and Stuart Piggin (eds), *Reviving Australia*, CSAC, Sydney, 1994, pp. 170–84.

—— 'The First World War as Holy War in German and Australian Perspective', *Colloquium*, 26.1, 1994, pp. 44–55.

Mukherjee, S. K., *Crime Trends in Twentieth Century Australia*, Australian Institute of Criminology and Allen & Unwin, Sydney, 1981.

—— *et al.*, *Source Book of Australian Criminal and Social Statistics, 1900–1980*, Australian Institute of Criminology, Canberra, 1981.

Murray, Iain H., *David Martyn Lloyd-Jones: The Fight of Faith*, Banner of Truth Trust, Edinburgh, 1990.

—— *Australian Christian Life from 1788*, Banner of Truth Trust, Edinburgh, 1988.

Nadel, George, *Australia's Colonial Culture*, Harvard UP, Cambridge, Mass., 1957.

Nairn, Bede, *Civilising Capitalism: The Labour Movement in New South Wales, 1870–1900*, ANU Press, Canberra, 1973.

Nanscawen, Anne, *With One Accord: The Beginning of an Aussie Awakening*, Anzea, Sydney, 1989.

Nelson, Warren, *T. C. Hammond: Irish Christian*, Banner of Truth Trust, Edinburgh, 1994.

Neuhaus, R. J. (ed.), *Unsecular America*, Eerdmans, Grand Rapids, Michigan, 1986.

Newton, K. J., 'A History of the Brethren in Australia, with Particular Reference to the Open Brethren', PhD thesis, Fuller Theological Seminary, 1990.

Nichols, Alan, *David Penman*, Albatross, Sydney, 1991.

O'Brien, Peter T., and Peterson, David G. (eds), *God who is Rich in Mercy*, Lancer, Homebush West, NSW, 1986.

O'Farrell, Patrick, 'Writing the General History of Australian Religion,' *Journal of Religious History*, 9.1, June 1976, pp. 65–73.

—— *Letters from Irish Australia, 1825–1929*, UNSW Press, Kensington, 1984.

—— *The Catholic Church and Community in Australia: A History*, Nelson, Melbourne, 1977; revised 1985 and 1992.

O'Leary, Patrick John, 'Queensland Baptists: The Development of Baptist Evangelicalism, 1846–1926', MA thesis, University of Queensland, 1991.

Olsen, Mervyn Keith, 'One Consuming Passion—To Tell the World: An Assessment of the Life and Ministry of Leslie Gordon Young', dissertation, Baptist Theological College of Queensland, Brisbane, 1986.

Orr, J. Edwin, *Evangelical Awakenings in the South Seas*, Bethany Fellowship, Minneapolis, 1976.

Otzen, Roslyn, *Whitley: The Baptist College of Victoria*, Hyland House, Melbourne, 1991.

Owen, J., *History of the British and Foreign Bible Society*, 3 vols, London, 1816–20.

A Pageant of Early Church History, Town Hall, Sydney, 20–22 May, 1937. Programme, CSAC Archives.

Paproth, Darrell, 'Revivalism in Melbourne from Federation to World War I: The Torrey–Alexander–Chapman Campaigns', in Mark Hutchinson and Stuart Piggin (eds), *Reviving Australia*, CSAC, Sydney, 1994, pp. 143–69.

—— 'C. H. Nash and his Influence', PhD thesis, School of Humanities, Deakin University, 1993.

Parker, David, 'Theological and Bible College Education in Australia', *Journal of Christian Education*, Papers 86, July 1986, pp. 5–18.

—— 'Fundamentalism and Conservative Protestantism in Australia 1920–1980', PhD thesis, University of Queensland, 1982.

—— 'The Bible College Movement in Australia', paper presented at the 9th Conference of the South Pacific Association of Bible Colleges, August 1980.

Patrick, Arthur, 'Christianity and Culture in Colonial Australia', PhD thesis, University of Newcastle, 1991.

Petras, Michael, *Extension or Extinction: Baptist Growth in New South Wales*, Baptist Historical Society, Eastwood, 1983.

Phillimore, Walter G. F., *Ecclesiastical Law of the Church of England*, 1873, second edition, Sweet and Maxwell, London, 1895.

Phillips, W. W., 'Religion', in W. Vamplew (ed.), *Australians: Historical Statistics*, Fairfax, Syme & Weldon, Sydney, 1987.

Phillips, Walter, *Defending 'A Christian Country': Churchmen and Society in New South Wales in 1880s and After*, UQP, St Lucia, 1981.

Piggin, Stuart, 'From Independence to Domesticity: Masculinity in Australian History and the Female Ordination Debate', in Mark Hutchinson and Edmund Campion (eds), *Long Patient Struggle: Essays on Women and Gender in Australian Christianity*, CSAC, Sydney, 1994, pp. 151–60.

—— 'Towards a Theoretical Understanding of Revival', in Mark Hutchinson and Stuart Piggin (eds), *Reviving Australia*, CSAC, Sydney, 1994, pp. 13–33.

—— 'Jonathan Edwards and the Revival Chronicles of the 1740s', *Lucas*, 15, June 1993, pp. 14–20.

—— 'Bicentennial History of Australian Evangelicalism: Thesis and Themes', *Lucas*, 4, September 1988, pp. 5–27.

—— 'Towards a Bicentennial History of Australian Evangelicalism', *Journal of Religious History*, 15.1, June 1988, pp. 20–37.

—— *Helpmeets and Heroines: Women and the History of Australian Evangelicalism*, Mothers' Union of Wollongong, Figtree, NSW, 1988.

—— 'Writing the History of the Church in a Secular, Pluralist Society: Reed's Theory and the Relevance of Ecclesiological Developments', *St Mark's Review*, 129, March 1987, pp. 20–32.

—— *Faith of Steel: A History of the Christian Churches in Illawarra, Australia*, University of Wollongong, Wollongong, 1984.

—— *Making Evangelical Missionaries*, Sutton Courtenay Press, Appleford, Oxford, 1984.

—— *The Fruitful Figtree, A History of All Saints Anglican Church Figtree, 1888–1983*, Figtree Anglican Church, Figtree, NSW, 1983.

Pike, Douglas, *Paradise of Dissent*, Melbourne UP, Carlton, 1967.

Pollock, John, *Crusades: 20 Years with Billy Graham*, World Wide Publications, Minneapolis, 1969.

—— *Billy Graham, The Authorised Biography*, Hodder & Stoughton, London, 1966.

Porter, Brian (ed.), *Colonial Tractarians*, Joint Board of Christian Education, Melbourne, 1989.

Porter, Muriel, 'The End of the "Great Debate": The 1992 General Synod Decision on Women Priests', in Mark Hutchinson and Edmund Campion (eds), *Long Patient Struggle: Essays on Women and Gender in Australian Christianity*, CSAC, Sydney, 1994, pp. 161–85.

—— *Women in the Church: The Great Ordination Debate in Australia*, Penguin, Ringwood, Vic., 1989.

Powell, Gordon, 'Six Months after Billy Graham, An Address delivered at the University of Sydney on October 8, 1959', Billy Graham Evangelistic Association, 1960.

Pratt, Ambrose, *Sidney Myer: A Biography*, Quartet, Melbourne, 1978.

Prince, John and Moyra, *Out of the Tower*, Anzea, Sydney, 1987.

—— *No Fading Vision: The First 50 Years of A.P.C.M.*, Asia Pacific Christian Mission, no place, 1981.

—— *Tuned in to Change: A History of the Australian Scripture Union, 1880–1980*, Scripture Union of Australia, Sydney, 1979.

Prior, A. C., *Some Fell on Good Ground: A History of the Beginnings and Development of the Baptist Church in New South Wales, Australia, 1831–1965*, Baptist Union of New South Wales, Sydney, 1966.

Pryor, Oswald, *Australia's Little Cornwall*, Rigby, Adelaide, 1962, reprinted 1980.

Pura, Murray A., and Lewis, Donald M., 'On Spiritual Symmetry: The Christian Devotion of William Wilberforce', in J. I. Packer and Loren

Wilkinson (eds), *Alive to God: Studies in Spirituality*, IVP, Downers Grove, 1992, pp. 176–89.

Ramsland, John, *The Struggle against Isolation: A History of the Manning Valley*, Library of Australian History, Greater Taree City Council, 1987.

Redman, Jess, *The Light Shines On: The Story of the Missionary Outreach of the Baptist People of Australia, 1882–1982*, Australian BMS, Hawthorn, Vic., 1982.

Reeson, Margaret, *Currency Lass*, Albatross, Sutherland, 1985.

Reiger, K., *The Disenchantment of the Home*, Oxford UP, 1985.

Renshaw, Will F., *Some Melbourne Notes and Comments*, 1–9, 1993–94.

Report of the Committee on the Future of Tertiary Education in Australia, (Martin Report), 3 vols, Government Printer, Melbourne, 1964–65.

Rien, E. T., *A Challenge to Holiness*, Wyee, NSW, n.d.

Robin, A. de Q., 'Theology and Theological Training in Australia: An Outline Historical Survey', *Journal of the Royal Australian Historical Society*, 54.4, 1968, pp. 356–67.

—— *Charles Perry, Bishop of Melbourne: The Challenges of a Colonial Episcopate, 1847–76*, UWA Press, Nedlands 1967.

Robinson, D. W. B., Presidential Address, *Yearbook of the Diocese of Sydney*, 1990.

—— 'Scripture, Apostolic Tradition and the Ordination of Women,' *AAM Australia Newsletter*, November 1990.

—— 'The Church Revisited: An Autobiographical Fragment,' *Reformed Theological Review*, I, January–April 1989.

—— 'The Doctrine of the Church and Its Implications for Evangelism,' *Interchange*, 1974.

—— 'The Church in the New Testament', *St Mark's Review*, 17, August 1959.

—— 'The Church Universal and Its Earthly Form', parts 1 and 2, *Australian Church Record*, 2, 16 February 1956.

Robinson, Portia, *The Hatch and Brood of Time: A Study of the First Generation of Native-born White Australians, 1788–1828*, Oxford UP, Melbourne, 1985.

Robson, L. L., *The Convict Settlers of Australia*, Melbourne UP, Carlton, 1965.

Roderick, C. (ed.), *Collected Verse of Henry Lawson*, 3 vols, Angus & Robertson, Sydney, 1967–69.

Roe, Jill, 'Challenge and Response: Religious Life in Melbourne, 1876–86', *Journal of Religious History*, December 1968, pp. 149–66.

Roe, Michael, *Quest for Authority in Eastern Australia, 1835–1857*, ANU/MUP, Carlton, 1965.

Rowland, E. C., *The Tropics for Christ*, Diocese of North Queensland, Townsville, 1960.

Runia, Klaas, *The Sermon under Attack*, Paternoster, Exeter, 1983.

—— *Reformed Dogmatics: Its Essence and Method*, Reformed Theological College, Geelong, 1957.

Sanders, J. Oswald, *Planting Men in Melanesia: The First Decade of Development of the Christian Leaders' Training College of Papua New Guinea*, Christian Leaders' Training College of PNG, Mt Hagen, 1978.

Schedvin, M. B. and C. B., 'The Nomadic Tribes of Urban Britain: A Prelude to Botany Bay', *Historical Studies: Australia and New Zealand*, 18, 1978, pp. 254–76.

Shaw, G. P., *Patriarch and Prophet: Willam Grant Broughton, 1788–1853: Colonial Statesman and Ecclesiastic*, Melbourne UP, Carlton, 1978.

Shaw, George, 'Judeo-Christianity and the Mid-Nineteenth Century Colonial Civil Order', in Mark Hutchinson and Edmund Campion (eds), *Re-Visioning Australian Colonial Christianity: New Essays in the Australian Christian Experience, 1788–1900*, CSAC, Sydney, 1994, pp. 29–39.

Smith, A. Christopher, 'The Spirit and Letter of Carey's Catalytic Watchword: A Study in the Transmission of Baptist Tradition', *Baptist Quarterly*, XXXIII.5, 1990, pp. 226–37.

Southwood, Martin, *John Howard: Prison Reformer*, Independent Press, London, 1958.

Spence, W. G., *Australia's Awakening*, Sydney, 1908.

Spong, J. S., *Resurrection—Myth or Reality?*, Harper, San Francisco, 1994.

—— *Born of a Woman: A Bishop Rethinks the Birth of Jesus*, Harper, San Francisco, 1992.

—— *Living in Sin: A Bishop Rethinks Human Sexuality*, Harper, San Francisco, 1988.

Strachan, Alexander, *The Life of the Rev. Samuel Leigh, Missionary to the Settlers and Savages of Australia and New Zealand, with a History of the Origin and Progress of the Missions in those Colonies*, London, 1870.

Sturmey, Ruth I., 'Women and the Anglican Church in Australia: Theology and Social Change', PhD thesis, University of Sydney, 1989.

Suttor, T. L., *Hierarchy and Democracy in Australia, 1788–1870*, Melbourne, 1965.

—— 'Australian Catholic Culture,' *Manna*, 4, 1961.

Swain, T., and Rose, D. B., *Aboriginal Australians and Christian Missions*, Australian Association for the Study of Religions, Adelaide, 1988.

The Missionary Heritage of Australian Baptists, Australian Baptist Foreign Missions, Glebe, NSW, n.d.

Thiering, Barbara, *Jesus the Man: A New Interpretation from the Dead Sea Scrolls*, Doubleday, Sydney, 1992.

—— *God's Experiment—Australian Religion*, Murdoch University, Perth, 1982.

Thompson, Roger C., *Religion in Australia*, Oxford UP, Melbourne, 1994.

Tomkins, Dorothea, and Hughes, Brian, *The Road from Gona*, Angus & Robertson, Sydney, 1969.

Torrey, R. A., *The Power of Prayer and the Prayer of Power*, 1924; Zondervan, Grand Rapids, Michigan, 1971.

Tress, N., *Caught for Life: A Story of the Anglican Deaconess Order in Australia*, Mission Publications, New South Wales, 1933.

Trollope, A., *Australia*, 1873; UQP, St Lucia, 1967.

Venn, Henry, *Memoir of Henry Venn*, London, 1834.

Walker, Alan, *The Whole Gospel for the Whole World*, Marshall, Morgan & Scott, London, 1958.

Walker, Harry, *et al.*, 'Minjung in Australia', *South Pacific Journal of Mission Studies*, 1.1, July 1989, pp. 8–10.

Walker, R. B., 'Presbyterian Church and People in the Colony of New South Wales in the Late Nineteenth Century', *Journal of Religious History*, 2.1, June 1969, pp. 49–65.

Wallis, N. W., *The Warhorse: The Life and Work of Rev. Dr. Harold J. Whitney*, Mission Publications of Australia, Lawson, NSW, 1986.

Walsh, J. D., 'The Magdalene Evangelicals', *Church Quarterly Review*, October–December 1958, pp. 499–511.

Ward, Rowland, 'Spiritual Awakenings in Scottish Gaelic Communities in Australia, 1837–1870', in Mark Hutchinson and Stuart Piggin (eds), *Reviving Australia*, CSAC, Sydney, 1994, pp. 75–96.

Ward, Rowland S., *The Bush Still Burns: The Presbyterian and Reformed Faith in Australia, 1788–1988*, published by the author, Wantirna, Vic., 1989.

Ward, Russel, *The Australian Legend*, Oxford UP, Melbourne, 1958, 1980.

Ward, W. R., *The Protestant Evangelical Awakening*, Cambridge UP, Cambridge, 1992.

Ward, Winifred L., 'Aspects of Secularised Religion within the Tradition of New South Wales Methodism since 1930', PhD thesis, University of Wollongong, 1988.

Warren, W., 'The Genesis of the Australian Revival', *The Missionary Review of the World*, 26, March 1903, p. 202f.

Watsford, John, *Glorious Gospel Triumphs*, Charles H. Kelly, London, 1900.

West, Janet, *Innings of Grace: A Life of Bishop W. G. Hilliard*, Trinity Grammar School, Sydney, 1987.

Westwood, Susan, 'A Study of the Attitudes and Activities of the Church of England in the Illawarra during the First World War', BA hons thesis, University of Wollongong, 1980.

Wetherell, David, *Reluctant Mission: The Anglican Church in Papua New Guinea, 1891–1942*, UQP, St Lucia, 1977.

—— (ed.) *The New Guinea Diaries of Philip Strong, 1936–1945*, Macmillan, South Melbourne, 1981.

White, Paul, *Alias Jungle Doctor: An Autobiography*, Paternoster, Exeter, 1977.

Whiteman, Darrell, *Melanesians and Missionaries: An Ethnohistorical Study of Social and Religious Change in the Southwest Pacific*, William Carey Library, Pasadena, 1983.

Whitney, Harold, *Pilgrimage with a Purpose*, Mission Publications of Australia, Lawson, NSW, 1988.

—— *Tell Australia*, W. R. Smith & Paterson, Brisbane, 1957.

Wilberforce, A. M. (ed.), *Private Papers of William Wilberforce*, London, 1897.

Wilberforce, R. I. and S., *Correspondence of William Wilberforce*, London, 1840.

Williams, Louise, 'A Hard Man of God', *Sydney Morning Herald*, 12 December 1992.

Wilson, B., *Can God Survive in Australia?*, Albatross, Sydney, 1983.

Wilson, J. F., 'Perspectives on the Historiography of Religious Awakenings', *Sociological Analysis*, 44, 1983, pp. 117–20.

Withycombe, R. S. M. (ed.), *Australian and New Zealand Religious History, 1788–1988: A Collection of Papers and Addresses*, ANZATS and STS, Canberra, 1988.

Wood, Arthur Skevington, *Thomas Haweis, 1743–1820*, Society for Promoting Christian Knowledge, London, 1957.

Woodhouse, John, 'The Use of the Bible in Modern Controversies; A Watershed among Evangelicals?', in B. G. Webb (ed.), *Personhood, Sexuality, and Christian Ministry*, Explorations: Moore Papers No. 1, Sydney, 1986, pp. 4–14.

Woolmington, Jean, 'Missionary Attitudes to the Baptism of Australian Aborigines before 1850', *Journal of Religious History*, 13.3, 1985, pp. 283–93.

Wright, Don, *The Mantle of Christ: A History of the Sydney Central Methodist Mission*, UQP, St Lucia, 1983.

—— and Clancy, Eric, *The Methodists: A History of Methodism in New South Wales*, Allen & Unwin, Sydney, 1993.

Yarwood, A. T., *Samuel Marsden: The Great Survivor*, Melbourne UP, Carlton, 1977.

Young, F. S. H., *Pearls from the Pacific*, Marshall Brothers, London and Edinburgh, n.d.

Zaunbrecher, Marion, 'Religious Attitudes in Australian Literature of the 1890s', MA thesis, University of Wollongong, 1979.

Index

Abbott, Len   123
Aboriginal people   viii, ix, xiii, 2, 8–9, 15,
    21–3, 67, 149, 180, 192, 197–202,
    224
  missions to   21–3, 26, 28, 31, 44–9, 51,
    66–7, 73, 82–3, 126, 140–2, 175,
    177
Aborigines Inland Mission   66–7
Adelaide   30, 41, 49, 65, 71, 81, 87–8, 91,
    103, 137, 168, 178–9, 184, 220
  see also South Australia
Adelaide Bible Institute   167
Africa Inland Mission   109
Agnew family   107–9
  Vera   109–10, 114, 119
  Nancy   109, 117, 119
  Del   109–10, 113, 117–21
Alexander, Charles   57, 60, 87
Andersen, Frank   139
Anderson, John   131
Andrews, Mary   167
Angas, George Fife   30–1, 91
Anglican Church League   130
Anglican Information Office   214
Anglicanism   xiii, 25, 56, 109, 119, 123, 131,
    151, 153, 162–3, 166, 169, 173,
    180–2, 188, 202–21
  evangelical   8, 13, 37, 83, 128–33, 147,
    170–1, 177
  see also Church of England; Sydney
    Anglicans
Anglo-Catholics   xiii, 24, 35, 73–4, 78, 103,
    151, 203, 219
  see also High Church
Angus, Samuel   92–4, 96, 98, 109, 134
Apostolic Church   103
Apostolic Faith Mission   102, 103

Appelman, Hyman 148
Archdale, Mervyn   76, 77
Arnhem Land (NT)   67, 140–2, 198
Arnold, Ellen   71, 82
Arrowsmith, Herbert Maxwell   152, 159,
    163
Asia Pacific Christian Mission   144
Assemblies of God   102–3, 161
Association for the Apostolic Ministry   203,
    206, 209–10, 219
Atkinson, Alan   26, 27
Atkinson, Basil   136
atonement   74–5, 80, 93, 99, 105, 139, 150,
    159, 176, 185, 201, 204, 225
Australasian Evangelisation Society   59
Australian and New Zealand Association of
    Theological Schools   178
Australian Baptist Missionary Society   71
Australian Board of Missions   68, 73, 83, 133
Australian Church   75
Australian College of Theology   137, 180,
    184
Australian Inland Mission   83
Australian Teachers' Christian Fellowship   120
Aveling, Marian   26, 27

Babbage, Neville   110
Babbage, Stuart Barton   126, 139, 152, 163,
    170, 184
Baeyertz, Emilia   57, 130
Ballantine-Jones, Bruce   214
Ballarat (Victoria)   41–3, 62, 68
Banner of Truth   181–3, 189
Banton, Albert   91, 103
baptism of the Holy Spirit   65, 69, 86–7,
    101–2, 105, 110–12, 129, 148, 149
  see also second blessing

Baptist Missionary Society   6, 58, 71
Baptist theological colleges   94, 98, 100, 134, 139, 179, 183–4
Baptist Union   29, 58, 75, 166, 181, 183
Baptists   2–3, 6, 30–1, 36, 50, 58, 70–2, 74–5, 91–2, 94, 97, 100–1, 126, 128, 134, 139, 166–7, 181–3, 194–5
Barker College, Sydney   123, 151
Barker, Frederic   29, 35–9, 76
Barker, Jane   37, 39
Barnett, Charles Benson   91–2
Barnett, Os   89
Barnett, Paul   180, 220
Barrett, David   73
Barth, Karl   134–5, 13
beach missions   137
Bebbington, David   x
Becroft, Colin   137
Begbie, Campbell   110, 116
Begbie, Hugh Smirnoff   78, 94, 129–30
Belgrave Heights Convention   72, 78, 144
Bellingham, Charles   110
Bendigo (Victoria)   41, 43, 62, 77
Bennelong, Thomas Coke Walker   21
Berry, Digby   77–8
Bethshan Holiness Mission   64
Betts, Walter   99
Bible   vii–xi, 8, 34, 36, 39, 44, 46, 49–51, 63, 65, 69, 75–8, 80, 92–5, 97–8, 101–3, 106, 107, 111–50 *passim*, 160, 162, 164, 173, 175–6, 181–2, 184–90, 195–225 *passim*
Bible Churchmen's Missionary Society   130
Bible colleges   79–80, 91–2, 103, 178
   see also colleges by name
Bible reading   ix, 69, 95–6, 167
Bible Society   xiii
Bible Union of Australia   99–100
Biblical criticism   49–50, 74–9, 104, 134, 138, 174
Bickford, James   43
Billy Graham crusades   ix, 59, 97, 104, 125, 136, 147, 154–71, 182, 185, 189, 191
Bingham, Geoffrey   122–3, 150, 196–7
Blacket, John   200
Bollen, David   51
Booth-Clibbon, William   148

Boreham, Frank William   165
Borneo Evangelical Mission   100
Bos, Robert   202
Bourke, Richard   28–9
Bowden, Thomas   18
Boyce, Fancis Bertie   56, 76–7
Bradley, William 'Cairo'   148
Brand, Alan   91, 93
Brennan, Patricia   208–9, 211, 213
Brethren   61, 72, 76, 97, 108–10, 120, 123, 144, 182
Brighton (Victoria)   41, 43, 145
Brisbane   30–1, 62, 68, 75, 87, 168, 178–9, 217
British Israelitism   103, 109, 113
Broken Hill (NSW)   62, 195
Brooker, Edna   199
Broughton, William Grant   22, 37, 131
Brown, George   71
Brown, William   61
Bryson, Allan   109, 114, 120
   Bruce   109–10, 144
   Stuart   109, 114
Buchanan, Florence   74
Buck, Len   144, 146–7, 164
Buck, William   99
Bullard, Narelle   82
Burgmann, Ernest Henry   90, 162
Burnard, Ian   137, 188–9
Burra (SA)   41, 43
Burrows, Eva   90
Bush Church Aid Society   59, 83
Bush Missionary Society   58

Cable, Ken   7, 23, 140
Call to Australia Party   191–2
Calvinism   viii, 18–19, 36–7, 74–6, 106, 131, 135, 139, 157, 172, 181–5, 195, 204
Calvinistic Methodism   2–3, 7–8, 17–19
Campaigners for Christ   99, 144–6, 162
Campion, Edmund   xiii
Campus Bible Study   190
Campus Crusade   189–90
Canada   85, 96, 128
Canberra   142, 162, 179, 192, 203, 210–11
Carey, Harvey   114–15, 120–1

Carnley, Peter 212–13
Cartwright, Richard 27
Carvosso, Benjamin 19
Cathcart, William 103
Catholic Church xi, xiii, 49, 52, 85–6,
89–90, 125, 137, 151–3, 170, 173,
176, 183, 224
Catholics 13, 24, 25, 29, 32, 34–5, 52–6,
67, 94, 127, 130, 191–3
Cavanagh, Jim 192
Centre for the Study of Australian Christianity
xiii, xiv
Chambers, George 82
Champion, Malcolm 199–200
Chant, Barry 178
Chapman, J. Wilbur 57, 60, 87, 91
Charismatic movement ix–x, xiii, 98, 105,
112, 122–3, 153, 173–6, 187, 190–6,
200, 221, 224–5
Cheek, Alison 211
Children's Special Service Mission 57, 105,
112, 116
China 1, 4, 45, 49, 66, 66–9, 70–3, 91, 112,
127–8, 133
China Inland Mission 57, 69, 72–3, 92
see also Hudson Taylor
Christian and Missionary Alliance 65
Christian Endeavour 57, 70, 191
Christian Leaders Training College 146
Christian Revival Crusade 103
Christian Outreach Centre 178
Church Army 57, 199
Church Missionary Association 68, 72–3
Church Missionary Society 7, 15–16, 22,
44–5, 72–3, 77, 82–3, 100, 112, 116,
123, 130, 133, 140–1, 149–51, 167,
194
Church of England 74, 76, 84–5, 88, 127,
138
in Britain 2, 7, 27, 59, 101, 192, 218–19
in NSW 17–19, 23, 29, 34–5, 58, 68,
77, 82, 184; see also Sydney
Anglicans
in Victoria 30, 68, 72, 77–8, 98
in SA 49, 137
in NT 67
in Tasmania 73

Churches of Christ 179, 183, 190, 195
City Men's Bible Class 99, 143
Clack, Bill 144
Clapham Sect viii, 5, 28
Clark, Manning xiii, 9
clergy xiii, 20, 23, 29, 31–2, 37–9, 42, 76–9,
81, 83–6, 92, 101, 120, 130–2, 144,
146, 150–1, 161–3, 170, 176, 180,
188, 194, 204, 206, 210–11, 214, 218
Cole, Alan 138
Cole, Keith xiii, 142, 180
Collard, Cecil 93
Collins, Paul xiii
Commonwealth and Continental Church
Society 83
Commonwealth Revival Crusade 103
Congregationalism 2, 7, 29–30, 36, 65, 75,
80–1, 87, 91–4, 97, 173, 178, 185,
191–2
conservative evangelicalism 50, 77, 79–80,
83, 88–94, 104, 109, 125, 129–31,
134, 138, 173–4, 183–8, 193, 203,
208–12, 223
convention movement 49–50, 57–8, 72,
78–80, 92, 97–100, 103, 108, 110,
112, 145, 150–1, 158–9, 199
conversion 15, 27, 42–3, 47, 61, 63, 67–9,
73, 76, 78, 86–9, 91, 96–7, 101–2,
144–5, 154–5, 157, 159–61, 164,
166–9, 191, 195, 197–8
convicts viii, xiii, 1, 4–5, 8–17, 20, 23, 27,
30–3, 35, 40, 45, 53
Cook, Joseph 56
Cook, Thomas 57
Coombe, Alfred 144, 147
Coombe, Sabina 144
Cordiner, Robert 84
Cornerstone 195
Cosh, James 48
Cotton, Frank 56
Cover, James Fleet 17
Cowper, William 19
Cranswick, Geoffrey 81
Creation Science 44, 175, 221
Croker Island Mission 82–3
Crook, William Pascoe 17
Crusader Union 105, 109–12, 116–17, 119

Curr, Edmund 35
Curtis, John 195–6
   Judy 195–6

Dagiar 141
Dahl, Jack 116
Dain, Jack 167
Daley, Eric 111, 144
Daley, Victor 54
Darwin (NT) 140–2, 180
Darwinism 49, 59, 74–5, 77–9
Davies, David John 88
Davies, Glenn 214
Davies, John Arthur 183
Davis family 145–6
   Norman Charles 145–6
   Ralph 144–7
Dayton, Don 64
Deaconess House 167
Deane, Arthur 167
Debenham, Margaret 117, 121
Deck family 107–8, 112, 118–19
   Brian 116
   Cathie 108
   Connie 108
   Humphrey 114
   Jack 110
   John Field 108
   Norman 108, 111
   Northcote 108, 111
   Philip 114, 116
   Roger 116
Depression, the 79–80, 88–91, 103, 125,
      127, 223
Diocese of Sydney see Sydney Anglicans
dispensationalism 80, 108
divorce 51, 80–1, 117, 195
doctrine ix, 11, 14, 23, 36, 44, 51, 53, 59, 65,
      77, 80, 88, 92, 95, 98, 100–1, 105–7,
      113–16, 120, 139, 176, 185, 223
Dowie, John Alexander 65
Dowling, Owen 203, 205–6, 210, 212,
      217–18
downgrade controversy 75
Doyle, Robert 204
Draper, Daniel James 145
Dredge, James 45–7

Drummond, Heather 116–17, 119, 120
Drummond, Henry 57
Dunkley, Win 119
Dunstan, Albert 89
Duthie, Gil 192
Dyer, Alf 140, 141
Dyer, Harry 99

Eagar, Edward 18, 26–7
Eclectic Society 5–6, 11
Edden, Alfred 56
education 21, 24, 29–34, 38, 46–51, 57,
      68–9, 82–3, 94–6, 136, 139, 177–80,
      188–90, 194, 223
Edwards, John 92
Edwards, Jonathan x–xi, 2, 59, 154–6, 159
Egglestone, Alex 99
Elcho Island 83, 197–8, 200
Elkin, Adolphus Peter 142
Elland Society 5
Eltham Holiness Convention 112
Ely, Richard 33, 51
entire sanctification 40, 105–24, 158
Eremos 175
Erskine, George 19
Evangelical Alliance 146, 177
Evangelical Council of NSW 63
Evangelical Fellowship of the Anglican
      Communion 204
Evangelical History Association xi
Evangelical Theological Association 183
Evangelical Unions 95–6, 105, 109–21, 137,
      144, 184, 189
evangelicalism see conservative evangelicalism;
      liberal evangelicalism
Evangelisation Society of Victoria 98
evangelism ix, xiii, 4, 8–9, 17–18, 37, 40,
      42, 49, 57–9, 61, 67–8, 70, 77, 80, 82,
      86, 89, 92, 96–100, 103, 106–8, 110,
      126, 128–30, 136, 142–3, 147–8,
      152, 154–71, 175–6, 184, 186, 189,
      194–5, 211, 221
evangelistic campaigns 42, 49–51, 57–64,
      72, 78, 87, 91, 101, 103, 112–13, 125,
      136, 144–5, 148–52, 154–71, 191,
      196–7, 223
Evatt, Herbert Vere 153

Everyman's Welfare Service   146
evolution   44, 79, 221
Exeter Hall   28

Fairfax Family Trust   xiv
Fairymead   108
family dynasties   18, 72, 81, 107, 108–9,
   118, 144
family life   17, 26–7, 47, 51, 58, 60, 80,
   89–91, 107–8, 112, 114, 116–18,
   120, 144–6, 152, 168, 195, 221
Farrell, Monica   130
Fawkner, John Pascoe   30
Fee, Gordon   204
Fellowship for Biblical Studies   137
feminism   66, 81–2, 174, 203, 208–10, 213,
   225
   see also women
Festival of Light   191–2
Finney, Charles   181
Fletcher, Lionel   86–7, 148
Flynn, John   83
Foord, Dudley   136, 151
Forbes, Chris   214
Ford, Patrick   55
foreign missions see overseas missions
Four-Square Church   103
Fuller Theological Seminary   204–5
fulness of the Spirit see baptism of the Holy
   Spirit
fundamentalism   59, 79–80, 94, 97, 125,
   128–9, 134, 138–9, 150, 161–2, 175,
   182, 189–92, 212
fundamentals   33, 96, 100, 102
Furlong, Monica   208
Fusion   193

Game, Phillip   88
Garland, David   87
Garnham, Florence   82
Gee, Donald   65
Gee, Thomas   152
Geelong (Victoria)   41, 58, 62,
   98
General Board of Religious Education   180
George, Ian   220
Gibson, Edward   166

Gilchrist, Alex   148
Giles, Kevin   214–15
Gillison, Andrew   86
Gillman, Ian   33
Gipps, George   44
Gippsland   47, 77, 81
Gleeson, Murray   210
Glover, Kelso   65
Glover, Susan   218
Goe, Field Flowers   77
Gondarra, Djiniyini   197–8, 201
Good News Hall   65–6
Goodhew, Harry   214, 221
Gospel   passim
Gossner, Johannes Evangelista   31
Gough, Hugh   96, 177
Goulburn (NSW)   41–2, 62, 77, 81, 90, 162,
   203, 210–11
Goulburn Island Mission   67, 83
Graham, Billy   128, 133, 149, 151, 154–71,
   182–3
   see also Billy Graham crusades
Grant family   107, 109–10, 112, 116, 118
   David   109–10, 116–17, 121
   Frances   109
   Lindsay   108–10, 112–15, 117–19,
      120–1
   Margaret   109
   Mary   117
   Ronald   109, 111, 117, 119, 120
Green, Michael   204
Greenwood, Charles   102
Griffiths family   107–9, 119
   James,   99
   John   99, 147
   Ken   109
   Leslie   109
Gribble, John   47
Groote Eylandt Mission   83
Grose, Francis   12–13
Grubb, George   57–8, 72, 76–8
Grubb, Norman   95
Guinness, Harry   57
Guinness, Howard   96, 109, 113, 119, 136

Hagenauer, Frederick   47
Hall, George   99–100

Hamilton, Gavin 148
Hammond, Elizabeth 220
Hammond, Robert Brodribb Stuart 76, 85, 88–9
Hammond, Thomas Chatterton 89, 107, 115–16, 120, 122, 126, 130–1, 135–6, 138, 150
Hampson, Margaret 57
Hannah, Horace John 99
Hare, Alice 119
Harper, Andrew 92
Harper, John 22
Harris, Cecil 103
Harris, John 22, 47, 67
Harris, Leo 103
Harris, Tim 214
Hart, Richard 43
Hassall, Mary Cover 16, 19
Hassall, Rowland 16–19
Hassall, Thomas 18
Haweis, Thomas xi, 1, 3, 7, 14
Haymaker, Willis 156
Hayward, Patricia 208, 216, 218, 220–1
healing 65, 101–3, 197–8, 200
heaven 73, 75, 87, 101, 186
Hebert, Gabriel 138
hell 66, 75, 97
Henry, William 17
Hercus, John 114, 116
heresy 3, 75, 105, 135
hermeneutics 77, 138, 187, 204, 215
Hervey, Fred 83
High Church 37, 38, 58, 76, 87
  see also Anglo-Catholics
Higher Criticism see Biblical criticism
Higinbotham, George 75
Hill, Thomas Ernest 76
Hilliard, David xiii
Hobart 40–1, 72
Hobbin, Bill 90–1, 93
Hodgson, William 37
Hogg, Anna 119, 139
Hogg, James 183
Holdsworth, W. H. 134
holiness movement viii, 50, 64, 72, 100
holiness vii, 57, 64–5, 76–7, 105–24, 135, 143, 150–1, 158, 176, 188, 193, 225

Hollingworth, Peter 217
Holman, William 85
Holt, Ian 110, 114, 116–17, 120
Holy Spirit vii, xi, xiii, 4, 8, 39, 42–3, 60, 63, 66, 69–70, 75, 99–101, 104–6, 111, 118, 121–3, 134, 145, 148–9, 154–5, 157, 164, 168, 175, 177, 181, 187–8, 197–9, 202, 206, 224–5
  see also baptism of the Holy Spirit
Home Mission Society 29, 130
home missions xiii, 4, 58, 71, 103, 129, 151
Honour Oak movement 111, 123
Hope, Robert Marsden 216
Hope, John 103
Howe, Robert 20
Hurst, Benjamin 45
humanitarianism 25, 51, 86, 142, 152
Hungerford, Hilda 119
Hunt, Arnold 42
Hunter, John 13, 17
Hurstville Christian Fellowship Centre 122–3
Hutchinson, Mark xiii, xiv
Hyde, Dudley 91, 93

India 1, 7–8, 45, 49, 61, 66, 71–2, 82, 123, 167
inerrancy 75, 78–80, 175, 184–5, 205
Inglis, Ken 163
inspiration 77, 80, 92, 94, 138, 187, 211
Intercessors, the 193
Interdenominational Missionary Fellowship 146–7
International Fellowship of Evangelical Students 133
Inter-Schools Christian Fellowship 105, 110, 137
Inter-Varsity Fellowship 95–6, 105, 109–10, 112, 116–19, 121, 128, 135–8, 184, 188–90
Irish 9, 27, 30, 32, 34–5, 38, 43, 52, 55–8, 61, 88, 110, 130, 138

Japan 49, 66, 72, 111, 126, 140, 141
Jem, Kum 68
Jensen, Peter 204

Jensen, Phillip   190, 212
Jesuit Theological College   178
Jesus   vii, xi, 1, 13–14, 20, 25, 42, 47, 54,
   60–71 *passim*, 80, 82, 87–9, 91–3, 99,
   101, 105–7, 120–1, 130–9, 144–60
   passim, 167–8, 176, 181–2, 185–6,
   195–6, 198–9, 201, 204, 206, 221–2,
   225
Jews   77, 99, 130
Jireh Baptist Church   71
John Knox Theological College   139, 181
Johnson, Mary   12, 17
Johnson, Milbah Mary   21
Johnson, Raynor   146
Johnson, Richard   3, 5–6, 11–13, 21, 23
Johnstone, Samuel Martin   130
Jones, Nathaniel   76–7
Joyful News Mission   57
Judd, Stephen   88
Judge, Edwin   140
justification   20, 105–6, 114, 187

Kanakas   49, 62, 66, 69–70
Katoomba Convention   70, 108, 110–12,
   151
Kentishbury (Tasmania)   61–3
Kerle, Ronald Clive   163, 170
Kerr, Alan   144, 147, 162
Kerr, Grahame   174
Kerr, William   30
Keswick movement   x, 57–8, 72, 76, 92, 97,
   99–100, 102, 106–8, 110, 112, 114,
   122, 150–1
Kiek, Winifred   81
King, Copeland   74
Kirkby, Sydney James   83
Kitchen, James Howard   72, 144
Kitchen, John James   72, 99
Kitchen, Philip Freeman   72
Kitchen, Ridley   144
Knox, Ailsa   188
Knox, David Broughton   107–8, 121, 159,
   184–8
Knox, David James   88, 94, 129–30
Korea   125, 127, 173
Kotlowski, Elizabeth   xiii
Kuring-gai Gospel Chapel   123

Kuyper, Abraham   138, 181
La Touche, Everard Digges   88, 130
Labor Party   52, 54–7, 85, 127, 153, 191–2
laity   xiii , 20, 30, 32, 37–9, 42, 58, 72, 75,
   78, 92, 98–100, 112, 118, 120, 131,
   142–8, 163, 170, 176–7, 180, 218
Lamb, Margaret   xiv
Lancaster, Janet   65–6
Lane, Alan   116
Lang, Jack   55
Lang, John Dunmore   26, 29, 31, 35–6, 47,
   135
Langford Smith, Sydney Edgar   129–30
Launceston (Tasmania)   18, 62, 71–2, 181
Lawry, Walter   16, 19, 27
Lawson, Henry   51–5
Lawton, Bill   185
lay preachers   17, 22, 25, 42, 56, 89, 99–100,
   147
Le Fanu, Henry   131
Ledger, Christine   189
Lee, Merv   192
Lee, Nigel   183
Leeper, Alexander   84
Leigh, Samuel   8, 13, 18–19
Len, George Ah   68
Leonard, Graham   209
liberal evangelicalism   ix, 50, 88, 91–2, 129,
   189
Liberal Party   153, 192
liberalism
   political   viii, 24–34, 37–9, 44, 50, 52,
      56, 223
   theological   ix, 36–7, 59, 74–80, 84,
      90–7, 104, 109, 128, 134–6, 148,
      173–7, 182–4, 188, 223–5
Lilley, William Osborne   75
Lincolne, J. Laurie   181
Linder, Robert D.   xiv
Liverpool (NSW)   18, 89, 211
Lloyd-Jones, David Martyn   133, 155, 176–7
Loane, Marcus   xii, xiii, 113, 117, 150, 154,
   161–3, 170
London Missionary Society   3, 7, 14–18, 22,
   31, 82
Long, Reginald Charles Michel   122

Long, Retta 67
Love, Garry 148
Lowe, Robert 37
Luther Seminary, Adelaide 178
Lutheran Church 178

Macarthur, John 12
Macartney, Hussey Burgh (Jr) 72–3
McCarthy, Tony 189
MacColl, D. Stewart 99
McColl, A. S. 140–1
McCracken, J. Harold 144
McEachran, Duncan Stewart 74–5
McGowan, Robert 93, 109
McGowen, James Sinclair Taylor 56
Macintyre, Ronald George 92
McIntire, Carl 162, 182
McIntyre, Allan 43
McKenzie, William 'Fighting Mac' 86
McKernan, Michael 85–6
Mackerras, Catherine 55
Mackintosh, Hugh 52
Maclaren, Albert 74
McLennan, Graham xii
McNamara, Bill 55
MacNeil, John 57, 60
McPherson, Aimee Semple 65, 101
Macquarie, Elizabeth 20
    Lachlan 18, 20–2
McQueen, Humphrey 9
Maitland (NSW) 41, 62, 68
Manning River (NSW) 41, 43, 62
Mannix, Daniel 153
Mansfield, Bruce 140
Mansfield, Ralph 13, 19
marriage 26, 63, 81, 105, 107–8, 117, 120,
    143, 196, 207
Marsden, Ann 18
    Elizabeth 17
    Samuel 8, 12–13, 15–20, 23, 46–47
Marshall, Walter 150
Mason, Keith 217
Masonic movement 27–8
mateship 52–4
Maranatha 190
Mahoney, Dennis Leslie 216
Meagher, Roderick Pitt 210

Mead, Silas 37, 70–1
Melanesian Mission 73
Melbourne 30, 35, 37–8, 41, 43, 45, 47,
    59–62, 65, 68, 72, 74, 77–8, 80, 84,
    89, 98–102, 107, 110, 112, 117–18,
    126, 135, 137, 139, 142–8, 151–3,
    156–8, 160–5, 170, 178–9, 183, 189,
    193–4, 203–5, 210, 220
    see also Victoria
Melbourne Bible Institute 72, 78, 92,
    99–100, 102, 111, 144, 167, 191
Melbourne College of Divinity 134, 137, 183
Melbourne Gospel Crusade 78–9
Men, Women and God 209
Menzies, Robert Gordon 127, 177
Metheringham, Deane 196
Methodism xi, 1, 3, 7–8, 12–13, 16, 18–20,
    25–6, 29, 31, 36, 40, 42–3, 49–50, 52,
    56–7, 63, 65, 67, 76, 80, 84–6, 89–
    97, 100–1, 126–7, 145–8, 152,
    162, 166, 170, 173, 178, 182, 191,
    196
    class meetings 3, 18, 20, 27,
    love feasts 43
    overseas missions 82, 83, 147
    see also Calvinistic Methodism; Central
        Methodist Missions; Wesleyan
        Methodism
millennialism viii, 2, 8, 76, 80, 108–9, 125,
    158–9
    see also second coming
Miller, Crawford 183
Miller, Katie 82
Mills, Ruth 211
Minniecon, Rodney 149
miracles 65, 74, 80, 168, 199–200
Mission Church, Launceston 71
Mission to the Nation 126, 152
missionaries xiii, 1, 3, 7, 14–21, 31, 44–5,
    47, 66–74, 82, 96, 109, 112, 114, 120,
    123, 140–2, 166–7, 194, 199, 201
    see also missionary societies by name; Aboriginal
        people, missions to
Missionary Aviation Fellowship 144, 146,
    198
missions see Aboriginal people, missions to;
    China; crusades; evangelistic

missions, *cont.*
  campaigns; home missions; Kanakas;
    overseas missions
modernism   x, 75, 79–80, 92, 95–6, 129,
    134, 191, 195
Mol, Hans   172
Moody Bible Institute   59
Moody, Dwight Lyman   57–9, 149, 165
Moonta (SA)   41, 49, 62
Moore Theological College   37, 39, 76, 88,
    115, 126, 130–1, 133, 158–9, 161,
    167, 180, 183–8, 204, 216
moralism, morality   8, 11, 22, 24–5, 28, 33,
    35, 50–1, 63, 83–4, 88, 90, 105,
    168–70, 174, 191–3, 199, 224
Moravians   31, 41, 47
Morgan, Peter   149
Morling, George Henry   94, 97–8, 100–1,
    107, 126, 139
Moroney, John Burbury   144
Morris, Leon   139, 152, 163, 170, 204
Morton, Archie   163
Morton, William Lockhart   91–2
Moses, John   84
Mothers' Union   81
Mott, John Raleigh   57, 95
Moule, Handley   106, 112
Movement for the Ordination of Women
    203, 208–9, 213, 218–21
Mowll, Howard   81, 88, 100, 107, 126,
    128–133, 159, 163, 170
Mowll, Dorothy   128–33
Moyes, Gordon   194
Moyse, Edward   61
Murray, Andrew   110, 150
Murray, Robert Lathrop   26
Myer, Sidney   99, 163

Nairn, Bede   55
Nash, Clifford Harris   92, 98–100, 102, 107,
    109–12, 117, 126, 142–8
National Missionary Council of Australia   142
National Revival Crusade   103
Navigators, the   189
Neil family   107–8, 110, 112
  Alan   109, 111–12, 118, 120
    Edwin Lee   98–9, 109, 112, 118, 143, 144

Phyllis   109
New Guinea   14, 71–4, 146
New Zealand   14–16, 58, 69, 72, 87, 100,
    103–4, 107–8, 117, 140, 167, 174,
    178, 219
Newcastle (NSW)   56, 68, 90, 211
Newman, Eben   93
Newton, John   xi, 1, 3, 11
Nicholl, George   71
Nicholls, Michael   219
Nichols, Alan   194
Nicholson, James Beath   96
Nicholson, William Patteson   110, 148
Nile, Elaine   191–2
Nile, Fred   191–2
Nimmo, John   144
North, Helen   123
Northern Territory   47, 82–3
Norton, John   51
Nungalinya College   142, 180

O'Donnell, David   64
Oenpelli Mission   83, 140
O'Farrell, Patrick   xiii
Open Air Campaigners   110
open-air preaching   99, 103, 146, 147
O'Reilly, Colleen   221
ordination   68, 81, 102, 178,
  see also women, ordination of
Ormond College   95, 178
Orr, James   92
Orthodox churches   172, 179
orthodoxy   vii, 2, 74–5, 92–4, 104, 109,
    116–17, 119, 122–3, 133, 173, 189
Orton, Joseph   19, 20
overseas missions   ix, xii–xiii, 1–8, 14–19, 27,
    29, 45, 48–9, 58, 66, 70–4, 79, 81, 91–2,
    95–6, 100, 103–4, 108–10, 126–9,
    146–7, 149–51, 173, 186, 209

Pacific   1, 4, 22, 49, 73, 126, 132, 147, 173,
    178
Packer, James   128, 138
Page, John   71
Parkes, Henry   50
Parliamentary Christian Fellowship   192
Parramatta   12, 17, 19, 21–2, 41–2, 48, 186

Parramatta Conference   214–16
Paterson, William   21
Patteson, John Coleridge   73
Paton, John Gibson   48
Peace Expedition   140–2
Pearson, George   144
Pell, Norman   191
Penman, David   189, 193–4
Pentecostal Church of Australia   102
pentecostalism   xiii , 64–6, 91, 101–3, 112,
        122, 138, 149, 173, 175–8, 225
Pepper, Nathaniel   47
perfectionism   ix, 25, 125, 193, 222, 225
    see also sinless perfectionism
Perry, Charles   30, 38, 77
Perth   21, 92, 131, 168, 178–9, 212–13
Peterson, David   214
philanthropy   31, 63, 71, 96, 152
Phillip, Arthur   11, 21
Pietism   vii, x, xi, 50, 78, 80, 110, 135, 150,
        175, 185, 189, 222, 225
piety   90, 92, 129, 131, 152, 176
Pike, Douglas   30
Plested, Martha   71
Pocklington, Arthur   144
Pomeroy, John   213
Pong, Le Ung   68
Porter, Jean   119
Porter, William   44
Powell, Gordon   154, 162, 166
prayer   ix, 13, 39–43, 50–2, 59–61, 64,
        69–70, 78, 87, 95–6, 114–15, 133,
        136, 140, 143, 147–8, 150–2, 156–8,
        160, 164–5, 185, 192–4, 197–8, 209,
        225
Prayer Book   88, 130, 177, 187
preaching   4, 11–12, 15–18, 20, 36–7, 42–3,
        51, 58–9, 61, 63, 81–2, 97–9, 100–1,
        103, 119, 129, 134, 145, 149, 155,
        165, 168, 175, 181, 186, 193
Presbyterian Church   3, 7, 29–30, 34, 36, 43,
        47–8, 68, 74–5, 80, 82–4, 86, 91–4,
        96, 109, 127, 135, 151–2, 154–5, 162,
        166, 173–4, 178, 181–3, 220
Presbyterian Church of Eastern Australia
        135, 181
Presbyterian Reformed Church   174

Prescott, Alwyn   114–15, 120
Priestley, Lancelot John   216–17
Primitive Methodists   49, 56
Primmer, Dalba   210
Protestant Reformation   vii–viii, xi, 59, 140,
        173, 181, 184–5, 218–19, 221
Puritanism   vii, 122, 175, 181, 191

Quakers   3, 81, 101
Queen's College, Melbourne   146, 178
Queensland   31, 36, 49, 62, 69–71, 83, 102,
        108, 118, 139, 149, 152, 161, 178,
        180, 183, 201
    see also Brisbane
Queensland Baptist Missionary Society   71
Queensland Kanaka Mission   69–70
Quinn, Rod   54

Rade, Martin   84
Ramsay, Jim   211–12
Rayner, Keith   212, 219
Rayward, Frank   126
Red Book Case   184
Reddell, Arthur   114
Reed, Henry   71
Reed, Mary   71–2
reform   vii–xiii, 1, 4–6, 8–10, 13, 24–8, 32,
        89, 212, 214
Reformation   see Protestant Reformation
Reformation Society (NSW)   35
Reformed Churches of Australia   135, 138,
        181
Reformed Evangelical Church   181
Reformed Evangelical Protestant Association
        (REPA)   211–12
Reformed Presbyterian Church   135
Reformed theology   ix, 59, 107, 122, 125,
        135, 138–9, 151, 172, 175–7, 180–9,
        200
Reid, Andrew   190
Renfrey, Lionel   220
Renshaw family   145
    David   144
    David Ernest   99, 144
    John   144
    Will   144
Rentoul, J. Laurence   74

revivalism   26, 53, 57, 69, 76, 78, 91, 105,
    118, 123, 135, 158–61, 188, 222, 225
Revivals, Australian   ix, xiii , 7, 25, 39–43,
    49–50, 58, 60–4, 70, 83, 86, 88, 91,
    100, 102, 110, 125, 147–52, 154–71,
    175, 182, 196–202,
    224–5
  Azusa Street   64
  East Africa   149–51
  eighteenth century   vii, x, 1–2, 11, 150,
    154
  Fiji   48
  Irish (Ulster)   43,
  Scottish   43
  Welsh   43, 63, 64
Ridley College   139, 147, 194, 204–5
Ridley, John   97, 126
Rien, Elliot John   64
ritualism   35, 49, 74, 76, 177, 184, 225
Robarts, David   210
Robert Menzies College   xiii , xiv, 180
Robinson, Donald William Bradley   116, 133,
    159, 173, 186–7, 203, 206–9, 214,
    216–18, 220
Robinson, John   144–5, 148
Robinson, Richard Bradley   94, 129–30
Rochardson, Maude   58
Rogers, Andrew J.   210
Rolls, Charles Jubilee   92
Roper River Mission   67, 140, 198–9
Roy, Doris   119
Roydan, Maude   81
Runia, Klaas   138, 139, 204

Sabbath observance   12, 15, 30, 51, 75, 84
St Andrew's Cathedral, Sydney   68, 81, 88,
    126, 132
St Andrew's College, Sydney   92, 183
St Mark's College of Ministry, Canberra   179
St Paul's College (Sydney)   37, 123
Salvation Army   49, 57, 71, 86, 90–1, 101
Samuels, Gordon   210
Sanders, John Oswald   144
Sandland, Charles Alfred   99, 144, 146–7
Saunders, Eliza   73
  John   37
  Nellie   73

Topsy   73
Scandrett, Laurie   210, 213, 216
Schep, John Adrian   138
School of Christian Studies   180
Schwarz, Fred   118
Scotland   34–5, 43, 61, 65, 75, 92, 108, 121
Scripture Union   57, 112, 116, 137, 147,
    166, 167
Scroggie, Graham   110
Sebald, William   163
second blessing   ix, 76, 113, 135, 195
  see also baptism of the Holy Spirit
second coming   50, 54, 69, 76–7, 80, 121,
    159, 176
  see also millennialism
sectarianism   3, 13, 24–8, 32, 34–7, 51, 53,
    55, 86, 130, 161, 173, 189
secularisation, secularism   ix–x, xii, 10–11,
    26, 29, 32–3, 50–1, 53, 57, 59, 74, 97,
    172, 174, 176, 190, 193–4, 212, 223,
    225
Selwyn, George Augustus   73
Shaw, George   32
Shepherd, James   16
Sherlock, Charles   204, 220
Shilton, Lance   166
Shindler, Robert   75
Shore Grammar School   123
Simeon, Charles   1, 15
Simpson, Albert Benjamin   65
sinless perfection   98, 105–24, 143, 158, 196
Smailes, George W.   56
Smee, Reginald   58
Smith, Alice   113, 119
Smith, Gipsy   57
Smith, Hervey Perceval   72, 78, 99–100,
    144, 146
Smith, James   71
Smith, Oswald   148
Smith, Tony Golsby   123
social class   1, 8–12, 20, 25–6, 30, 33, 35,
    39, 49, 52–6,
    71, 95, 119, 127, 153,
    168
social gospel   ix, 79–80, 90, 93, 152
social reform or action   viii–ix, 4–5, 24, 31,
    39, 49, 51, 76–7, 80, 88–91, 96, 104,

152–3, 175–6, 189, 193–6, 198, 221–2, 224–5
see also reform
social welfare see welfare
socialism 54, 57, 79, 90–1, 153
Society Islands 7, 17–18
Solomon Islands 70, 108, 111
Soltau, George 72
Sommerlad, Lloyd 114
South Africa 58, 66, 103, 219
South Australia 27, 30–1, 36, 40–3, 49, 56, 62, 65, 71, 84, 87, 102, 149, 161, 191, 196
see also Adelaide
South Sea Evangelical Mission 69–70, 73, 108–12
South Sea islanders viii, xiii, 2–4, 7, 9, 14, 17, 23, 45, 66, 69, 73, 108
Spence, William Guthrie 52, 54
Spry, Ian 206, 210
Spurgeon, Charles Haddon 58, 75, 149, 165, 183
Spurgeon, Thomas 57
Stace, Arthur 97
Stanway, Alf 144
Stebbins, Ivan 93
Stephenson, Noel 115
Stewart, Charles 36
Stewart. Robert 72–3
Stirling, James 21
Stock, Eugene 72
Stott, John 138
Strehlow, Carl 47
Strong, Charles 74–5
Student Christian Movement 95–6, 188–9
Student Life 190
Students for Christ 190
Sudan Interior Mission 209
Sutton, Ralph 90
Sunday Observance Act (1780) 51, 191
Sunday schools 3, 18–20, 25–56, 83, 151, 223
Swan, James 31
Swanton, Howell 144, 146
Swanton, Robert 135, 183
Switzerland 135

Sydney 7, 14–18, 21, 29–31, 35, 37–41, 51, 56, 63, 68, 72, 77, 80–2, 88–90, 92, 96–7, 102–3, 107, 110, 114, 117, 121–2, 126, 131, 133, 151, 154–5, 158–60, 162–5, 167, 169, 170, 174, 178, 191, 196, 206
Sydney Anglicans ix, xiv, 35, 37–9, 76–8, 83, 85, 88, 93–4, 100, 107, 131–2, 151, 163, 176, 184–8, 203–21
see also Anglicanism, evangelical
Sydney College of Divinity 179–80, 183–4
Sydney Teachers' College 139
synods 29, 38, 187, 206, 209–10, 214, 217–19, 221

Tabor Bible College 178
Tahiti 7, 14–15
Talbot, Albert Edward 88
Tasmania 18, 26, 35, 40–1, 61, 68, 72–3, 107, 109–10, 114, 181, 192
see also Hobart; Launceston
Taylor, Clark 178
Taylor, Hudson 57, 69–72, 91
Taylor, James 37
Taylor, Ruth Minton 82
Taylor, William 'California' 57
temperance 24, 49, 51–2, 56, 58, 63, 65, 76, 84–9, 145, 169–70, 191, 198–9
Ten, Soo Hoo 68
Tench, Watkin 4
theological colleges xiii, 38, 42, 57–8, 74, 91–3, 98, 125, 134, 137–40, 142, 166–7, 177–81, 194–5, 212
see also colleges by name
theology 19, 21, 38, 50, 58–9, 65–6, 74, 76, 83–4, 91, 94–5, 97–8, 103–4, 107–13, 118, 120, 122, 129, 131, 134–9, 150, 156–7, 175–80, 185, 187, 195, 204, 206, 212, 215, 218, 224
Thiering, Barbara 23, 174
Thomson, John 98, 137, 139
Threlkeld, Lancelot 22–3
Tinsley, Allan 100
Tinsley, Charles James 94, 97

Tonga   14, 16, 27
tongues. gift of   64–5, 149, 197, 200
Torres Strait Islanders   74
Torrey, Reuben Archer   57, 59–60, 78, 98,
        100, 165
Tress, Thomas Broughton   86
Tress, Herbert Langley   130
Trinity College, Brisbane   179
Trinity College, Melbourne   84
Trinity Grammar School, Sydney   109, 120,
        151
Troutman, Charles   126, 136–7, 188
Tuckfield, Francis   45
Turnbull, Eric   181

Unevangelised Fields Mission   100
United Aborigines Mission   66–7, 83, 144
United Faculty of Theology   92, 183
United Presbyterian Church   36, 68
Uniting Church   173–4, 179, 183, 197, 202
universities   177–80, 188–90
    Melbourne   39, 84, 95–6, 109, 118, 135,
        137, 144, 146
    NSW   114, 190, 212
    Queensland   139
    Sydney   37, 92, 94–6, 105, 110–14, 116,
        119, 121, 123, 131, 136, 140, 142,
        179–80, 183–4, 189
university student work   xiii, 79, 94–6, 103,
        110–14, 119, 126, 130–1, 133,
        135–6, 164, 177, 188–90, 212
Upwey Convention   72, 78, 99–100, 144,
        147–8
Urquhart, Carment   92

Valdez, Alfred C. sen.   102
Van Eyk, Frederick   65, 102, 91, 103
Varley, Frank   99
Varley, Henry   57, 99
Vickery, Ebenezer   63
Victoria   29, 38, 40–1, 43, 45, 47–8, 60, 62,
        68, 71, 73–7, 89, 153, 164, 182, 184
    see also Melbourne
Voller, James   37

Waddingham, Stan   144

Wai, John Young   68
Wales   34, 43, 64, 103, 176
Walker, Alan   91, 126, 152, 162, 170
Walker, Keith   144
Walker, William   21–2, 42
war   53, 83, 84, 127
    see also World War I; World
        War II
Ward, Russell   30
Warren, Hubert   140–1
Warren, Max   100
Warren, William   60
Warriner, Thomas   139
Wartheim, R.L.   64
Watsford, John   40, 42, 48
Watson, David   204
Watson, Peter   187
Watson, Richard   40
Watson, William   44, 45
Watts, Bill   148, 149
Webb, Allan   60
welfare   24, 31, 33, 51, 57, 71, 88–91, 223
Wentworth, William Charles   26
Wesley, John   x–xi, 8, 15, 18, 20, 25, 59, 90,
        106, 118, 122, 154–5
Wesleyan Methodism   2, 7–8, 13, 18–20, 30,
        34, 36, 40, 49, 51, 56, 71, 111, 114,
        161
Wesleyan Methodist Missionary Society   8,
        16, 19, 22, 40, 45, 48
Western Australia   26, 41, 47,
        68, 83, 92, 102, 181, 198, 199
Westminster Confession   36, 59, 93
Westminster Presbyterian Church   181
Whale, William   75
Wheeler, Ray   151
White, Gilbert   74
White, Paul   95, 110, 112, 119–21, 126,
        136–7
Whitefield, George   3, 154–5
Whitham, Alan   93
Whitlam, Freda   193
    Gough   184, 192–3
Whitley College   183
Whitney, Harold   151, 155, 162
Wigglesworth, Smith   101

Wilberforce, William   viii, 3–8, 25, 28, 77,
        89
Wilkes, Paget   111, 114
Williams, Basil   117
Williams, Spencer   40
Wilson, Grady   156
Wilson, William   39
Windsor (NSW)   18, 27, 41, 42
women   xiii, 8, 11–12, 44, 46, 49, 52–3, 58,
        64–5, 71, 80–1, 84–5, 101, 113,
        118–19, 130, 132, 141, 144–5, 198,
        203–21
    ordination of ix, 81, 194, 203–21
    missionaries 16, 66, 69–74, 79, 82, 92,
        128–9, 170, 209
Woodforde, James   7
Woodhouse, John   204, 212, 221
Woods. Frank   151
World Council of Churches   127, 133
World Evangelisation Crusade   181
World Vision   175
World War I   24, 77, 79–80, 83–8, 94, 103,
        132, 142

World War II   73, 88–9, 121, 125,
        127, 132, 143, 148, 150, 152–3,
        214
Worldwide Evangelisation Crusade   95–6
wowserism   51–2, 84, 191
Wran, Neville   191, 193
Wright, John Charles   81, 85
Wudinna (SA)   196–7

Yatman, Charles   57
Youl, John   17, 19
Young family   107–8, 118–19
    Emily Baring   108
    Ernest   119
    Florence   69, 70, 72, 108, 112, 119
    Henry   108
    Margaret   119
Young, Gordon   194
Young Men's Christian Association   68, 95
Youth with a Mission (YWAM)   193

Zadok   175
Zenana missions   71